The Cry for Justice

An Anthology of the Literature of Social Protest

Selected and edited by

Upton Sinclair

New edition, revised and edited

with the cooperation of

EDWARD SAGARIN and ALBERT TEICHNER

THE

CRY

FOR

JUSTICE

BARRICADE BOOKS · NEW YORK

Published by Barricade Books Inc.
150 Fifth Avenue
New York, NY 10011

Printed in the United States of America.

Library of Congress Cataloging-in-Publication Data

The cry for justice: an anthology of the great social protest
literature of all time / [edited] by Upton Sinclair.
p.   cm.
        Includes bibliographical references and index.
        ISBN 1-56980-069-3
        1. Social problems. 2. Social justice. I. Sinclair, Upton.
        1878-1968.
        HN5.C79   1996
        303.3'72—dc20   95-51076
                                                              CIP

First Trade Paperback Printing

The Heavy Sledge, *Mahonri Young*

A Personal Note from the Publisher

In my lifetime, I have had contact with many world leaders ranging from Marshal Tito to Fidel Castro. I had a falling out with Fidel when the leaders of the Cuban Revolution lied to me about a political prisoner. (I pressured them to finally release him, but that was the end of my relationship with Fidel.) Nevertheless, to this day my automobile license plate reads simply: CHE, in honor of Major Ernesto "Che" Guevara, who, like Upton Sinclair, has been one of my heroes.

African-Americans are impressed to discover that I knew and worked with W.E.B. DuBois.

However, of all the so-called celebrities I've known, people seem most impressed that I knew and worked with Upton Sinclair. He was my partner in the publication of this anthology. My last meeting with him was in a small room in New York's famed Algonquin Hotel where we sat together while he cooked rice over a small stove that he'd spirited into his room. He was a delightful man who changed the perception of our world. And whose books like *The Jungle* vastly improved it for all of us.

Last year, two good friends died who were also my authors. One was the amazing Ferdinand Lundberg. His *America's 60 Families* became the touchstone for Franklin D. Roosevelt's New Deal. And Lundberg's *The Rich and the Super-Rich*, which I published, did more than add the word super-rich to our language. It showed us who really owned America.

The Rich and the Super-Rich was a #1 bestseller throughout the world. When *Forbes* magazine launched its "Forbes 400," it credited Lundberg as its inspiration.

The other man, dead at the age of 104, was George Seldes. He exposed the bias of daily newspapers, even as Sinclair had done earlier with his *The Brass Ring*.

Seldes did it with his newsletter *In fact* and with such books as *Lords of the Press; Never Tire of Protesting;* and *Tell the Truth and Run!*

Many years ago, thanks to the determination of my friend, Irving Caesar (he wrote lyrics to such hit songs as "Tea for Two"; "Swannee"; "I Want To Be Happy," etc.), I published my first anthology *The Great Quotations*. (At this writing, Irving is alive and well and 100 years old.)

I was able to publish *The Great Quotations* by George Seldes only with the help of more than seventy "patrons." These included, Dr.

7

Albert Ellis, Ira Gershwin, "Yip" Harburg, Oscar Hammerstein, and Steve Allen.

It was quite a job. I determined never to tackle the work and cost of producing another anthology.

And then, one peaceful day in May 1962, I was approached by Upton Sinclair's friend, Dr. Harry W. Laidler. Upton Sinclair wanted to meet me to persuade me to update and put back into print his collection of social protest literature titled, *The Cry for Justice*. It was originally published in 1915 and had been out of print for decades.

How could I refuse the king of muckrakers and one of America's true heroes?

Edward Sagarin and Albert Teichner revised and updated the book. It was successful. When I sold Lyle Stuart, Inc., in 1989, *The Cry for Justice* was one of the few titles I bought back from my former company.

This edition has been updated and continues in the spirit and tradition of our publishing philosophy.

No single volume can contain all the worthwhile treasures that comprise the best of protest literature. This then is but a sampling. But I find it a rich and inspiring sampling—and I hope you do too.

Lyle Stuart
April, 1996
New York City

Postscript: A word about the cover illustration. It depicts Stjepan Filipovic, a Yugoslavian metalworker, at the moment of his death.

Stjepan Filipovic joined Tito's partisans in their uprising against the Nazi occupation. He was captured and ordered hung in the public square in the Serbian village of Valjevo. The Nazis rounded up the townspeople and ordered them to watch. The hanging was intended to frighten the local inhabitants into obeying their German occupiers.

When the Nazis put the rope around his neck, Stjepan Filipovic flung his arms out, cursed the Germans as murderers, and even as he was hung, shouted to his fellow Yugoslavians to continue their resistance.

At the moment of death, a Nazi solder snapped a photograph. The soldier was later captured by the Allies and the photo seized. It became the basis for a sculpture by Vojin Bakiu. The statue is now a monument and sits in a garden fronting the house where Tito hid as he prepared for his partisan uprising against the Nazis.

When I saw the statue in that Belgrade garden, I telephoned New York and ordered the jackets we'd already printed for *The Cry for Justice* destroyed and a photo of the statue converted into art.

I knew nothing could be more appropriate to cover this book.

Introduction to the First Edition

by JACK LONDON

This anthology, I take it, is the first edition, the first gathering together of the body of the literature and art of the humanistic thinkers of the world. As well done as it has been done, it will be better done in the future. There will be much adding, there will be a little subtracting, in the succeeding editions that are bound to come. The result will be a monument of the ages, and there will be none fairer.

Since reading of the Bible, the Koran, and the Talmud has enabled countless devout and earnest right-seeking souls to be stirred and uplifted to higher and finer planes of thought and action, then the reading of this humanist Holy Book cannot fail similarly to serve the needs of groping, yearning humans who seek to discern truth and justice amid the dazzle and murk of the thought-chaos of the present-day world.

No person, no matter how soft and secluded his own life has been, can read this Holy Book and not be aware that the world is filled with a vast mass of unfairness, cruelty, and suffering. He will find that it has been observed, during all the ages, by the thinkers, the seers, the poets, and the philosophers.

And such person will learn, possibly, that this fair world so brutally unfair, is not decreed by the will of God nor by any iron law of Nature. He will learn that the world can be fashioned a fair world indeed by the humans who inhabit it, by the very simple, and yet most difficult process of coming to an understanding of the world. Understanding, after all, is merely sympathy in its fine correct sense. And such sympathy, in its genuineness, makes toward unselfishness. Unselfishness inevitably connotes service. And service is the solution of the entire vexatious problem of man.

He, who by understanding becomes converted to the gospel of service, will serve truth to confute liars and make of them truth-tellers; will serve kindness so that brutality will perish; will serve beauty to the erasement of all that is not beautiful. And he who is strong will serve the weak that they may become strong. He will devote his strength, not to the debasement and defilement of his weaker fellows, but to the making of opportunity for them to make themselves into men rather than into slaves and beasts.

One has but to read the names of the men and women whose words burn in these pages, and to recall that by far more than average intelligence have they won to their place in the world's eye and in the world's brain long after the dust of them has vanished, to realize that due credence must be placed in their report of the world herein recorded. They were not tyrants and wastrels, hypocrites and liars, brewers and gamblers, market-riggers and stock-brokers. They were givers and servers, and seers and humanists. They were unselfish. They conceived of life, not in terms of profit, but of service.

Life tore at them with its heart-break. They could not escape the hurt of it by selfish refuge in the gluttonies of brain and body. They saw, and steeled themselves to see, clear-eyed und unafraid. Nor were they afflicted by some strange myopia. They all saw the same thing. They are all agreed upon what they saw: The totality of their evidence proves this with unswerving consistency. They have brought the report, the commissioners of humanity. It is here in these pages. It is a true report.

But not merely have they reported the human ills. They have proposed the remedy. And their remedy is of no part of all the jangling sects. It has nothing to do with the complicated metaphysical processes by which one may win to other worlds and imagined gains beyond the sky. It is a remedy for this world, since worlds must be taken one at a time. And yet, that not even the jangling sects should receive hurt by the making fairer of this world for this own world's sake, it is well, for all future worlds of them that need future worlds, that their splendor be not tarnished by the vileness and ugliness of this world.

It is so simple a remedy, merely service. Not one ignoble thought or act is demanded of any one of all men and women in the world to make fair the world. The call is for nobility of thinking, nobility of doing. The call is for service, and, such is the wholesomeness of it, he who serves all, best serves himself.

Times change, and men's minds with them. Down the past, civilizations have exposited themselves in terms of power, of world-power or of other-world power. No civilization has yet exposited itself in terms of love-of-man. The humanists have no quarrel with the previous civilizations. They were necessary in the development of man. But their purpose is fulfilled, and they may well pass, leaving man to build the new and higher civilization that will exposit itself in terms of love and service and brotherhood.

To see gathered here together this great body of human beauty and fineness and nobleness is to realize what glorious humans have already existed, do exist, and will continue increasingly to exist until all the world beautiful be made over in their image. We know how gods are made. Comes now the time to make a world.

HONOLULU, March 6, 1915.

Acknowledgments

The editors of the present edition have made every effort to obtain permission from authors and publishers for the use of all new material in this volume protected by copyright. Material from the following authors is used by permission:

James Baldwin, from *Notes of a Native Son*, reprinted by permission of Beacon Press, © 1955 by James Baldwin.

Carleton Beals, from *America South*, J. B. Lippincott Co., publisher.

Albert Camus, from *Resistance, Rebellion and Death*, and from *The Rebel*, Alfred A. Knopf, Inc., publisher.

Clarence Darrow, from *Crime: Its Cause and Treatment*, copyright 1922, 1950 by the publishers, Thomas Y. Crowell Co., New York.

Milovan Djilas from *The New Class*, Frederick A. Praeger, Inc., publishers.

Danilo Dolci, from *Report from Palermo*, copyright 1956 Giulo Einaudi Editore S. p. A., copyright 1959 The Orion Press, Inc. Reprinted by permission of The Orion Press.

Theodore Dreiser, from *An American Tragedy*. Reprinted by arrangement with The World Publishing Co.

Albert Einstein, from *The Fight Against War*, edited by Alfred Leif, reprinted by permission of The John Day Co., publisher.

Sigmund Freud, from *The Future of an Illusion*, and from *Civilization and Its Discontents*, reprinted by permission of Liveright Publishing Corp. and Hogarth Press, Ltd.

Erich Fromm, from *The Sane Society*, copyright 1955 by Erich Fromm. Reprinted by permission of Holt, Rinehart and Winston, Inc.

Michael Harrington, from *The Other America*, copyright 1962 by Michael Harrington. Reprinted with permission of The Macmillan Company.

Langston Hughes, *Scottsboro*, reprinted by permission of Langston Hughes, copyright 1932 by Prentiss Taylor; also *I Dream a World* from the opera *Troubled Island*, music by William Grant Still, copyright 1941 by Leeds Music Corp., poem used by permission of Langston Hughes.

Charles Hurd, from *A Treasury of Great American Speeches*, copyright 1959 by Hawthorn Books, Inc., New York, for excerpts from speeches by Eugene Debs, William Faulkner, Harold Ickes, John L. Lewis, and Franklin D. Roosevelt.

V. I. Lenin, from *Imperialism,* by permission of Lawrence and Wishart.

Walter Lord, from *A Night to Remember,* copyright 1955 by Walter Lord. Reprinted by permission of Holt, Rinehart and Winston, Inc.

Carey McWilliams, from *Witch Hunt: The Revival of Heresy,* copyright 1950 by Carey McWilliams, reprinted by permission of Little, Brown and Company.

Thomas Mann, from *The Coming Victory of Democracy,* reprinted by permission of Alfred A. Knopf, Inc.

Mao Tse-Tung, from *Selected Works,* reprinted by permission of International Publishers, New York.

Katherine Mayo, from *Mother India,* copyright 1927 by Harcourt, Brace & World, Inc.; renewed 1955 by M. Moyca Newell, and reprinted by permission of the publishers.

Edna St. Vincent Millay, from *The Murder of Lidice,* published by Harper & Brothers, copyright 1942 by Edna St. Vincent Millay, reprinted by permission of Norma Millay Ellis.

C. Wright Mills, from *The Power Elite,* copyright 1956 by Oxford University Press, Inc. Reprinted by permission.

Christopher Morley, from *Ballad of New York.* "Children's Crusade," copyright 1950 by The Saturday Review Associates, Inc. Reprinted by permission of Doubleday & Co., Inc.

Lewis Mumford, from *The Condition of Man,* copyright 1944 by Lewis Mumford. Reprinted by permission of Harcourt, Brace & World, Inc.

John Reed, from *Ten Days that Shook the World,* reprinted by permission of International Publishers, New York.

David Rousset, from *The Other Kingdom,* copyright 1947 by Harcourt, Brace & World, Inc., and reprinted with their permission.

Bertrand Russell, from *Has Man a Future?,* copyright 1961 by Bertrand Russell, and reprinted by permission of Simon and Schuster, Inc.

Carl Sandburg, from *The People, Yes,* copyright 1936 by Harcourt, Brace &World, Inc., and reprinted with their permission.

Jean-Paul Sartre, from *Portrait of the Anti-Semite,* by permsision of Martin Secker and Warburg, Ldt.

George Seldes, from *Sawdust Caesar,* by permission of the author.

Lincoln Steffens, from *The Autobiography of Lincoln Steffens,* copyright 1931 by Harcourt, Brace & World, Inc.; renewed 1959 by Peter Steffens. Reprinted by permission of the publishers.

Adlai E. Stevenson, from *Major Campaign Speeches of Adlai E. Stevenson,* by permission of Random House, Inc.

Harvey Swados, from *A Radical's America,* copyright 1957 by Harvey Swados, reprinted by permission of Little, Brown and Company–Atlantic Monthly Press.

Norman Thomas, from *The Conscientious Objector in War,* by permission of the author.

Leon Trotsky, from *The Revolution Betrayed,* by permission of Pioneer Publishers, New York.

Veterans of the Abraham Lincoln Brigade, for permission to use two poems from Songs of the Spanish Civil War; permission granted by M. Fishman for Veterans of the Abraham Lincoln Brigade.

Yevgeny Yevtushenko, from *Selected Poems,* translated by R. Milner-Gulland and Peter Levi, reprinted by permission of Penguin Books, Inc.

In the first edition of this book, acknowledgment was made to many publishers and authors who had granted permission for use of material. It is almost half a century since that edition was published; most of the material used at that time is now in the public domain. Some of the publishers are no longer in existence, and some of the excerpts and writings are not retained in this edition. We wish to repeat the original thanks to authors, publishers and artists, who permitted their work to be used in the original edition of this book. The full list of acknowledgments appears on pages 7 to 12 of that edition.

Contents

List of Illustrations

Preface to the First Edition
by UPTON SINCLAIR

When the idea of this collection was first thought of, it was a matter of surprise that the task should have been so long unattempted. There exist small collections of Socialist songs for singing, but apparently this is the first effort that has been made to cover the whole field of the literature of social protest, both in prose and poetry, and from all languages and times.

The reader's first inquiry will be as to the qualifications of the editor. Let me say that I gave nine years of my life to a study of literature under academic guidance, and then, emerging from a great endowed university, discovered the modern movement of proletarian revolt, and have given fifteen years to the study and interpretation of that. The present volume is thus a blending of two points of view. I have reread the favorites of my youth, choosing from them what now seemed most vital; and I have sought to test the writers of my own time by the touchstone of the old standards.

The size of the task I did not realize until I had gone too far to retreat. It meant not merely the rereading of the classics and the standard anthologies; it meant going through a small library of volumes by living writers, the files of many magazines, and a dozen or more scrap-books and collections of fugitive verse. At the end of this labor I found myself with a pile of typewritten manuscript a foot high; and the task of elimination was the most difficult of all.

To a certain extent, of course, the selection was self-determined. No anthology of social protest could omit "The Song of the Shirt," and "The Cry of the Children," and "A Man's a Man for A' That"; neither could it omit the "Marseillaise" and the "Internationale." Equally inevitable were selections from Shelley and Swinburne, Ruskin, Carlyle and Morris, Whitman, Tolstoy and Zola. The same was true of Wells and Shaw and Kropotkin, Hauptmann and Maeterlinck, Romain Rolland and Anatole France. When it came to the newer writers, I sought first their own judgment as to their best work; and later I submitted the manuscript to several friends, the best qualified men and women I knew. Thus the final version was the product of a number of minds; and the collection may be said to represent, not its editor, but a whole movement, made and sustained by the master-spirits of all ages.

For this reason I may without suspicion of egotism say what I think about the volume. It was significant to me that several persons reading the manuscript and writing quite independently, referred to it as "a new Bible." I believe that it is, what literally and simply what the old Bible was—a selection by the living minds of a living time of the best and truest writings known to them. It is a Bible of the future, a Gospel of the new hope of the race. It is a book for the apostles of a new dispensation to carry about with them; a book to cheer the discouraged and console the wounded in humanity's last war of liberation.

The standards of the book are those of literature. If there has been any letting down, it has been in the case of old writings, which have an interest apart from that of style. It brings us a thrill of wonder to find, in an ancient Egyptian parchment, a father setting forth to his son how easy is the life of the lawyer, and what a dog's life is that of the farmer. It amuses us to read a play, produced in Athens two thousand, two hundred and twenty-three years ago, in which is elaborately propounded the question which thousands of Socialist "soap-boxers" are answering every night: "Who will do the dirty work?" It makes us shudder, perhaps, to find a Spaniard of the thirteenth century analyzing the evil devices of tyrants, and expounding in detail the labor-policy of some present-day great corporations in America.

Let me add that I have not considered it my function to act as censor to the process of social evolution. Every aspect of the revolutionary movement has found a voice in this book. Two questions have been asked of each writer: Have you had something vital to say? and Have you said it with some special effectiveness? The reader will find for example, one or two of the hymns of the "Christian Socialists"; he will also find one of the parodies on Christian hymns which are sung by the Industrial Workers of the World in their "jungles" in the Far West. The Anarchists and the apostles of insurrection are also represented; and if some of the things seem to the reader the mere unchaining of furies, I would say, let him not blame the faithful anthologist, let him not blame even the writer—let him blame himself, who has acquiesced in the existence of conditions which have driven his fellow-men to the extremes of madness and despair.

In the preparation of this work I have placed myself under obligation to so many people that it would take much space to make complete acknowledgments. I must thank those friends who went through the bulky manuscript, and gave me the benefit of their detailed criticism: George Sterling, Max Eastman, Floyd Dell, Clement Wood, Louis Untermeyer, and my wife. I am under obligation to a number of people, some of them strangers, who went to the trouble of sending me scrap-books which represented years and even decades of collecting: Elisabeth Balch, Elizabeth Magie Phillips, Frank B. Norman, Frank Stuhlman, J. M. Maddox, Edward J. O'Brien, and Clement Wood. Among those who helped me with valuable suggestions were: Edwin Björkman, Reginald Wright Kauffman, Thomas Seltzer, Jack London, Rose Pastor Stokes, May Beals, Elizabeth Freeman, Arthur W. Calhoun, Frank Shay, Alexander Berkman, Joseph F. Gould, Louis Untermeyer, Harold Monro, Morris Hillquit, Peter Kropotkin, Dr. James P. Warbasse, and the Baroness von Blomberg. The fullness of the section devoted to ancient writings is in part due to the advice of a number of scholars: Dr. Paul Carus, Professor Crawford H. Toy, Professor William Cranston Lawton, Professor Charles Burton Gulick, Professor Thomas D. Goodell, Professor Walton Brooks Mc Daniels, Rev. John Haynes Holmes, Professor George F. Moore, Prof. Walter Rauschenbusch, and Professor Charles R. Lanman.

With regard to the illustrations in the volume, I endeavored to repeat in the field of art what had been done in the field of literature: to obtain the best material, both old and new, and select the most interesting and vital.

I have to record my indebtedness to a number of friends who made suggestions in this field—Ryan Walker, Art Young, John Mowbray-Clarke, Martin Birnbaum, Odon Por, and Walter Crane. Also I must thank Mr. Frank Weitenkampf and Dr. Herman Rosenthal of the New York Public Library, and Dr. Clifford of the Library of the Metropolitan Museum of Art. To the artists whose copyrighted work I have used I owe my thanks for their permission: as likewise to the many writers whose copyrighted books I have quoted. Elsewhere in the volume I have made acknowledgments to publishers for the rights they have kindly granted. Let me here add this general caution: *The copyrighted passages used have been used by permission, and any one who desires to reprint them must obtain similar permission.*

One or two hundred contemporary authors responded to my invitation and sent me specimens of their writings. Of these authors, probably three-fourths will not find their work included—for which seeming discourtesy I can only offer the plea of the limitations of space which were imposed upon me. I am not being diplomatic, but am stating a fact when I say that I had to leave out much that I thought was of excellent quality.

What was chosen will now speak for itself. Let my last word be of the hope, which has been with me constantly, that the book may be to others what it has been to me. I have spent with it the happiest year of my lifetime: the happiest, because occupied with beauty of the greatest and truest sort. If the material in this volume means to you, the reader, what it has meant to me, you will live with it, yearn and hunger with it, and, above all, resolve with it. You will carry it with you about your daily tasks, you will be utterly possessed by it; and again and again you will be led to dedicate yourself to the greatest hope, the most wondrous vision which has ever thrilled the soul of humanity. In this spirit and to this end the book is offered to you. If you will read it through consecutively, skipping nothing, you will find it has a form. You will be led from one passage to the next, and when you reach the end you will be a wiser, a humbler, and a more tender-hearted person.

A Consecration
by JOHN MASEFIELD
English Poet Laureate, 1878–1967

Not of the princes and prelates with periwigged charioteers
Riding triumphantly laurelled to lap the fat of the years,
Rather the scorned—the rejected—the men hemmed in with the
    spears;

The men of the tattered battalion which fights till it dies,
Dazed with the dust of the battle, the din and the cries,
The men with the broken heads and the blood running into their
    eyes.

Not the be-medalled Commander, beloved of the throne,
Riding cock-horse to parade when the bugles are blown,
But the lads who carried the koppie and cannot be known.

Not the ruler for me, but the ranker, the tramp of the road,
The slave with the sack on his shoulders pricked on with the goad,
The man with too weighty a burden, too weary a load.

The sailor, the stoker of steamers, the man with the clout,
The chantyman bent at the halliards putting a tune to the shout,
The drowsy man at the wheel and the tired lookout.

Others may sing of the wine and the wealth and the mirth,
The portly presence of potentates goodly in girth;—
Mine be the dirt and the dross, the dust and scum of the earth!

Theirs be the music, the color, the glory, the gold;
Mine be a handful of ashes, a mouthful of mould.
Of the maimed, of the halt and the blind in the rain and the
    cold—

Of these shall my songs be fashioned, my tale be told.

                                        AMEN.

BOOK I

Toil

The dignity and tragedy of labor; pictures of the actual conditions under which men and women work in mills and factories, fields and mines.

The Man With the Hoe

by EDWIN MARKHAM
American poet, 1852-1940

Bowed by the weight of centuries he leans
Upon his hoe and gazes on the ground,
The emptiness of ages in his face,
And on his back the burden of the world.
Who made him dead to rapture and despair,
A thing that grieves not and that never hopes,
Stolid and stunned, a brother to the ox?
Who loosened and let down this brutal jaw?
Whose was the hand that slanted back this brow?
Whose breath blew out the light within this brain?

Is this the thing the Lord God made and gave
To have dominion over sea and land;
To trace the stars and search the heavens for power;
To feel the passion of Eternity?
Is this the dream He dreamed who shaped the suns
And marked their ways upon the ancient deep?
Down all the stretch of Hell to its last gulf
There is no shape more terrible than this—
More tongued with censure of the world's blind greed—
More filled with signs and portents for the soul—
More fraught with menace to the universe.

What gulfs between him and the seraphim!
Slave of the wheel of labor, what to him
Are Plato and the swing of Pleiades?
What the long reaches of the peaks of song,
The rift of dawn, the reddening of the rose?
Through this dread shape the suffering ages look;
Time's tragedy is in that aching stoop;
Through this dread shape humanity betrayed,
Plundered, profaned and disinherited,
Cries protest to the Judges of the World,
A protest that is also prophecy.

29

O masters, lords and rulers in all lands,
Is this the handiwork you give to God,
This monstrous thing distorted and soul-quenched?
How will you ever straighten up this shape;
Touch it again with immortality;
Give back the upward looking and the light;
Rebuild in it the music and the dream;
Make right the immemorial infamies,
Perfidious wrongs, immedicable woes?

O masters, lords and rulers in all lands,
How will the Future reckon with this **Man?**
How answer his brute question in that hour
When whirlwinds of rebellion shake the world?
How will it be with kingdoms and with kings—
With those who shaped him to the thing he is—
When this dumb Terror shall reply to God,
After the silence of the centuries?

Country Life

by GEORGE CRABBE
One of the earliest of English realistic poets, called
'The Poet of the Poor'; 1754-1832

Or will you deem them amply paid in health,
Labor's fair child, that languishes with wealth?
Go then! and see them rising with the sun,
Through a long course of daily toil to run;
See them beneath the dog-star's raging heat,
When the knees tremble and the temples beat;
Behold them, leaning on their scythes, look o'er
The labor past, and toils to come explore;
See them alternate suns and showers engage,
And hoard up aches and anguish for their age;
Through fens and marshy moors their steps pursue,
Where their warm pores imbibe the evening dew;
Then own that labor may as fatal be
To these thy slaves, as thine excess to thee.

Farm Laborers

by James Matthew Barrie
Scottish playwright, 1860-1937

Grand, patient, long-suffering fellows these men were, up at five, summer and winter, foddering their horses, maybe, hours before there would be food for themselves, miserably paid, housed like cattle, and when rheumatism seized them, liable to be flung aside like a broken graip. As hard was the life of the women: coarse food, chaff beds, damp clothes their portion, their sweethearts in the service of masters who were loath to fee a married man. Is it to be wondered that these lads who could be faithful unto death drank soddenly on their one free day; that these girls, starved of opportunities for womanliness, of which they could make as much as the finest lady, sometimes woke after a holiday to wish that they might wake no more?

Helotage
(*From "Sartor Resartus"*)
by Thomas Carlyle
British historian and essayist, 1795-1881

It is not because of his toils that I lament for the poor: we must all toil, or steal (howsoever we name our stealing), which is worse; no faithful workman finds his task a pastime. The poor is hungry and athirst; but for him also there is food and drink: he is heavy-laden and weary; but for him also the Heavens send sleep, and of the deepest; in his smoky cribs, a clear dewy haven of rest envelops him, and fitful glitterings of cloud-skirted dreams. But what I do mourn over is, that the lamp of his soul should go out; that no ray of heavenly, or even of earthly, knowledge should visit him; but only, in the haggard darkness, like two spectres, Fear and Indignation bear him company. Alas, while the body stands so broad and brawny, must the soul lie blinded, dwarfed, stupefied, almost annihilated! Alas, was this too a Breath of God; bestowed in heaven, but on earth never to be unfolded!—That there should one Man die ignorant who had capacity for Knowledge, this I call a tragedy, were it to happen more than twenty times in the minute, as by some computations it does. The miserable fraction of Science which our united Mankind, in a wide universe of Nescience, has acquired, why is not this, with all diligence, imparted to all?

The Man with the Hoe, *Jean François Millet*

Played Out

(From "Songs of the Dead End")
by PATRICK MACGILL
Irish working-class poet, born 1890

As a bullock falls in the crooked ruts, he fell when the day was
    o'er,
The hunger gripping his stinted guts, his body shaken and sore.
They pulled it out of the ditch in the dark, as a brute is pulled
    from its lair,
The corpse of the navvy, stiff and stark, with the clay on its face
    and hair.

In Christian lands, with calloused hands, he labored for others'
    good,
In workshop and mill, ditchway and drill, earnest, eager, and rude;
Unhappy and gaunt with worry and want, a food to the whims of
    fate,
Hashing it out and booted about at the will of the goodly and
    great.

To him was applied the scorpion lash, for him the gibe and the
    goad—
The roughcast fool of our moral wash, the rugous wretch of the
    road.
Willing to crawl for a pittance small to the swine of the tinsel sty,
Beggared and burst from the very first, he chooses the ditch to
    die—
. . . Go, pick the dead from the sloughy bed, and hide him from
    mortal eye.

He tramped through the colorless winter land, or swined in the
    scorching heat,
The dry skin hacked on his sapless hands or blistering on his feet;
He wallowed in mire unseen, unknown, where your houses of
    pleasure rise,
And hapless, hungry, and chilled to the bone, he builded the
    edifice.
In cheerless model and filthy pub, his sinful hours were passed,
Or footsore, weary, he begged his grub, in the sough of the
    hail-whipped blast,

So some might riot in wealth and ease, with food and wine be
    crammed,
He wrought like a mule, in muck to his knees, dirty, dissolute,
    damned.

Arrogant, adipose, you sit in the homes he builded high;
Dirty the ditch, in the depths of it he chooses a spot to die,
Foaming with nicotine-tainted lips, holding his aching breast,
Dropping down like a cow that slips, smitten with rinderpest;
Drivelling yet of the work and wet, swearing as sinners swear,
Raving the rule of the gambling school, mixing it up with a
    prayer.

He lived like a brute as the navvies live, and went as the cattle go,
No one to sorrow and no one to shrive, for heaven ordained it so—
He handed his check to the shadow in black, and went to the
    misty lands,
Never a mortal to close his eyes or a woman to cross his hands.

As a bullock falls in the rugged ruts
He fell when the day was o'er,
Hunger gripping his weasened guts,
But never to hunger more—

They pulled it out of the ditch in the dark,
The chilling frost on its hair,
The mole-skinned navvy stiff and stark
From no particular where.

Conventional Lies of Our Civilization
by MAX NORDAU
Hungarian physician and social commentator, 1849-1923

The modern day laborer is more wretched than the slave of
former times, for he is fed by no master nor any one else, and if his
position is one of more liberty than the slave, it is principally the
liberty of dying of hunger. He is by no means so well off as the
outlaw of the Middle Ages, for he has none of the gay independence of the free-lance. He seldom rebels against society, and has
neither means nor opportunity to take by violence or treachery
what is denied him by the existing conditions of life. The rich
is thus richer, the poor poorer than ever before since the begin-
nings of history.

Rounding the Horn
(From "Dauber")
by JOHN MASEFIELD

Then came the cry of "Call all hands on deck!"
The Dauber knew its meaning; it was come:
Cape Horn, that tramples beauty into wreck,
And crumples steel and smites the strong man dumb.
Down clattered flying kites and staysails: some
Sang out in quick, high calls: the fair-leads skirled,
And from the south-west came the end of the world . . .

"Lay out!" the Bosun yelled. The Dauber laid
Out on the yard, gripping the yard, and feeling
Sick at the mighty space of air displayed
Below his feet, where mewing birds were wheeling.
A giddy fear was on him; he was reeling.
He bit his lip half through, clutching the jack.
A cold sweat glued the shirt upon his back.

The yard was shaking, for a brace was loose.
He felt that he would fall; he clutched, he bent,
Clammy with natural terror to the shoes
While idiotic promptings came and went.
Snow fluttered on a wind-flaw and was spent;
He saw the water darken. Someone yelled,
"Frap it; don't stay to furl! Hold on!" He held.

Darkness came down—half darkness—in a whirl;
The sky went out, the waters disappeared.
He felt a shocking pressure of blowing hurl
The ship upon her side. The darkness speared
At her with wind; she staggered, she careered,
Then down she lay. The Dauber felt her go;
He saw her yard tilt downwards. Then the snow

Whirled all about—dense, multitudinous, cold—
Mixed with the wind's one devilish thrust and shriek,
Which whiffled out men's tears, defeated, took hold,
Flattening the flying drift against the cheek.
The yards buckled and bent, man could not speak.
The ship lay on her broadside; the wind's sound
Had devilish malice at having got her downed. . . .

How long the gale had blown he could not tell,
Only the world had changed, his life had died.
A moment now was everlasting hell
Nature an onslaught from the weather side,
A withering rush of death, a frost that cried,
Shrieked, till he withered at the heart; a hail
Plastered his oilskins with an icy mail. . . .

"Up!" yelled the Bosun; "up and clear the wreck!"
The Dauber followed where he led; below
He caught one giddy glimpsing of the deck
Filled with white water, as though heaped with snow.
He saw the streamers of the rigging blow
Straight out like pennons from the splintered mast,
Then, all sense dimmed, all was an icy blast

Roaring from nether hell and filled with ice,
Roaring and crashing on the jerking stage,
An utter bridle given to utter vice,
Limitless power mad with endless rage
Withering the soul; a minute seemed an age.
He clutched and hacked at ropes, at rags of sail,
Thinking that comfort was a fairy-tale

Told long ago—long, long ago—long since
Heard of in other lives—imagined, dreamed—
There where the basest beggar was a prince.
To him in torment where the tempest screamed,
Comfort and warmth and ease no longer seemed
Things that a man could know; soul, body, brain,
Knew nothing but the wind, the cold, the pain.

Stokers

(From "The Harbor")
by ERNEST POOLE
American playwright and novelist, 1880-1950

We crawled down a short ladder and through low passageways, dripping wet, and so came into the stokehole.

This was a long narrow chamber with a row of glowing furnace doors. Wet coal and coal-dust lay on the floor. At either end a small steel door opened into bunkers that ran along the sides of the ship, deep down near the bottom, containing thousands of tons of soft coal. In the stokehole the fires were not yet up, but by the time the ship was at sea the furnace mouths would be white hot and the men at work half naked. They not only shovelled coal into the flames, they had to spread it as well, and at intervals rake out the "clinkers" in fiery masses on the floor. On these a stream of water played, filling the chamber with clouds of steam. In older ships, like this one, a "lead stoker" stood at the head of the line and set the pace for the others to follow. He was paid more to keep up the pace. But on the big new liners this pacer was replaced by a gong.

"And at each stroke of the gong you shovel," said Joe. "You do this till you forget your name. Every time the boat pitches the floor heaves you forward, the fire spurts at you out of the doors, and the gong keeps on like a sledge-hammer coming down on top of your mind. And all you think of is your bunk and the time when you're to tumble in."

From the stokers' quarters presently there came a burst of singing.

"Now let's go back," he ended, "and see how they're getting ready for this."

As we crawled back, the noise increased, and swelled to a roar as we entered. The place was pandemonium. Those groups I had noticed around the bags had been getting out the liquor, and now at eight o'clock in the morning half the crew were already well soused. Some moved restlessly about. One huge bull of a creature with limpid shining eyes stopped suddenly with a puzzled stare, and then leaned back on a bunk and laughed uproariously. From there he lurched over the shoulder of a thin, wiry, sober man who, sitting on the edge of a bunk, was slowly spelling out the words of a newspaper aeroplane story. The big man laughed again and spit, and the thin man jumped half up and snarled.

Louder rose the singing. Half the crew was crowded close around a little red-faced cockney. He was the modern "chanty man." With sweat pouring down his cheeks and the muscles of his neck drawn taut, he was jerking out verse after verse about women. He sang to an old "chanty" tune, one that I remembered well. But he was not singing out under the stars, he was screaming at steel walls down here in the bottom of the ship. And although he kept speeding up his song, the crowd were too drunk to wait for the chorus; their voices kept tumbling in over his, and soon it was only a frenzy of sound, a roar with yells rising out of it. The singers kept pounding each other's backs or waving bottles over their heads. Two bottles smashed together and brought a still higher burst of glee.

"I'm tired!" Joe shouted. "Let's get out!"

I caught a glimpse of his strained frowning face. Again it came over me in a flash, the years he had spent in holes like this, in this hideous rotten world of his, while I had lived joyously in mine. And as though he had read the thought in my disturbed and troubled eyes, "Let's go up where *you* belong," he said.

I followed him up and away from his friends. As we climbed ladder after ladder, fainter and fainter on our ears rose that yelling from below. Suddenly we came out on deck and slammed an iron door behind us. And I was where *I* belonged.

I was in dazzling sunshine and keen, frosty autumn air. I was among gay throngs of people. Dainty women brushed me by. I felt the softness of their furs, I breathed the fragrant scent of them and of the flowers that they wore, I saw their trim, fresh, immaculate clothes. I heard the joyous tumult of their talking and their laughing to the regular crash of the band—all the life of the ship I had known so well.

And I walked through it all as though in a dream. On the dock I watched it spellbound—until with handkerchiefs waving and voices calling down goodbyes, that throng of happy travellers moved slowly out into midstream.

And I knew that deep below all this, down in the bottom of the ship, the stokers were still singing.

The Fertilizer Man
(From "The Jungle")
by UPTON SINCLAIR
American novelist, essayist, dramatist and social reformer, 1878–1968

His labor took him about one minute to learn. Before him was one of the vents of the mill in which the fertilizer was being ground—rushing forth in a great brown river, with a spray of the finest dust floating forth in clouds. Jurgis was given a shovel, and along with half a dozen others it was his task to shovel this fertilizer into carts. That others were at work he knew by the sound, and by the fact that he sometimes collided with them; otherwise they might as well not have been there, for in the blinding dust-storm a man could not see six feet in front of his face. When he had filled one cart he had to grope around him until another came, and if there was none on hand he continued to grope till one arrived. In five minutes he was, of course, a mass of fertilizer from head to feet; they gave him a sponge to tie over his mouth, so that he could breathe, but the sponge did not prevent his lips and eyelids from caking up with it and his ears from filling solid. He looked like a brown ghost at twilight—from hair to shoes he became the color of the building and of everything in it, and for that matter a hundred yards outside it. The building had to be left open, and when the wind blew Durham and Company lost a great deal of fertilizer.

Working in his shirt-sleeves, and with the thermometer at over a hundred, the phosphates soaked in through every pore of Jurgis' skin, and in five minutes he had a headache, and in fifteen was almost dazed. The blood was pounding in his brain like an engine's throbbing; there was a frightful pain in the top of his skull, and he could hardly control his hands. Still, with the memory of his four jobless months behind him, he fought on, in a frenzy of determination; and half an hour later he began to vomit—he vomited until it seemed as if his inwards must be torn into shreds. A man could get used to the fertilizer-mill, the boss had said, if he would only make up his mind to it; but Jurgis now began to see that it was a question of making up his stomach.

At the end of that day of horror, he could scarcely stand. He had to catch himself now and then, and lean against a building and get his bearings. Most of the men, when they came out, made straight for a saloon—they seemed to place fertilizer and rattle-snake poison in one class. But Jurgis was too ill to think of drinking—he could only make his way to the street and stagger on to a car. He had a sense of humor, and later on, when he became an old hand, he used to think it fun to board a streetcar and see what happened. Now, however, he was too ill to notice it—how the people in the car began to gasp and sputter, to put their handkerchiefs to their noses, and transfix him with furious glances. Jurgis only knew that a man in front of him immediately got up and gave him a seat; and that half a minute later the two people on each side of him got up; and that in a full minute the crowded car was nearly empty—those passengers who could not get room on the platform having gotten out to walk.

Of course, Jurgis had made his home a miniature fertilizer mill a minute after entering. The stuff was half an inch deep in his skin—his whole system was full of it, and it would have taken a week not merely of scrubbing, but of vigorous exercise, to get it out of him. As it was, he could be compared with nothing known to man, save that newest discovery of the savants, a substance which emits energy for an unlimited time, without being itself in the least diminished in power. He smelt so that he made all the food at the table taste, and set the whole family to vomiting; for himself it was three days before he could keep anything upon his stomach—he might wash his hands, and use a knife and fork, but were not his mouth and throat filled with the poison?

And still Jurgis stuck it out! In spite of splitting headaches he would stagger down to the plant and take up his stand once more, and begin to shovel in the blinding clouds of dust. And so at the end of the week he was a fertilizer-man for life—he was able to eat again, and though his head never stopped aching, it ceased to be so bad that he could not work.

Pittsburgh
by JAMES OPPENHEIM
American poet, 1882-1932

Over his face his gray hair drifting hides his Labor-glory in smoke,
Strange through his breath the soot is sifting, his feet are buried
    in coal and coke.
By night hands twisted and lurid in fires, by day hands blackened
    with grime and oil,
He toils at the foundries and never tires, and ever and ever his lot
    is toil.

He speeds his soul till his body wrestles with terrible tonnage and
    terrible time,
Out through the yards and over the trestles the flat-cars clank and
    the engines chime,
His mills through windows seem eaten with fire, his high cranes
    travel, his ingots roll,
And billet and wheel and whistle and wire shriek with the speed-
    ing up of his soul.
Lanterns with reds and greens a-glisten wave the way and the
    head-light glares,

The back-bent laborers glance and listen and out through the
    night the tail-light flares—
Deep in the mills like a tipping cradle the huge converter turns
    on its wheel
And sizzling spills in the ten-ton ladle a golden water of molten
    steel.

Yet screwed with toil his low face searches shadow-edged fires and
    whited pits,
Gripping his levers his body lurches, grappling his irons he prods
    and hits,
And deaf with the roll and clangor and rattle with its sharp
    escaping staccato of steam,
And blind with flame and worn with battle, into his tonnage he
    turns his dream.

The world he has builded rises around us, our wonder-cities and
    weaving rails,
Over his wires a marvel has found us, a glory rides in our wheeled
    mails,
For the Earth grows small with strong Steel woven, and they come
    together who plotted apart—
But he who has wrought this thing in his oven knows only toil and
    the tired heart.

The Song of the Wage Slave
(From "The Spell of the Yukon")
by ROBERT W. SERVICE
Canadian poet, 1874-1958

When the long, long day is over, and the Big Boss gives me my pay,
I hope that it won't be hell-fire, as some of the parsons say.
And I hope that it won't be heaven, with some of the parsons I've
    met—
All I want is just quiet, just to rest and forget.
Look at my face, toil-furrowed; look at my calloused hands;
Master, I've done Thy bidding, wrought in Thy many lands—
Wrought for the little masters, big-bellied they be, and rich;
I've done their desire for a daily hire, and I die like a dog in a
    ditch. . . .
I, the primitive toiler, half naked and grimed to the eyes,

Once Ye Have Seen My Face, Ye Dare Not Mock

Sweating it deep in their ditches, swining it stark in their styes;
Hurling down forests before me, spanning tumultuous streams;
Down in the ditch building o'er me palaces fairer than dreams;
Boring the rock to the ore-bed, driving the road through the fen,
Resolute, dumb, uncomplaining, a man in a world of men.
Master, I've filled my contract, wrought in Thy many lands;
Not by my sins wilt Thou judge me, but by the work of my hands.
Master, I've done Thy bidding, and the light is low in the west,
And the long, long shift is over. . . . Master, I've earned it—Rest.

A Cry from the Ghetto
by MORRIS ROSENFELD

Yiddish poet of New York's East Side tenements, 1862-1923. The following translation is by Charles Weber Linn.

The roaring of the wheels has filled my ears,
    The clashing and the clamor shut me in;
Myself, my soul, in chaos disappears,
    I cannot think or feel amid the din.
Toiling and toiling and toiling—endless toil.
    For whom? For what? Why should the work be done?
I do not ask, or know. I only toil.
    I work until the day and night are one.

The clock above me ticks away the day,
    Its hands are spinning, spinning, like the wheels.
It cannot sleep or for a moment stay,
    It is a thing like me, and does not feel.
It throbs as tho' my heart were beating there—
    A heart? My heart? I know not what it means.
The clock ticks, and below I strive and stare.
    And so we lose the hour. We are machines.

Noon calls a truce, an ending to the sound,
    As if a battle had one moment stayed—
A bloody field! The dead lie all around;
    Their wounds cry out until I grow afraid.
It comes—the signal! See, the dead men rise,
    They fight again, amid the roar they fight.
Blindly, and knowing not for whom, or why,
    They fight, they fall, they sink into the night.

Trousers
(From "A Motley")
by JOHN GALSWORTHY
English novelist and dramatist, Nobel Prize for Literature 1932; 1867-1933

She held in one hand a threaded needle, in the other a pair of trousers, to which she had been adding the accessories demanded by our civilization. One had never seen her without a pair of trousers in her hand, because she could only manage to supply them with decency at the rate of seven or eight pairs a day, working twelve hours. For each pair she received seven farthings, and used nearly one farthing's worth of cotton; and this gave her an income, in good times, of six to seven shillings a week. But some weeks there were no trousers to be had and then it was necessary to live on the memory of those which had been, together with a little sum put by from weeks when trousers were more plentiful. Deducting two shillings and threepence for rent of the little back room, there was therefore, on an average, about two shillings and ninepence left for the sustenance of herself and husband, who was fortunately a cripple, and somewhat indifferent whether he ate or not. And looking at her face, so furrowed, and at her figure, of which there was not much, one could well understand that she, too, had long established within her such internal economy as was suitable to one who had been "in trousers" twenty-seven years, and, since her husband's accident fifteen years before, in trousers only, finding her own cotton. . . . He was a man with a round, white face, a little grey mustache curving down like a parrot's beak, and round whitish eyes. In his aged and unbuttoned suit of grey, with his head held rather to one side, he looked like a parrot—a bird clinging to its perch, with one grey leg shortened and crumpled against the other. He talked, too, in a toneless, equable voice, looking sideways at the fire, above the rims of dim spectacles, and now and then smiling with a peculiar disenchanted patience.

No—he said—it was no use to complain; did no good! Things had been like this for years, and so, he had no doubt, they always would be. There had never been much in trousers; not this common sort that anybody'd wear, as you might say. Though he'd never seen anybody wearing such things; and where they went to he didn't know—out of England, he should think. Yes, he had been a carman; ran over by a dray. Oh! yes, they had given him something—four bob a week; but the old man had died and the four bob had died too. Still, there he was, sixty years old—not so very bad for his age. . . .

They were talking, he had heard said, about doing something for trousers. But what could you do for things like these, at half a crown a pair? People must have 'em, so you'd got to make 'em. There you were, and there you would be! *She* went and heard them talk. They talked very well, she said. It was intellectual for her to go. He couldn't go himself owing to his leg. He'd like to hear them talk. Oh, yes! and he was silent, staring sideways at the fire as though in the thin crackle of the flames attacking the fresh piece of wood, he were hearing the echo of that talk from which he was cut off. "Lor' bless you!" he said suddenly. "They'll do nothing! Can't!" And, stretching out his dirty hand he took from his wife's lap a pair of trousers, and held it up. "Look at 'em! Why you can see right throu' 'em, linings and all. Who's goin' to pay more than 'alf a crown for that? Where they go to I can't think. Who wears 'em? Some institution I should say. They talk, but dear me, they'll never do anything so long as there's thousands like us, glad to work for what we can get. Best not to think about it, I says."

And laying the trousers back on his wife's lap he resumed his sidelong stare into the fire.

The Song of the Shirt
by THOMAS HOOD
English poet and humorist, 1799-1845

With fingers weary and worn,
   With eyelids heavy and red,
A woman sat, in unwomanly rags,
   Plying her needle and thread,—
     Stitch! stitch! stitch!
   In poverty, hunger, and dirt;
And still with a voice of dolorous pitch
   She sang the "Song of the Shirt!"

"Work! work! work!
   While the cock is crowing aloof!
And work—work—work
   Till the stars shine through the roof!
It's O! to be a slave
   Along with the barbarous Turk,

Where woman has never a soul to save,
   If this is Christian work!

"Work—work—work
   Till the brain begins to swim!
Work—work—work
   Till the eyes are heavy and dim!
Seam, and gusset, and band,
   Band, and gusset, and seam,—
Till over the buttons I fall asleep,
   And sew them on in a dream!

"O Men, with sisters dear!
   O Men, with mothers and wives!
It is not linen you're wearing out,
   But human creatures' lives!
     Stitch—stitch—stitch
   In poverty, hunger, and dirt,—
Sewing at once, with a double thread,
   A shroud as well as a Shirt!

"But why do I talk of Death—
   That phantom of grisly bone?
I hardly fear his terrible shape,
   It seems so like my own—
It seems so like my own
   Because of the fasts I keep;
O God! that bread should be so dear,
   And flesh and blood so cheap!

"Work—work—work!
   My labor never flags;
And what are its wages? A bed of straw,
   A crust of bread—and rags.
That shattered roof—and this naked floor—
   A table—a broken chair—
And a wall so blank my shadow I thank
   For something falling there!

"Work—work—work!
   From weary chime to chime!
Work—work—work

As prisoners work for crime!
Band, and gusset, and seam,
    Seam, and gusset, and band,
Till the heart is sick and the brain benumbed,
    As well as the weary hand.

"Work—work—work
    In the dull December light!
And work—work—work
    When the weather is warm and bright!
While underneath the eaves
    The brooding swallows cling,
As if to show me their sunny backs
    And twit me with the Spring.

"O! but to breathe the breath
    Of the cowslip and primrose sweet—
With the sky above my head,
    And the grass beneath my feet!
For only one short hour
    To feel as I used to feel,
Before I knew the woes of want,
    And the walk that costs a meal!

"O! but for one short hour—
    A respite however brief!
No blessed leisure for Love or Hope,
    But only time for Grief!
A little weeping would ease my heart;
    But in their briny bed
My tears must stop, for every drop
    Hinders needle and thread!"

With fingers weary and worn,
    With eyelids heavy and red,
A woman sat, in unwomanly rags,
    Plying her needle and thread—
        Stitch! stitch! stitch!
    In poverty, hunger, and dirt;
And still, with a voice of dolorous pitch,
Would that its tone could reach the rich!—
    She sang this "Song of the Shirt!"

A London Sweating Den
(From "The People of the Abyss")
by JACK LONDON
California novelist and socialist, 1876-1916

A spawn of children cluttered the slimy pavement, for all the world like tadpoles just turned frogs on the bottom of a dry pond. In a narrow doorway, so narrow that perforce we stepped over her, sat a woman with a young babe, nursing at breasts grossly naked and libelling all the sacredness of motherhood. In the black and narrow hall behind her we waded through a mess of young life, and essayed an even narrower and fouler stairway. Up we went, three flights, each landing two feet by three in area, and heaped with filth and refuse.

There were seven rooms in this abomination called a house. In six of the rooms, twenty-odd people, of both sexes and all ages, cooked, ate, slept, and worked. In size the rooms averaged eight feet by eight, or possibly nine. The seventh room we entered. It was the den in which five men sweated. It was seven feet wide by eight long, and the table at which the work was performed took up the major portion of the space. On this table were five lasts, and there was barely room for the men to stand to their work, for the rest of the space was heaped with cardboard, leather, bundles of shoe uppers, and a miscellaneous assortment of materials used in attaching the uppers of shoes to their soles.

In the adjoining room lived a woman and six children. In another vile hole lived a widow, with an only son of sixteen who was dying of consumption. The woman hawked sweetmeats on the street, I was told, and more often failed than not to supply her son with the three quarts of milk he daily required. Further, this son, weak and dying, did not taste meat oftener than once a week; and the kind and quality of this meat cannot possibly be imagined by people who have never watched human swine eat.

"The w'y 'e coughs is somethin' terrible," volunteered my sweated friend, referring to the dying boy. "We 'ear 'im 'ere, w'ile we're workin', an' it's terrible, I say, terrible!"

And, what of the coughing and the sweetmeats, I found another menace added to the hostile environment of the children of the slums.

My sweated friend, when work was to be had, toiled with four other men in his eight-by-seven room. In the winter a lamp burned nearly all the day and added its fumes to the overloaded air, which was breathed, and breathed, and breathed again.

In good times, when there was a rush of work, this man told me that he could earn as high as "thirty bob a week."—Thirty shillings! Seven dollars and a half!

"But it's only the best of us can do it," he qualified. "An' then we work twelve, thirteen, and fourteen hours a day, just as fast as we can. An' you should see us sweat! Just runnin' from us! If you could see us, it'd dazzle your eyes—tacks flyin' out of mouth like from a machine. Look at my mouth."

I looked. The teeth were worn down by the constant friction of the metallic brads, while they were coal-black and rotten.

"I clean my teeth," he added, "else they'd be worse."

After he had told me that the workers had to furnish their own tools, brads, "grindery," cardboard, rent, light, and what not, it was plain that his thirty bob was a diminishing quantity.

"But how long does the rush season last, in which you receive this high wage of thirty bob?" I asked.

"Four months," was the answer; and for the rest of the year, he informed me, they average from "half a quid" to a "quid," a week, which is equivalent to from two dollars and a half to five dollars. The present week was half gone, and he had earned four bob, or one dollar. And yet I was given to understand that this was one of the better grades of sweating.

The Hop-pickers

So far has the divorcement of the worker from the soil proceeded, that the farming districts, the civilized world over, are dependent upon the cities for the gathering of the harvests. Then it is, when the land is spilling its ripe wealth to waste, that the street folk, who have been driven away from the soil, are called back to it again. But in England they return, not as prodigals, but as outcasts still, as vagrants and pariahs, to be doubted and flouted by their country brethren, to sleep in jails or casual wards, or under the hedges, and to live the Lord knows how.

It is estimated that Kent alone requires eighty thousand of the street people to pick her hops. And out they come, obedient to the call, which is the call of their bellies and of the lingering dregs of adventure-lust still in them. Slums, stews, and ghetto pour them forth, and the festering contents of slums, stews, and ghetto are undiminished. Yet they overrun the country like an army of ghouls, and the country does not want them. They are out of place. As they drag their squat, misshapen bodies along the highways and byways, they resemble some vile spawn from underground. Their very presence, the fact of their existence, is an outrage to the fresh, bright sun and the green and growing things. The clean, upstanding trees cry shame upon them and their withered crookedness, and their rottenness is a slimy desecration of the sweetness and purity of nature.

Is the picture overdrawn? It all depends. For one who sees and thinks life in terms of shares and coupons, it is certainly overdrawn. But for one who sees and thinks life in terms of manhood and womanhood, it cannot be overdrawn. Such hordes of beastly wretchedness and inarticulate misery are no compensation for a millionaire brewer who lives in a West End palace, sates himself with the sensuous delights of London's golden theatres, hobnobs with lordlings and princelings, and is knighted by the king. Wins his spurs—God forbid! In old time the great blonde beasts rode in the battle's van and won their spurs by cleaving men from pate to chin. And, after all, it is finer to kill a strong man with a clean-slicing blow of singing steel than to make a beast of him, and of his seed through the generations, by the artful and spidery manipulation of industry and politics.

Environment
(From "Merrie England")
by ROBERT BLATCHFORD
Widely read English socialist author; his works sold well over three million copies; 1851-1943

Some years ago a certain writer, much esteemed for his graceful style of saying silly things, informed us that the poor remain poor because they show no efficient desire to be anything else. Is that true? Are only the idle poor? Come with me and I will show you where men and women work from morning till night, from week to week, from year to year, at the full stretch of their powers, in dim and fetid dens, and yet are poor—aye, destitute—have for their wages a crust of bread and rags. I will show you where men work in dirt and heat, using the strength of brutes, for a dozen hours a day, and sleep at night in styes, until brain and muscle are exhausted, and fresh slaves are yoked to the golden car of commerce, and the broken drudges filter through the poor-house or the prison to a felon's or a pauper's grave! I will show you how men and women thus work and suffer and faint and die, generation after generation; and I will show you how the longer and the harder these wretches toil the worse their lot becomes; and I will show you the graves, and find witnesses to the histories of brave and noble and industrious poor men whose lives were lives of toil, *and* poverty, and whose deaths were tragedies.

And all these things are due to sin—but it is to the sin of the smug hypocrites who grow rich upon the robbery and the ruin of their fellow creatures.

The Failure of Civilization
by FREDERIC HARRISON
English positivist philosopher, 1831-1923

I cannot myself understand how any one who knows what the present manner is can think that it is satisfactory. To me, at least, it would be enough to condemn modern society as hardly an advance on slavery or serfdom, if the permanent condition of industry were to be that which we behold; that ninety per cent of the actual producers of wealth have no home that they can call their own beyond the end of the week; have no bit of soil, or so much as a room that belongs to them; have nothing of value of any kind, except as much old furniture as will go in a cart; have the precarious chance of weekly wages, which barely suffice to keep them in health; are housed for the most part in places that no man thinks fit for his horse; are separated by so narrow a margin from destitution that a month of bad trade, sickness or unexpected loss brings them face to face with hunger and pauperism. In cities, the increasing organization of factory work makes life more and more crowded, and work more and more a monotonous routine; in the country, the increasing pressure makes rural life continually less free, healthful and cheerful; whilst the prizes and hopes of betterment are now reduced to a minimum. This is the normal state of the average workman in town or country, to which we must add the record of preventable disease, accident, suffering and social oppression with its immense yearly roll of death and misery. But below this normal state of the average workman there is found the great band of the destitute outcasts —the camp-followers of the army of industry, at least one-tenth of the whole proletarian population, whose normal condition is one of sickening wretchedness. If this is to be the permanent arrangement of modern society, civilization must be held to bring a curse on the great majority of mankind.

Work and Pray
by GEORG HERWEGH
German revolutionary poet, 1817-1875

Pray and work! proclaims the world;
Briefly pray, for Time is gold.
On the door there knocketh dread—
Briefly pray, for Time is bread.

And ye plow and plant to grow.
And ye rivet and ye sow.
And ye hammer and ye spin—
Say, my people, what ye win.

Weave at loom both day and night,
Mine the coal to mountain height;
Fill right full the harvest horn—
Full to brim with wine and corn.

Yet where is thy meal prepared?
Yet where is thy rest-hour shared?
Yet where is thy warm hearth-fire?
Where is thy sharp sword of ire?

Labor Has Many Sorrows
by JOHN L. LEWIS
American trade union leader, organizer of the Congress of Industrial Organizations 1880-1969

Certainly labor wants a fairer share of the national income. Assuredly labor wants a larger participation in increased productive efficiency. Obviously the population is entitled to participate in the fruits of the genius of our men of achievement in the field of material sciences.

Labor has suffered just as our farm population has suffered from a viciously unequal distribution of the national income. In the exploitation of both classes of workers has been the source of panic and depression, and upon the economic welfare of both rests the best assurance of a sound and permanent prosperity.

Under the banner of the Committee for Industrial Organization American labor is on the march. Its objectives today are those it had in the beginning: to strive for the unionization of our unorganized millions of workers and for the acceptance of collective bargaining as a recognized American institution.

It seeks a peace with the industrial world. It seeks cooperation and mutuality of effort with the agricultural population. It would avoid strikes. It would have its rights determined under the law by the peaceful negotiations and contract relationships that are supposed to characterize American commercial life.

Until an aroused public opinion demands that employers accept that rule, labor has no recourse but to surrender its rights or struggle for their realization with its own economic power.

Labor, like Israel, has many sorrows. Its women weep for their fallen and they lament for the future of the children of the race. It ill behooves one who has supped at labor's table and who has been sheltered in labor's house to curse with equal fervor and fine impartiality both labor and its adversaries when they become locked in deadly embrace.

The Happy Worker
by HARVEY SWADOS
American novelist and social critic, 1920–1968

The plain truth is that factory work is degrading. It is degrading to any man who ever dreams of doing something worth while with his life; and it is about time we faced the fact. The more a man is exposed to middle-class values, the more sophisticated he becomes and the more production-line work is degrading to him. The immigrant who slaved in the poorly lighted, foul, vermin-ridden sweatshop found his work less degrading than the native-born high school graduate who reads "Judge Parker," "Rex Morgan, M.D.," and "Judd Saxon, Business Executive," in the funnies, and works in a fluorescent factory with ticker-tape production-control machines. For the immigrant laborer, even the one who did not dream of socialism, his long hours were going to buy him freedom. For the factory worker of the Fifties, his long hours are going to buy him commodities . . . and maybe reduce a few of his debts.

Almost without exception, the men with whom I worked on the assembly line last year felt like trapped animals. Depending on their age and circumstances, they were either resigned to their fate, furiously angry at *themselves* for what they were doing, or desperately hunting other work that would pay as well and in

addition offer some variety, some prospect of change and betterment. They were sick of being pushed around by harried foremen
(themselves more pitied than hated), sick of working like blink-
ered donkeys, sick of being dependent for their livelihood on a
maniacal production-merchandising setup, sick of working in a
place where there was no spot to relax during the twelve-minute
rest period. (Someday—let us hope—we will marvel that production was still so worshipped in the Fifties that new factories could
be built with every splendid facility for the storage and movement of essential parts, but with no place for a resting worker to
sit down for a moment but on a fireplug, the edge of a packing
case, or the sputum- and oil-stained stairway of a toilet.)

The older men stay put and wait for their vacations. But since
the assembly line demands young blood (you will have a hard
time getting hired if you are over thirty-five), the factory in which
I worked was aswarm with new faces every day; labor turnover
was so fantastic and absenteeism so rampant, with the young men
knocking off a day or two every week to hunt up other jobs, that
the company was forced to overhire in order to have sufficient
workers on hand at the starting siren. . . .

If this is what we want, let's be honest enough to say so. If we
conclude that there is nothing noble about repetitive work, but
that it is nevertheless good enough for the lower orders, let's say
that, too, so we will at least know where we stand. But if we cling
to the belief that other men are our brothers, not just Egyptians
or Israelis or Hungarians, but *all* men, including millions of
Americans who grind their lives away on an insane treadmill,
then we will have to start thinking about how their work and
their lives can be made meaningful. That is what I assume the
Hungarians, both workers and intellectuals, have been thinking
about. Since no one has been ordering us what to think, since no
one has been forbidding our intellectuals to fraternize with our
workers, shouldn't it be a little easier for us to admit, first, that
our problems exist, then to state them, and then to see if we can
resolve them?

BOOK II

The Chasm

The contrast between riches and poverty; the protest of common sense against a condition of society where one-tenth of the people own nine-tenths of the wealth.

Wat Tyler

by ROBERT SOUTHEY
English poet, 1774-1843

"When Adam delved and Eve span,
Who was then the gentleman?"

Wretched is the infant's lot,
Born within the straw-roof'd cot;
Be he generous, wise, or brave,
He must only be a slave.
Long, long labor, little rest,
Still to toil, to be oppress'd;
Drain'd by taxes of his store,
Punish'd next for being poor:
This is the poor wretch's lot,
Born within the straw-roof'd cot.

While the peasant works,—to sleep,
What the peasant sows,—to reap,
On the couch of ease to lie,
Rioting in revelry;
Be he villain, be he fool,
Still to hold despotic rule,
Trampling on his slaves with scorn!
This is to be nobly born.

"When Adam delved and Eve span,
Who was then the gentleman?"

The Poor-Slave Household
(From "Sartor Resartus")
by THOMAS CARLYLE

"The furniture of this Caravanserai consisted of a large iron
Pot, two oaken Tables, two Benches, two Chairs, and a Potheen
Noggin. There was a Loft above (attainable by a ladder), upon
which the inmates slept; and the space below was divided by a
hurdle into two apartments; the one for their cow and pig, the
other for themselves and guests. On entering the house we dis-

57

covered the family, eleven in number, at dinner; the father sitting at the top, the mother at the bottom, the children on each side, of a large oaken Board, which was scooped out in the middle, like a trough, to receive the contents of their Pot of Potatoes. Little holes were cut at equal distances to contain Salt; and a bowl of Milk stood on the table; all the luxuries of meat and beer, bread, knives and dishes, were dispensed with." The Poor-Slave himself our Traveller found, as he says, broad-backed, black-browed, of great personal strength, and mouth from ear to ear. His Wife was a sun-browned but well-featured woman; and his young ones, bare and chubby, had the appetite of ravens. Of their Philosophical or Religious tenets or observances, no notice or hint.

But now, secondly, of *the Dandiacal Household*:

"A Dressing-room splendidly furnished; violet-colored curtains, chairs and ottomans of the same hue. Two full-length Mirrors are placed, one on each side of a table, which supports the luxuries of the Toilet. Several Bottles of Perfume, arranged in a peculiar fashion, stand upon a smaller table of mother-of-pearl; opposite to these are placed the appurtenances of Lavation richly wrought in frosted silver. A Wardrobe of Buhl is on the left; the doors of which, being partly open, discover a profusion of Clothes; Shoes of a singularly small size monopolize the lower shelves." Fronting the wardrobe a door ajar gives some slight glimpse of the Bath-room. Folding-doors in the background.—"Enter the Author," our Theogonist in person, "obsequiously preceded by a French Valet, in white silk Jacket and cambric Apron."

Such are the two sects which, at this moment, divide the more unsettled portion of the British People; and agitate that ever-vexed country. To the eye of the political Seer, their mutual relation, pregnant with the elements of discord and hostility, is far from consoling. These two principles of Dandiacal Self-worship or Demon-worship, and Poor-Slavish or Drudgical Earth-worship, or whatever that same Drudgism may be, do as yet indeed manifest themselves under distant and nowise considerable shapes: nevertheless, in their roots and subterranean ramifications, they extend through the entire structure of Society, and work unweariedly in the secret depths of English national Existence; striving to separate and isolate it into two contradictory, uncommunicating masses.

In numbers, and even individual strength, the Poor-Slaves or

Drudges, it would seem, are hourly increasing. The Dandiacal, again, is by nature no proselytizing Sect; but it boasts of great hereditary resources, and is strong by union; whereas the Drudges, split into parties, have as yet no rallying-point; or at best only co-operate by means of partial secret affiliations. If, indeed, there were to arise a *Communion of Drudges*, as there is already a Communion of Saints, what strangest effects would follow therefrom! Dandyism as yet affects to look down on Drudgism; but perhaps the hour of trial, when it will be practically seen which ought to look down, and which up, is not so distant.

To me it seems probable that the two Sects will one day part England between them; each recruiting itself from the intermediate ranks, till there be none left to enlist on either side. These Dandiacal Manicheans, with the host of Dandyizing Christians, will form one body; the Drudges, gathering round them whosoever is Drudgical, be he Christian or Infidel Pagan; sweeping-up likewise all manner of Utilitarians, Radicals, refractory Potwallopers, and so forth, into their general mass, will form another. I could liken Dandyism and Drudgism to two bottomless boiling Whirlpools that had broken-out on opposite quarters of the firm land; as yet they appear only disquieted, foolishly bubbling wells, which man's art might cover-in; yet mark them, their diameter is daily widening; they are hollow Cones that boil-up from the infinite Deep, over which your firm land is but a thin crust or rind! Thus daily is the intermediate land crumbling-in, daily the empire of the two Buchan-Bullers extending; till now there is but a foot-plank, a mere film of Land between them; this too is washed away; and then—we have the true Hell of Waters, and Noah's Deluge is outdeluged!

Or better, I might call them two boundless, and indeed unexampled Electric Machines (turned by the "Machinery of Society"), with batteries of opposite quality; Drudgism the Negative, Dandyism the Positive; one attracts hourly towards it and appropriates all the Positive Electricity of the nation (namely, the Money thereof); the other is equally busy with the Negative (that is to say the Hunger) which is equally potent. Hitherto you see only partial transient sparkles and sputters; but wait a little, till the entire nation is in an electric state; till your whole vital Electricity, no longer healthfully Neutral, is cut into two isolated portions of Positive and Negative (of Money and of Hunger); and stands there bottled-up in two World-Batteries! The stirring

of a child's finger brings the two together; and then—What then?
The Earth is but shivered into impalpable smoke by that Doom's-
thunderpeal; the Sun misses one of his Planets in Space, and
thenceforth there are no eclipses of the Moon.

The Lotus Eaters

by ALFRED, LORD TENNYSON
English Poet Laureate; 1809-1892

Let us swear an oath, and keep it with an equal mind,
In the hollow Lotos-land to live and lie reclined
On the hills like Gods together, careless of mankind.
For they lie beside their nectar, and the bolts are hurl'd
Far below them in the valleys, and the clouds are lightly curl'd
Round their golden houses, girdled with the gleaming world:
Where they smile in secret, looking over wasted lands,
Blight and famine, plague and earthquake, roaring deeps and fiery
    sands,
Clanging fights and flaming towns, and sinking ships, and praying
    hands.
But they smile, they find a music centred in a doleful song
Steaming up, a lamentation and an ancient tale of wrong,
Like a tale of little meaning tho' the words are strong;
Chanted from an ill-used race of men that cleave the soil,
Sow the seed, and reap the harvest with enduring toil,
Storing yearly little dues of wheat, and wine and oil;
Till they perish and they suffer—some, 'tis whisper'd—down in hell.

Rich and Poor

by LEO TOLSTOY
Russian novelist and reformer, 1828-1910

The present position which we, the educated and well-to-do
classes, occupy, is that of the Old Man of the Sea, riding on the
poor man's back; only, unlike the Old Man of the Sea, we are
very sorry for the poor man, very sorry; and we will do almost
anything for the poor man's relief. We will not only supply him
with food sufficient to keep him on his legs, but we will teach and
instruct him and point out to him the beauties of the landscape;
we will discourse sweet music to him and give him abundance of
good advice.

Yes, we will do almost anything for the poor man, anything but
get off his back.

Looking Backward
by Edward Bellamy
American writer, 1850-1898. A socialist classic, this book sold over four hundred
thousand copies within a year of publication.

By way of attempting to give the reader some general impression
of the way people lived together in those days, and especially of
the relations of the rich and poor to one another, perhaps I cannot
do better than compare society as it then was to a prodigious coach
which the masses of humanity were harnessed to and dragged
toilsomely along a very hilly and sandy road. The driver was
hunger, and permitted no lagging, though the pace was necessarily
very slow. Despite the difficulty of drawing the coach at all along
so hard a road, the top was covered with passengers who never got
down, even at the steepest ascents. The seats on top were very
breezy and comfortable. Well up out of the dust their occupants
could enjoy the scenery at their leisure, or critically discuss the
merits of the straining team. Naturally such places were in great
demand and the competition for them was keen, every one seeking
as the first end in life to secure a seat on the coach for himself
and to leave it to his child after him. By the rule of the coach a
man could leave his seat to whom he wished, but on the other
hand there were many accidents by which it might at any time
be wholly lost. For all that they were so easy, the seats were very
insecure, and at every sudden jolt of the coach persons were slip-
ping out of them and falling to the ground, where they were
instantly compelled to take hold of the rope and help to drag the
coach on which they had before ridden so pleasantly. It was
naturally regarded as a terrible misfortune to lose one's seat, and
the apprehension that this might happen to them or their friends
was a constant cloud upon the happiness of those who rode.

But did they think only of themselves? you ask. Was not their
very luxury rendered intolerable to them by comparison with
the lot of their brothers and sisters in the harness, and the knowledge that their own weight added to their toil! Had they no compassion for fellow beings from whom fortune only distinguished
them? Oh, yes; commiseration was frequently expressed by those
who rode for those who had to pull the coach, especially when
the vehicle came to a bad place in the road, as it was constantly
doing, or to a particularly steep hill. At such times, the desperate
straining of the team, their agonized leaping and plunging under

the pitiless lashing of hunger, the many who fainted at the rope and were trampled in the mire, made a very distressing spectacle, which often called forth highly creditable displays of feeling on the top of the coach. At such times the passengers would call down encouragingly to the toilers of the rope, exhorting them to patience, and holding out hopes of possible compensation in another world for the hardness of their lot, while others contributed to buy salves and liniments for the crippled and injured. It was agreed that it was a great pity that the coach should be so hard to pull, and there was a sense of general relief when the specially bad piece of road was gotten over. This relief was not, indeed, wholly on account of the team, for there was always some danger at these bad places of a general overturn in which all would lose their seats.

It must in truth be admitted that the main effect of the spectacle of the misery of the toilers at the rope was to enhance the passengers' sense of the value of their seats upon the coach, and to cause them to hold on to them more desperately than before. If the passengers could only have felt assured that neither they nor their friends would ever fall from the top, it is probable that, beyond contributing to the funds for liniments and bandages, they would have troubled themselves extremely little about those who dragged the coach.

My Religion
by LEO TOLSTOY

What is the law of nature? Is it to know that my security and that of my family, all my amusements and pleasures, are purchased at the expense of misery, deprivation, and suffering to thousands of human beings—by the terror of the gallows; by the misfortune of thousands stifling within prison walls; by the fears inspired by millions of soldiers and guardians of civilization, torn from their homes and besotted by discipline, to protect our pleasures with loaded revolvers against the possible interference of the famishing! Is it to purchase every fragment of bread that I put in my mouth and the mouths of my children by the numberless privations that are necessary to procure my abundance? Or is it to be certain that my piece of bread only belongs to me when I know that everyone else has a share, and that no one starves while I eat?

A Tale of Two Cities

by CHARLES DICKENS

Most popular of all English novelists, 1812-1870. The following scene shows one
of Monseigneur's guests driving away from the palace.

Not many people had talked with him at the reception; he had
stood in a little space apart, and Monseigneur might have been
warmer in his manner. It appeared under the circumstances,
rather agreeable to him to see the common people dispersed before his horses, and often barely escaping from being run down.
His man drove as if he were charging an enemy, and the furious
recklessness of the man brought no check into the face, or to the
lips, of the master. The complaint had sometimes made itself
audible, even in that deaf city and dumb age, that, in the narrow
streets without footways, the fierce patrician custom of hard driving endangered and maimed the mere vulgar in a barbarous
manner. But few cared enough for that to think of it a second
time, and, in this matter, as in all others, the common wretches
were left to get out of their difficulties as they could.

With a wild rattle and clatter, and an inhuman abandonment
of consideration not easy to be understood in these days, the
carriage dashed through streets and swept round corners, with
women screaming before it, and men clutching each other and
clutching children out of its way. At last, swooping at a street
corner by a fountain, one of its wheels came to a sickening little
jolt, and there was a loud cry from a number of voices, and the
horses reared and plunged.

But for the latter inconvenience, the carriage probably would
not have stopped; carriages were often known to drive on, and
leave their wounded behind, and why not? But the frightened
valet had got down in a hurry, and there were twenty hands at the
horses' bridles.

"What has gone wrong?" said Monsieur, calmly looking out.

A tall man in a nightcap had caught up a bundle from among
the feet of the horses, and had laid it on the basement of the
fountain, and was down in the mud and wet, howling over it like
a wild animal.

"Pardon, Monsieur the Marquis!" said a ragged and submissive
man, "it is a child."

"Why does he make that abominable noise? Is it his child?"

"Excuse me, Monsieur the Marquis—it is a pity—yes."

The Hand of Fate, *William Balfour Ker*

The fountain was a little removed; for the street opened, where it was, into a space some ten or twelve yards square. As the tall man suddenly got up from the ground, and came running at the carriage, Monsieur the Marquis clapped his hand for an instant on his swordhilt.

"Killed!" shrieked the man, in wild desperation, extending both arms at their length above his head, and staring at him. "Dead!"

The people closed round, and looked at Monsieur the Marquis. There was nothing revealed by the many eyes that looked at him but watchfulness and eagerness; there was no visible menacing or anger. Neither did the people say anything; after the first cry, they had been silent, and they remained so. The voice of the submissive man who had spoken, was flat and tame in its extreme submission. Monsieur the Marquis ran his eyes over them all, as if they had been mere rats come out of their holes.

He took out his purse.

"It is extraordinary to me," said he, "that you people cannot take care of yourselves and your children. One or the other of you is for ever in the way. How do I know what injury you have done my horses. See! Give him that."

He threw out a gold coin for the valet to pick up, and all the heads craned forward that all the eyes might look down at it as it fell. The tall man called out again with a most unearthly cry "Dead!"

Paris

by EMILE ZOLA

French novelist and foremost defender of Captain Dreyfus against judicial persecution and racial bigotry; 1840-1902

Pierre remembered that frightful house in the Rue des Saules, where so much want and suffering were heaped up. He saw again the yard filthy like a quagmire, the evil-smelling staircases, the sordid, bare, icy rooms, the families fighting for messes which even stray dogs would not have eaten; the mothers, with exhausted breasts, carrying screaming children to and fro; the old men who fell in corners like brute beasts, and died of hunger amidst filth. And then came his other hours with the magnificence or the quietude or the gaiety of the *salons* through which he had passed, the whole insolent display of financial Paris, and political Paris, and society Paris. And at last he came to the dusk, and to that

Paris-Sodom and Paris-Gomorrah before him, which was lighting itself up for the night, for the abominations of that accomplice night which, like fine dust, was little by little submerging the expanse of roofs. And the hateful monstrosity of it all howled aloud under the pale sky where the first pure, twinkling stars were gleaming.

A great shudder came upon Pierre as he thought of all that mass of iniquity and suffering, of all that went on below amid wealth and vice. The *bourgeoisie,* wielding power, would relinquish naught of the sovereignty which it had conquered, wholly stolen; while the people, the eternal dupe, silent so long, clenched its fists and growled, claiming its legitimate share. And it was that frightful injustice which filled the growing gloom with anger. From what dark-breasted cloud would the thunderbolt fall? For years he had been waiting for that thunderbolt, which low rumbles announced on all points of the horizon. And if he had written a book full of candour and hope, if he had gone in all innocence to Rome, it was to avert that thunderbolt and its frightful consequences. But all hope of the kind was dead within him; he felt that the thunderbolt was inevitable, that nothing henceforth could stay the catastrophe. And never before had he felt it to be so near, amidst the happy impudence of some, and the exasperated distress of others. It was gathering, and it would surely fall over that Paris, all lust and bravado, which, when evening came, thus stirred up its furnace.

King Hunger

by LEONID ANDREYEV

Russian novelist and dramatist of social protest, 1871-1919

In the first scene King Hunger is shown inciting the starving factory-slaves to revolt; in the second, he presides over a gathering of the outcasts of society, who meet in a cellar to discuss projects of ferocious vengeance upon the idlers in the ballroom over their heads, but break up in a drunken brawl instead. In the present scene, King Hunger turns traitor to his victims, and presides as a judge passing sentence upon them. The leisure class attend as spectators in the courtroom, the women in evening gowns and jewels, "the men in dress coats and surtouts, carefully shaven and dressed at the wig-makers."

KING HUNGER: Show in the first starveling.

(*The first starveling, a ragged old man with lacerated feet, is conducted into the courtroom. A wire muzzle encases his face.*)

KING HUNGER: Take the muzzle off the starveling. What's your offense, Starveling?

OLD MAN (*speaking in a broken voice*): Theft.

KING HUNGER: How much did you steal?

OLD MAN: I stole a five-pound loaf, but it was wrested from me. I had only time to bite a small piece of it. Forgive me, I will never again——

KING HUNGER: How? Have you acquired an inheritance? Or won't you eat hereafter?

OLD MAN: No. It was wrested from me. I only chewed off a small piece——

KING HUNGER: But how won't you steal? Why haven't you been working?

OLD MAN: There's no work.

KING HUNGER: But where's your brood, Starveling? Why don't they support you?

OLD MAN: My children died of hunger.

KING HUNGER: Why did you not starve to death, as they?

OLD MAN: I don't know. I had a mind to live.

KING HUNGER: Of what use is life to you, Starveling?

(*Voices of Spectators.*)

—Indeed, how do they live? I don't comprehend it.

—To work.

—To glorify God and be confirmed in the consciousness that life—

—Well, I don't suppose they exalt Him.

—It were better if he were dead.

—A rather wearisome old fellow. And what style of trousers!

—Listen! Listen!

KING HUNGER (*rising, speaks aloud*): Now, ladies and gentlemen, we will feign to meditate. Honorable judges, I beg you to simulate a meditative air.

(*The judges for a brief period appear in deep thought—they knit their brows, gaze up at the ceiling, prop up their noses, sigh and obviously endeavor to think. Venerable silence. Then with faces profoundly solemn and earnest, silent as before, the judges rise, and simultaneously they turn around facing Death. And all together they bow low and lingering, stretching forward.*)

KING HUNGER (*with bent head*): What is your pleasure?

DEATH (*swiftly rising, wrathfully strikes the table with his clenched fist and speaks in a grating voice*): Condemned—in the name of Satan!

(*Then as quickly he sits down and sinks into a malicious inflexibility. The judges resume their places.*)

KING HUNGER: Starveling, you're condemned.

OLD MAN: Have mercy!

KING HUNGER: Put the muzzle over him. Bring the next starveling. . . .

(*The next starveling is led into the room. She is a graceful, but extremely emaciated young woman, with a face pallid and tragic to view. The black, fine eyebrows join over her nose; her luxuriant hair is negligently tied in a knot, falling down her shoulders. She makes no bows nor looks around, as if seeing nobody. Her voice is apathetic and dull.*)

KING HUNGER: What's your offense, Starveling?

YOUNG WOMAN: I killed my child.

(*Spectators.*)

—Oh, horrors! This woman is altogether destitute of motherly feelings.

—What do you expect of them? You astonish me.

—How charming she is. There's something tragical about her.

—Then marry her.

—Crimes of infanticide were not regarded as such in ancient times, and were looked upon as a natural right of parents. Only with the introduction of humanism into our customs——

—Oh, please, just a second, professor.

—But science, my child——

KING HUNGER: Tell us, Starveling, how it happened.

(*With drooping hands and motionless, the woman speaks up dully and dispassionately.*)

YOUNG WOMAN: One night my baby and I crossed the long bridge over the river. And since I had long before decided, so then approaching the middle, where the river is deep and swift, I said: "Look, baby dear, how the water is a-roaring below." She said, "I can't reach, mamma, the railing is so high." I said, "Come, let me lift you, baby dear." And when she was gazing down into the black deep, I threw her over. That's all.

KING HUNGER: Did she grip you?

YOUNG WOMAN: No.

KING HUNGER: She screamed?

YOUNG WOMAN: Yes, once.

KING HUNGER: What was her name?

YOUNG WOMAN: Baby dear.

KING HUNGER: No, her name. How was she called?

YOUNG WOMAN: Baby dear.

KING HUNGER (*covering his face, he speaks in sad, quivering voice*): Honorable judges, I beg you to simulate a meditative air. (*The judges knit their brows, gaze on the ceiling, chew their lips. Venerable silence. They they rise and gravely bow to Death.*)

DEATH: Condemned—in the name of Satan!

KING HUNGER (*rising speaks aloud, extending his hands to the woman, as if veiling her in an invisible, black shroud*): You're condemned, woman, do you hear? Death awaits you. In blackest hell you will be tormented and burnt on everlasting, slakeless fires! Devils will rack your heart with their iron talons! The most venomous serpents of the infernal abyss will suck your brain and sting, sting you, and nobody will heed your agonizing cries, for you'll be silenced. Let eternal night be over you. Do you hear, Starveling?

YOUNG WOMAN: Yes.

KING HUNGER: Muzzle her.

(*The starveling is led away. King Hunger addresses the spectators in a frank and joyous manner.*) Now, ladies and gentlemen, I propose recess for luncheon. Adjudication is a fatiguing affair, and we need to invigorate ourselves. (*Gallantly.*) Especially our charming matrons and the young ladies. Please!

(*Joyful exclamations.*)

—To dine! To dine!

—'Tis about time!

—Mamma dear, where are the bonbons?

—Your little mind is only on bonbons!

—Which—is tried? (*Waking up.*)

—Dinner is ready, Your Excellency.

—Ah! Why didn't you wake me up before?

(*Everything assumes at once a happy, amiable, homelike aspect. The judges pull off their wigs, exposing their bald heads, and gradually they lose themselves in the crowd, shake hands, and with feigned indifference they look askance, contemplating the dining. Portly waiters in rich liveries, with difficulty and bent under the weight of immense dishes, bring gigantic portions; whole mutton trunks, colossal hams, high, mountain-like roasts. Before the stout man, on a low stool, they place a whole roasted pig, which is brought in by three. Doubtful, he looks at it.)*

—Would you assist me, Professor?

—With pleasure, Your Excellency.

—And you, Honorable Judge?

—Although I am not hungry—but with your leave—

—I may, perhaps, be suffered to— *(the Abbot modestly speaks, his mouth watering.)*

(The four seat themselves about the pig and silently they carve it greedily with their knives. Occasionally the eyes of the Professor and of the Abbot meet, and with swollen cheeks, powerless to chew, they are smitten with reciprocal hatred and contempt. Then choking, they ardently champ on. Everywhere small groups eating. Death produces a dry cheese sandwich from his pocket and eats in solitude. A heavy conversation of full-crammed mouths. Munching.)

London
by WILLIAM BLAKE
English poet and painter of strange visions, 1757-1827

I wander through each chartered street,
　　Near where the chartered Thames does flow;
A mark in every face I meet,
　　Marks of weakness, marks of woe.

In every cry of every man,
　　In every infant's cry of fear,
In every voice, in every ban,
　　The mind-forged manacles I hear:

How the chimney-sweeper's cry
　　Every blackening church appalls,
And the hapless soldier's sigh
　　Runs in blood down palace-walls.

But most, through midnight streets I hear
　　How the youthful harlot's curse
Blasts the new-born infant's tear,
　　And blights with plagues the marriage-hearse.

London

by HEINRICH HEINE
German poet and essayist, 1797-1856

It is in the dusky twilight that Poverty with her mates, Vice and Crime, glide forth from their lairs. They shun daylight the more anxiously, the more cruelly their wretchedness contrasts with the pride of wealth which glitters everywhere; only Hunger sometimes drives them at noonday from their dens, and then they stand with silent, speaking eyes, staring beseechingly at the rich merchant who hurries along, busy and jingling gold, or at the lazy lord who, like a surfeited god, rides by on his high horse, casting now and then an aristocratically indifferent glance at the mob below, as though they were swarming ants, or, at all events, a mass of baser beings, whose joys and sorrows have nothing in common with his feelings. . . .

Poor Poverty! how agonizing must thy hunger be where others swell in scornful superfluity! And when some one casts with indifferent hand a crust into thy lap, how bitter must the tears be wherewith thou moistenest it! Thou poisonest thyself with thine own tears. Well art thou in the right when thou alliest thyself to Vice and Crime. Outlawed criminals often bear more humanity in their hearts than those cold, blameless citizens of virtue, in whose white hearts the power of evil is quenched; but also the power of good. I have seen women on whose cheeks red vice was painted, and in whose hearts dwelt heavenly purity.

Reflections Upon Poverty

(From "The New Grub Street")

by GEORGE GISSING
English novelist who endured the genteel poverty he described, 1857-1903

As there was sunshine Amy accompanied her husband for his walk in the afternoon; it was long since they had been out together. An open carriage that passed, followed by two young girls on horseback, gave a familiar direction to Reardon's thoughts.

"If one were as rich as those people. They pass so close to us; they see us, and we see them; but the distance between is infinity. They don't belong to the same world as we poor wretches. They see everything in a different light; they have powers which would seem supernatural if we were suddenly endowed with them."

"Of course," assented his companion with a sigh.

"Just fancy, if one got up in the morning with the thought that no reasonable desire that occurred to one throughout the day need remain ungratified! And that it would be the same, any day and every day, to the end of one's life! Look at those houses; every detail, within and without, luxurious. To have such a home as that!"

"And they are empty creatures who live there."

"They do *live*, Amy, at all events. Whatever may be their faculties, they all have free scope. I have often stood staring at houses like these until I couldn't believe that the people owning them were mere human beings like myself. The power of money is so hard to realize, one who has never had it marvels at the completeness with which it transforms every detail of life. Compare what we call our home with that of rich people; it moves one to scornful laughter. I have no sympathy with the stoical point of view; between wealth and poverty is just the difference between the whole man and the maimed. If my lower limbs are paralyzed I may still be able to think, but then there is no such thing in life as walking. As a poor devil I may live nobly; but one happens to be made with faculties of enjoyment, and those have to fall into atrophy. To be sure, most rich people don't understand their happiness; if they did, they would move and talk like gods—which indeed they are."

Amy's brow was shadowed. A wise man, in Reardon's position, would not have chosen this subject to dilate upon.

"The difference," he went on, "between the man with money and the man without is simply this: the one thinks, 'How shall I use my life?' and the other, 'How shall I keep myself alive?' A physiologist ought to be able to discover some curious distinction between the brain of a person who has never given a thought to the means of subsistence, and that of one who has never known a day free from such cares. There must be some special cerebral development representing the mental anguish kept up by poverty."

"I should say," put in Amy, "that it affects every function of the brain. It isn't a special point of suffering, but a misery that colors every thought."

"True. Can I think of a single object in all the sphere of my experience without the consciousness that I see it through the medium of poverty? I have no enjoyment which isn't tainted by that thought, and I can suffer no pain which it doesn't increase.

The curse of poverty is to the modern world just what that of slavery was to the ancient. Rich and destitute stand to each other as free man and bond. You remember the line of Homer I have often quoted about the demoralizing effect of enslavement; poverty degrades in the same way."

"It has had its effect upon me—I know that too well," said Amy, with bitter frankness.

Reardon glanced at her, and wished to make some reply, but he could not say what was in his thoughts.

The Veins of Wealth
by JOHN RUSKIN
English critic, 1819-1900

Primarily, which is very notable and curious, I observe that men of business rarely know the meaning of the word "rich." At least if they know, they do not in their reasonings allow for the fact, that it is a relative word, implying its opposite "poor" as positively as the word "north" implies its opposite "south." Men nearly always speak and write as if riches were absolute, and it were possible, by following certain scientific precepts, for everybody to be rich. Whereas riches are a power like that of electricity, acting only through inequalities or negations of itself. The force of the guinea you have in your pocket depends wholly on the default of a guinea in your neighbor's pocket. If he did not want it, it would be of no use to you; the degree of power it possesses depends accurately upon the need or desire he has for it,—and the art of making yourself rich, in the ordinary mercantile economist's sense, is therefore equally and necessarily the art of keeping your neighbor poor.

The Octopus
by FRANK NORRIS
American novelist, 1870-1902. In the following scene the hero is at a dinner party in San Francisco, at the same time that the widow and child of a victim of the railroad "octopus" are wandering the streets outside.

All around the table conversations were going forward gayly. The good wines had broken up the slight restraint of the early part of the evening and a spirit of good humor and good fellowship prevailed. Young Lambert and Mr. Gerard were deep in

reminiscences of certain mutual duck-shooting expeditions. Mrs.
Gerard and Mrs. Cedarquist discussed a novel—a strange mingling
of psychology, degeneracy, and analysis of erotic conditions—which
had just been translated from the Italian. Stephen Lambert and
Beatrice disputed over the merits of a Scotch collie just given to
the young lady. The scene was gay, the electric bulbs sparkled,
the wine flashing back the light. The entire table was a vague
glow of white napery, delicate china, and glass as brilliant as
crystal. Behind the guests the serving-men came and went, filling
the glasses continually, changing the covers, serving the entrées,
managing the dinner without interruption, confusion, or the
slightest unnecessary noise.

But Presley could find no enjoyment in the occasion. From that
picture of feasting, that scene of luxury, that atmosphere of
decorous, well-bred refinement, his thoughts went back to Los
Muertos and Quien Sabe and the irrigating ditch at Hooven's.
He saw them fall, one by one, Harran, Annixter, Osterman,
Broderson, Hooven. The clink of the wine glasses was drowned
in the explosion of revolvers. The Railroad might indeed be a
force only, which no man could control and for which no man
was responsible, but his friends had been killed, but years of
extortion and oppression had wrung money from all the San
Joaquin, money that had made possible this very scene in which
he found himself. Because Magnus had been beggared, Gerard
had become Railroad King; because the farmers of the valley
were poor, these men were rich.

The fancy grew big in his mind, distorted, caricatured, terrible.
Because the farmers had been killed at the irrigating ditch, these
others, Gerard and his family, fed full. They fattened on the
blood of the People, on the blood of the men who had been killed
at the ditch. It was a half-ludicrous, half-horrible "dog eat dog,"
an unspeakable cannibalism. Harran, Annixter, and Hooven
were being devoured there under his eyes. These dainty women,
his cousin Beatrice and little Miss Gerard, frail, delicate; all these
fine ladies with their small fingers and slender necks, suddenly
were transfigured in his tortured mind into harpies tearing human
flesh. His head swam with the horror of it, the terror of it. Yes,
the People *would* turn some day, and, turning, rend those who
now preyed upon them. It would be "dog eat dog" again, with
positions reversed, and he saw for an instant of time that splendid
house sacked to its foundations, the tables overturned, the pictures

torn, the hangings blazing, and Liberty, the red-handed Man in the Street, grimed with powder smoke, foul with the gutter, rush yelling, torch in hand, through every door.

At ten o'clock Mrs. Hooven fell.

Luckily she was leading Hilda by the hand at the time and the little girl was not hurt. In vain had Mrs. Hooven, hour after hour, walked the streets. After a while she no longer made any attempt to beg; nobody was stirring, nor did she even try to hunt for food with the stray dogs and cats. She had made up her mind to return to the park in order to sit upon the benches there, but she had mistaken the direction, and, following up Sacramento Street, had come out at length, not upon the park, but upon a great vacant lot at the very top of the Clay Street hill. The ground was unfenced and rose above her to form the cap of the hill, all overgrown with bushes and a few stunted live-oaks. It was in trying to cross this piece of ground that she fell. . . .

"You going to sleep, mammy?" inquired Hilda, touching her face.

Mrs. Hooven roused herself a little.

"Hey? Vat you say? Asleep? Yais, I guess I wass asleep."

Her voice trailed unintelligibly to silence again. She was not, however, asleep. Her eyes were open. A grateful numbness had begun to creep over her, a pleasing semi-insensibility. She no longer felt the pain and cramps of her stomach, even the hunger was ceasing to bite.

"These stuffed artichokes are delicious, Mrs. Gerard," murmured young Lambert, wiping his lips with a corner of his napkin. "Pardon me for mentioning it, but your dinner must be my excuse."

"And this asparagus—since Mr. Lambert has set the bad example," observed Mrs. Cedarquist, "so delicate, such an exquisite flavor. How *do* you manage?"

"We get all our asparagus from the southern part of the State, from one particular ranch," explained Mrs. Gerard. "We order it by wire and get it only twenty hours after cutting. My husband sees to it that it is put on a special train. It stops at this ranch just to take on our asparagus. Extravagant, isn't it, but I simply can not eat asparagus that has been cut more than a day."

"Nor I," exclaimed Julian Lambert, who posed as an epicure.

"I can tell to an hour just how long asparagus has been picked."

"Fancy eating ordinary market asparagus," said Mrs. Gerard, "that has been fingered by Heaven knows how many hands."

"Mammy, mammy, wake up," cried Hilda, trying to push open Mrs. Hooven's eyelids, at last closed. "Mammy, don't. You're just trying to frighten me."

Feebly Hilda shook her by the shoulder. At last Mrs. Hooven's lips stirred. Putting her head down, Hilda distinguished the whispered words:

"I'm sick. Go to schleep. . . . Sick. . . . Noddings to eat."

The dessert was a wonderful preparation of alternate layers of biscuit, glacés, ice cream, and candied chestnuts.

"Delicious, is it not?" observed Julian Lambert, partly to himself, partly to Miss Cedarquist. "This *Moscovite fouetté*—upon my word, I have never tasted its equal."

"And you should know, shouldn't you?" returned the young lady.

"Mammy, mammy, wake up," cried Hilda. "Don't sleep so. I'm frightened."

Repeatedly she shook her; repeatedly she tried to raise the inert eyelids with the point of her finger. But her mother no longer stirred. The gaunt, lean body, with its bony face and sunken eye-sockets, lay back, prone upon the ground, the feet upturned and showing the ragged, worn soles of the shoes, the forehead and gray hair beaded with fog, the poor, faded bonnet awry, the poor, faded dress soiled and torn.

Hilda drew close to her mother, kissing her face, twining her arms around her neck. For a long time she lay that way, alternately sobbing and sleeping. Then, after a long time, there was a stir. She woke from a doze to find a police officer and two or three other men bending over her. Some one carried a lantern. Terrified, smitten dumb, she was unable to answer the questions put to her. Then a woman, evidently the mistress of the house on the top of the hill, arrived and took Hilda in her arms and cried over her.

"I'll take the little girl," she said to the police officer. "But the mother, can you save her? Is she too far gone?"

"I've sent for a doctor," replied the other.

Just before the ladies left the table, young Lambert raised his glass of Madeira. Turning towards the wife of the Railroad King, he said:

"My best compliments for a delightful dinner."

The doctor, who had been bending over Mrs. Hooven, rose.

"It's no use," he said; "she has been dead some time—exhaustion from starvation."

By ANATOLE FRANCE

French author, 1844–1924

The law in its majestic equality forbids the rich as well as the poor to sleep under bridges, to beg in the streets and to steal bread.

Progress and Poverty

by HENRY GEORGE

Founder of single tax movement; 1839-1897

Unpleasant as it may be to admit it, it is at last becoming evident that the enormous increase in productive power which has marked the present century and is still going on with accelerating ratio, has no tendency to extirpate poverty or to lighten the burdens of those compelled to toil. It simply widens the gulf between Dives and Lazarus, and makes the struggle for existence more intense. The march of invention has clothed mankind with powers of which a century ago the boldest imagination could not have dreamed. But in factories where labor-saving machinery has reached its most wonderful development, little children are at work; wherever the new forces are anything like fully utilized, large classes are maintained by charity or live on the verge of recourse to it; amid the greatest accumulations of wealth, men die of starvation, and puny infants suckle dry breasts; while everywhere the greed of gain, the worship of wealth, shows the force of the fear of want. The promised land flies before us like the mirage. The fruits of the tree of knowledge turn, as we grasp them, to apples of Sodom that crumble at the touch. . . .

This association of poverty with progress is the great enigma of our times. It is the central fact from which spring industrial, social, and political difficulties that perplex the world, and with which statesmanship and philanthropy and education grapple in vain. From it come the clouds that overhang the future of the most progressive and self-reliant nations. It is the riddle which the

Sphinx of Fate puts to our civilization, and which not to answer is to be destroyed. So long as all the increased wealth which modern progress brings goes but to build up great fortunes, to increase luxury and make sharper the contrast between the House of Have and the House of Want, progress is not real and cannot be permanent. The reaction must come. The tower leans from its foundations, and every new story but hastens the final catastrophe. To educate men who must be condemned to poverty, is but to make them restive; to base on a state of most glaring social inequality political institutions under which men are theoretically equal, is to stand a pyramid on its apex.

Isabella, or The Pot of Basil
by JOHN KEATS
English romantic poet, 1795-1821

With her two brothers this fair lady dwelt,
    Enrichèd from ancestral merchandise,
And for them many a weary hand did swelt
    In torchèd mines and noisy factories,
And many once proud-quiver'd loins did melt
    In blood from stinging whip,—with hollow eyes
Many all day in dazzling river stood,
To take the rich-ored driftings of the flood.

For them the Ceylon diver held his breath,
    And went all naked to the hungry shark;
For them his ears gushed blood; for them in death
    The seal on the cold ice with piteous bark
Lay full of darts; for them alone did seethe
    A thousand men in troubles wide and dark;
Half-ignorant, they turn'd an easy wheel,
That set sharp wracks at work, to pinch and peel.

When the Rich Came First
(From "A Night to Remember")
by WALTER LORD
Contemporary American writer, born 1917

Actually, there were boats for 1178—the White Star Line complained that nobody appreciated their thoughtfulness. Even so, this took care of only 52 per cent of the 2207 people on board, and only 30 per cent of her total capacity. From now on the rules and formulas were simple indeed—lifeboats for everybody.

And it was the end of class distinction in filling the boats. The White Star Line always denied—and the investigators backed them up—yet there's overwhelming evidence that the steerage took a beating. Daniel Buckley kept from going into First Class . . . Olaus Abelseth released from the poop deck as the last boat pulled away . . . Stewart Hart convoying two little groups of women topside, while hundreds were kept below . . . steerage passengers crawling along the crane from the well deck aft . . . others climbing vertical ladders to escape the well deck forward.

Then there were the people Colonel Gracie, Lightroller and others saw surging up from below, just before the end. Until this moment Gracie was sure the women were all off—they were so hard to find when the last boats were loading. Now, he was appalled to see dozens of them suddenly appear. The statistics suggest who they were—the *Titanic's* casualty list included four of 143 First Class women (three by choice) . . . 15 of 93 Second Class women . . . and 81 of 179 Third Class women.

Not to mention the children. Except for Lorraine Allison, all 29 First and Second Class children were saved, but only 23 out of 76 steerage children.

Neither the chance to be chivalrous nor the fruits of chivalry seemed to go with a Third Class passage.

It was better, but not perfect, in Second Class. Lawrence Beesley remembered an officer stopping two ladies as they started through the gate to First Class. "May we pass to the boats?" they asked.

"No, madam; your boats are down on your own deck."

In fairness to the White Star Line, these distinctions grew not so much from set policy as from no policy at all. At some points the crew barred the way to the Boat Deck; at others they opened the gates but didn't tell anyone; at a few points there were well-meaning efforts to guide the steerage up. But generally Third Class was left to shift for itself. A few of the more enterprising met the challenge, but most milled helplessly about their quarters —ignored, neglected, forgotten.

If the White Star Line was indifferent, so was everybody else. No one seemed to care about Third Class—neither the press, the official Inquiries, nor even the Third Class passengers themselves.

In covering the *Titanic,* few reporters bothered to ask the

The Bowery, *Reginald Marsh*

Third Class passengers anything. The New York *Times* was justly proud of the way it handled the disaster. Yet the famous issue covering the *Carpathia's* arrival in New York contained only two interviews with Third Class passengers. This apparently was par for the course—of 43 survivor accounts in the New York *Herald,* two again were steerage experiences.

Certainly their experiences weren't as good copy as Lady Cosmo Duff (one New York newspaper had her saying, "The last voice I heard was a man shouting, 'My God, My God!' "). But there was indeed a story. The night was a magnificent confirmation of "women and children first," yet somehow the loss rate was higher for Third Class children than First Class men. It was a contrast which would never get by the social consciousness (or news sense) of today's press.

Nor did Congress care what happened to Third Class. Senator Smith's *Titanic* investigation covered everything under the sun, including what an iceberg was made of ("Ice," explained Fifth Officer Lowe), but the steerage received little attention. Only three of the witnesses were Third Class passengers. Two of these said they were kept from going to the Boat Deck, but the legislators didn't follow up. Again, the testimony doesn't suggest any deliberate hush-up—it was just that no one was interested.

An Atmosphere of Corruption
(From "Ten Days That Shook the World")
by JOHN REED
American journalist, 1887-1920

A large section of the propertied classes preferred the Germans to the Revolution—even to the Provisional Government—and didn't hesitate to say so. In the Russian household where I lived the subject of conversation at the dinner table was almost invariably the coming of the Germans, bringing "law and order." . . . One evening I spent at the house of a Moscow merchant; during tea we asked the eleven people at the table whether they preferred "Wilhelm or the Bolsheviki." The vote was ten to one for Wilhelm. . . .

The speculators took advantage of the universal disorganization to pile up fortunes, and to spend them in fantastic revelry or the corruption of Government officials. Foodstuffs and fuel were

hoarded, or secretly sent out of the country to Sweden. In the
first four months of the Revolution, for example, the reserve
food supplies were almost openly looted from the great Municipal
warehouses of Petrograd, until the two-years' provision of grain
had fallen to less than enough to feed the city for one month. . . .
According to the official report of the last Minister of Supplies in
the Provisional Government coffee was bought wholesale in
Vladivosfok for two rubles a pound, and the consumer in Petrograd paid thirteen. In all the stores of the large cities were tons
of food and clothing; but only the rich could buy them.

In a provincial town I knew a merchant family turned specu-
lator—*maradior* (bandit, ghoul) the Russians call it. The three
sons had bribed their way out of military service. One gambled
in foodstuffs. Another sold illegal gold from the Lena mines to
mysterious partners in Finland. The third owned a controlling
interest in a chocolate factory, which supplied the local Cooperative societies—on condition that the Cooperatives furnished him
everything he needed. And so, while the masses of the people
got a quarter pound of black bread on their bread cards, he had
an abundance of white bread, sugar, tea, candy, cake and butter.
. . . Yet when the soldiers at the front could no longer fight from
cold, hunger and exhaustion, how indignantly did this family
scream "Cowards!"—how "ashamed" they were "to be Russians."
. . . When finally the Bolsheviki found and requisitioned vast
hoarded stores of provisions, what "Robbers" they were.

Beneath all this external rottenness moved the old-time Dark
Forces, unchanged since the fall of Nicholas the Second, secret
still and very active. The agents of the notorious *Okhrana* still
functioned, for and against the Tsar, for and against Kerensky
—whoever would pay. . . . In the darkness, underground organizations of all sorts, such as the Black Hundreds, were busy attempting to restore reaction in some form or other.

In this atmosphere of corruption, of monstrous half-truths, one
clear note sounded day after day, the deepening chorus of the
Bolsheviki, "All Power to the Soviets! All power to the direct
representatives of millions of common workers, soldiers, peasants.
Land, bread, an end to the senseless war, an end to secret di-
plomacy, speculation, treachery. . . . The Revolution is in danger,
and with it the cause of the people all over the world!"

The struggle between the proletariat and the middle class,
between the Soviets and the Government, which had begun in

the first March days, was about to culminate. Having at one bound leaped from the Middle Ages into the twentieth century, Russia showed the startled world two systems of Revolution—the political and the social—in mortal combat.

What a revelation of the vitality of the Russian Revolution, after all these months of starvation and disillusionment! The bourgeoisie should have better known its Russia. Not for a long time in Russia will the "sickness" of Revolution have run its course. . . .

Too Small a Share
(From "The Future of an Illusion")
by SIGMUND FREUD
Founder of psychoanalysis, 1856-1939

If we turn to those restrictions that only apply to certain classes of society, we encounter a state of things which is glaringly obvious and has always been recognized. It is to be expected that the neglected classes will grudge the favored ones their privileges and that they will do everything in their power to rid themselves of their own surplus of privation. Where this is not possible a lasting measure of discontent will obtain within this culture, and this may lead to dangerous outbreaks. But if a culture has not gone beyond the stage in which the satisfaction of one group of its members necessarily involves the suppression of another, perhaps the majority—and this is the case in all modern cultures— it is intelligible that these suppressed classes should develop an intense hostility to the culture; a culture, whose existence they make possible by their labor, but in whose resources they have too small a share. In such conditions one must not expect to find an internalization of the cultural prohibitions among the suppressed classes; indeed they are not even prepared to acknowledge these prohibitions, intent, as they are, on the destruction of the culture itself and perhaps even of the assumptions on which it rests. These classes are so manifestly hostile to culture that on that account the more latent hostility of the better provided social strata has been overlooked. It need not be said that a culture which leaves unsatisfied and drives to rebelliousness so large a number of its members neither has a prospect of continued existence, nor deserves it.

The Ballad of the Pleasant Life

(From "The Threepenny Opera")

by BERTOLT BRECHT
German dramatist, 1898-1956

Some say that we should live like famous sages
On empty stomachs and ascetic reading
Within a hovel where the rats are breeding.
Preserve me from such lunatics in cages!
Let those who like it live the simple way
I've had (between ourselves) too much by far.
No animal from here to Zanzibar
Would live that simple life a single day.
What help is freedom? What good to me?
Only the well-to-do live pleasantly!

Those brave adventurers of light and leading
Who risk their skins in search of new sensations
In order that their truthful publications
May give the bourgeoisie exciting reading—
Just look at them in their domestic station
See how they go with frigid wife to bed,
Their gloomy thoughts five thousand years ahead
And one ear cocked for further acclamation.
Can we call that living? Don't you agree:
Only the well-to-do live pleasantly?

And I myself have felt the inclination
To lead a great and solitary existence
But when I saw such men at shorter distance
I told myself—that's not your occupation.
Poverty makes you sad as well as wise
And bravery brings with fame a bitter grave:
So you are poor and lonely, wise and brave,
And now not even greatness satisfies.
Then let this adage your motto be:
Only the well-to-do live pleasantly.

By WILLIAM HOWARD TAFT
President of the United States; 1857-1930

"What is a man to do who is starving, and cannot find work?"
"God knows."

The Medical Fraternity
(*From "Generation of Vipers"*)
by PHILIP WYLIE
American novelist and moralist, 1902–1971

The doctors are condemned as a whole, again, by their infuriated defiance of a public tendency toward health insurance and toward any step that may be called the socialization of medicine. If this defiance were accompanied by a practicable plan, agreeable to all, whereby the mordant and the miserable of this republic could get themselves a fair measure of mere physical care, the emotion could be interpreted as an urge to restrain man from foolishness and guide him into wisdom. Such is not the case. With a few notable distinctions, the medicos have merely bellowed wrathfully at progress, and there is in the sound of their voices too much of the tone of a baby bereaved of its candy. The exceptions, moreover, irrespective of the merits of their various plans, have been persecuted, except only for physical torture, which, to hear some doctors talk, is none too good for them. Because they have tried to solve the clinical dilemmas of groups, rather than poor or paying individuals, they have been thrown out of societies, castigated by name in the newspapers, refused the fraternal and scientific rights of the profession, and in some instances driven beyond poverty to suicide, which is the handy modern equivalent of the rack, and a more hideous one if you happen to be stretched by it.

A New Class Emerges
by MILOVAN DJILAS
Yugoslav ex-communist, imprisoned several times by the
regime he helped bring to power, 1911–1995

There are fundamental differences between professional politicians in other systems and in the Communist system. In extreme cases, politicians in other systems use the government to secure privileges for themselves and their cohorts, or to favor the economic interests of one social stratum or another. The situation is different with the Communist system where the power and, the government are identical with the use, enjoyment, and disposition of almost all the nation's goods. He who grabs power grabs privileges and indirectly grabs property. Consequently, in Communism, power or politics as a profession is the ideal of those who have the desire or the prospect of living as parasites at the expense of others.

Membership in the Communist Party before the Revolution meant sacrifice. Being a professional revolutionary was one of the highest honors. Now that the party has consolidated its power, party membership means that one belongs to a privileged class. And at the core of the party are the all-powerful exploiters and masters.

For a long time the Communist revolution and the Communist system have been concealing their real nature. The emergence of the new class has been concealed under socialist phraseology and, more important, under the new collective forms of property ownership. The so-called socialist ownership is a disguise for the real ownership by the political bureaucracy. And in the beginning this bureaucracy was in a hurry to complete industrialization, and hid its class composition under that guise. . . .

In Communist systems, thefts and misappropriations are inevitable. It is not just poverty that motivates people to steal the "national property"; but the fact that the property does not seem to belong to anyone. All valuables are somehow rendered valueless, thus creating a favorable atmosphere for theft and waste. In 1954, in Yugoslavia alone, over 20,000 cases of theft of "socialist property" were discovered. The Communist leaders handle national property as their own, but at the same time they waste it as if it were somebody else's. Such is the nature of ownership and government of the system.

The greatest waste is not even visible. This is the waste of manpower. The slow, unproductive work of disinterested millions, together with the prevention of all work not considered "socialist," is the calculable, invisible, and gigantic waste which no Communist regime has been able to avoid. Even though they are adherents of Smith's theory that labor creates value, a theory which Marx adopted, these power-wielders pay the least attention to labor and manpower, regarding them as something of very little value which can be readily replaced.

The fear which Communists have of "the renewal of capitalism," or of economic consequences that would arise from narrow class "ideological" motives, has cost the nation tremendous wealth and put a brake on its development. Entire industries are destroyed because the state is not in a position to maintain or develop them; only that which is the state's is considered "socialist."

Nobody Starves
(From "The Other America")
by MICHAEL HARRINGTON
American social worker and journalist, 1928–1989

It is much easier in the United States to be decently dressed than to be decently housed, fed, or doctored. Even people with terribly depressed incomes can look prosperous.

This is an extremely important factor in defining our emotional and existential ignorance of poverty. In Detroit the existence of social classes became much more difficult to discern the day the companies put lockers in the plants. From that moment on, one did not see men in work clothes on the way to the factory, but citizens in slacks and white shirts. The process has been magnified with the poor throughout the country. There are tens of thousands of Americans in the big cities who are wearing shoes, perhaps even a stylishly cut suit or dress, and yet are hungry. It is not a matter of planning, though it almost seems as if the affluent society had given out costumes to the poor so that they would not offend the rest of society with the sight of rags. . . .

In 1929 there were almost 1,700,000 low-income farms. They constituted 35.8 per cent of the total of commercial farms. During the depression their number rose as the unemployed came back to the land. In 1939 they were 39.2 per cent of all the commercial farms. During the war the figures dropped sharply. (The agricultural population gained because of the way in which price and wage stabilization worked during the war.) But in the postwar period the old pattern reasserted itself. In 1949 these low-income farms were 30.3 per cent of the total, and in 1954, 32.2 per cent. In a period of a quarter of a century, the number of low-income farms had declined to about a million. But despite this enormous change, their percentage drop was only a little better than 3 per cent. In 1929 a third of the commercial farms in America were centers of poverty; in 1954 the same relative figure still held. . . .

Taken all in all, men, women, children, and counting the Braceros, there are around 2,000,000 human beings who live and work under these inhuman conditions. In 1959 the Secretary of Labor computed the average Bracero wage which is a fair index of what all these people are paid: it came to $0.50 an hour. In the same period a congressional study estimated that a family of Texas migrants, with five workers in the field, would make just over

$3,000 a year. That means $600 to each worker for a full year's work.

One argument used to justify this system of impoverishment is that the migrant and the hired hand are not efficient workers. Yet a special Senate study concluded that the average farm hand in 1955 was 110 per cent more efficient than he had been twenty-five years earlier. With 37 per cent fewer workers, there was 54 per cent more production. The migrants and the hands contributed profits to this development, but they did not receive benefits from it.

But perhaps the most dramatic deprivation in all this is visited upon children. They work in the fields, of course. (There are laws against it, but they are inadequately enforced, and the desperate families need every bit of labor they can get.) Among the Texas Mexicans, for instance, the upper educational limit is six years of schooling, and the chances are that it was received on the fly, that it was constantly interrupted, and that it was inferior.

All of this was made specific and unmistakable by a study of the National Educational Association: in Florida, Texas, and Illinois 75 per cent of the migrant children were retarded.

These educational statistics get at a basic problem of the rural poor, both migrants and hired hands. More and more of them are being driven from the land. The average size of farms is going up; the number of opportunities is going down. In 1950 the Department of Agriculture estimated that 40 per cent of the rural youth could be spared in the coming decade. At the decade's end, a group of rural sociologists decided that this had been an understatement. In short, the vast exodus from the land is heavily weighted in the direction of the young. . . .

Loneliness, isolation, and sickness are the afflictions of the aged in every economic class. But for those who are poor, there is an intensification of each of these tragedies: they are more lonely, more isolated, sicker. So it is that a Government report unwittingly stated a social paradox. It noted that only a society of abundance could produce such a high proportion of old people. We can afford them, we create them, because we are so rich. But later, in discussing the reality of life for the aged, the same report noted that these human products of abundance were denied its fruits. We tolerate them as long as they are poor.

The 1960 Senate report stated the issue clearly enough: ". . . at least one-half of the aged—approximately eight million people

—cannot afford today decent housing, proper nutrition, adequate medical care, preventive or acute, or necessary recreation." The same grim picture emerged from the White House Conference on Aging in 1961. As one volume put it, "Many states report that half their citizens over 65 have incomes too low to meet their basic needs."

Here are the statistics. They are some of the most incredible figures to be found in American society:

The Bureau of the Census figures for 1958 show almost 60 per cent of the population over sixty-five with incomes under $1,000 a year. This must be measured against the Government computation that an adequate budget for a retired couple in the autumn of 1959 would range from an urban low of $2,681 in Scranton to a high of $3,304 in Chicago. In short, the top couples in the 60 per cent would have a budget 20 per cent below adequacy in the cheapest city, and almost 40 per cent below adequacy in the most expensive.

Over half of these people are covered by some kind of Federal program (social security, old-age assistance, and so on). Yet, the social security payments are, by Federal admission, completely inadequate to a decent life. In 1959, for instance, they averaged a little better than $70 a month. Or, to take another expression of the same fact, the Senate report concluded that if aged couples could live within the low-cost minimum food budget of the Department of Agriculture, a quarter of them would be spending more than half their income on food alone. . . .

The poor in America constitute about 25 per cent of the total population. They number somewhere between 40,000,000 and 50,000,000, depending on the criterion of low income that is adopted.

The majority of the poor in America are white, although the nonwhite minorities suffer from the most intense and concentrated impoverishment of any single group.

A declining number and percentage of the poor are involved in farm work, and although rural poverty is one of the most important components of the culture of poverty, it does not form its mass base.

In addition to the nonwhite minorities, the groups at a particular disadvantage are: the aged, the migrant workers, the industrial rejects, children, families with a female head, people of low education. These various characteristics of the culture of poverty tend to cluster together. (The large families have had the least gain of all family groups in recent years, and hence more children among the poor.)

The people who are in this plight are at an enormous physical disadvantage, suffering more from chronic diseases and having less possibility of treatment.

The citizens of the culture of poverty also suffer from more mental and emotional problems than any group in American society. . . .

These are the figures and there is legitimate reason for sincere men to argue over the details, to claim that a particular interpretation is too high or too low.. At this point I would begf the reader to forget the numbers game. Whatever the precise calibrations, it is obvious that these statistics represent an enormous, an unconscionable amount of human suffering in this land. They should be read with a sense of outrage.

From his inaugural address, January 20, 1961

BY JOHN F. KENNEDY

President of the United States, 1917-1963

If a free society cannot help the many who are poor, it cannot save the few who are rich.

Letter to the Viceroy

BY MAHATMA GANDHI

Exponent of nonviolence, hero of India's struggle
for independence, assassinated by right-wing Hindu fanatic; 1869-1948

Sent March 1, 1930

Dear Friend, Before embarking on Civil Disobedience and taking risk I have dreaded to take all these years, I would fain approach you and find a way out.

My personal faith is absolutely clear. I cannot intentionally hurt anything that lives, much less human beings, even though they may do the greatest wrong to me and mine. Whilst, therefore, I hold the British rule to be a curse, I do not intend harm to a single Englishman or to any legitimate interest he may have in India.

And why do I regard the British rule a curse?

It has impoverished the dumb millions by a system of progressive exploitation and by a ruinous expensive military and civil administration which the country can never afford.

It has reduced us politically to serfdom. It has sapped the foundations of our culture. And by the policy of cruel disarmament, it has degraded us spiritually. . . .

I fear...there never has been any intention of granting...Dominion Status to India in the immediate future. . . .

It seems as clear as daylight that responsible British statesman do not contemplate any alteration in British policy that might adversely affect Britain's commerce with India. . . . If nothing is done to end the process of exploitation India must be bled with an ever increasing speed. . . .

Let me put before you some salient points.

The terrific pressure of land revenue, which furnishes a large part of the total, must undergo considerable modification in an Independent India...the whole revenue system has to be so revised as to make the peasant's good its primary concern. But the British system seems to be designed to crush the very life out of him. Even the salt he must use to live is so taxed as to make the burden fall heaviest on him, if only because of the heartless impartiality of its incidence. The tax shows itself still more burdensome on the poor man when it is remembered that salt is the one thing he must eat more than the rich man. . . . The drink and drug revenue, too, is derived from the poor. It saps the foundations both of their health and morals.

The iniquities sampled above are maintained in order to carry on a foreign administration demonstrably the most expensive in the world. Take your own salary. It is over 21,000 rupees per month, besides many other indirect additions. . . . You are getting over 700 rupees [approximately $100] a day against India's average income of less than two annas [four cents] per day. Thus you are getting much over five thousand times India's average income. The British Prime Minister is getting ninety times Britain's average income. On bended knee, I ask you to ponder over this phenomenon. I have taken a personal illustration to drive home a painful truth. I have too great a regard for you as a man to wish to hurt your feelings. I know that you do not need the salary you get. Probably the whole of your salary goes to charity. But a system that provides such an arrangement deserves to be summarily scrapped. What is true of the Viceregal salary is true generally of the whole administration. . . . Nothing but organized non-violence can check the organized violence of the British government. . . .

This non-violence will be expressed through civil disobedience, for the moment confined to the inmates of the Satyagraha Ashram, but ultimately designed to cover all those who choose to join the movement. . . .

My ambition is no less than to convert the British people through non-violence, and thus make them see the wrong they have done to India. I do not seek to harm your people. I want to serve them even as I want to serve my own. . . .

If the people [of India] join me as I expect they will, the sufferings they will undergo, unless the British nation sooner retraces its steps, will be enough to melt the stoniest hearts.

The plan through Civil Disobedience will be to combat such evils as I have sampled out. . . . I respectfully invite you to pave the way for the immediate removal of those evils, and thus open a way for real conference between equals. . . . But if you cannot see your way to deal with these evils and if my letter makes no appeal to your heart, on the eleventh day of this month, I shall proceed with such co-workers of the Ashram as I can take, to disregard the provisions of the Salt Laws. . . . It is, I know, open to you to frustrate my design by arresting me. I hope there will be tens of thousands ready, in a disciplined manner, to take up the work after me. . . .

If you care to discuss matters with me, and if to that end you would like me to postpone publication of this letter, I shall gladly refrain on receipt of a telegram. . . .

This letter is not in any way intended as a threat but it is a simple and sacred duty peremptory on a civil resister. Therefore I am having it specially delivered by a young English friend who believes in the Indian cause. . . .

> I remain
> Your sincere friend,
> M.K. Gandhi

The New Poverty
(From "The Soul and the Operator")
BY JOHN BERGER
British author and critic, born 1926

The poverty of our century is unlike that of any other. It is not, as poverty was before, the result of natural scarcity, but of a set of priorities imposed upon the rest of the world by the rich. Consequently, the modern poor are not pitied...but written off as trash. The twentieth-century consumer economy has produced the first culture for which a beggar is a reminder of nothing.

BOOK III

The Outcast

The life of the underworld, of those thrown upon the scrapheap of the modern industrial machine; vivid and powerful passages portraying the lives of social pariahs.

Not Guilty
by ROBERT BLATCHFORD

In defending the Bottom Dog I do not deal with hard science only; but with the dearest faiths, the oldest wrongs and the most awful relationships of the great human family, for whose good I strive and to whose judgment I appeal. Knowing, as I do, how the hardworking and hard-playing public shun laborious thinking and serious writing, and how they hate to have their ease disturbed or their prejudices handled rudely, I still make bold to undertake this task, because of the vital nature of the problems I shall probe.

The case for the Bottom Dog should touch the public heart to the quick, for it affects the truth of our religions, the justice of our laws and the destinies of our children and our children's children. Much golden eloquence has been squandered in praise of the successful and the good; much stern condemnation has been vented upon the wicked. I venture now to plead for those of our poor brothers and sisters who are accursed of Christ and rejected of men.

Hitherto all the love, all the honors, all the applause of this world, and all the rewards of heaven, have been lavished on the fortunate and the strong; and the portion of the unfriended Bottom Dog, in his adversity and weakness, has been curses, blows, chains, the gallows and everlasting damnation. I shall plead, then, for those who are loathed and tortured and branded as the sinful and unclean; for those who have hated us and wronged us, and have been wronged and hated by us. I shall defend them for right's sake, for pity's sake and for the benefit of society and the race. For these also are of our flesh, these also have erred and gone astray, these also are victims of an inscrutable and relentless Fate.

If it concerns us that the religions of the world are childish dreams or nightmares; if it concerns us that our penal laws and moral codes are survivals of barbarism and fear; if it concerns us that our most cherished and venerable ideas of our relations to God and to each other are illogical and savage, then the case for the Bottom Dog concerns us nearly.

If it moves us to learn that disease may be prevented, that ruin may be averted, that broken hearts and broken lives may be made whole; if it inspires us to hear how beauty may be conjured out of loathsomeness and glory out of shame; how waste may be turned

97

to wealth and death to life, and despair to happiness, then the case
for the Bottom Dog is a case to be well and truly tried.

By Horace Greeley
American editor and candidate for President; 1811-1872

Morality and religion are but words to him who fishes in gutters
for the means of sustaining life, and crouches behind barrels in
the street for shelter from the cutting blasts of a winter night.

The Punishment of Thieves
(From "Utopia")
by Sir Thomas More
English statesman, executed by Henry VIII; 1478-1535

In this poynte, not you onlye, but also the most part of the
world, be like evyll scholemaisters, which be readyer to beate,
than to teache, their scholers. For great and horrible punishmentes
be appointed for theves, whereas much rather provision should
have ben made, that there were some meanes, whereby they myght
get their livyng, so that no man should be dryven to this extreme
necessitie, firste to steale, and then to dye.

The Unemployed Problem
(From "Past and Present")
by Thomas Carlyle

And truly this first practical form of the Sphinx-question, in-
articulately and so audibly put there, is one of the most impressive
ever asked in the world. "Behold us here, so many thousands,
millions, and increasing at the rate of fifty every hour. We are
right willing and able to work; and on the Planet Earth is plenty
of work and wages for a million times as many. We ask, If you
mean to lead us towards work; to try to lead us—by ways new,
never yet heard of till this new unheard-of Time? Or if you declare that you cannot lead us? And expect that we are to remain
quietly unled, and in a composed manner perish of starvation?
What is it you expect of us? What is it you mean to do with us?"
This question, I say, has been put in the hearing of all Britain;
and will be again put, and ever again, till some answer be given it.

The Parish Workhouse
by GEORGE CRABBE

Theirs is yon house that holds the parish poor,
Whose walls of mud scarce bear the broken door;
There, where the putrid vapors flagging play,
And the dull wheel hums doleful through the day;
There children dwell who know no parents' care;
Parents, who know no children's love, dwell there;
Heart-broken matrons on their joyless bed,
Forsaken wives and mothers never wed;
Dejected widows with unheeded tears,
And crippled age with more than childhood-fears;
The lame, the blind, and—far the happiest they!—
The moping idiot and the madman gay.

Here too the sick their final doom receive,
Here brought amid the scenes of grief to grieve,
Where the loud groans from some sad chamber flow,
Mixed with the clamors of the crowd below;
Here, sorrowing, they each kindred sorrow scan,
And the cold charities of man to man:
Whose laws indeed for ruined age provide,
And strong compulsion plucks the scrap from pride;
But still that scrap is bought with many a sigh,
And pride imbitters what it can't deny.

Say ye, oppressed by some fantastic woes,
Some jarring nerve that baffles your repose;
Who press the downy couch while slaves advance
With timid eye, to read the distant glance;
Who with sad prayers the weary doctor tease,
To name the nameless ever-new disease;
Who with mock patience dire complaints endure,
Which real pain and that alone can cure:
How would ye bear in real pain to lie,
Despised, neglected, left alone to die?
How would ye bear to draw your latest breath
Where all that's wretched paves the way for death?

Ecce Homo, *Constantin Meunier*

The Bread Line
by Berton Braley
American poet, 1882–1966

Well, here they are—they stand and stamp and shiver
  Waiting their food from some kind stranger hand,
Their weary limbs with eagerness a-quiver
  Hungry and heartsick in a bounteous land.

"Beggars and bums?" Perhaps, and largely worthless.
  Shaky with drink, unlovely, craven, low,
With obscene tongues and hollow laughter mirthless;
  But who shall give them scorn for being so?

Yes, here they are—with gaunt and pallid faces,
  With limbs ill-clad and fingers stiff and blued,
Shuffling and stamping on their pavement places,
  Waiting and watching for their bit of food.

We boast of vast achievements and of power,
  Of human progress knowing no defeat,
Of strange new marvels every day and hour—
  And here's the bread line in the wintry street!

Ten thousand years of war and peace and glory,
  Of hope and work and deeds and golden schemes,
Of mighty voices raised in song and story,
  Of huge inventions and of splendid dreams;

Ten thousand years replete with every wonder,
  Of empires risen and of empires dead;
Yet still, while wasters roll in swollen plunder,
  These broken men must stand in line—for bread!

From the Psalms

He hath looked down from the height of his sanctuary . . . to hear the sighing of the prisoner; to loose those that are appointed to death.

The Bread of Affliction
(From "Children of the Ghetto")
by ISRAEL ZANGWILL
English poet and novelist, 1864-1926

At half-past five the stabledoors were thrown open, and the crowd pressed through a long, narrow whitewashed stone corridor into a barn-like compartment, with a whitewashed ceiling traversed by wooden beams. Within this compartment, and leaving but a narrow circumscribing border, was a sort of cattle-pen, into which the paupers crushed, awaiting amid discomfort and universal jabber the divine moment. The single jet of gas-light depending from the ceiling flared upon the strange simian faces, and touched them into a grotesque picturesqueness that would have delighted Doré.

They felt hungry, these picturesque people; their near and dear ones were hungering at home. Voluptuously savoring in imagination the operation of the soup, they forgot its operation as a dole in aid of wages; were unconscious of the grave economical possibilities of pauperization and the rest, and quite willing to swallow their independence with the soup. Even Esther, who had read much, and was sensitive, accepted unquestioningly the theory of the universe that was held by most people about her, that human beings were distinguished from animals in having to toil terribly for a meagre crust, but that their lot was lightened by the existence of a small and semi-divine class called *Takeefim*, or rich people, who gave away what they didn't want. How these rich people came to be, Esther did not inquire; they were as much a part of the constitution of things as clouds and horses. The semi-celestial variety was rarely to be met with. It lived far away from the Ghetto, and a small family of it was said to occupy a whole house. Representatives of it, clad in rustling silks or impressive broadcloth, and radiating an indefinable aroma of superhumanity, sometimes came to the school, preceded by the beaming Head Mistress; and then all the little girls rose and curtseyed, and the best of them, passing as average members of the class, astonished the semi-divine persons by their intimate acquaintance with the topography of the Pyrenees and the disagreements of Saul and David, the intercourse of the two species ending in effusive smiles and general satisfaction. But the dullest of the girls was alive to the comedy, and had a good-humored contempt for the unworld-liness of the semi-divine persons, who spoke to them as if they were not going to recommence squabbling, and pulling one another's hair, and copying one another's sums, and stealing one another's needles, the moment the semi-celestial backs were turned.

No. 5 John Street
by RICHARD WHITEING
English author, 1840-1928

After midnight the gangs return in carousal from the gin shops, the more thoughtful of them with stored liquor for the morning draft. Now it is three stages of man—no more: man gushing, confiding, uplifted, as he feels the effect of the lighter fumes; disputatious, quarrelsome, as the heavier mount in a second brew of hell; raging with wrath and hate, as the very dregs send their emanations to the tortured brain.

The embrace, the wrangle, and the blow—this is the order of succession. Till one—to mark it by the clock—we sing, " 'Art to 'art an' 'and to 'and." At about one forty-five you may expect the tribal row between the gangs, who prey on one another for recreation, and on society for a living. Our brutes read the current gospel of the survival of the fittest in their own way, and they dimly apprehend that mankind is still organized as a predatory horde. The ever-open door brings us much trouble from the outside. The unlighted staircase is a place of rendezvous, and, not unfrequently, of deadly quarrel, in undertones of concentrated fury, between wretches who seek seclusion for the work of manslaughter. Our latest returning inmate, the other night, stumbled over the body of a woman not known at No. 5. She had been kicked to death within sight and sound of lodgers who, believing it to be a matrimonial difference, held interference to be no business of theirs.

The first thud of war between the "Hooligans" is generally for two sharp. The seconds set to, along with their principals, as in the older duel. For mark that in most things we are as our betters were just so many centuries ago, and are simply belated with our flint age. And now our shapelier waves of sound break into a mere foam of oath and shriek. At times there is an interval of silence more awful than the tumult; and you may know that the knife is at its silent work, and that the whole meaner conflict is suspended for an episode of tragedy. If it is a hospital case, it closes the celebration. If it is not, the entertainment probably dies out in a slanging match between two of the fair; and the unnamable in invective and vituperation rises, as in blackest vapor, from our pit to the sky. At this, every room that holds a remnant of decency closes its window, and all withdraw, except, perhaps, the little boys and girls, who are beginning to pair according to the laws of the ooze and of the slime.

Night in the Slums
by JACK LONDON

I was glad the keepers were there, for I did not have on my "seafaring" clothes, and I was what is called a "mark" for the creatures of prey that prowled up and down. At times, between keepers, these males looked at me sharply, hungrily, gutter-wolves that they were, and I was afraid of their hands, of their naked hands, as one may be afraid of the paws of a gorilla. They reminded me of gorillas. Their bodies were small, ill-shaped, and squat. There were no swelling muscles, no abundant thews and wide-spreading shoulders. They exhibited, rather, an elemental economy of nature, such as the cave-men must have exhibited. But there was strength in those meagre bodies, the ferocious, primordial strength to clutch and tear and gripe and rend. When they spring upon their human prey they are known even to bend the victim backward and double its body till the back is broken. They possess neither conscience nor sentiment, and they will kill for half a sovereign, without fear or favor. . . .

The dear soft people of the golden theatres and wonder-mansions of the West End do not see these creatures, do not dream that they exist. But they are here, alive, very much alive in their jungle. And woe the day when England is fighting in her last trench, and her ablebodied men are on the firing line! For on that day they will crawl out of their dens and lairs, and the people of the West End will see them, as the dear soft aristocrats of Feudal France saw them and asked one another, "Whence come they?" "Are they men?"

But they were not the only beasts that ranged the menagerie. They were only here and there, lurking in dark courts and passing like grey shadows along the walls; but the women from whose rotten loins they spring were everywhere. They whined insolently, and in maudlin tones begged me for pennies, and worse. They held carouse in every boozing den, slatternly, unkempt, bleary-eyed, and tousled, leering and gibbering, overspilling with foulness and corruption, and, gone in debauch, sprawling across benches and bars, unspeakably repulsive, fearful to look upon.

And there were others, strange, weird faces and forms and twisted monstrosities that shouldered me on every side, inconceivable types of sodden ugliness, the wrecks of society, the perambulating carcasses, the living deaths—women, blasted by disease and drink till their shame brought not tuppence in the open mart; and men, in fantastic rags, wrenched by hardship and exposure out of all semblance of men, their faces in a perpetual writhe of pain, grinning idiotically, shambling like apes, dying with every step they took and every breath they drew. And there were young girls, of eighteen and twenty, with trim bodies and faces yet untouched with twist and bloat, who had fetched the bottom of the Abyss plump, in one swift fall. And I remember a lad of fourteen, and one of six or seven, white-faced and sickly, homeless, the pair of them, who sat upon the pavement with their backs against a railing and watched it all. . . .

The unfit and the unneeded! The miserable and despised and forgotten, dying in the social shambles. The progeny of prostitution—of the prostitution of men and women and children, of flesh and blood, and sparkle and spirit; in brief, the prostitution of labor. If this is the best that civilization can do for the human, then give us howling and naked savagery. Far better to be a people of the wilderness and desert, of the cave and the squatting place, than to be a people of the machine and the Abyss.

By Kenko Hoshi
Japanese Buddhist priest of the Fourteenth Century

It is desirable for a ruler that no man should suffer from cold and hunger under his rule. Man cannot maintain his standard of morals when he has no ordinary means of living.

So long as people, being ill-governed, suffer from hunger, criminals will never disappear. It is extremely unkind to punish those who, being sufferers from hunger, are compelled to violate laws.

The governing class should stop their luxurious expenditures in order to help the governed class. For only when a man has been provided with the ordinary means of living, and yet steals, may he be really called a thief.

A Night's Lodging

by Maxim Gorky

Russian novelist, portrayer of the Lower Depths; 1868-1936

LUKA: Treat everyone with friendliness—injure no one.

NATASHA: How good you are, grandfather! How is it that you are so good?

LUKA: I am good, you say. Nyah—if it is true, all right. But you see, my girl—there must be some one to be good. We must have pity on mankind. Christ, remember, had pity for us all and so taught us. Have pity when there is still time, believe me, that is right. I was once, for example, employed as a watchman, at a country place which belonged to an engineer, not far from the city of Tomsk, in Siberia. The house stood in the middle of the forest, an out-of-the-way location; and it was winter and I was all alone in the country house. It was beautiful there—magnificent! And once—I heard them scrambling up!

NATASHA: Thieves?

LUKA: Yes. They crept higher, and I took my rifle and went outside. I looked up—two men, opening a window, and so busy that they did not see anything of me at all. I cried to them: Hey, there, get out of that! And would you think it, they fell on me with a hand ax! I warned them. Halt, I cried, or else I fire! Then I aimed first at one and then at the other. They fell on their knees saying, Pardon us! I was pretty hot—on account of the hand ax, you remember. You devils, I cried, I told you to clear out and you didn't! And now, I said, one of you go into the brush and get a switch. It was done. And now, I commanded, one of you stretch out on the ground, and the other thrash him. And so they whipped each other at my command. And when they had each had a sound beating, they said to me: Grandfather, said they, for the sake of Christ give us a piece of bread. We haven't a bite in our bodies. They, my daughter, were the thieves who had fallen upon me with the hand ax. Yes, they were a pair of splendid fellows. I said to them, If you had asked for bread! Then they answered: We had gotten past that. We had asked and asked, and nobody would give us anything. Endurance was worn out. Nyah—and so they remained with me the whole winter. One of them, Stephen by name, liked to take the rifle and go into the woods. And the other, Jakoff, was constantly ill, always coughing. The three of us watched the place, and when spring came they said, Farewell, grandfather, and went away—to Russia.

NATASHA: Were they convicts, escaping?

LUKA: They were fugitives—they had left their colony. A pair of splendid fellows. If I had not had pity on them—who knows what would have happened? They might have killed me. Then they would be taken to court again, put in prison, sent back to Siberia—why all that? You can learn nothing good in prison, nor in Siberia. But a man, what can he not learn!

The Menagerie
by UPTON SINCLAIR

Oh come, ye lords and ladies of the realm,
Come from your couches soft, your perfumed halls,
Come watch with me throughout the weary hours.
Here are there sounds to thrill your jaded nerves,
Such as the cave-men, your forefathers, heard,
Crouching in forests of primeval night;
Here tier on tier in steel-barred cages pent
The beasts ye breed and hunt throughout the world.
Hark to that snore—some beast that slumbers deep;
Hark to that roar—some beast that dreams of blood;
Hark to that moan—some beast that wakes and weeps;
And then in sudden stillness mark the sound—
Some beast that rasps his vermin-haunted hide!

Oh come, ye lords and ladies of the realm,
Come keep the watch with me; this show is yours.
Behold the source of all your joy and pride,
The beasts ye harness fast and set to draw
The chariots of your pageantry and pomp!
It is their blood ye shed to make your feasts,
It is their treadmill that moves all your world.
Come gather now, and think how it will be
When God shall send his flaming angel down
And break these bars—so hath he done of yore,
So doeth he to lords and ladies grand—
And loose these beasts to raven in your streets!

Cold, *Roger Bloche*

Prisons

by Emma Goldman

Anarchist lecturer and writer, 1869-1940

Year after year the gates of prison hells return to the world an emaciated, deformed, will-less shipwrecked crew of humanity, with the Cain mark on their foreheads, their hopes crushed, all their natural inclinations thwarted. With nothing but hunger and inhumanity to greet them, these victims soon sink back into crime as the only possibility of existence. It is not at all an unusual thing to find men and women who have spent half their lives —nay, almost their entire existence—in prison. I know a woman on Blackwell's Island, who has been in and out thirty-eight times; and through a friend I learn that a young boy of seventeen, whom he had nursed and cared for in the Pittsburgh penitentiary, had never known the meaning of liberty. From the reformatory to the penitentiary had been the path of this boy's life, until, broken in body, he died a victim of social revenge. These personal experiences are substantiated by extensive data giving overwhelming proof of the futility of prisons as a means of deterrence or reform.

The Prison System

(From "Resurrection")

by Leo Tolstoy

"It is just as if a problem had been set: to find the best, the surest means, of depraving the greatest number of people!" thought Nehlúdof, while getting an insight into the deeds that were being done in the prisons and halting-stations. Every year hundreds of thousands were brought to the highest pitch of depravity, and when completely depraved they were liberated to spread broadcast the moral disease they had caught in prison.

In the prisons of Tumén, Ekáterinburg, Tomsk, and at the halting-stations, Nehlúdof saw how successfully the object society seemed to have set itself was attained. Ordinary simple men holding the Russian peasant social and Christian morality lost this conception, and formed a new prison, one founded chiefly on the idea that any outrage to or violation of human beings is justifiable, if it seems profitable. After living in prison these people became conscious with the whole of their being that, judging by what was happening to themselves, all those moral laws of respect and sympathy for others which the Church and the moral teachers preach, were set aside in real life, and that therefore they, too, need not keep these laws. Nehlúdof noticed this effect of prison life in all the prisoners he knew. He learnt, during his journey, that tramps who escape into the marshes will persuade comrades to escape with them, and will then kill them and feed on their flesh. He saw a living man who was accused of this, and acknowledged the act. And the most terrible thing was, that this was not a solitary case of cannibalism, but that the thing was continually recurring.

Only by a special cultivation of vice such as was carried on in these establishments, could a Russian be brought to the state of these tramps, who excelled Nietzsche's newest teaching, holding everything allowable and nothing forbidden, and spreading this teaching, first among the convicts and then among the people in general.

The only explanation of what was being done was that it aimed at the prevention of crime, at inspiring awe, at correcting offenders, and at dealing out to them "lawful vengeance," as the books said. But in reality nothing in the least resembling these results came to pass. Instead of vice being put a stop to, it only spread farther; instead of being frightened, the criminals were encouraged (many a tramp returned to prison of his own free will); instead of correction, every kind of vice was systematically instilled; while the desire for vengeance, far from being weakened by the measures of Government, was instilled into the people to whom it was not natural.

"Then why is it done?" Nehlúdof asked himself, and could find no answer.

A Sentiment on Social Reform

by Eugene V. Debs
Most popular of all social leaders, three times candidate for President,
1855–1926

> While there is a lower class, I am in it.
> While there is a criminal element, I am of it.
> While there is a soul in jail, I am not free.

A Hanging in Prison

(From "The Ballad of Reading Goal")

by OSCAR WILDE

Anglo-Irish poet and dramatist, 1856-1900. The poem from which these extracts are
taken was the fruit of his long imprisonment.

With slouch and swing around the ring
 We trod the Fools' Parade;
We did not care; we knew we were
 The Devil's Own Brigade:
And shaven head and feet of lead
 Make a merry masquerade.

We tore the tarry rope to shreds
 With blunt and bleeding nails;
We rubbed the doors, and scrubbed the floors,
 And cleaned the shining rails:
And, rank by rank, we soaped the plank,
 And clattered with the pails.

We sewed the sacks, we broke the stones,
 We turned the dusty drill:
We banged the tins, and bawled the hymns,
 And sweated on the mill:
But in the heart of every man
 Terror was lying still.

So still it lay that every day
 Crawled like a weed-clogged wave;
And we forgot the bitter lot
 That waits for fool and knave,
Till once, as we tramped in from work,
 We passed an open grave.

With yawning mouth the yellow hole
 Gaped for a living thing;
The very mud cried out for blood
 To the thirsty asphalt ring:
And we knew that ere one dawn grew fair
 Some prisoner had to swing.

Right in we went, with soul intent
  On Death and Dread and Doom:
The hangman, with his little bag,
  Went shuffling through the gloom:
And each man trembled as he crept
  Into his numbered tomb.

That night the empty corridors
  Were full of forms of Fear,
And up and down the iron town
  Stole feet we could not hear,
And through the bars that hide the stars
  White faces seemed to peer. . . .

We were as men who through a fen
  Of filthy darkness grope:
We did not dare to breathe a prayer,
  Or to give our anguish scope:
Something was dead in each of us,
  And what was dead was Hope.

For Man's grim Justice goes its way,
  And will not swerve aside:
It slays the weak, it slays the strong,
  It has a deadly stride:
With iron heel it slays the strong,
  The monstrous parricide.

We waited for the stroke of eight:
  Each tongue was thick with thirst:
For the stroke of eight is the stroke of Fate
  That makes a man accursed,
And Fate will use a running noose
  For the best man and the worst.

We had no other thing to do,
  Save to wait for the sign to come:
So, like things of stone in a valley lone,
  Quiet we sat and dumb:
But each man's heart beat thick and quick
  Like a madman on a drum!

With sudden shock the prison-clock
   Smote on the shivering air,
And from all the gaol rose up a wail
   Of impotent despair,
Like the sound that frightened marshes hear
   From some leper in his lair.

And as one sees most fearful things
   In the crystal of a dream,
We saw the greasy hempen rope
   Hooked to the blackened beam,
And heard the prayer the hangman's snare
   Strangled into a scream.

And all the woe that moved him so
   That he gave that bitter cry,
And the wild regrets, and the bloody sweats,
   None knew so well as I:
For he who lives more lives than one
   More deaths than one must die.

There is no chapel on the day
   On which they hang a man:
The Chaplain's heart is far too sick,
   Or his face is far too wan,
Or there is that written in his eyes
   Which none should look upon.

So they kept us close till nigh on noon,
   And then they rang the bell,
And the Warders with their jingling keys
   Opened each listening cell,
And down the iron stairs we tramped,
   Each from his separate Hell.

Out into God's sweet air we went,
   But not in wonted way,
For this man's face was white with fear,
   And that man's face was grey,
And I never saw sad men who looked
   So wistfully at the day.

I never saw sad men who looked
  With such a wistful eye
Upon that little tent of blue
  We prisoners call the sky,
And at every careless cloud that passed
  In happy freedom by. . . .

The Warders strutted up and down,
  And kept their herd of brutes,
Their uniforms were spick and span,
  And they were their Sunday suits,
But we knew the work they had been at
  By the quicklime on their boots.

For where a grave had opened wide
  There was no grave at all:
Only a stretch of mud and sand
  By the hideous prison-wall,
And a little heap of burning lime,
  That the man should have his pall.

For he has a pall, this wretched man,
  Such as few men can claim;
Deep down below a prison-yard,
  Naked for greater shame,
He lies, with fetters on each foot,
  Wrapt in a sheet of flame! . . .

I know not whether Laws be right,
  Or whether Laws be wrong;
All that we know who lie in jail
  Is that the wall is strong;
And that each day is like a year,
  A year whose days are long.

But this I know, that every Law
  That men have made for Man,
Since first Man took his brother's life,
  And the sad world began,
But straws the wheat and saves the chaff
  With a most evil fan.

This too I know—and wise it were
    If each could know the same—
That every prison that men build
    Is built with bricks of shame,
And bound with bars lest Christ should see
    How men their brothers maim.

With bars they blur the gracious moon,
    And blind the goodly sun:
And they do well to hide their Hell,
    For in it things are done
That Son of God nor son of Man
    Ever should look upon!

The vilest deeds like poison weeds
    Bloom well in prison-air:
It is only what is good in Man
    That wastes and withers there:
Pale Anguish keeps the heavy gate,
    And the Warder is Despair.

For they starve the little frightened child
    Till it weeps both night and day:
And they scourge the weak, and flog the fool,
    And gibe the old and grey,
And some grow mad, and all grow bad,
    And none a word may say.

If This Great World

by WILLIAM WORDSWORTH
English romantic poet, 1770–1850

If this great world of joy and pain
    Revolve in one sure track;
If freedom, set, will rise again,
    And virtue, flown, come back;
Woe to the purblind crew who fill
    The heart with each day's care;
Nor gain, from past or future, skill
    To bear, and to forbear!

The Priestess of Humanity
(From "A History of European Morals")
by WILLIAM E. H. LECKY
English historian and philosopher, 1838-1903

Under these circumstances, there has arisen in society a figure which is certainly the most mournful, and in some respects the most awful, upon which the eye of the moralist can dwell. That unhappy being whose very name is a shame to speak; who counterfeits with a cold heart the transports of affection, and submits herself as the passive instrument of lust; who is scorned and insulted as the vilest of her sex, and doomed, for the most part, to disease and abject wretchedness and an early death, appears in every age as the perpetual symbol of the degradation and sinfulness of man. Herself the supreme type of vice, she is ultimately the most efficient guardian of virtue. But for her, the unchallenged purity of countless happy homes would be polluted, and not a few who, in the pride of their untempted chastity, think of her with an indignant shudder, would have known the agony of remorse and despair. On that one degraded and ignoble form are concentrated the passions that might have filled the world with shame. She remains, while creeds and civilizations rise and fall, the eternal priestess of humanity, blasted for the sins of the people.

Sisterhood
by MARY CRAIG SINCLAIR
American author and journalist, 1883-1961

Last night I woke, and in my tranquil bed
I lay, and thanked my God with fervent prayer
That I had food and warmth, a cosy chair
Beside a jolly fire, and roses red
To give my room a touch of light and grace.
And I thanked God, oh thanked Him! that my face
Was beautiful, that it was fair to men:
I thought awhile, then thanked my God again.
For yesterday, on Broadway I had walked,
And I had stopped to watch them as they stalked
Their prey; and I was glad I had no sons
To look with me upon those woeful ones—
Paint on their lips, and from a corpse their hair,
And eyes of simulated lust, astare!

The Bridge of Sighs
by THOMAS HOOD

One more Unfortunate
  Weary of breath,
Rashly importunate,
  Gone to her death!

Take her up tenderly,
  Lift her with care;
Fashion'd so slenderly,
  Young, and so fair!

Look at her garments
Clinging like cerements;
  Whilst the wave constantly
Drips from her clothing;
  Take her up instantly,
Loving, not loathing.

Touch her not scornfully;
Think of her mournfully,
  Gently and humanly;
Not of the stains of her—
All that remains of her
  Now is pure womanly.

Make no deep scrutiny
Into her mutiny
  Rash and undutiful:
Past all dishonor
Death has left on her
  Only the beautiful.

Loop up her tresses
  Escaped from the comb,
Her fair auburn tresses;
Whilst wonderment guesses
  Where was her home?

Who was her father?
  Who was her mother?
Had she a sister?
  Had she a brother?
Or was there a dearer one
  Yet, than all other?

Alas! for the rarity
Of Christian charity
  Under the sun!
O! it was pitiful!
Near a whole city full,
  Home she had none.

Sisterly, brotherly,
Fatherly, motherly,
  Feelings had changed;
Love, by harsh evidence,
Thrown from its eminence;
Even God's providence
  Seeming estranged.

Where the lamps quiver
So far in the river,
  With many a light
From window and casement,
From garret to basement,
She stood, with amazement,
  Houseless by night.

The bleak wind of March
  Made her tremble and shiver;
But not the dark arch,
  Or the black flowing river;
Mad from life's history,
Glad to death's mystery
  Swift to be hurl'd—
Anywhere, anywhere
  Out of the world!

In she plunged boldly,
No matter how coldly
  The rough river ran;
Over the brink of it,—
Picture it, think of it,
  Dissolute Man!
Lave in it, drink of it
  Then, if you can!

Take her up tenderly,
  Lift her with care;
Fashion'd so slenderly,
  Young, and so fair!

Ere her limbs frigidly
Stiffen too rigidly,
  Decently, kindly,
Smooth and compose them;
And her eyes, close them,
  Staring so blindly!

Dreadfully staring
  Thro' muddy impurity,
As when with the daring
Last look of despairing
  Fix'd on futurity.

Perishing gloomily,
Spurr'd by contumely,
Cold inhumanity,
Burning insanity,
  Into her rest.
—Cross her hands humbly
As if praying dumbly,
  Over her breast!

Owning her weakness,
Her evil behavior,
And leaving, with meekness,
  Her sins to her Saviour!

The White Slave, *Abastenia St. Leger Eberle*

In the Strand

by ARTHUR SYMONS
English critic and poet, 1865-1945

With eyes and hands and voice convulsively
She craves the bestial wages. In her face
What now is left of woman? whose lost place
Is filled with greed's last eating agony.
She lives to be rejected and abhorred,
Like a dread thing forgotten. One by one
She hails the passers, whispers blindly; none
Heeds now the voice that had not once implored
Those alms in vain. The hour has struck for her,
And now damnation is scarce possible
Here on the earth; it waits for her in hell.
God! to be spurned of the last wayfarer
That haunts a dark street after midnight! Now
Shame's last disgrace is hot upon her brow.

The Weak Voice of Mercy

by CLARENCE DARROW
American criminal lawyer and leading fighter in civil liberties causes, most notable
of which was the defense of free scientific thought in the Tennessee evolution case;
1857-1938

The first necessary to lessen crime and to relieve victims from
the cruelty of moral judgments is a change of public opinion as
to human responsibility. When scientific ideas on this important
subject shall be generally accepted, all things that are possible will
follow from it. Some headway has already been made in the direction of considering heredity and environment. Theoretically we
no longer hold the insane responsible and some allowance is
made for children and the obviously defective. The discouraging
thing is that the public is fickle and changeable, and any temporary feeling overwhelms the patient effort of years. In the
present mad crusade against crime consequent upon the Great
War, penalties have been increased, new crimes created, and
paroles and pardons have been made almost impossible. The
public and press virtually declare that even insanity should not
save the life of one who slays his fellow. Repeatedly the insane
are hanged without a chance, and sentences of death are pro-

nounced, where before, a term of years, or life imprisonment would have been the penalty for the offense. Individual men and collections of men are ruled not by judgment but by impulse; the voice of conscience and mercy is always very weak and drowned by the hoarse cry for vengeance.

As long as men collectively impose their will upon the individual units, they should consider that this imposition calls for intelligence, kindliness, tolerance and a large degree of sympathy and understanding. In considering the welfare of the public, the accused, his family and his friends should be included as a part. It need not be expected that all maladjustments can ever be wiped out. Organization with its close relation of individual units implies conflicts. Nevertheless, the effort should be to remove all possible inducement for the violent clashing of individuals and to minimize the severity of such conflicts as are inevitable.

Portrait of the Anti-Semite
by JEAN-PAUL SARTRE
French dramatist, novelist and philosopher, 1905–1980

The anti-semite willingly admits that the Jew is intelligent and hard-working; he may even acknowledge his own inferiority in this respect. Such a concession costs him little: he has put these virtues, as it were, in parentheses. Or rather, their value depends on the person who possesses them: where the Jew is concerned, the more virtues he has, the more dangerous he is. The anti-semite cherishes no illusions about himself. He regards himself as an average man, as a representative of the common man, and basically of the mediocre: one does not find instances of an anti-semite claiming individual superiority over the Jews. But it must not be thought that he is ashamed of his mediocrity: on the contrary, he vaunts it: for he has in fact chosen it. Such a man dreads every kind of solitude, that of the genius as much as that of the murderer: he is the man of the crowd, and no matter how insignificant his stature, he takes the precaution of stooping lower for fear of emerging above the herd and coming face to face with himself. If he has become anti-semitic, it is because that is something one cannot become alone. The expression, "I hate the Jews," is something one always says in front of others: and in uttering the words, one affirms one's link with a tradition and a community whose hallmark is mediocrity.

It may be pointed out at this juncture that to have accepted mediocrity does not mean to be humble, or even modest. Exactly the opposite in fact. The mediocre have their own passionate pride, and anti-semitism is an attempt to give value to mediocrity for its own sake, to create an elite of the mediocre. Intelligence, for the anti-semite, is a Jewish attribute, hence he is free to despise it to his heart's content, as he is free to despise all the other virtues the Jew may possess: these are ersatz qualities which the Jews use in place of the balanced mediocrity which they will always lack.

The Untouchables
(From "Mother India")
by KATHERINE MAYO
American author, 1867-1940

The first time that I, personally, approached a realizing sense of what the doctrine of Untouchability means in terms of man's inhumanity to man, was during a visit to a child-welfare center in a northerly Indian city.

The place was crowded with Indian women who had brought their babies to be examined by the English professional in charge, a trained public health nurse. Toward her their attitude was that of children toward a wise and loving mother—confiding, affectionate, trusting. And their needs were inclusive. All morning I had been watching babies washed and weighed and examined, simple remedies handed out, questions answered, advice and friendly cautions given, encouragement and praise. Just now I happened to be looking at a matronly high-caste woman with an intelligent, clean-cut face. She was loaded with heavy gold and silver jewelry and wore a silk mantle. She sat down on the floor to show her baby, unrolling him from the torn fragment of an old quilt, his only garment. This revealed his whole little body caked in a mass of dry and half-dry excreta.

"She appears unconcerned," I remarked to the Sister. The Sister replied:

"We try to get such women to have napkins for their babies, but they won't wash them themselves and they won't pay washers to wash them, although they are quite able to do so. This woman is well born. Her husband is well educated—a technical man— and enjoys a good salary. Sometimes it may please her to hang that bit of quilt out in the sun in her courtyard, and, when it is dry, to brush off what will come off. That's all. This, incidentally, helps explain why infantile diarrhea spreads through the families in a district. They will make no attempt whatever to keep things clean."

As the Sister spoke, a figure appeared before the open doorway —a young woman so graceful and with a face so sweet and appealing as to rivet attention at once. She carried an ailing baby on her arm, but came no farther—just stood still beyond the doorway, wistfully smiling. The Sister, looking up, smiled back.

"Why does she not come in?" I asked.

"She dare not. If she did, all those others would go. She is an Untouchable—an outcast. She herself would feel it wicked to set her foot upon that sill."

"She looks at least as decent as they," I remarked.

"Untouchables may be as intelligent as anyone else—and you see for yourself that they couldn't be dirtier," said the Sister. "But such is the custom of India. Since we can't alter it, we just plod on, trying to help them all, as best we can."

And so the gentle suppliant waited outside, among a crowd of others of her kind till Sister could go to them, bring to this one ointment for baby's eyes, to that one a mixture for baby's cough, and hearing the story of another.

But they might not bring their little ones in to the mercy of the warm bath, as the other women were doing at will. They might not come to the sewing class. They might not defile the scales by laying their babies in its basket, to see what the milk-dole was doing. For they were all horrible sinners in aeons past, deserving now neither help nor sympathy while they worked out their curse.

The Empire of Cruelty
by DAVID ROUSSET
French veteran of Nazi concentration camps

This concept of inferior beings, organically wicked, was so natural and inborn among the SS and went along with such contempt, such a long familiarity with every form of depravity, and such complete reliance on the power of their system to crush all human dignity, that they came to consider it a favor to a prisoner to assign him to some chosen task—which explains the burlesque idea of relegating some of the prisoners to laboratory research projects.

This inner certitude that they were predestined to rule and that it was a sacrilege ever to feel the slightest doubt of their mission stirred the SS to insatiable rages against the women prisoners. That they should so much as exist was an act of defiance that sent them into paroxysms of fury. And the sharp necessity for expiation, mingled with all the sexual impulsions that were given free rein, explains the reprisals against them.

The blind hatred that ordains and presides over all these enterprises is the outcropping of all the rancors, all the thwarted petty ambitions, all the cravings and despair engendered by the extraordinary dissolution of the German middle class in the period between the two wars. To attribute it to any racial atavism is only to echo the very fallacy on which the SS mentality is based. At each economic cataclysm, each financial collapse, whole sections of German society crumbled away. Tens of thousands of persons were torn from the traditional forms of existence to which they physically belonged, and condemned to a social death that was a degradation and a torture to them. Amid the corpses of faiths and the haunting memory of erstwhile comforts, the most established intellectual horizons gone askew, there remained only an extraordinary nakedness made up of impotent rage, and a sullen and criminal thirst for revenge.

National Socialism endowed all the turpitudes released by the earthquake in German society with a mythlike glamor. Its propaganda rose to genius in poisoning brains and mobilizing seething hatred. The need for mystifying the masses to the advantage of the masters led their propagandists to create amazing characters embodying all despairs, battening on all crimes: the Communist, the Jew, the Democrat. It was a fabulous setting of crude, highly colored caricatures that formed the background of the SS mentality. In the frightful nullity that this mystification imposed, appetites were launched like aimless tempests against these straw men planted among the ruins, who made a convenient target at least. Propaganda injected into the world a passion for lynching. Lynching, realized and systematized, created this astonishing empire of the camps, as a sop to a desperate and humiliated mob.

Babiy Yar

by YEVGENY YEVTUSHENKO

Soviet poet, born 1933. The translation is by R. Milner-Gulland and P. Levi.

Over Babiy Yar
there are no memorials.
The steep hillside like a rough inscription.
I am frightened.
Today I am as old as the Jewish race.
I seem to myself a Jew at this moment.
I, wandering in Egypt.
I, crucified. I perishing.
Even today the mark of the nails.
I think also of Dreyfus. I am he.
The Philistine my judge and my accuser.
Cut off by bars and cornered,
ringed round, spat at, lied about;
the screaming ladies with the Brussels lace
poke me in the face with parasols.
I am also a boy in Belostok,
the dropping blood spreads across the floor,
the public-bar heroes are rioting
in an equal stench of garlic and of drink.
I have no strength, go spinning from a boot,
shriek useless prayers that they don't listen to,
with a cackle of 'Thrash the kikes and save **Russia!**'
the corn-chandler is beating up my mother.
I seem to myself like Anne Frank
to be transparent as an April twig
and am in love, I have no need for words,
I need for us to look at one another.
How little we have to see or to smell
separated from foliage and the sky,
how much, how much in the dark room
gently embracing each other.
They're coming. Don't be afraid.
The booming and banging of the spring.
It's coming this way. Come to me.
Quickly, give me your lips.

They're battering in the door. Roar of the ice.
Over Babiy Yar
rustle of the wild grass.
The trees look threatening, look like judges
And everything is one silent cry.
Taking my hat off
I feel myself slowly going grey.
And I am one silent cry
over the many thousands of the buried;
am every old man killed here,
every child killed here.
O my Russian people, I know you.
Your nature is international.
Foul hands rattle your clean name.
I know the goodness of my country.
How terrible it is that pompous title
the anti-semites calmly call themselves,
Society of the Russian Race.
No part of me can ever forget it.
When the last anti-semite on the earth
is buried for ever
let the International ring out.
No Jewish blood runs among my blood,
but I am as bitterly and hardly hated
by every anti-semite
as if I were a Jew. By this
I am a Russian.

BOOK IV

Out of the Depths

*The protest of the soul of man who is confronted with social
injustice and is groping for a remedy.*

The People's Anthem

by Ebenezer Elliott

A leader of the Chartist movement in England, 1781–1849

When wilt thou save the people?
   O God of mercy! when?
Not kings and lords, but nations!
   Not thrones and crowns, but men!
Flowers of thy heart, O God, are they!
Let them not pass, like weeds, away!
Their heritage a sunless day!
      God save the people!

Shall crime bring crime for ever,
   Strength aiding still the strong?
Is it thy will, O Father!
   That man shall toil for wrong?
"No!" say thy mountains; "No!" thy skies;
"Man's clouded sun shall brightly rise,
And songs be heard instead of sighs."
      God save the people!

When wilt thou save the people?
   O God of mercy! when?
The people, Lord! the people!
   Not thrones and crowns, but men!
God save the people! thine they are;
Thy children, as thy angels fair;
Save them from bondage and despair!
      God save the people!

A Hymn

by GILBERT K. CHESTERTON
English essayist and poet, 1874-1936

O God of earth and altar
   Bow down and hear our cry,
Our earthly rulers falter,
   Our people drift and die;
The walls of gold entomb us,
   The swords of scorn divide,
Take not Thy thunder from us,
   But take away our pride.

From all that terror teaches,
   From lies of tongue and pen,
From all the easy speeches
   That comfort cruel men,
From sale and profanation
   Of honor and the sword,
From sleep and from damnation,
   Deliver us, good Lord.
Tie in a living tether
   The priest and prince and thrall,

Bind all our lives together,
   Smite us and save us all;
In ire and exultation
   Aflame with faith, and free,
Lift up a living nation,
   A single sword to Thee.

By MATTHEW ARNOLD
English critic and poet, 1822-1888

Our inequality materializes our upper class, vulgarizes our middle class, brutalizes our lower class.

The World's Way

by WILLIAM SHAKESPEARE
England's greatest poet and dramatist, 1564-1616

Tired with all these, for restful death I cry—
    As, to behold desert a beggar born,
And needy nothing trimm'd in jollity,
    And purest faith unhappily forsworn,

And gilded honor shamefully misplaced,
    And maiden virtue rudely strumpeted,
And right perfection wrongfully disgraced,
    And strength by limping sway disablèd,

And art made tongue-tied by authority,
    And folly, doctor-like, controlling skill,
And simple truth miscall'd simplicity,
    And captive Good attending captain Ill:—

Tired with all these, from these would I be gone,
Save that, to die, I leave my Love alone.

Written in London, September, 1802

by WILLIAM WORDSWORTH
English poet, 1770-1850

O friend! I know not which way I must look
For comfort, being, as I am, opprest
To think that now our life is only drest
For show; mean handy-work of craftsman, cook,
Or groom!—We must run glittering like a brook
In the open sunshine, or we are unblest;
The wealthiest man among us is the best;
No grandeur now in nature or in book
Delights us. Rapine, avarice, expense,
This is idolatry; and these we adore;
Plain living and high thinking are no more:
The homely beauty of the good old cause
Is gone; our peace, our fearful innocence,
And pure religion breathing household laws.

These Populations
by EDWARD CARPENTER
English social reformer and poet, 1844-1929

These populations—
So puny, white-faced, machine-made,
Turned out by factories, out of offices, out of drawingrooms, by thousands all alike—
Huddled, stitched up, in clothes, fearing a chill, a drop of rain, looking timidly at the sea and sky as at strange monsters, or running back so quick to their suburban runs and burrows,
Dapper, libidinous, cute, with washed-out small eyes—
What are these?
Are they men and women?
Each denying himself, hiding himself?
Are they men and women?
So timorous, like hares—a breath of propriety or custom, a draught of wind, the mere threat of pain or of danger?
O for a breath of the sea and the great mountains!
A bronzed hardy live man walking his way through it all;
Thousands of men companioning the waves and the storms, splendid in health, naked-breasted, catching the lion with their hands;
A thousand women swift-footed and free—owners of themselves, forgetful of themselves, in all their actions—full of joy and laughter and action;
Garbed not so differently from the men, joining with them in their games and sports, sharing also their labors;
Free to hold their own, to grant or withhold their love, the same as the men;
Strong, well-equipped in muscle and skill, clear of finesse and affectation—
(The men, too, clear of much brutality and conceit)—
Comrades together, equal in intelligence and adventure,
Trusting without concealment, loving without shame but with discrimination and continence towards a perfect passion.
O for a breath of the sea!
The necessity and directness of the great elements themselves!
Swimming the rivers, braving the sun, the cold, taming the animals and the earth, conquering the air with wings, and each other with love—
The true, the human society!

Freedom
by JAMES RUSSELL LOWELL
American poet and scholar, 1819-1891

Men! whose boast it is that ye
Come of fathers brave and free,
If there breathe on earth a slave,
Are ye truly free and brave?
If ye do not feel the chain
When it works a brother's pain,
Are ye not base slaves indeed,
Slaves unworthy to be freed?

Is true Freedom but to break
Fetters for our own dear sake,
And, with leathern hearts, forget
That we owe mankind a debt?
No! True Freedom is to share
All the chains our brothers wear,
And, with heart and hand, to be
Earnest to make others free!

They are slaves who fear to speak
For the fallen and the weak;
They are slaves who will not choose
Hatred, scoffing and abuse,
Rather than in silence shrink
From the truth they needs must think:
They are slaves who dare not be
In the right with two or three.

The Land Question
by CARDINAL MANNING
British prelate, 1808-1892

The land question means hunger, thirst, nakedness, notice to quit, labor spent in vain, the toil of years seized upon, the breaking up of homes; the misery, sickness, deaths of parents, children, wives; the despair and wildness which springs up in the hearts of the poor, when legal force, like a sharp harrow, goes over the most sensitive and vital rights of mankind. All this is contained in the land question.

Far From the Madding Crowd
(From "Elegy Written in a Country Churchyard")
by THOMAS GRAY
English poet and scholar, 1716-1771

Oft did the harvest to their sickle yield,
    Their furrow oft the stubborn glebe has broke;
How jocund did they drive their team afield!
    How bow'd the woods beneath their sturdy stroke!

Let not Ambition mock their useful toil,
    Their homely joys, and destiny obscure;
Nor Grandeur hear with a disdainful smile
    The short and simple annals of the Poor.

The boast of heraldry, the pomp of power,
    And all that beauty, all that wealth, e'er gave
Await alike th' inevitable hour:—
    The paths of glory lead but to the grave. . . .

Can storied urn, or animated bust,
    Back to its mansion call the fleeting breath?
Can honor's voice provoke the silent dust,
    Or flattery soothe the dull cold ear of death?

Perhaps in this neglected spot is laid
    Some heart once pregnant with celestial fire;
Hands, that the rod of empire might have swayed,
    Or waked to ecstasy the living lyre;

But knowledge to their eyes her ample page,
    Rich with the spoils of time, did ne'er unroll;
Chill penury repressed their noble rage,
    And froze the genial current of the soul.

Full many a gem of purest ray serene
    The dark unfathomed caves of ocean bear;
Full many a flower is born to blush unseen,
    And waste its sweetness on the desert air.

Some village Hampden, that, with dauntless breast,
　　The little tyrant of his fields withstood,
Some mute inglorious Milton here may rest,
　　Some Cromwell guiltless of his country's blood.

The applause of listening senates to command,
　　The threats of pain and ruin to despise,
To scatter plenty o'er a smiling land,
　　And read their history in a nation's eyes,

Their lot forbade: nor circumscribed alone
　　Their growing virtues, but their crimes confined;
Forbade to wade through slaughter to a throne,
　　And shut the gates of mercy on mankind;

The struggling pangs of conscious truth to hide,
　　To quench the blushes of ingenuous shame,
Or heap the shrine of luxury and pride
　　With incense kindled at the Muse's flame.

Far from the madding crowd's ignoble strife,
　　Their sober wishes never learned to stray;
Along the cool sequestered vale of life
　　They kept the noiseless tenor of their way.

The Preface to "Les Miserables"
by Victor Hugo
French poet and humanitarian novelist, 1802-1885

So long as there shall exist, by reason of law and custom, a social condemnation, which, in the face of civilization, artificially creates hells on earth, and complicates a destiny that is divine, with human fatality; so long as the three problems of the age—the degradation of man by poverty, the ruin of women by starvation, and the dwarfing of childhood by physical and spiritual night—are not solved; so long as, in certain regions, social asphyxia shall be possible; in other words, and from a yet more extended point of view, so long as ignorance and misery remain on earth, books like this cannot be useless.

Preface to "Major Barbara"
by GEORGE BERNARD SHAW
Irish dramatist, critic and major spokesman for Fabian socialism, 1856-1950

The thoughtless wickedness with which we scatter sentences of imprisonment, torture in the solitary cell and on the plank bed, and flogging, on moral invalids and energetic rebels, is as nothing compared to the stupid levity with which we tolerate poverty as if it were either a wholesome tonic for lazy people or else a virtue to be embraced as St. Francis embraced it. If a man is indolent, let him be poor. If he is drunken, let him be poor. If he is not a gentleman, let him be poor. If he is addicted to the fine arts or to pure science instead of to trade and finance, let him be poor. If he chooses to spend his urban eighteen shillings a week or his agricultural thirteen shillings a week on his beer and his family instead of saving it up for his old age, let him be poor. Let nothing be done for "the undeserving": let him be poor. Serves him right! Also—somewhat inconsistently—blessed are the poor!

Now what does this Let Him Be Poor mean? It means let him be weak. Let him be ignorant. Let him become a nucleus of disease. Let him be a standing exhibition and example of ugliness and dirt. Let him have rickety children. Let him be cheap and let him drag his fellows down to his price by selling himself to do their work. Let his habitations turn our cities into poisonous congeries of slums. Let his daughters infect our young men with the diseases of the streets and his sons revenge him by turning the nation's manhood into scrofula, cowardice, cruelty, hypocrisy, political imbecility, and all the other fruits of oppression and malnutrition. Let the undeserving become still less deserving; and let the deserving lay up for himself, not treasures in heaven, but horrors in hell upon earth. This being so, is it really wise to let him be poor? Would he not do ten times less harm as a prosperous burglar, incendiary, ravisher, or murderer, to the utmost limits of humanity's comparatively negligible impulses in these directions? Suppose we were to abolish all penalties for such activities, and decide that poverty is the one thing we will not tolerate—that every adult with less than, say, £365 a year, shall be painlessly but inexorably killed, and every hungry half naked child forcibly fattened and clothed, would not that be an enormous improvement on our existing system, which has already destroyed so many civilizations, and is visibly destroying ours in the same way?

The Jungle
by UPTON SINCLAIR

Now the dreadful winter was come upon them. In the forests, all summer long, the branches of the trees do battle for light, and some of them lose and die; and then come the raging blasts, and the storms of snow and hail, and strew the ground with these weaker branches. Just so it was in Packingtown; the whole district braced itself for the struggle that was an agony, and those whose time was come died off in hordes. All the year round they had been serving as cogs in the great packing-machine; and now was the time for the renovating of it, and the replacing of damaged parts. There came pneumonia and grippe, stalking among them, seeking for weakened constitutions; there was the annual harvest of those whom tuberculosis had been dragging down. There came cruel cold, and biting winds, and blizzards of snow, all testing relentlessly for failing muscles and impoverished blood. Sooner or later came the day when the unfit one did not report for work; and then, with no time lost in waiting, and no inquiries or regrets, there was a chance for a new hand. . . .

Home was not a very attractive place—at least not this winter. They had only been able to buy one stove, and this was a small one, and proved not big enough to warm even the kitchen in the bitterest weather. This made it hard for Teta Elzbieta all day, and for the children when they could not get to school. At night they would sit huddled around this stove, while they ate their supper off their laps; and then Jurgis and Jonas would smoke a pipe, after which they would all crawl into their beds to get warm, after putting out the fire to save the coal. Then they would have some frightful experiences with the cold. They would sleep with all their clothes on, including their overcoats, and put over them all the bedding and spare clothing they owned; the children would sleep all crowded into one bed, and yet even so they could not keep warm. The outside ones would be shivering and sobbing, crawling over the others and trying to get down into the center, and causing a fight. This old house with the leaky weather-boards was a very different thing from their cabins at home, with great thick walls plastered inside and outside with mud; and the cold which came upon them was a living thing, a demon-presence in the room. They would waken in the midnight hours, when everything was black; perhaps they would hear it yelling outside, or perhaps there would be deathlike stillness—and that would be worse yet. They could feel the cold as it crept in through the cracks, reaching out for them with its icy, death-dealing fingers; and they would crouch and cower, and try to hide from it, all in vain. It would come, and it would come; a grisly thing, a spectre born in the black caverns of terror; a power primeval, cosmic, shadowing the tortures of the lost souls flung out to chaos and destruction. It was cruel, iron-hard; and hour after hour they would cringe in its grasp, alone, alone. There would be no one to hear them if they cried out; there would be no help, no mercy. And so on until morning—when they would go out to another day of toil, a little weaker, a little nearer to the time when it would be their turn to be shaken from the tree.

By JOHN STUART MILL
English philosopher, 1806-1873

Hitherto, it is questionable if all the mechanical inventions yet made have lightened the day's toil of any human being.

To a Foil'd European Revolutionaire
by WALT WHITMAN
American poet and vigorous exponent of democratic hope, 1819-1892

Not songs of loyalty alone are these,
But songs of insurrection also;
For I am the sworn poet of every dauntless rebel, the world over,
And he going with me leaves peace and routine behind him,
And stakes his life, to be lost at any moment. . . .

When liberty goes out of a place, it is not the first to go, nor the
    second or third to go,
It waits for all the rest to go—it is the last.
When there are no more memories of martyrs and heroes,
And when all life, and all the souls of men and women are
    discharged from any part of the earth,
Then only shall liberty, or the idea of liberty, be discharged from
    that part of the earth,
And the infidel come into full possession.

The Man Under the Stone
by EDWIN MARKHAM

When I see a workingman with mouths to feed,
Up, day after day, in the dark before the dawn,
And coming home, night after night, thro' the dusk,
Swinging forward like some fierce silent animal,
I see a man doomed to roll a huge stone up an endless steep.
He strains it onward inch by stubborn inch,
Crouched always in the shadow of the rock. . . .
See where he crouches, twisted, cramped, misshapen!
　　He lifts for their life;
　　The veins knot and darken—
　　Blood surges into his face. . . .
　　Now he loses—now he wins—
　　Now he loses—loses— (God of my soul!)
　　He digs his feet into the earth—
　　There's a movement of terrified effort. . . .
　　It stirs—it moves!
　　Will the huge stone break his hold
　　And crush him as it plunges to the Gulf?

The silent struggle goes on and on,
Like two contending in a dream.

Robinson Crusoe Sees Inequality
by DANIEL DEFOE
English novelist and pamphleteer, 1661-1731; many times imprisoned
for satires upon the authorities

I saw the world round me, one part laboring for bread, and
the other part squandering in vile excess or empty pleasures,
equally miserable, because the end they proposed still fled from
them; for the man of pleasure every day surfeited of his vice, and
heaped up work for sorrow and repentance; and the man of labor
spent his strength in daily struggling for bread to maintain the
vital strength he labored with; so living in a daily circulation of
sorrow, living but to work, and working but to live, as if daily
bread were the only end of a wearisome life, and a wearisome
life the only occasion of daily bread.

Echo of a Scream, *David Alfaro Siqueiros*

Fomá Gordyéeff
by Maxim Gorky

Yozhov drank his tea at one draught, thrust the glass on the saucer, placed his feet on the edge of the chair, and clasping his knees in his hands, rested his chin upon them. In this pose, small sized and flexible as rubber, he began:

"The student Sachkov, my former teacher, who is now a doctor of medicine, a whist player and a mean fellow all around, used to tell me whenever I knew my lesson well: 'You're a fine fellow, Kolya! You are an able boy. We proletarians, plain and poor people, coming from the backyard of life, we must study and study, in order to come to the front, ahead of everybody. Russia is in need of wise and honest people. Try to be such, and you will be master of your fate and a useful member of society. On us commoners rest the best hopes of the country. We are destined to bring into it light, truth,' and so on. I believed him, the brute. And since then about twenty years have elapsed. We proletarians have grown up, but have neither appropriated any wisdom nor brought light into life. As before, Russia is suffering from its chronic disease—a superabundance of rascals; while we, the proletarians, take pleasure in filling their dense throngs."

Yozhov's face wrinkled into a bitter grimace, and he began to laugh noiselessly, with his lips only. "I, and many others with me, we have robbed ourselves for the sake of saving up something for life. Desiring to make myself a valuable man, I have underrated my individuality in every way possible. In order to study and not die of starvation, I have for six years in succession taught blockheads how to read and write, and had to bear a mass of abominations at the hands of various papas and mammas, who humiliated me without any constraint. Earning my bread and tea, I could not, I had not the time to earn my shoes, and I had to turn to charitable institutions with humble petitions for loans on the strength of my poverty. If the philanthropists could only reckon up how much of the spirit they kill in man while supporting the life of his body! If they only knew that each rouble they give for bread contains ninety-nine copecks worth of poison for the soul! If they could only burst from excess of their kindness and pride, which they draw from their holy activity! There is no one on earth more disgusting and repulsive than he who gives alms. No one so miserable as he who accepts them."

Concerning Women
(From "Aurora Leigh")
by ELIZABETH BARRETT BROWNING
English poet and champion of Italian liberty, 1806-1861

I call you hard
To general suffering. Here's the world half blind
With intellectual light, half brutalized
With civilization, having caught the plague
In silks from Tarsus, shrieking east and west
Along a thousand railroads, mad with pain
And sin too! . . . does one woman of you all,
(You who weep easily) grow pale to see
This tiger shake his cage?—does one of you
Stand still from dancing, stop from stringing pearls,
And pine and die because of the great sum
Of universal anguish?—Show me a tear
Wet as Cordelia's, in eyes bright as yours,
Because the world is mad. You cannot count,
That you should weep for this account, not you!
You weep for what you know. A red-haired child
Sick in a fever, if you touch him once,
Though but so little as with a finger-tip,
Will set you weeping; but a million sick—
You could as soon weep for the rule of three
Or compound fractions. Therefore, this same world.
Uncomprehended by you.—Women as you are,
Mere women, personal and passionate,
You give us doting mothers, and perfect wives,
Sublime Madonnas, and enduring saints!
We get no Christ from you,—and verily
We shall not get a poet, in my mind.

The Wrongfulness of Riches
by GRANT ALLEN
English essayist and naturalist, 1848-1899

If you are on the side of the spoilers, then you are a bad man.
If you are on the side of social justice, then you are a good one.
There is no effective test of high morality at the present day
save this.

Critics of the middle-class type often exclaim, of reasoning like this, "What on earth makes him say it? What has *he* to gain by talking in that way? What does he expect to get by it?" So bound up are they in the idea of a self-interest as the one motive of action that they never even seem to conceive of honest conviction as a ground for speaking out the truth that is in one. To such critics I would answer, "The reason why I write all this is because I profoundly believe it. I believe the poor are being kept out of their own. I believe the rich are for the most part selfish and despicable. I believe wealth has been generally piled up by cruel and unworthy means. I believe it is wrong in us to acquiesce in the wicked inequalities of our existing social state, instead of trying our utmost to bring about another, where right would be done to all, where poverty would be impossible. I believe such a system is perfectly practicable, and that nothing stands in its way save the selfish fears and prejudices of individuals. And I believe that even those craven fears and narrow prejudices are wholly mistaken; that everybody, including the rich themselves, would be infinitely happier in a world where no poverty existed, where no hateful sights and sounds met the eye at every turn, where all slums were swept away, and where everybody had their just and even share of pleasures and refinements in a free and equal community."

Each Against All
by CHARLES FOURIER
One of the early Utopian writers, 1772-1837.

The present social order is a ridiculous mechanism, in which portions of the whole are in conflict and acting against the whole. We see each class in society desire, from interest, the misfortune of the other classes, placing in every way individual interest in opposition to public good. The lawyer wishes litigations and suits, particularly among the rich; the physician desires sickness. (The latter would be ruined if everybody died without disease, as would the former if all quarrels were settled by arbitration.) The soldier wants a war, which will carry off half his comrades and secure him promotion; the undertaker wants burials; monopolists and forestallers want famine, to double or treble the price of grain; the architect, the carpenter, the mason, want conflagrations, that will burn down a hundred houses to give activity to their branches of business.

Despair
by LADY WILDE
Irish poet, mother of Oscar Wilde, 1826-1896

Before us dies our brother, of starvation;
  Around are cries of famine and despair!
Where is hope for us, or comfort or salvation—
  Where—oh! where?
If the angels ever hearken, downward bending,
  They are weeping, we are sure,
At the litanies of human groans ascending
  From the crushed hearts of the poor.

We never knew a childhood's mirth and gladness,
  Nor the proud heart of youth free and brave;
Oh, a death-like dream of wretchedness and sadness
  Is life's weary journey to the grave!
Day by day we lower sink, and lower,
  Till the God-like soul within
Falls crushed beneath the fearful demon power
  Of poverty and sin.

So we toil on, on with fever burning
  In heart and brain;
So we toil on, on through bitter scorning,
  Want, woe, and pain.
We dare not raise our eyes to the blue heavens
  Or the toil must cease—
We dare not breathe the fresh air God has given
  One hour in peace.

Inequality of Wealth
by GEORGE BERNARD SHAW

I am not bound to keep my temper with an imposture so outrageous, so abjectly sycophantic, as the pretence that the existing inequalities of income correspond to and are produced by moral and physical inferiorities and superiorities—that Barnato was five million times as great and good a man as William Blake, and committed suicide because he lost two-fifths of his superiority; that the life of Lord Anglesey has been on a far higher plane than that of John Ruskin; that Mademoiselle Liane de Pougy has been raised by her successful sugar speculation to moral heights never attained by Florence Nightingale; and that an arrangement to establish economic equality between them by duly adjusted pensions would be impossible. I say that no sane person can be expected to treat such impudent follies with patience, much less with respect.

The Two Songs
by WILLIAM BLAKE

I heard an Angel singing
When the day was springing:
"Mercy, pity, and peace,
Are the world's release."

So he sang all day
Over the new-mown hay,
Till the sun went down,
And haycocks looked brown.

I heard a Devil curse
Over the heath and the furze:
"Mercy could be no more
If there were nobody poor,
And pity no more could be

If all were happy as ye:
And mutual fear brings peace.
Misery's increase
Are mercy, pity, peace."

At his curse the sun went down,
And the heavens gave a frown.

By JAMES ANTHONY FROUDE
English historian, 1818-1894

The endurance of the inequalities of life by the poor is the marvel of human society.

Savva

by Leonid Andreyev

(In this strange drama, which might be called a symbolic tragi-comedy, the Russian writer has set forth the plight of the educated people of his country, confronted by the abject superstition of the peasantry. Savva, a fanatical revolutionist, endeavors to wipe out this superstition by blowing up monastery full of drunken monks. But the plot is revealed to the monks, who carry out the ikon, or sacred image, before the explosion, and afterwards carry it back into the ruins. The peasants, arriving on the scene and finding the ikon uninjured, hail a supreme miracle; the whole country is swept by a wave of religious frenzy, in the course of which Savva is trampled to death by a mob.

In the following scene Savva argues with his sister, a religious believer. The tramp of pilgrims is heard outside).

SAVVA (*smiling*): The tramp of death!

LIPA: Remember that each one of these would consider himself happy in killing you, in crushing you like a reptile. Each one of these is your death. Why, they beat a simple thief to death, a horse thief. What would they not do to you? You who wanted to steal their God!

SAVVA: Quite true. That's property too.

LIPA: You still have the brazenness to joke? Who gave you the right to do such a thing? Who gave you the power over people? How dare you meddle with what to them is right? How dare you interfere with their life?

SAVVA: Who gave me the right? You gave it to me. Who gave me the power? You gave it to me—you with your malice, your ignorance, your stupidity! You with your wretched impotence! Right! Power! They have turned the earth into a sewer, an outrage, an abode of slaves. They worry each other, they torture each other, and they ask: "Who dares to take us by the throat?" I! Do you understand? I!

LIPA: But to destroy all! Think of it!

SAVVA: What could you do with them? What would *you* do? Try to persuade the oxen to turn away from their bovine path? Catch each one by his horn and pull him away? Would you put on a frock-coat and read a lecture? Haven't they had plenty to teach them? As if words and thought had any significance to them! Thought—pure, unhappy thought! They have perverted it. They have taught it to cheat and defraud. They have made it a salable commodity, to be bought at auction in the market.

No, sister, life is short, and I am not going to waste it in arguments with oxen. The way to deal with them is by fire. That's what they require—fire!

LIPA: But what do you want? What do you want?

SAVVA: What do I want? To free the earth, to free mankind. Man—the man of today—is wise. He has come to his senses. He is ripe for liberty. But the past eats away his soul like a canker. It imprisons him within the iron circle of things already accomplished. I want to do away with everything behind man, so that there is nothing to see when he looks back. I want to take him by the scruff of his neck and turn his face toward the future!

The Man Forbid
by JOHN DAVIDSON
Scotch poet and dramatist, 1857-1909

This Beauty, this Divinity, this Thought,
This hallowed bower and harvest of delight
Whose roots ethereal seemed to clutch the stars,
Whose amaranths perfumed eternity,
Is fixed in earthly soil enriched with bones
Of used-up workers; fattened with the blood
Of prostitutes, the prime manure; and dressed
With brains of madmen and the broken hearts
Of children. Understand it, you at least
Who toil all day and writhe and groan all night
With roots of luxury, a cancer struck
In every muscle: out of you it is
Cathedrals rise and Heaven blossoms fair;
You are the hidden putrefying source
Of beauty and delight, of leisured hours,
Of passionate loves and high imaginings;
You are the dung that keeps the roses sweet.
I say, uproot it; plough the land; and let
A summer-fallow sweeten all the World.

Peasantry

by STEPHEN CRANE
American novelist and poet, 1871-1900

These stupid peasants, who, throughout the world, hold potentates on their thrones, make statesmen illustrious, provide generals with lasting victories, all with ignorance, indifference, or half-witted hatred, moving the world with the strength of their arms, and getting their heads knocked together, in the name of God, the king, or the stock exchange—immortal, dreaming, hopeless asses, who surrender their reason to the care of a shining puppet, and persuade some toy to carry their lives in his purse.

Out of the Dark

by HELEN KELLER
America's most celebrated blind deaf-mute, who triumphed over all handicaps, 1880–1968

Step by step my investigation of blindness led me into the industrial world. And what a world it is! I must face unflinchingly a world of facts—a world of misery and degradation, of blindness, crookedness, and sin, a world struggling against the elements, against the unknown, against itself. How reconcile this world of fact with the bright world of my imagining? My darkness had been filled with the light of intelligence, and behold, the outer day-lit world was stumbling and groping in social blindness. At first I was most unhappy; but deeper study restored my confidence. By learning the sufferings and burdens of men, I became aware as never before of the life-power that has survived the forces of darkness—the power which, though never completely victorious, is continuously conquering. The very fact that we are still here carrying on the contest against the hosts of annihilation proves that on the whole the battle has gone for humanity. The world's great heart has proved equal to the prodigious undertaking which God set it. Rebuffed, but always persevering; self-reproached, but ever regaining faith; undaunted, tenacious, the heart of man labors towards immeasurably distant goals. Discouraged not by difficulties without, or the anguish of ages within, the heart listens to a secret voice that whispers: "Be not dismayed; in the future lies the Promised Land."

A South Sea Islander

by FRANCIS W. L. ADAMS
English poet, 1862-1893; dead by his own hand after a life of poverty

Aloll in the warm clear water,
    On her back with languorous limbs
She lies. The baby upon her breast
    Paddles and falls and swims.

With half-closed eyes she smiles,
    Guarding it with her hands;
And the sob swells up in my heart—
    In my heart that understands.

Dear, in the English country,
    The hatefullest land on earth,
The mothers are starved and the children die
    And death is better than birth!

Heirs of Time

by THOMAS WENTWORTH HIGGINSON
American writer, colonel of first Black regiment during the Civil War, 1823–1911

From street and square, from hill and glen,
    Of this vast world beyond my door,
I hear the tread of marching men,
    The patient armies of the poor.

Not ermine-clad or clothed in state,
    Their title-deeds not yet made plain,
But waking early, toiling late,
    The heirs of all the earth remain.

The peasant brain shall yet be wise,
    The untamed pulse grow calm and still;
The blind shall see, the lowly rise,
    And work in peace Time's wondrous will.

Some day, without a trumpet's call
    This news will o'er the world be blown:
"The heritage comes back to all;
    The myriad monarchs take their own."

London, Paul Gustave Doré

Beyond Human Might

by BJORNSTJERNE BJORNSON

Norwegian dramatist, 1832-1910. Here a young clergyman is speaking to a crowd
of miners in the midst of a bitterly-fought strike

BRATT: Here it is dark and cold. Here few work hopefully,
and no one joyfully. Here the children won't thrive—they yearn
for the sea and the daylight. They crave the sun. But it lasts
only a little while, and then they give up. They learn that among
those who have been cast down here there is rarely one who can
climb up again.

SEVERAL: That's right! . . .

BRATT: What is there to herald the coming of better things?
A new generation up there? Listen to what their young people
answer for themselves: "We want a good time!" And their
books? The books and the youth together make the future. And
what do the books say? Exactly the same as the youth: "Let us
have a good time! Ours are the light and the lust of life, its colors
and its joys!" That's what the youth and their books say.—They
are right! It is all theirs! There is no law to prevent their taking
life's sunlight and joy away from the poor people. For those who
have the sun have also made the law.—But then the next question is whether we might not scramble up high enough to take
part in the writing of a new law. (*This is received with thunder-
ing cheers.*) What is needed is that one generation makes an
effort strong enough to raise all coming generations into the
vigorous life of full sunlight.

MANY: Yes, yes!

BRATT: But so far every generation has put it off on the next
one. Until at last *our* turn has come—to bear sacrifices and sufferings like unto those of death itself!

New Prophets and Old

by DOROTHY DAY

American Catholic and radical reformer, 1897–1980

Jesus said, "Blessed are the meek," but I could not be meek at
the thought of injustice. I wanted a Lord who would scourge the
money-changers out of the temple, and I wanted to help all those
who raised their hand against oppression.

For me Christ no longer walked the streets of this world. He
was two thousand years dead and new prophets had risen up in
His place.

Weavers
by HEINRICH HEINE

Their eyelids are drooping, no tears lie beneath;
They stand at the loom and grind their teeth;
"We are weaving a shroud for the doubly dead,
And a threefold curse in its every thread—
    We are weaving, still weaving.

"A curse for the Godhead to whom we have bowed
In our cold and our hunger, we weave in the shroud;
For in vain have we hoped and in vain have prayed;
He has mocked us and scoffed at us, sold and betrayed—
    We are weaving, still weaving.

"A curse for the king of the wealthy and proud,
Who for us had no pity, we weave in the shroud;
Who takes our last penny to swell out his purse,
While we die the death of a dog—yea, a curse—
    We are weaving, still weaving.

"A curse for our country, whose cowardly crowd
Hold her shame in high honor, we weave in the shroud;
Whose blossoms are blighted and slain in the germ,
Whose filth and corruption engender the worm—
    We are weaving, still weaving.

"To and fro flies our shuttle—no pause in its flight,
'Tis a shroud we are weaving by day and by night;
We are weaving a shroud for the worse than dead,
And a threefold curse in its every thread—
    We are weaving—still weaving."

By ROBERT HERRICK
English lyric poet, 1591-1674

To mortal man great loads allotted be;
But of all packs, no pack like poverty.

An Italian Restaurant
(From "A Bed of Roses")
by W. L. GEORGE
English novelist, 1857-1903

They sat at a marble topped table, flooded with light by incandescent gas. In the glare the waiters seemed blacker, smaller and more stunted than by the light of day. Their faces were pallid, with a touch of green: their hair and moustaches were almost blue black. Their energy was that of automata. Victoria looked at them, melting with pity.

"There's life for you," said Farwell, interpreting her look. "Sixteen hours' work a day in an atmosphere of stale food. For meals, plate scourings. For sleep and time to get to it, eight hours. For living, the rest of the day."

"It's awful, awful," said Victoria. "They might as well be dead."

"They will be soon," said Farwell, "but what does that matter? There are plenty of waiters. In the shadow of the olive groves tonight in far-off Calabria, at the base of the vine-clad hills, couples are walking hand in hand, with passion flashing in their eyes. Brown peasant boys are clasping to their breast young girls with dark hair, white teeth, red lips, hearts that beat and quiver with ecstasy. They tell a tale of love and hope. So we shall not be short of waiters."

Death House
(From "An American Tragedy")
by THEODORE DREISER
American novelist, 1871-1945

The "death house" in this particular prison was one of those crass erections and maintenances of human insensitiveness and stupidity principally for which no one primarily was responsible. Indeed, its total plan and procedure were the results of a series of primary legislative enactments, followed by decisions and compulsions as devised by the temperaments and seeming necessities of various wardens, until at last—by degrees and without anything worthy of the name of thinking on any one's part—there had been gathered and was now being enforced all that could possibly be imagined in the way of unnecessary and really unauthorized cruelty or stupid and destructive torture. And to the end that a

man, once condemned by a jury, would be compelled to suffer
not alone the death for which his sentence called but a thousand
others before that. For the very room by its arrangement, as well
as the rules governing the lives and actions of the inmates, was
sufficient to bring about this torture, willy-nilly. . . .

Worse yet, and productive of perhaps the most grinding and
destroying of all the miseries here—the transverse passage leading
between the old death house on the one hand and the execution-
chamber on the other. For this from time to time—alas, how
frequently—was the scene or stage for at least a part of the tragedy
that was here so regularly enacted—the final business of execution.

For through this passage, on his last day, a man was transferred
from his *better* cell in the new building, where he might have
been incarcerated for so much as a year or two, to one of the older
ones in the death house, in order that he might spend his last
hours in solitude, although compelled at the final moment, none-
theless (the death march), to retrace his steps along this narrower
cross passage—and where all might see—into the execution chamber
at the other end of it.

Reflections on the Guillotine
by ALBERT CAMUS
French novelist and essayist, Nobel Prize for Literature 1957; 1913-1960

In relation to crime, how can our civilization be defined? The
reply is easy: for thirty years now, State crimes have been far more
numerous than individual crimes. I am not even speaking of wars,
general or localized, although bloodshed too is an alcohol that
eventually intoxicates like the headiest of wines. But the number
of individuals killed directly by the State has assumed astronomi-
cal proportions and infinitely outnumbers private murders. There
are fewer and fewer condemned by common law and more and
more condemned for political reasons. The proof is that each of
us, however honorable he may be, can foresee the possibility of
being someday condemned to death, whereas that eventuality
would have seemed ridiculous at the beginning of the century.
Alphonse Karr's witty remark, "Let the noble assassins begin" has
no meaning now. Those who cause the most blood to flow are the
same ones who believe they have right, logic, and history on their
side.

Hence our society must now defend herself not so much against
the individual as against the State. It may be that the proportions

will be reversed in another thirty years. But, for the moment, our self-defense must be aimed at the State first and foremost. Justice and expediency command the law to protect the individual against a State given over to the follies of sectarianism or of pride. "Let the State begin and abolish the death penalty" ought to be our rallying cry today.

Scottsboro
by LANGSTON HUGHES
Black American poet and writer, 1902–1967

8 BLACK BOYS IN A SOUTHERN JAIL.
WORLD, TURN PALE!

8 black boys and one white lie.
Is it much to die?

Is it much to die when immortal feet
March with you down Time's street,
When beyond steel bars sound the deathless drums
Like a mighty heart-beat as they come?

Who comes?

Christ,
Who fought alone.

John Brown.

That mad mob
That tore the Bastille down
Stone by stone.

Moses

Jeanne d'Arc

Dessalines

Nat Turner

Fighters for the free.

Lenin with the flag blood red.

(Not dead! Not dead!
None of these is dead.)

Gandhi

Sandino

Evangelista, too,
To walk with you—

8 BLACK BOYS IN A SOUTHERN JAIL.
WORLD, TURN PALE!

The Empire of Hate
by DAVID ROUSSET

It is only normal that, when all the vital forces of a social class
are the stake in the most total warfare ever yet conceived, the adversaries shall be rendered incapable of doing any harm and, if
necessary, exterminated. The purpose of the camps is indeed
physical destruction, but the actual aim of the concentrationary
universe, goes far beyond this. The SS does not conceive of his
adversary as a normal man. The enemy, according to the philosophy of the SS, is the physical and intellectual embodiment of the
Power of Evil. The Communist, the Socialist, the German liberal,
the revolutionary, the resistants in foreign countries, are the *active*
manifestations of Evil. But the very existence of certain peoples,
of certain races, such as the Jews, the Poles, and the Russians, is
the *static* expression of Evil. It is not necessary that a Jew, a Pole,
a Russian, actively combat National Socialism: he is by birth, by
predestination, a non-assimilable heretic doomed to hellfire. Death
is therefore not enough. Only expiation can assuage and soothe
the Master Race. The concentration camps are an amazing and
complex mechanism of expiation. Those who are to die go to
their deaths slowly, at a rate so calculated that their physical and
moral disintegration, realized by degrees, shall make them finally

aware that they are creatures accursed, incarnations of Evil, not men. And the high priest of this punishment feels a secret pleasure, an inner thrill of ecstasy, in wrecking their bodies.

This philosophy alone explains the inspired niceties of the tortures, the intricate refinements that prolong them, their systematization, and all the other elements that go to make the camps what they are. The presence of the criminals; the brutal lumping of all nationalities while abolishing any possibility of understanding between them; the deliberate mixture of all strata of society and of all age groups; hunger, beatings, fear permanently drilled into every brain—all these are but so many factors whose logical result, without any need for further intervention, can only be that total dissolution of the individual which is the ultimate expression of expiation.

Such a philosophy is not a fortuitous one, a mere sop to unbalanced brains. It fulfills an important social function. Death by itself gives forth but little terror. The long silent rows of gallows have only limited potentialities of dread. Torture, permanently established as a natural condition of existence, breeds a much more potent fear. The camps, by the simple fact of their existence, set up in society a destructive nightmare, eternally present and accessible. Death fades away. Torture triumphant, always living and active, spreads like a vault above the cowed world of men. It is not simply a question of crushing or paralyzing an opposition. This weapon has a much greater scope of efficiency. The camps castrate free brains.

Democracy and Justice

(From "The Children of Light and the Children of Darkness")
BY REINHOLD NIEBUHR

Man's capacity for justice makes democracy possible, but man's inclination to injustice makes democracy necessary.

The Revolutionary Fire

(From a letter written in 1953)
BY FIDEL CASTRO
Cuban revolutionary and premier, born 1926

I feel my belief in sacrifice and struggle getting stronger. I despise the kind of existence that clings to the miserly trifles of comfort and self-interest. I think that a man should not live beyond the age when he begins to deteriorate, when the flame that lighted the brightest moment of his life has weakened.

Conscience

(From a letter written to three students, October 1967)
BY ALEXANDER SOLZHENITSYN
Russian novelist, won the Nobel Prize for literature in 1970, born 1918

Justice *is* conscience, not a personal conscience but the conscience of the whole of humanity. Those who clearly recognize the voice of their own conscience usually recognize also the voice of justice.

BOOK V

Revolt

The struggle to abolish injustice; the battle cries of the new army which is gathering for the deliverance of humanity.

A Man's a Man for a' That

by ROBERT BURNS
Scotland's foremost poet, 1759-1796

Is there, for honest poverty,
　　That hangs his head, and a' that?
The coward slave, we pass him by,
　　We daur be puir, for a' that!
　　　　For a' that, and a' that,
　　Our toils obscure and a' that,
The rank is but the guinea's stamp—
　　The man's the gowd for a' that.

What though on hamely fare we dine,
　　Wear hoddin-grey and a' that;
Gie fools their silks, and knaves their wine—
　　A man's a man for a' that.
　　　　For a' that, and a' that,
　　Their tinsel show and a' that,
The honest man, though e'er sae puir,
　　Is king o' men for a' that.

Ye see yon birkie, ca'ed a lord,
　　Wha struts, and stares, and a' that;
Though hundreds worship at his word,
　　He's but a coof for a' that:
　　　　For a' that, and a' that,
　　His riband, star, and a' that;
The man of independent mind,
　　He looks and laughs at a' that.

A king can make a belted knight,
　　A marquis, duke, and a' that;
But an honest man's aboon his might,
　　Gude faith, he maunna fa' that!
　　　　For a' that, and a' that,
　　Their dignities and a' that,
The pith o' sense and pride o' worth
　　Are higher rank than a' that.

> Then let us pray that come it may,
>   (As come it will for a' that)
> That sense and worth, o'er a' the earth,
>   May bear the gree and a' that.
>   For a' that, and a' that—
>   It's coming yet, for a' that,
> When man to man, the warld o'er,
>   Shall brithers be for a' that.

By Thomas Jefferson
President of the United States and author of the Declaration of Independence,
1743-1826

All eyes are opened or opening to the rights of man. The general spread of the light of science has already laid open to every view the palpable truth, that the mass of mankind has not been born with saddles on their backs, nor a favored few booted and spurred, ready to ride them legitimately, by the grace of God.

A Vindication of Natural Society
by Edmund Burke
British statesman and orator, defender of American colonies during the
Revolutionary War; 1729-1797

Ask of politicians the ends for which laws were originally designed, and they will answer that the laws were designed as a protection for the poor and weak, against the oppression of the rich and powerful. But surely no pretence can be so ridiculous; a man might as well tell me he has taken off my load, because he has changed the burden. If the poor man is not able to support his suit according to the vexatious and expensive manner established in civilized countries, has not the rich as great an advantage over him as the strong has over the weak in a state of nature? . . .

The most obvious division of society is into rich and poor, and it is no less obvious that the number of the former bear a great disproportion to those of the latter. The whole business of the poor is to administer to the idleness, folly, and luxury of the rich, and that of the rich, in return, is to find the best methods of confirming the slavery and increasing the burdens of the poor. In a state of nature it is an invariable law that a man's acquisitions are in proportion to his labors. In a state of artificial society it is a law as constant and invariable that those who labor most enjoy the fewest things, and that those who labor not at all have the greatest number of enjoyments. A constitution of things this, strange and ridiculous beyond expression! We scarce believe a thing when we are told it which we actually see before our eyes every day without being in the least surprised. I suppose that there are in Great Britain upwards of an hundred thousand people employed in lead, tin, iron, copper, and coal mines; these unhappy wretches scarce ever see the light of the sun; they are buried in the bowels of the earth; there they work at a severe and dismal task, without the least prospect of being delivered from it; they subsist upon the coarsest and worst sort of fare; they have their health miserably impaired, and their lives cut short, by being perpetually confined in the close vapors of these malignant minerals. An hundred thousand more at least are tortured without remission by the suffocating smoke, intense fires, and constant drudgery necessary in refining and managing the products of those mines. If any man informed us that two hundred thousand innocent persons were condemned to so intolerable slavery, how should we pity the unhappy sufferers, and how great would be our just indignation against those who inflicted so cruel and ignominious a punishment! This is an instance—I could not wish a stronger—of the numberless things which we pass by in their common dress, yet which shock us when they are nakedly represented. . . .

In a misery of this sort, admitting some few lenitives, and those too but a few, nine parts in ten of the whole race of mankind drudge through life. It may be urged, perhaps, in palliation of this, that at least the rich few find a considerable and real benefit from the wretchedness of the many. But is this so in fact? . . .

The poor by their excessive labor, and the rich by their enormous luxury, are set upon a level, and rendered equally ignorant of any knowledge which might conduce to their happiness. A dismal view of the interior of all civil society! The lower part broken and ground down by the most cruel oppression; and the rich by their artificial method of life bringing worse evils on themselves than their tyranny could possibly inflict on those below them.

By WENDELL PHILLIPS
American abolitionist, 1811-1884

If there is anything that cannot bear free thought, let it crack.

Barricade, *José Orozco*

The Antiquity of Freedom
by WILLIAM CULLEN BRYANT
American poet, 1794-1878

O freedom! thou art not, as poets dream,
A fair young girl, with light and delicate limbs,
And wavy tresses gushing from the cap
With which the Roman master crowned his slave
When he took off the gyves. A bearded man,
Armed to the teeth, art thou; one mailed hand
Grasps the broad shield, and one the sword; thy brow,
Glorious in beauty though it be, is scarred
With tokens of old wars; thy massive limbs
Are strong with struggling. Power at thee has launched
His bolts, and with his lightnings smitten thee;
They could not quench the life thou hast from heaven.
Merciless Power has dug thy dungeon deep,
And his swart armorers, by a thousand fires,
Have forged thy chain; yet, while he deems thee bound,
The links are shivered, and the prison walls
Fall outward; terribly thou springest forth,
As springs the flame above a burning pile,
And shoutest to the nations, who return
Thy shoutings, while the pale oppressor flies.

By LORD BYRON
English poet, died while participating in the Greek War of Liberation; 1788-1824

Hereditary bondsmen! know ye not
Who would be free themselves must strike the blow?
By their right arms the conquest must be wrought?

Concerning Moderation
by LAFCADIO HEARN
Essayist, most noted as commentator on Japanese culture, 1850-1904

Permit me to say something in opposition to a very famous and
very popular Latin proverb—In medio tutissimus ibis—"Thou wilt
go most safely by taking the middle course." In speaking of two
distinct tendencies in literature, you might expect me to say that
the aim of the student should be to avoid extremes, and to try

not to be either too conservative or too liberal. But I should certainly never give any such advice. On the contrary, I think that the proverb above quoted is one of the most mischievous, one of the most pernicious, one of the most foolish, that ever was invented in the world. I believe very strongly in extremes—in violent extremes; and I am quite sure that all progress in this world, whether literary, or scientific, or religious, or political, or social, has been obtained only with the assistance of extremes. But remember that I say, "With the assistance,"—I do not mean that extremes alone accomplish the aim: there must be antagonism, but there must also be conservatism. What I mean by finding fault with the proverb is simply this—that it is very bad advice for a young man. To give a young man such advice is very much like telling him not to do his best, but only to do half of his best —or, in other words, to be half-hearted in his undertaking. . . . It is not the old men who ever prove great reformers: they are too cautious, too wise. Reforms are made by the vigor and courage and the self-sacrifice and the emotional conviction of young men, who did not know enough to be afraid, and who feel much more deeply than they think. Indeed great reforms are not accomplished by reasoning, but by feeling.

Battle Hymn of the Chinese Revolution

Freedom, one of the greatest blessings of Heaven,
United to Peace, thou wilt work on this earth ten thousand
    wonderful new things.

Grave as a spirit, great as a giant rising to the very skies,
With the clouds for a chariot and the wind for a steed,
Come, come to reign over the earth!

For the sake of the black hell of our slavery,
Come, enlighten us with a ray of thy sun! . . .

In this century we are working to open a new age.
In this century, with one voice, all virile men
Are calling for a new making of heaven and earth.

Hin-Yun, our ancestor, guide us!
Spirit of Freedom, come and protect us!

Working and Taking

(From the Lincoln-Douglas debates, 1858)

by ABRAHAM LINCOLN
Civil War President of the United States; 1809-1865

That is the real issue that will continue in this country when these poor tongues of Judge Douglas and myself shall be silent. It is the eternal struggle between these two principles, right and wrong, throughout the world. They are the two principles that have stood face to face from the beginning of time. The one is the common right of humanity, the other the divine right of kings. It is the same principle in whatever shape it develops itself. It is the same spirit that says "you toil and work and earn bread and I'll eat it."

Address to President Lincoln

by the INTERNATIONAL WORKINGMEN'S ASSOCIATION
(Drafted by Karl Marx)

When an oligarchy of three hundred thousand slaveholders, for the first time in the annals of the world, dared to inscribe "Slavery" on the banner of armed revolt; when on the very spot where hardly a century ago the idea of one great democratic republic had first sprung up, whence the first declaration of the Rights of Man was issued, and the first impulse given to the European revolution of the eighteenth century, when on that very spot the counter-revolution cynically proclaimed property in man to be "the corner-stone of the new edifice"—then the working classes of Europe understood at once that the slaveholders' rebellion was to sound the tocsin for a general holy war of property against labor; and that for the men of labor, with their hopes for the future, even their past conquests were at stake in that tremendous conflict on the other side of the Atlantic.

"New" Women

by OLIVE SCHREINER
South African writer, 1859-1922

We are not new! If you would understand us, go back two thousand years, and study our descent; our breed is our explanation. We are the daughters of our fathers as well as our mothers.

In our dreams we still hear the clash of the shields of our forebears, as they struck them together before battle and raised the shout of "Freedom!" In our dreams it is with us still, and when we wake it breaks from our own lips. We are the daughters of these men. . . .

Thrown into strict logical form, our demand is this: We do not ask that the wheels of time should reverse themselves, or the stream of life flow backward. We do not ask that our ancient spinning-wheels be again resuscitated and placed in our hands; we do not demand that our old grindstones and hoes be returned to us, or that man should again betake himself entirely to his ancient province of war and the chase, leaving to us all domestic and civil labor. We do not even demand that society shall immediately so reconstruct itself that every woman may be again a childbearer (deep and overmastering as lies the hunger for motherhood in every virile woman's heart!); neither do we demand that the children we bear shall again be put exclusively into our hands to train. This, we know, cannot be. The past material conditions of life have gone for ever; no will of man can recall them. But *this* is our demand: We demand that, in that strange new world that is arising alike upon the man and the woman, where nothing is as it was, and all things are assuming new shapes and relations, that in this new world we also shall have our share of honored and socially useful human toil, our full half of the labor of the Children of Woman. We demand nothing more than this, and will take nothing less. *This is our* "WOMAN'S RIGHT!"

Boston Hymn
by RALPH WALDO EMERSON
American essayist, philosopher and poet, 1803-1882

Today unbind the captive,
　　So only are ye unbound;
Lift up a people from the dust,
　　Trump of their rescue, sound!

Pay ransom to the owner
　　And fill the bag to the brim.
Who is the owner? The slave is owner,
　　And ever was. Pay him.

The Revolution

by RICHARD WAGNER

German operatic composer, political activist in German Revolution of 1848;
1813-1883

I am the secret of perpetual youth, the everlasting creator of
life; where I am not, death rages. I am the comfort, the hope, the
dream of the oppressed. I destroy what exists; but from the rock
whereon I light new life begins to flow. I come to you to break all
chains which bear you down; to free you from the embrace of
death, and instill a new life into your veins. All that exists must
perish; that is the eternal condition of life, and I the all-destroying
fulfill that law to create a fresh, new existence. I will renovate to
the very foundations the order of things in which you live, for it
is the offspring of sin, whose blossom is misery and whose fruit
is crime. The grain is ripe, and I am the reaper. I will dissipate
every delusion which has mastery over the human race. I will destroy the authority of the one over the many; of the lifeless over the
living; of the material over the spiritual. I will break into pieces
the authority of the great; of the law of property. Let the will of
each be master of mankind, one's own strength be one's one
property, for the freeman is the sacred man, and there is nothing
sublimer than he....

I will destroy the existing order of things which divides one
humanity into hostile peoples, into strong and weak, into privileged and outlawed, into rich and poor; for that makes unfortunate creatures of one and all. I will destroy the order of things
which makes millions the slaves of the few, and those few the
slaves of their own power, of their own wealth. I will destroy the
order of things which severs enjoyment from labor, which turns
labor into a burden and enjoyment into a vice, which makes one
man miserable through want and another miserable through
superabundance. I will destroy the order of things which consumes the vigor of manhood in the service of the dead, of inert
matter, which sustains one part of mankind in idleness or useless
activity, which forces thousands to devote their sturdy youth to
the indolent pursuits of soldiery, officialism, speculation and
usury, and the maintenance of such like despicable conditions,
while the other half, by excessive exertion and sacrifice of all the
enjoyment of life, bears the burden of the whole infamous structure. I will destroy even the very memory and trace of this de-
lirious order of things which, pieced together out of force, false-

hood, trouble, tears, sorrow, suffering, need, deceit, hypocrisy and crime is shut up in its own reeking atmosphere, and never receives a breath of pure air, to which no ray of pure joy ever penetrates. . . .

Arise, then, ye people of the earth, arise, ye sorrow-stricken and oppressed. Ye, also, who vainly struggle to clothe the inner desolation of your hearts, with the transient glory of riches, arise! Come and follow in my track with the joyful crowd, for I know not how to make distinction between those who follow me. There are but two peoples from henceforth on earth—the one which follows me, and the one which resists me. The one I will lead to happiness, but the other I will crush in my progress. For I am the Revolution, I am the new creating force. I am the divinity which discerns all life, which embraces, revives, and rewards.

Ladies in Rebellion
by ABIGAIL ADAMS
The wife of one President of the United States and mother of another, 1744-1818. From a letter to her husband written in 1774, during the first Continental Congress.

I long to hear that you have declared an independency. And in the new code of laws which I suppose it will be necessary for you to make, I desire you would remember the ladies, and be more generous and favorable to them than your ancestors. . . . If particular care and attention is not paid to the ladies, we are determined to foment a rebellion, and will not hold ourselves bound by any laws in which we have no voice or representation.

A Doll's House
by HENRIK IBSEN
Norwegian dramatist, 1828-1906. A play which may be called the literary source of the modern feminist movement. In this scene a young wife announces her revolt.

NORA: While I was at home with father, he used to tell me his opinions, and I held the same opinions. If I had others, I concealed them, because he wouldn't have liked it. He used to call me his doll-child, and played with me as I played with my dolls. Then I came to live in your house—

HELMER: What an expression to use about our marriage!

NORA (*undisturbed*): I mean I passed from father's hands into yours. You settled everything according to your taste; and I got the same tastes as you; or I pretended to—I don't know which—both ways, perhaps. When I look back on it now, I seem to have been living here like a beggar, from hand to mouth. I lived by performing tricks for you, Torvald. But you would have it so. You and father have done me a great wrong. It is your fault that my life has been wasted.

HELMER: Why, Nora, how unreasonable and ungrateful you are. Haven't you been happy here?

NORA: No, only merry. And you have always been so kind to me. But your house has been nothing but a play-room. Here I have been your doll-wife, just as at home I used to be papa's doll-child. And the children, in their turn, have been my dolls. I thought it fun when you played with me, just as the children did when I played with them. That has been our marriage, Torvald. . . . And that is why I am now leaving you!

HELMER (*jumping up*): What—do you mean to say—

NORA: I must stand quite alone, to know myself and my surroundings; so I can't stay with you.

HELMER: Nora! Nora!

NORA: I am going at once. Christina will take me for tonight.

HELMER: You are mad! I shall not allow it. I forbid it.

NORA: It is no use your forbidding me anything now. I shall take with me what belongs to me. From you I will accept nothing, either now or afterwards. . . .

HELMER: To forsake your home, your husband, and your children! You don't consider what the world will say.

NORA: I can pay no heed to that. I only know what I must do.

HELMER: It is exasperating! Can you forsake your holiest duties in this world?

NORA: What do you call my holiest duties?

HELMER: Do you ask me that? Your duties to your husband and your children.

NORA: I have other duties equally sacred.

HELMER: Impossible! What duties do you mean?

NORA: My duties towards myself.

HELMER: Before all else you are a wife and a mother.

NORA: That I no longer believe. I think that before all else I am a human being, just as much as you are—or at least I will try to become one.

The Great Strike

by FREDERIK VAN EEDEN
Dutch physician and novelist, 1860-1932

About forty of us were sent as delegates to different towns to lead and encourage the strikers there. The password was given and a date and hour secretly appointed. On Monday morning, the sixth of April, 1903, no train was to run on any railway in the Netherlands.

Sunday evening I set out, as one of the forty delegates, on the warpath. I took leave of my family, filled a suitcase with pamphlets and fly-leaves, and arrived in the middle of the night at the little town of Amersfoort, an important railway junction, to bring my message from headquarters that a strike would be declared that night in the whole country. Expecting the Government to be very active and energetic and not unlikely to arrest me, I took an assumed name, and was dressed like a laborer. . . .

I stayed a week in that little town, living in the houses of the strikers, sharing their meals and their hours of suspense and anxiety. There was a dark, dingy meeting-room where they all preferred to gather, rather than stay at home. The women also regularly attended these meetings, sometimes bringing their children, and they all sought the comfort of being in company, talking of hopes and fears, cheering each other up by songs, and trying to raise each other's spirits during the long days of inaction. I addressed them, three or four times a day, trying to give them sound notions on social conditions and preparing them for the defeat which I soon knew to be inevitable. I may say, however, that, though I was of all the forty delegates the least hopeful of ultimate success, my little party was the last to surrender and showed the smallest percentage of fugitives.

I saw in those days of strife that of the two contending parties, the stronger, the victorious one, was by far the least sympathetic in its moral attitude and methods. The strikers were pathetically stupid and ignorant about the strength of their opponents and their own weakness. If they had unexpectedly gained a complete victory they would have been utterly unable to use it. If the political power had shifted from the hands of the Government to those of the leading staff of that general strike, the result would have been a terrible confusion. There was no mind strong enough, no hand firm enough among them to rule and reorganize that mass of workers, unaccustomed to freedom, untrained to self-control, unable to work without severe authority and discipline. Yet the feelings and motives of that multitude were fair and just —they showed a chivalry, a generosity, an idealism and an enthusiasm with which the low methods of their powerful opponents contrasted painfully.

Every striker had to fight his own fight at home. Every evening he had to face the worn and anxious face of his wife, the sight of his children in danger of starvation and misery. He had to notice the hidden tears of the woman, or to answer her doubts and reproaches, with a mind itself far from confident. He had to fight in his own heart the egotistical inclination to save himself and give up what he felt to be his best sentiment, solidarity, the faith towards his comrades.

I believe no feeling man of the leisure class could have gone through a week in those surroundings and taken part in a struggle like this without acquiring a different conception of the ethics of socialism and class war.

For on the other side there were the Government, the companies, the defendants of existing order, powerful by their wealth, by their routine, by their experience, and supported by the servility of the great public and the army. They had not to face any real danger (the strikers showed no inclination to deeds of violence), and the arms they used were intimidation and bribery. The only thing for them to do was to demoralize the striker, to make him an egoist, a coward, a traitor to his comrades. And this was done quietly and successfully.

Demoralizing the enemy may be the lawful object of every war —the unavoidable evil to prevent a greater wrong; yet in this case, where the method of corruption could be used only on one side, it showed the ugly character of the conflict. This was no fair battle with common moral rules of chivalry and generosity; it was a pitiful and hopeless struggle between a weak slave and a strong usurper, between an ill-treated, revolting child and a brutal oppressor, who cared only for the restoration of his authority, not for the morals of the child.

FROM ECCLESIASTES
Surely oppression maketh a wise man mad.

The Uprising, *Honoré Daumier*

What Meaneth a Tyrant
by ALFONSO THE WISE
A Spanish king of great learning, 1226-1284

A tyrant doth signify a cruel lord, who, by force or by craft, or by treachery, hath obtained power over any realm or country; and such men be of such nature, that when once they have grown strong in the land, they love rather to work their own profit, though it be to the harm of the land, than the common profit of all, for they always live in an ill fear of losing it. And that they may be able to fulfill this their purpose unencumbered, the wise of old have said that they use their power against the people in three manners. The first is, that they strive that those under their mastery be ever ignorant and timorous, because, when they be such, they may not be bold to rise against them, nor to resist their wills; and the second is, that their victims be not kindly and united among themselves, in such wise that they trust not one another, for while they live in disagreement, they shall not dare to make any discourse against their lord, for fear faith and secrecy should not be kept among themselves; and the third way is, that they strive to make them poor, and to put them upon great undertakings, which they can never finish, whereby they may have so much harm that it may never come into their hearts to devise anything against their ruler. And above all this, have tyrants ever striven to make spoil of the strong and to destroy the wise; and have forbidden fellowship and assemblies of men in their land, and striven always to know what men said or did; and do trust their counsel and the guard of their person rather to foreigners, who will serve at their will, than to them of the land, who serve from oppression.

An Open Letter to the Employers
by GEORGE W. RUSSELL ("A.E.")
Irish poet, 1867-1935; published in the Dublin *Times* at the time of the great strike of 1913

Sirs: I address this warning to you, the aristocracy of industry in this city, because, like all aristocracies, you tend to grow blind in long authority, and to be unaware that you and your class and its every action are being considered and judged day by day by those who have power to shake or overturn the whole social order,

and whose restlessness in poverty today is making our industrial
civilization stir like a quaking bog. You do not seem to realize
that your assumption that you are answerable to yourselves alone
for your actions in the industries you control is one that becomes
less and less tolerable in a world so crowded with necessitous life.
Some of you have helped Irish farmers to upset a landed aristocracy in the island, an aristocracy richer and more powerful in
its sphere than you are in yours, with its roots deep in history.
They, too, as a class, though not all of them, were scornful or
neglectful of the workers in the industry by which they profited;
and to many who knew them in their pride of place and thought
them all-powerful they are already becoming a memory, the good
disappearing with the bad. If they had done their duty by those
from whose labor came their wealth, they might have continued
unquestioned in power and prestige for centuries to come. The
relation of landlord and tenant is not an ideal one, but any relations in a social order will endure if there is infused into them
some of that spirit of human sympathy which qualifies life for
immortality. Despotisms endure while they are benevolent, and
aristocracies while *"noblesse oblige"* is not a phrase to be referred
to with a cynical smile. Even an oligarchy might be permanent if
the spirit of human kindness, which harmonizes all things otherwise incompatible, were present. . . .

Those who have economic power have civic power also, yet you
have not used the power that was yours to right what was wrong in
the evil administration of this city. You have allowed the poor to
be herded together so that one thinks of certain places in Dublin
as of a pestilence. There are twenty thousand rooms, in each of
which live entire families, and sometimes more, where no functions of the body can be concealed, and delicacy and modesty are
creatures that are stifled ere they are born. The obvious duty of
you in regard to these things you might have left undone, and
it be imputed to ignorance or forgetfulness; but your collective
and conscious action as a class in the present labor dispute has
revealed you to the world in so malign an aspect that the mirror
must be held up to you, so that you may see yourself as every
humane person sees you.

The conception of yourselves as altogether virtuous and
wronged is, I assure you, not at all the one which onlookers hold
of you. . . . The representatives of labor unions in Great Britain
met you, and you made of them a preposterous, an impossible

demand, and because they would not accede to it you closed the Conference; you refused to meet them further; you assumed that no other guarantees than those you asked were possible, and you determined deliberately, in cold anger, to starve out one-third of the population of this city, to break the manhood of the men by the sight of the suffering of their wives and the hunger of their children. We read in the Dark Ages of the rack and thumb-screw. But these iniquities were hidden and concealed from the knowledge of men in dungeons and torture-chambers. Even in the Dark Ages humanity could not endure the sight of such suffering, and it learnt of such misuse of power by slow degrees, through rumor, and when it was certain it razed its Bastilles to their foundations. It remained for the twentieth century and the capital city of Ireland to see an oligarchy of four hundred masters deciding openly upon starving one hundred thousand people, and refusing to consider any solution except that fixed by their pride. You, masters, asked men to do that which masters of labor in any other city in these islands had not dared to do. You insolently demanded of these men who were members of a trade union that they should resign from that union; and from those who were not members you insisted on a vow that they would never join it.

Your insolence and ignorance of the rights conceded to workers universally in the modern world were incredible, and as great as your inhumanity. If you had between you collectively a portion of human soul as large as a three-penny bit, you would have sat night and day with the representatives of labor, trying this or that solution of the trouble, mindful of the women and children, who at least were innocent of wrong against you. But no! You reminded labor you could always have your three square meals a day while it went hungry. You went into conference again with representatives of the State, because, dull as you are, you knew public opinion would not stand your holding out. You chose as your spokesman the bitterest tongue that ever wagged in this island, and then, when an award was made by men who have an experience in industrial matters a thousand times transcending yours, who have settled disputes in industries so great that the sum of your petty enterprises would not equal them, you withdraw again, and will not agree to accept their solution, and fall back again on your devilish policy of starvation. Cry aloud to Heaven for new souls! The souls you have got cast upon the screen of pub-

licity appear like the horrid and writhing creatures enlarged from
the insect world, and revealed to us by the cinematograph.

You may succeed in your policy and ensure your own damnation by your victory. The men whose manhood you have broken
will loathe you, and will always be brooding and scheming to
strike a fresh blow. The children will be taught to curse you.
The infant being molded in the womb will have breathed into
its starved body the vitality of hate. It is not they—it is you who
are blind Samsons pulling down the pillars of the social order.
You are sounding the death-knell of autocracy in industry. There
was autocracy in political life, and it was superseded by democracy. So surely will democratic power wrest from you the
control of industry. The fate of you, the aristocracy of industry,
will be as the fate of the aristocracy of land if you do not show
that you have some humanity still among you. Humanity abhors,
above all things, a vacuum in itself, and your class will be cut
off from humanity as the surgeon cuts the cancer and alien growth
from the body. Be warned ere it is too late.

The Two "Reigns of Terror"
(From "A Connecticut Yankee in King Arthur's Court")
by MARK TWAIN

America's greatest humorist, 1835-1910, creator of "Tom Sawyer" and "Huckleberry
Finn." The pseudonym Mark Twain was adopted by Samuel L. Clemens from his
early days as a river pilot.

There were two "Reigns of Terror," if we would but remember
it and consider it; the one wrought murder in hot passion, the
other in heartless cold blood; the one lasted mere months, the
other had lasted a thousand years; the one inflicted death upon
ten thousand persons, the other upon a hundred millions; but
our shudders are all for the "horrors" of the minor Terror, the
momentary Terror, so to speak; whereas, what is the horror of
swift death by the axe, compared with lifelong death from hunger,
cold, insult, cruelty and heartbreak? What is swift death by lightning compared with death by slow fire at the stake? A city cemetery could contain the coffins filled by that brief Terror which
we have all been so diligently taught to shiver at and mourn
over; but all France could hardly contain the coffins filled by that
older and real Terror—that unspeakably bitter and awful Terror
which none of us has been taught to see in its vastness or pity as it
deserves.

Europe: The 72nd and 73rd Years of These States
by WALT WHITMAN

Suddenly out of its stale and drowsy lair, the lair of slaves,
Like lightning it le'pt forth half startled at itself,
Its feet upon the ashes and the rags, its hands tight to the throats
    of kings.

O hope and faith!
O aching close of exiled patriots' lives!
O many a sicken'd heart!
Turn back unto this day, and make yourselves afresh.

And you, paid to defile the People! you liars, mark!
Not for numberless agonies, murders, lusts,
For court thieving in its manifold mean forms, worming from his
    simplicity the poor man's wages,
For many a promise sworn by royal lips, and broken, and laugh'd
    at in the breaking,
Then in their power, not for all these, did the blows strike revenge,
    or the heads of the nobles fall;
The People scorn'd the ferocity of kings.

But the sweetness of mercy brew'd bitter destruction, and the
    frighten'd monarchs come back;
Each comes in state, with his train—hangman, priest, taxgatherer,
Soldier, lawyer, lord, jailer, and sycophant.

Yet behind all, lowering, stealing—lo, a Shape,
Vague as the night, draped interminable, head, front, and form,
    in scarlet folds,
Whose face and eyes none may see,
Out of its robes only this—the red robes, lifted by the arm,
One finger, crook'd, pointed high over the top, like the head of a
    snake appears.

Meanwhile, corpses lie in new-made graves—bloody corpses of
    young men;
The rope of the gibbet hangs heavily, the bullets of princes are
    flying, the creatures of power laugh aloud,
And all these things bear fruits—and they are good.

Those corpses of young men,
Those martyrs that hang from the gibbets—those hearts pierc'd by
the gray lead,
Cold and motionless as they seem, live elsewhere with
unslaughter'd vitality.

They live in other young men, O kings!
They live in brothers again ready to defy you!
They were purified by death—they were taught and exalted.

Not a grave of the murder'd for freedom, but grows seed for
freedom, in its turn to bear seed,
Which the winds carry afar and re-sow, and the rains and the
snows nourish.
Not a disembodied spirit can the weapons of tyrants let loose,
But it stalks invisibly over the earth, whispering, counseling,
cautioning.

Liberty! let others despair of you! I never despair of you.

Is the house shut? Is the master away?
Nevertheless, be ready—be not weary of watching;
He will return soon—his messengers come anon.

Free Speech
by Sir Leslie Stephen
English essayist and critic, 1832-1904

I, for one, am fully prepared to listen to any arguments for the
propriety of theft or murder, or if it be possible, of immorality in
the abstract. No doctrine, however well established, should be
protected from discussion. If, as a matter of fact, any appreciable
number of persons are so inclined to advocate murder on principle, I should wish them to state their opinions openly and fearlessly, because I should think that the shortest way of exploding
the principle and of ascertaining the true causes of such a perversion of moral sentiment. Such a state of things implies the
existence of evils which cannot be really cured till their cause
is known, and the shortest way to discover the cause is to give a
hearing to the alleged reasons.

The Mask of Anarchy
by PERCY BYSSHE SHELLEY
English poet, 1792-1822

Men of England, Heirs of Glory,
Heroes of unwritten story,
Nurslings of one mighty mother,
Hopes of her, and one another!

Rise, like lions after slumber,
In unvanquishable number,
Shake your chains to earth like dew,
Which in sleep had fall'n on you.
Ye are many, they are few.

What is Freedom! Ye can tell
That which Slavery is too well,
For its very name has grown
To an echo of your own.

'Tis to work, and have such pay
As just keeps life from day to day
In your limbs as in a cell
For the tyrants' use to dwell:

So that ye for them are made,
Loom, and plough, and sword, and spade;
With or without your own will, bent
To their defence and nourishment.

'Tis to see your children weak
With their mothers pine and peak,
When the winter winds are bleak:—
They are dying whilst I speak.

'Tis to hunger for such diet
As the rich man in his riot
Casts to the fat dogs that lie
Surfeiting beneath his eye.

'Tis to be a slave in soul,
And to hold no strong control
Over your own wills, but be
All that others make of ye.

Real Liberty
by HENRIK IBSEN

Away with the State! I will take part in that revolution. Undermine the whole conception of a state, declare free choice and
spiritual kinship to be the only all-important conditions of any
union, and you will have the commencement of a liberty that is
worth something.

Christmas in Prison
(From "The Jungle")
by UPTON SINCLAIR

In the distance there was a church-tower bell that tolled the
hours one by one. When it came to midnight Jurgis was lying
upon the floor with his head in his arms, listening. Instead of
falling silent at the end, the bell broke out into a sudden clangor.
Jurgis raised his head; what could that mean—a fire? God! suppose
there were to be a fire in this jail! But then he made out a melody
in the ringing; there were chimes. And they seemed to waken the
city—all around, far and near, there were bells, ringing wild
music; for fully a minute Jurgis lay lost in wonder, before, all at
once, the meaning of it broke over him—that this was Christmas
Eve!

Christmas Eve—he had forgotten it entirely! There was a breaking of flood-gates, a whirl of new memories and new griefs rushing
into his mind. In far Lithuania they had celebrated Christmas;
and it came to him as if it had been yesterday—himself a little
child, with his lost brother and his dead father in the cabin in
the deep black forest, where the snow fell all day and all night
and buried them from the world. It was too far off for Santa Claus
in Lithuania, but it was not too far for peace and good-will to
men, for the wonder-bearing vision of the Christ-child.

But no, their bells were not ringing for him—their Christmas
was not meant for him, they were simply not counting him at all.
He was of no consequence, like a bit of trash, the carcass of some
animal. It was horrible, horrible! His wife might be dying, his
baby might be starving, his whole family might be perishing in

the cold—and all the while they were ringing their Christmas chimes! And the bitter mockery of it—all this was punishment for him! They put him in a place where the snow could not beat in, where the cold could not eat through his bones; they brought him food and drink—why, in the name of heaven, if they must punish him, did they not put his family in jail and leave him outside—why could they find no better way to punish him than to leave three weak women and six helpless children to starve and freeze?

That was their law, that was their justice! Jurgis stood upright, trembling with passion, his hands clenched and his arms upraised, his whole soul ablaze with hatred and defiance. Ten thousand curses upon them and their law! Their justice—it was a lie, a sham and a loathsome mockery. There was no justice, there was no right, anywhere in it—it was only force, it was tyranny, the will and the power, reckless and unrestrained!

These midnight hours were fateful ones to Jurgis; in them was the beginning of his rebellion, of his outlawry and his unbelief. He had no wit to trace back the social crime to its far sources— he could not say it was the thing men have called "the system" that was crushing him to the earth; that it was the packers, his masters, who had bought up the law of the land, and had dealt out their brutal will to him from the seat of justice. He only knew that he was wronged, and that the world had wronged him; that the law, that society, with all its powers, had declared itself his foe. And every hour his soul grew blacker, every hour he dreamed new dreams of vengeance, of defiance, of raging, frenzied hate.

Robbers and Governments
by Leo Tolstoy

The robber generally plundered the rich, the governments generally plunder the poor and protect those rich who assist in their crimes. The robber doing his work risked his life, while the governments risk nothing, but base their whole activity on lies and deception. The robber did not compel anyone to join his band, the governments generally enroll their soldiers by force. ... The robber did not intentionally vitiate people, but the governments, to accomplish their ends, vitiate whole generations from childhood to manhood with false religions and patriotic instruction.

"Gunmen" in Israel
by Louis Wallis
American writer, born 1876

We saw that the great revolt under David was put down by the assistance of mercenary troops, or hired "strong men," and that by their aid Solomon was elevated to the throne against the wishes of the peasantry. In the Hebrew text, these men of power are called *gibborim*. They were among the principal tools used by the kings in maintaining the government. It was the *gibborim* who garrisoned the royal strongholds that held the country in awe. In cases where the peasants refused to submit, bands of *gibborim* were sent out by the kings and the great nobles. Through them the peasantry were "civilized"; and through them, apparently, the Amorite law was enforced in opposition to the old justice.

Hence the prophets were very bitter against these tools of the ruling class. Hosea writes: "Thou didst trust in thy way, in the multitude of thy *gibborim;* therefore shall a tumult arise against thy people; and all thy fortresses shall be destroyed." Amos, the shepherd, says that when Jehovah shall punish the land, the *gibborim* shall fall: "Flight shall perish from the swift . . . neither shall he stand that handeth the bow; and he that is swift of foot shall not deliver himself; . . . and he that is courageous among the *gibborim* shall flee away naked in that day, saith Jehovah."

"Gunmen" in West Virginia
(*Written during the terrible strike of 1911-1912*)
by a Paint Creek Miner

The hills are very bare and cold and lonely;
  I wonder what the future months will bring.
The strike is on—our strength would win, if only—
  O, Buddy, how I'm longing for the spring!

They've got us down—their martial lines enfold us;
  They've thrown us out to feel the winter's sting,
And yet, by God, those curs can never hold us,
  Nor could the dogs of hell do such a thing!

It isn't just to see the hills beside me
    Grow fresh and green with every growing thing;
I only want the leaves to come and hide me,
    To cover up my vengeful wandering.

I will not watch the floating clouds that hover
    Above the birds that warble on the wing;
I want to use this GUN from under cover—
    O, Buddy, how I'm longing for the spring!

You see them there, below, the damned scab-herders!
    Those puppets on the greedy Owners' String;
We'll make them pay for all their dirty murders—
    We'll show them how a starveling's hate can sting!

They riddled us with volley after volley;
    We heard their speeding bullets zip and ring,
But soon we'll make them suffer for their folly—
    O, Buddy, how I'm longing for the spring!

Political Violence

(From an anarchist pamphlet published in London; author unknown)

Under miserable conditions of life, any vision of the possibility of better things makes the present misery more intolerable, and spurs those who suffer to the most energetic struggles to improve their lot; and if these struggles only result in sharper misery, the outcome is sheer desperation. In our present society, for instance, an exploited wage worker, who catches a glimpse of what life and work ought to be, finds the toilsome routine and the squalor of his existence almost intolerable; and even when he has the resolution and courage to continue steadily working his best, and waiting until new ideas have so permeated society as to pave the way for better times, the mere fact that he has such ideas and tries to spread them, brings him into difficulties with his employers. How many thousands of Socialists, and above all Anarchists, have lost work and even the chance of work, solely on the ground of their opinions. It is only the specially gifted craftsman who, if he be a zealous propagandist, can hope to retain permanent employment.

And what happens to a man with his brain working actively with a ferment of new ideas, with a vision before his eyes of a new hope dawning for toiling and agonizing men, with the knowledge that his suffering and that of his fellows in misery is not caused by the cruelty of fate, but by the injustice of other human beings, —what happens to such a man when he sees those dear to him starving, when he himself is starved? Some natures in such a plight, and those by no means the least social or the least sensitive, will become violent, and will even feel that their violence is social and not antisocial, that in striking when and how they can, they are striking, not for themselves, but for human nature, outraged and despoiled in their persons and in those of their fellow sufferers. And are we, who ourselves are not in this horrible predicament, to stand by and coldly condemn those piteous victims of the Furies and Fates? Are we to decry as miscreants these human beings who act with heroic self-devotion, sacrificing their lives in protest, where less social and less energetic natures would lie down and grovel in abject submission to injustice and wrong? Are we to join the ignorant and brutal outcry which stigmatizes such men as monsters of wickedness, gratuitously running amuck in a harmonious and innocently peaceful society? No! We hate murder with a hatred that may seem absurdly exaggerated to apologists for Matabele massacres, to callous acquiescers in hangings and bombardments; but we decline in such cases of homicide, or attempted homicide, as those of which we are treating, to be guilty of the cruel injustice of flinging the whole responsibility of the deed upon the immediate perpetrator. The guilt of these homicides lies upon every man and woman who, intentionally or by cold indifference, helps to keep up social conditions that drive human beings to despair. The man who flings his whole life into the attempt, at the cost of his own life, to protest against the wrongs of his fellow men, is a saint compared to the active and passive upholders of cruelty and injustice, even if his protest destroys other lives besides his own. Let him who is without sin in society cast the first stone at such an one.

By ROBERT G. INGERSOLL
American lecturer and free-thought spokesman, 1833-1899

Whoever produces anything by weary labor, does not need a revelation from heaven to teach him that he has a right to the thing produced.

The Orator on the Barricade
(From "Les Miserables")
by Victor Hugo

Friends, the hour in which we live, and in which I speak to you, is a gloomy hour, but of such is the terrible price of the future. A revolution is a toll-gate. Oh! the human race shall be delivered, uplifted and consoled! We affirm it on this barricade. Whence shall arise the shout of love, if it be not from the summit of sacrifice? O my brothers, here is the place of junction between those who think and those who suffer; this barricade is made neither of paving-stones, nor of timbers, nor of iron; it is made of two mounds, a mound of ideas and a mound of sorrows. Misery here encounters the ideal. Here day embraces night, and says: I will die with thee and thou shalt be born again with me. From the pressure of all desolations faith gushes forth. Sufferings bring their agony here, and ideas their immortality. This agony and this immortality are to mingle and compose our death. Brothers, he who dies here dies in the radiance of the future, and we are entering a grave illumined by the dawn.

The Bomb
by Frank Harris
English author whose works were frequently banned, 1856-1931

A meeting was called on a waste space in Packingtown, and over a thousand workmen came together. I went there out of curiosity. Lingg, I may say here, always went alone to these strike meetings. Ida told me once that he suffered so much at them that he could not bear to be seen, and perhaps that was the explanation of his solitary ways. Fielden, the Englishman, spoke first, and was cheered to the echo; the workmen knew him as a working-man and liked him; besides, he talked in a homely way, and was easy to understand. Spies spoke in German and was cheered also. The meeting was perfectly orderly when three hundred police tried to disperse it. The action was ill-advised, to say the best of it, and tyrannical; the strikers were hurting no one and interfering with no one. Without warning or reason the police tried to push their way through the crowd to the speakers; finding a sort of passive resistance and not being able to overcome it, they used their clubs savagely. One or two of the strikers, hot-headed, bared their knives, and at once the police, led on by that madman,

Schaack, drew their revolvers and fired. It looked as if the police had been waiting for the opportunity. Three strikers were shot dead on the spot, and more than twenty were wounded, several of them dangerously, before the mob drew sullenly away from the horrible place. A leader, a word, and not one of the police would have escaped alive; but the leader was not there, and the word was not given, so the wrong was done, and went unpunished.

I do not know how I reached my room that afternoon. The sight of the dead men lying stark there in the snow had excited me to madness. The picture of one man followed me like an obsession; he was wounded to death, shot through the lungs; he lifted himself up on his left hand and shook the right at the police, crying in a sort of frenzy till the spouting blood choked him—

"Bestien! Bestien!" ("Beasts! Beasts!")

I can still see him wiping the blood-stained froth from his lips; I went to help him; but all he could gasp was, "Weib! Kinder! (Wife, children!)" Never shall I forget the despair in his face. I supported him gently; again and again I wiped the blood from his lips; every breath brought up a flood; his poor eyes thanked me, though he could not speak, and soon his eyes closed; flickered out, as one might say, and he lay there still enough in his own blood; "murdered," as I said to myself when I laid the poor body back; "murdered!"

(As a result of this police action, the narrator goes to the next meeting of the strikers with a bomb in his pocket.)

The crowd began to drift away at the edges. I was alone and curiously watchful. I saw the mayor and the officials move off towards the business part of the town. It looked for a few minutes as if everything was going to pass over in peace; but I was not relieved. I could hear my own heart beating, and suddenly I felt something in the air; it was sentient with expectancy. I slowly turned my head. I was on the very outskirts of the crowd, and as I turned I saw that Bonfield had marched out his police, and was minded to take his own way with the meeting now that the mayor had left. I felt personal antagonism stiffen my muscles. . . . It grew darker and darker every moment. Suddenly there came a flash, and then a peal of thunder. At the end of the flash, as it seemed to me, I saw the white clubs falling, saw the police striking down the men running along the sidewalk. At once my mind was made up. I put my left hand on the outside of my trousers to hold the bomb tight, and my right hand into the pocket, and drew the tape. I heard a little rasp. I began to count slowly, "One, two, three, four, five, six, seven;" as I got to seven the police were quite close to me bludgeoning every one furiously. Two or three of the foremost had drawn their revolvers. The crowd were flying in all directions. Suddenly there was a shot, and then a dozen shots, all, it seemed to me, fired by the police. Rage blazed in me.

I took the bomb out of my pocket, careless whether I was seen or not, and looked for the right place to throw it; then I hurled it over my shoulder high in the air, towards the middle of the police, and at the same moment I stumbled forward, just as if I had fallen, throwing myself on my hands and face, for I had seen the spark. It seemed as if I had been on my hands for an eternity, when I was crushed to the ground, and my ears split with the roar. I scrambled to my feet again, gasping. Men were thrown down in front of me, and were getting up on their hands. I heard groans and cries, and shrieks behind me. I turned around; as I turned a strong arm was thrust through mine, and I heard Lingg say—

"Come, Rudolph, this way;" and he drew me to the sidewalk, and we walked past where the police had been.

"Don't look," he whispered suddenly; "don't look."

But before he spoke I had looked, and what I saw will be before my eyes till I die. The street was one shambles; in the very center of it a great pit yawned, and round it men lying, or pieces of men, in every direction, and close to me, near the side-walk as I passed, a leg and foot torn off, and near by two huge pieces of bleeding red meat, skewered together with a thigh-bone. My soul sickened; my senses left me; but Lingg held me up with superhuman strength, and drew me along.

"Hold yourself up, Rudolph," he whispered; "come on, man," and the next moment we had passed it all, and I clung to him, trembling like a leaf. When we got to the end of the block I realized that I was wet through from head to foot as if I had been plunged in cold water.

"I must stop," I gasped. "I cannot walk, Lingg."

"Nonsense," he said; "take a drink of this," and he thrust a flask of brandy into my hand. The brandy I poured down my throat set my heart beating again, allowed me to breathe, and I walked on with him.

"How you are shaking," he said. "Strange, you neurotic people; you do everything perfectly, splendidly, and then break down like women. Come, I am not going to leave you; but for God's sake throw off that shaken, white look. Drink some more."

I tried to; but the flask was empty. He put it back in his pocket.

"Here is the bottle," he said. "I have brought enough; but we must get to the depot."

We saw fire engines with police on them, galloping like madmen in the direction whence we had come. The streets were crowded with people, talking, gesticulating, like actors. Every one seemed to know of the bomb already, and to be talking about it. I noticed that even here, fully a block away, the pavement was covered with pieces of glass; all the windows had been broken by the explosion.

As we came in front of the depot, just before we passed into the full glare of the arc-lamps, Lingg said—

"Let me look at you," and as he let go my arm, I almost fell; my legs were like German sausages; they felt as if they had no bones in them, and would bend in any direction; in spite of every effort they would shake.

"Come, Rudolph," he said, "we'll stop and talk; but you must come to yourself. Take another drink, and think of nothing. I will save you; you are too good to lose. Come, dear friend, don't let them crow over us."

My heart seemed to be in my mouth, but I swallowed it down. I took another swig of brandy, and then a long drink of it. It might have been water for all I tasted; but it seemed to do me some little good. In a minute or so I had got hold of myself.

"I'm all right," I said; "what is there to do now?"

"Simply to go through the depot," he said, "as if there were nothing the matter, and take the train."

The Rising of the Peasants
by MAO TSE-TUNG
Chairman of Chinese Communist Politburo, 1893–1976

The revolt of the peasants in the countryside disturbed the sweet dreams of the gentry. When news about the countryside reached the cities, the gentry there immediately burst into an uproar. When I first arrived in Changsha, I met people from various circles and picked up a good deal of street gossip. From the middle strata upwards to the right-wingers of the Kuomintang, there was not a single person who did not summarise the whole thing in one phrase: "An awful mess!" Even quite revolutionary people, carried away by the opinion of the "awful mess" school which prevailed like a storm over the whole city, became downhearted at the very thought of the conditions in the countryside, and could not deny the word "mess." Even very progressive people could only remark, "Indeed a mess, but inevitable in the course of the revolution." In a word, nobody could categorically deny the word "mess."

But the fact is, as stated above, that the broad peasant masses have risen to fulfill their historic mission, that the democratic forces in the rural areas have risen to overthrow the rural feudal power. The patriarchal-feudal class of local bullies, bad gentry and lawless landlords has formed the basis of autocratic government for thousands of years, the cornerstone of imperialism, warlordism and corrupt officialdom. To overthrow this feudal power is the real objective of the national revolution. What Dr. Sun Yat-Sen wanted to do in the forty years he devoted to the national revolution but failed to accomplish, the peasants have accomplished in a few months. This is a marvellous feat which has never been achieved in the last forty or even thousands of years. It is very good indeed. It is not a "mess" at all. It is anything but an "awful mess."

The Unswerving Arrow
(From "The Rebel")
by ALBERT CAMUS

Absolute revolution, in fact, supposes the absolute malleability of human nature and its possible reduction to the condition of an historic force. But rebellion, in man, is the refusal to be treated as an object and to be reduced to simple historical terms. It is the affirmation of a nature common to all men, which eludes the world of power. History, undoubtedly, is one of the limits of man's experience; in this sense the revolutionaries are right. But man, by rebelling, imposes in his turn a limit to history and at this limit the promise of a value is born. It is the birth of this value which the Caesarian revolution implacably combats today because it presages its final defeat and the obligation to renounce its principles. The fate of the world is not being played out at present, as it seemed it would be, in the struggle between bour-

geois production and revolutionary production: their end-results
will be the same. It is being played out between the forces of
rebellion and those of the Caesarian revolution. The triumphant
revolution must prove by means of its police, its trials and its
excommunications, that there is no such thing as human nature.
Humiliated rebellion, by its contradictions, its sufferings, its
continuous defeats, and its inexhaustible pride, must give its
content of hope and suffering to this nature. . . .

Those who find no rest in God or in history are condemned
to live for those who, like themselves, cannot live: in fact, for the
humiliated. The most pure form of the movement of rebellion is
thus crowned with the heartrending cry of Karamazov: if all are
not saved, what good is the salvation of one only? Thus Catholic
prisoners, in the prison cells of Spain, refuse communion today
because the priests of the regime have made it obligatory in certain prisons. These lonely witnesses to the crucifixion of innocence refuse salvation, too, if it must be paid for by injustice and
oppression. This insane generosity is the generosity of rebellion,
which unhesitatingly gives the strength of its love and refuses
injustice without a moment's delay. Its merit lies in making no
calculations, distributing everything that it possesses to life and
to living men. It is thus that it is prodigal in its gifts to men to
come. Real generosity towards the future lies in giving all to the
present.

Rebellion proves, in this way, that it is the very movement of
life and that it cannot be denied without renouncing life. Its
purest outburst, on each occasion, gives birth to existence. Thus,
it is love and fecundity or it is nothing at all. Revolution without
honor, calculated revolution which, in preferring an abstract
concept of man to a man of flesh and blood, denies existence as
many times as is necessary, puts resentment in the place of love.
Immediately rebellion, forgetful of its generous origins, allows
itself to be contaminated by resentment, it denies life, dashes
toward destruction and raises up the grimacing cohorts of petty
rebels, slaves all of them, who end by offering themselves for sale,
in all the market-places of Europe, to no matter what form of
servitude. It is no longer either revolution or rebellion but rancour, malice and tyranny. Then, when revolution in the name
of power and of history becomes that immoderate and mechanical
murderer, a new rebellion is consecrated in the name of moderation and of life. We are at the extremity now. However, at the

end of this tunnel of darkness, there is inevitably a light, which we already divine and for which we only have to fight to ensure its coming. All of us, among the ruins, are preparing a renaissance beyond the limits of nihilism. But few of us know it. . . .

Our brothers are breathing under the same sky; justice is a living thing. Now is born that strange joy which helps one live and die, and which we shall never again renounce to a later time. On' the sorrowing earth it is the unresting thorn, the bitter food, the harsh wind off the sea, the ancient dawn forever renewed. With this joy, through long struggle, we shall remake the soul of our time, and a Europe which will exclude nothing. Not even that phantom Nietzsche who, for twelve years after his downfall, was continually invoked by the West as the ruined image of its loftiest knowledge and its nihilism; nor the prophet of justice without mercy who rests, by mistake, in the unbelievers' plot at Highgate Cemetery; nor the deified mummy of the man of action in his glass coffin; nor any part of what the intelligence and energy of Europe have ceaselessly furnished to the pride of a contemptible period. All may indeed live again, side by side with the martyrs of 1905, but on condition that they shall understand how they correct one another, and that a limit, under the sun, shall curb them all. Each tells the other that he is not God; this is the end of romanticism. At this moment, when each of us must fit an arrow to his bow and enter the lists anew, to reconquer, within history and in spite of it, that which he owns already, the thin yield of his fields, the brief love of this earth, at this moment when at last a man is born, it is time to forsake our age and its adolescent rages. The bow bends; the wood complains. At the moment of supreme tension there will leap into flight an unswerving arrow, a shaft that is inflexible and free.

Armed Crisis

(From "Minimanual of the Urban Guerilla")
BY CARLOS MARIGHELLA
Brazilian guerrilla fighter, died 1969

It is necessary to turn crisis into armed crisis by performing violent actions that will force those in power to transform the military situation into a political situation. That will alienate the masses, who,

from then on, will revolt against the army and the police and blame
them for this state of things.

A Call for Non-Collaboration

(From "The Struggle is My Life," a statement given in 1961)

BY NELSON MANDELA

South African apartheid foe sentenced to life imprisonment
in 1964 and not released until 1990. He won the Noble Peace Prize
in 1993 and was elected president of South Africa in 1994; born 1918

Those who are voteless cannot be expected to continue paying
taxes to a government which is not responsible to them. People who
live in poverty and starvation cannot be expected to pay exorbitant
house rents to the government and local authorities. We furnish the
sinews of agriculture and industry. We produce the work of the gold
mines, the diamonds and the coal, of the farms and industry, in
return for miserable wages. Why should we continue enriching those
who steal the products of our sweat and blood? Those who exploit us
and refuse us the right to organise trade unions? Those who side
with the government when we stage peaceful demonstrations to
assert our claims and aspirations? How can Africans serve on School
Boards and Committees which are part of Bantu Education, a sinister scheme of the Nationalist government to deprive the African people of real education in return for tribal education? Can Africans be
expected to be content with serving on Advisory Boards and Bantu
Authorities when the demand all over the continent of Africa is for
national independence and self-government? Is it not an affront to
the African people that the government should now seek to extend
Bantu Authorities to the cities, when people in the rural areas have
refused to accept the same system and fought against it tooth and
nail? Which African does not burn with indignation when thousands
of our people are sent to the gaol every month under the cruel pass
laws? Why should we continue carrying these badges of slavery? Non-
collaboration is a dynamic weapon. We must refuse. We must use it
to send this government to its grave. It must be used vigorously and
without delay. The entire resources of the Black people must be
mobilised to withdraw all co-operation with the Nationalist government. Various forms of industrial and economic action will be
employed to undermine the already tottering economy of the coun-

try. We will call upon international bodies to expel South Africa and upon nations of the world to sever economic and diplomatic relations with the country.

The Purpose of Revolution

(From "Prisoner of Love")
BY JEAN GENET
French playwright and novelist, 1910-1986

The main object of a revolution is the liberation of man...not the interpretation and application of some transcendental ideology.

The Oath

(An oath taken by thousands of Chinese students occupying Tiananmen Square in June 1989 shortly before the tanks rolled in.)

I swear, for the democratic movement and the prosperity of the country, for our motherland not to be overturned by a few conspirators, for our one billion people not to be killed in the white terror, that I am willing to defend Tiananmen, defend the republic, with my young life. Our heads can be broken, our blood can be shed, but we will not lose the People's square. We will fight to the end with the last person.

Moral Persuasion

BY STEVEN BIKO
Black South African political leader
who died while in police custody, 1946-1977

The power of the movement lies in the fact that it can indeed change the habits of people. This change is not the result of force but of dedication, of moral persuasion.

BOOK VI

Martyrdom

Messages and records of the heroes of past and present who have sacrificed themselves for the sake of the future.

Le Père Perdrix

by CHARLES-LOUIS PHILIPPE

French novelist, 1874-1909. The following scene is in the home of a workingman, who by heavy sacrifice has succeeded in educating his only son. One day the son unexpectedly returns home.

Pierre Bousset said, "How does it happen that you come today?"

Jean sat down with slowness enough, and one saw yet another thing sit down in the house. The mother said, "I guess you haven't eaten. I'll make a little chocolate before noon-time."

Jean's tongue was loosed. "Here it is. There is something new. It is necessary to tell you: I have left my place!"

"How! You have left your place!" They sat up all three—Pierre Bousset with his apron and his back of labor; and Jean saw that he had gray hair. The mother held a saucepan in her hand, careful like a kitchen-servant, but with feelings as if the saucepan were about to fall. Marguerite, the sister, was already weeping: "Ah, my God! I who was so proud!"

Pierre Bousset said, "And how did you manage that clever stroke?"

It was then that Jean felt his soul wither, and there rose up from the depths of his heart all the needs, all the mists of love. It was necessary that they should live side by side and understand one another, and it was necessary that someone should begin to weaken. He said, "Does one ever know what one does?"

"Ah, indeed!" said the father. "You don't know what you do?"

"There are moments," answered Jean, "when one loses his head, and afterwards I don't say one should not have regrets."

"For the matter of losing one's head, I know only one thing: It is that they pay you, and it is up to you always to obey whatever they command."

The mother watched the chocolate, from which the steam rose with a warmth of strong nutriment. They loved that in the family, like a Sunday morning indulgence, like a bourgeois chocolate for holiday folk. She said, "Anyhow, let it be as it will, he's got to eat."

Jean went on to speak. His blue eyes had undergone the first transformation which comes in a man's life, when he is no longer Jean, son of Pierre, pupil at the Central school, but Jean Bousset, engineer of applied chemistry. There remained in them, however, the shining of a young girl, that emotion which wakens two rays

201

of sunlight in a spring. And now they kept a sort of supplication, like the sweetness of a naked infant.

"Oh, I know everything that you are going to say. You cannot excuse me, because you are not in my place, and I cannot condemn a movement of my heart. You know—I wrote it to you—the workers were about to go on strike. At once I said to myself that these were matters which did not concern me; because, when you are taking care of yourself, it is not necessary to look any farther. But Cousin François explained it all to me."

"Ah, I told you so!" cried Pierre Bousset. "When you wanted to take Cousin François into your factory, I said to you: 'Relatives, it is necessary always to kep them at a distance. They push themselves forward, and sometimes, to excuse them one is led to commit whole heaps of lowness.' "

"In truth," said Jean, "I would never have had to complain of him. On the contrary, he wore his heart on his sleeve."

"Oh, all drunkards are like that. One says: 'They wear their hearts on their sleeve,' and one does not count all the times when they lead the others away."

"Ah, I have understood many things, father. How can I explain everything that I have understood! There are moments still when, to see and to realize—that makes in my head a noise as if the world would not stay in place. I tell you again it was François who made me understand. I saw, in the evenings. I would say to him: 'I am bored, I haven't even a comrade, and I eat at hotel-tables a dinner too well served.' He said: 'Come to my house. You don't know what it is to eat good things, because you don't work, and because hunger makes a part of work. You will have some soup with us, and we will tell you at least that you are happy to be where you are, and to look upon the workingman while playing the amateur.' I said to him: 'But I work, also. To see, to understand, to analyze, to be an engineer! You, it's your arms; me, it's my head and my heart that ache.' He laughed: 'Ha! ha! ha! ha! ha! When I come home in the evening with my throat dry and I eat my soup, I also have a headache, and I laugh at you with your heartache. I am as tired as a wolf. What's that you call your heart?' "

"Yes, he was right there," said Pierre Bousset. "For my part, I don't understand at all how you are going to pull through. You have understood a lot of things! As for me, I understand but one thing, which is you are unhappy over being too happy."

Jean went on speaking, with his blue eyes, like a madness,

like a ribbon, like a rosette without any reason which a young girl puts on her forehead. A sweetness came out of his heart to spread itself in the room, where the furniture gave off angular and waxy reflections. Marguerite listened, with restlessness, listened to her father, like a child whose habit it is to be guided by her parents. The mother saw to the chocolate, in a state of confusion, shaking her head.

"Yesterday I was in the office of the superintendent. It was then that the delegation arrived. It seems to me that I see them again. There were three workingmen. They had taken to white shirts, and they had just washed their hands. You know how the poor come into the homes of the rich. There was a great racket, and their steps were put down with so much embarrassment that one felt in the hearts of the three men the shame of crushed things. I had already thought about that poverty which, knowing that it soils, hides itself, and dares not even touch an object. They said: 'Well, Mr. Superintendent, we have been sent to talk to you. For more than ten years now we have worked in the factory. We get seventy cents a day. That's not much to tell about. We have wives and children, and our seventy cents hardly carries us farther than a glass of brandy and a little plate of soup. We understand that you also have expenses. But we should like to get eighty cents a day, and for us to explain everything to you, it is necessary that you should consent, because money gives courage to the workingman.' The other received them with that assurance of the rich, sitting straight up in his chair and holding his head as if it dominated your own. He would not have had much trouble, with his education, his habits of a master, his stability as a man of affairs, to put them all three ill at ease. 'Gentlemen, from the first word I say to you: No. The company cannot take account of your wishes. We pay you seventy cents a day, and we judge that it is up to you to lower your life to your wages. As for your insinuations, I shall employ such means as please me to fortify your courage. For the rest, our profits are not what you imagine, you who know neither our efforts nor our disappointments.' It was then, father, that I felt myself your son, and that I recalled your hands, your back which toils, and the carriage wheels that you make. The three workingmen seemed three children in their father's home, with hearts that swell and can feel no more. Ah, it was in vain I thought myself an engineer! On the benches of the school I imagined that my head was full of science, and that that sufficed. But all the blood of my father, the days that I passed in your shop, the storms which go to one's head and seem to come from far off, all that cried out like a grimace, like a lock, like a key. I took up the argument. 'Mr. Superintendent, I know these men. There is my cousin who works in the factory. Do you understand what it is, the life of acids, and that of charcoal?' If you could have seen him! He looked at me with eyes, as if their pupils had turned to ice. 'Mr. Engineer, I don't permit either you, who are a child, or these, who are workingmen, a single word to discuss my sayings and my actions! Gentlemen, you may retire.' I went straight off the handle. A door opened at a single burst. We have at least insolence, we poor, and blows of the mouth, since their weapons stop our blows of the teeth. I went away like them. They lowered their heads and thought. For my part I cried out, I turned about and cried, 'You be hanged!' "

"Ah, now, indeed! I didn't expect anything like that," said Pierre Bousset. "One raises children to make gentle-folk of them, so that they will work a little less than you. Now then, in God's name! go and demand a place of those for whom you have lost your own!"

By JOHANN WOLFGANG VON GOETHE
German poet and natural philosopher, 1749-1832

All those who oppose intellectual truths merely stir up the fire; the cinders fly about and set fire to that which else they had not touched.

The Subjection of Women
by JOHN STUART MILL
English philosopher and economist, 1806-1873

In struggles for political emancipation, everybody knows how often its champions are bought off by bribes, or daunted by terrors. In the case of women, each individual of the subject class is in a chronic state of bribery and intimidation combined. In setting up the standard of resistance, a large number of the leaders, and still more of the followers, must make an almost complete sacrifice of the pleasures or the alleviations of their own individual lot. If ever any system of privilege and enforced subjection had its yoke tightly riveted on the necks of those who are kept down by it, this has.

The Old Suffragist

by MARGARET WIDDEMER

American novelist and poet, 1884–1978

She could have loved—her woman-passions beat
  Deeper than theirs, or else she had not known
How to have dropped her heart beneath their feet
  A living stepping-stone:

The little hands—did they not clutch her heart?
  The guarding arms—was she not very tired?
Was it an easy thing to walk apart,
  Unresting, undesired?

She gave away her crown of woman-praise,
  Her gentleness and silent girlhood grace
To be a merriment for idle days,
  Scorn for the market-place:

She strove for an unvisioned, far-off good,
  For one far hope she knew she should not see:
These—not *her* daughters—crowned with motherhood
  And love and beauty—free.

On Liberty

by JOHN STUART MILL

Mankind can hardly be too often reminded, that there was once a man named Socrates, between whom and the legal authorities and public opinion of his time, there took place a memorable collision. Born in an age and country abounding in individual greatness, this man has been handed down to us by those who best knew both him and the age, as the most virtuous man in it; while *we* know him as the head and prototype of all subsequent teachers of virtue, the source equally of the lofty inspiration of Plato and the judicious utilitarianism of Aristotle, the two headsprings of ethical as of all other philosophy. This acknowledged master of all the eminent thinkers who have since lived—whose fame, still growing after more than two thousand years, all but outweighs the whole remainder of the names which make his native city illustrious—was put to death by his countrymen, after a judicial conviction, for impiety and immorality. Impiety, in denying the Gods recognized by the State; indeed his accusers asserted (see the "Apologia") that he believed in no gods at all. Immorality, in being, by his doctrines and instructions, a "corrupter of youth." Of these charges the tribunal, there is every ground for believing, honestly found him guilty, and condemned the man who probably of all then born had deserved best of mankind, to be put to death as a criminal.

Forcible Feeding
by E. SYLVIA PANKHURST
Militant English suffragette, 1857-1928

She was then surrounded and held down, whilst the chair was tilted backwards. She clenched her teeth, but the doctor pulled her mouth away to form a pouch and the wardress poured in milk and brandy, some of which trickled in through the crevices. Later in the day the doctors and wardresses again appeared. They forced her down on to the bed and held her there. One of the doctors then produced a tube two yards in length with a glass junction in the center and a funnel at one end. He forced the other end of the tube up her nostril, hurting her so terribly that the matron and two of the wardresses burst into tears and the second doctor interfered. At last the tube was pushed down into the stomach. She felt the pain of it to the end of the breast bone. Then one of the doctors stood upon a chair holding the funnel end of the tube at arm's length, and poured food down whilst the wardress and the other doctor all gripped her tight. She felt as though she would suffocate. There was a rushing, burning sensation in her head, the drums of her ears seemed to be bursting. The agony of pain in the throat and breast bone continued. The thing seemed to go on for hours. When at last the tube was withdrawn, she felt as though all the back of her nose and throat were being torn out with it.

Then almost fainting she was carried back to the punishment cell and put to bed. For hours the pain in the chest, nose and ears continued and she felt terribly sick and faint. Day after day the struggle continued; she used no violence, but each time resisted and was overcome by force of numbers. Often she vomited during the operation. When the food did not go down quickly enough the doctor pinched her nose with the tube in it, causing her even greater pain.

Going to the People

(From "Memoirs of a Revolutionist")

by PETER KROPOTKIN

Russian prince turned revolutionary who suffered imprisonment and exile; 1842-1921

"It is bitter, the bread that has been made by slaves," our poet Nekrasoff wrote. The young generation actually refused to eat that bread, and to enjoy the riches that had been accumulated in their fathers' houses by means of servile labor, whether the laborers were actual serfs or slaves of the present industrial system.

All Russia read with astonishment, in the indictment which was produced at the court against Karakozoff and his friends, that these young men, owners of considerable fortunes, used to live three or four in the same room, never spending more than ten roubles (five dollars) apiece a month for all their needs, and giving at the same time their fortunes for co-operative associations, co-operative workshops (where they themselves worked), and the like. Five years later, thousands and thousands of the Russian youth—the best part of it—were doing the same. Their watch-word was, "V naród!" (To the people; be the people.) During the years 1860-65 in nearly every wealthy family a bitter struggle was going on between the fathers, who wanted to maintain the old traditions, and the sons and daughters, who defended their right to dispose of their life according to their own ideals. Young men left the military service, the counter and the shop, and flocked to the university towns. Girls, bred in the most aristocratic families, rushed penniless to St. Petersburg, Moscow, and Kieff, eager to learn a profession which would free them from the domestic yoke, and some day, perhaps, also from the possible yoke of a husband. After hard and bitter struggles, many of them won that personal freedom. Now they wanted to utilize it, not for their own personal enjoyment, but for carrying to the people the knowledge that had emancipated them.

In every town of Russia, in every quarter of St. Petersburg, small groups were formed for self-improvement and self-education; the works of the philosophers, the writings of the economists, the researches of the young Russian historical school, were carefully read in these circles, and the reading was followed by endless discussions. The aim of all that reading and discussion was to solve the great question which rose before them: In what way could they be useful to the masses? Gradually, they came to the idea that the only way was to settle among the people and to live

The Liberators, *Alfredo Zalce*

the people's life. Young men went into the villages as doctors, doctors' assistants, teachers, village scribes, even as agricultural laborers, blacksmiths, woodcutters and so on, and tried to live there in closest contact with the peasants. Girls passed teachers' examinations, learned midwifery or nursing, and went by the hundred into the villages, devoting themselves entirely to the poorest part of the population. . . .

Here and there small groups of propagandists had settled in towns and villages in various capacities. Blacksmiths' shops and small farms had been started, and young men of the wealthier classes worked in the shops or on the farms, to be in daily contact with the toiling masses. At Moscow, a number of young girls, of rich families, who had studied at the Zurich university and had started a separate organization, went even so far as to enter cotton factories, where they worked from fourteen to sixteen hours a day, and lived in the factory barracks the miserable life of the Russian factory girls. It was a grand movement, in which, at the lowest estimate, from two to three thousand persons took an active part while twice or thrice as many sympathizers and supporters helped the active vanguard in various ways. With a good half of that army our St. Petersburg circle was in regular correspondence—always, of course, in cipher.

The literature which could be published in Russia under a rigorous censorship—the faintest hint of Socialism being prohibited—was soon found insufficient, and we started a printing office of our own abroad. Pamphlets for the workers and the peasants had to be written, and our small "literary committee," of which I was a member, had its hands full of work. Serghei wrote a couple of such pamphlets—one in the Lammenais style, and another containing an exposition of Socialism in a fairy tale—and both had a wide circulation. The books and pamphlets which were printed abroad were smuggled into Russia by thousands, stored at certain spots, and sent out to the local circles, which distributed them amongst the peasants and the workers. All this required a vast organization as well as much traveling about, and a colossal correspondence, particularly for protecting our helpers and our bookstores from the police. We had special ciphers for different provincial circles, and often, after six or seven hours had been passed in discussing all details, the women, who did not trust to our accuracy in the cipher correspondence, spent all the night in covering sheets of paper with cabalistic figures.

The Revolutionist

by IVAN TURGENEV

Russian novelist who was imprisoned and later exiled for his liberal views, 1818-
1883. In the original this extract is a prose poem; it was translated into English
poetry by Arthur Guiterman.

I saw a spacious house. O'erhung with pall,
A narrow doorway pierced the sombre wall.
Within was chill, impenetrable shade;
Without there stood a maid—a Russian maid,
To whom the icy dark sent forth a slow
And hollow-sounding Voice:

      "And dost thou know,
When thou hast entered, what awaits thee here?"
"I know," she said, "and knowing do not fear."
"Cold, hunger, hatred, Slander's blighting breath,"
The Voice still chanted, "suffering—and Death?"
"I know," she said.

    "Undaunted, wilt thou dare
The sneers of kindred? Art thou steeled to bear
From those whom most thou lovest, spite and scorn?"
"Though Love be paid with Hate, that shall be borne,"
She answered.

    "Think! Thy doom may be to die
By thine own hand, with none to fathom why,
Unthanked, unhonored, desolate, alone,
Thy grave unmarked, thy toil, thy love unknown,
And none in days to come shall speak thy name."
She said: "I ask no pity, thanks or fame."
"Art thou prepared for crime?"

      She bowed her head.
"Yes, crime, if that shall need," the maiden said.
Now paused the Voice before it asked anew:
"But knowest thou that all thou holdest true
Thy soul may yet deny in bitter pain,
So thou shalt deem thy sacrifice in vain?"
"E'en this I know," she said, "and yet again
I pray thee, let me enter."

"Enter then!"
That hollow Voice replied. She passed the door.
A sable curtain fell—and nothing more.
"A fool!" snarled some one, gnashing. Like a prayer
"A saint!" the whispered answer thrilled the air.

In a Russian Prison
(From "Memoirs of a Revolutionist")
by PETER KROPOTKIN

One day in the summer of 1875, in the cell that was next to mine I distinctly heard the light steps of heeled boots, and a few minutes later I caught fragments of a conversation. A feminine voice spoke from the cell, and a deep bass voice—evidently that of the sentry—grunted something in reply. Then I recognized the sound of the colonel's spurs, his rapid steps, his swearing at the sentry, and the click of the key in the lock. He said something, and a feminine voice loudly replied: "We did not talk. I only asked him to call the noncommissioned officer." Then the door was locked, and I heard the colonel swearing in whispers at the sentry.

So I was alone no more. I had a lady neighbor, who at once broke down the severe discipline which had hitherto reigned among the soldiers. From that day the walls of the fortress, which had been mute during the last fifteen months, became animated. From all sides I heard knocks with the foot on the floor: one, two, three, four, . . . eleven knocks; twenty-four knocks, fifteen knocks; then an interruption, followed by three knocks, and a long succession of thirty-three knocks. Over and over again these knocks were repeated in the same succession, until the neighbor would guess at last that they were meant for "Kto vy?" (Who are you?), the letter *v* being the third letter in our alphabet. Thereupon conversation was soon established, and usually was conducted in the abridged alphabet; that is, the alphabet being divided into six rows of five letters, each letter marked by its row and its place in the row.

I discovered with great pleasure that I had at my left my friend Serdukóff, with whom I could soon talk about everything, especially when we used our cipher. But intercourse with men brought its sufferings as well as its joys. Underneath me was lodged a peasant, whom Serdukóff knew. He talked to him by means of knocks; and even against my will, often unconsciously during my work, I followed their conversations. I also spoke to him. Now, if solitary confinement without any sort of work is hard for educated men, it is infinitely harder for a peasant who is accustomed to physical work, and not at all wont to spend years in reading. Our peasant friend felt quite miserable, and having been kept for nearly two years in another prison before he was brought to the fortress—his crime was that he had listened to Socialists—he was already broken down. Soon I began to notice, to my terror, that from time to time his mind wandered. Gradually his thoughts grew more and more confused, and we two perceived, step by step, day by day, evidences that his reason was failing, until his talk became at last that of a lunatic. Frightful noises and wild cries came next from the lower story; our neighbor was mad, but was still kept for several months in the casemate before he was removed to an asylum, from which he never emerged. To witness the destruction of a man's mind, under such conditons, was terrible. I am sure it must have contributed to increase the nervous irritability of my good and true friend Serdukóff. When, after four years' imprisonment, he was acquitted by the court and released, he shot himself.

The Martyrdom of an Anarchist
by HUTCHINS HAPGOOD
American radical, 1869-1944; the following passage is from his introduction to
"Prison Memoirs of an Anarchist," by Alexander Berkman.

Not only has this book the interest of the human document, but it is also a striking proof of the power of the human soul. Alexander Berkman spent fourteen years in prison, under perhaps more than commonly harsh and severe conditions. Prison life tends to destroy the body, weaken the mind and pervert the character. Berkman consciously struggled with these adverse, destructive conditions. He took care of his body. He took care of his mind. He did so strenuously. It was a moral effort. He felt insane ideas trying to take possession of him. Insanity is a natural result of prison life. It always tends to come. This man felt it, consciously struggled against it, and overcame it. That the prison affected him is true. It always does. But he saved himself, essentially. Society tried to destroy him, but failed.

If people will read this book carefully it will tend to do away with prisons. The public, once vividly conscious of what prison life is and must be, would not be willing to maintain prisons. This is the only book that I know which goes deeply into the corrupting, demoralizing psychology of prison life. It shows, in picture after picture, sketch after sketch, not only the obvious brutality, stupidity, ugliness permeating the institution, but, very touching, it shows the good qualities and instincts of the human heart perverted, demoralized, helplessly struggling for life; beautiful tendencies basely expressing themselves. And the personality of Berkman goes through it all; idealistic, courageous, uncompromising, sincere, truthful; not untouched, as I have said, by his surroundings, but remaining his essential self. . . .

The Russian Nihilistic origin of Berkman, his Anarchistic experience in America, his attempt on the life of Frick—an attempt made at a violent industrial crisis, an attempt made as a result of a sincere if fanatical belief that he was called on by his destiny to strike a psychological blow for the oppressed of the community—this part of the book will arouse extreme disagreement and disapproval of his ideas and his act. But I see no reason why this, with the rest, should not rather be regarded as an integral part of a human document, as part of the record of a life, with its social and psychological suggestions and explanations. Why not try to understand an honest man even if he feels called on to kill? There, too, it may be deeply instructive. There, too, it has its lessons. Read it not in a combative spirit. Read to understand. Do not read to agree, of course, but read to see.

Prison Memoirs of an Anarchist
by ALEXANDER BERKMAN
American anarchist leader, 1870-1936

The Dungeon

In the storeroom I am stripped of my suit of dark gray, and clad in the hateful stripes. Coatless and shoeless, I am led through hallways and corridors, down a steep flight of stairs, and thrown into the dungeon.

.   .   .   .   .   .

Total darkness. The blackness is massive, palpable—I feel its hand upon my head, my face. I dare not move, lest a misstep thrust me into the abyss. I hold my hand close to my eyes—I feel the touch of my lashes upon it, but I cannot see its outline. Motionless I stand on the spot, devoid of all sense of direction.

The silence is sinister; it seems to me I can hear it. Only now and then the hasty scrambling of nimble feet suddenly rends the stillness, and the gnawing of invisible river rats haunts the fearful solitude.

Slowly the blackness pales. It ebbs and melts; out of the sombre gray, a wall looms above; the silhouette of a door rises dimly before me, sloping upward and growing compact and impenetrable.

The hours drag in unbroken sameness. Not a sound reaches me from the cell-house. In the maddening quiet and darkness I am bereft of all consciousness of time, save once a day when the heavy rattle of keys apprises me of the morning: the dungeon is unlocked, and the silent guards hand me a slice of bread and a cup of water. The double doors fall heavily to, the steps grow fainter and die in the distance, and all is dark again in the dungeon.

The numbness of death steals upon my soul. The floor is cold and clammy, the gnawing grows louder and nearer, and I am filled with dread lest the starving rats attack my bare feet. I snatch a few unconscious moments leaning against the door; and then again I pace the cell, striving to keep awake, wondering whether it be night or day, yearning for the sound of a human voice.

Utterly forsaken! Cast into the stony bowels of the underground, the world of man receding, leaving no trace behind. . . . Eagerly I strain my ear—only the ceaseless, fearful gnawing. I clutch the bars in desperation—a hollow echo mocks the clanking iron. My hands tear violently at the door—"Ho, there! Any one here?" All is silent. Nameless terrors quiver in my mind, weaving nightmares of mortal dread and despair. Fear shapes convulsive thoughts: they rage in wild tempest, then become calm, and again rush through time and space in a rapid succession of strangely familiar scenes, wakened in my slumbering consciousness.

Exhausted and weary I droop against the wall. A slimy creeping on my face startles me in horror, and again I pace the cell. I feel cold and hungry. Am I forgotten? Three days must have passed, and more. Have they forgotten me? . . .

The clank of keys sends a thrill of joy to my heart. My tomb will open—oh, to see the light, and breathe the air again. . . .

"Officer, isn't my time up yet?"

"What's your hurry? You've only been here one day."

The doors fall to. Ravenously I devour the bread, so small and thin, just a bite. Only *one* day! Despair enfolds me like a pall. Faint with anguish, I sink to the floor. . . .

The Sick Line

One by one the men augment the row; they walk slowly, bent and coughing, painfully limping down the steep flights. From every range they come; the old and decrepit, the young consumptives, the lame and asthmatic, a tottering old Negro, an idiotic white boy. All look withered and dejected,—a ghastly line, palsied and blear-eyed, blanched in the valley of death.

The rotunda door opens noisily, and the doctor enters, accompanied by Deputy Warden Graves and Assistant Deputy Hopkins. Behind them is a prisoner, dressed in dark gray and carrying a medicine box. Dr. Boyce glances at the long line, and knits his brows. He looks at his watch, and the frown deepens. He has much to do. Since the death of the senior doctor, the young graduate is the sole physician of the big prison. He must make the rounds of the shops before noon, and visit the hospital before the Warden or the Deputy drops in.

Mr. Graves sits down at the officers' desk, near the hall entrance. The Assistant Deputy, pad in hand, places himself at the head of the sick line. The doctor leans against the door of the rotunda, facing the Deputy. The block officers stand within call, at respectful distances.

"Two-fifty-five!" the Assistant Deputy calls out.

A slender young man leaves the line and approaches the doctor. He is tall and well featured, the large eyes lustrous in the pale face. He speaks in a hoarse voice:

"Doctor, there is something the matter with my side. I have pains, and I cough bad at night, and in the morning——"

"All right," the doctor interrupts, without looking up from his note book. "Give him some salts," he adds, with a nod to his assistant.

"Next!" the Deputy calls.

"Will you please excuse me from the shop for a few days?" the sick prisoner pleads, a tremor in his voice.

The physician glances questioningly at the Deputy. The latter cries, impatiently, "Next, next man!" striking the desk twice, in quick succession, with the knuckles of his hand.

"Return to the shop," the doctor says to the prisoner.

"Next," the Deputy calls, spurting a stream of tobacco juice in the direction of the cuspidor. It strikes sidewise, and splashes over the foot of the approaching new patient, a young Negro, his neck covered with bulging tumors.

"Number?" the doctor inquires.

"One-thirty-seven, A one-thirty-seven!" the Deputy mumbles, his head thrown back to receive a fresh handful of "scrap" tobacco.

"Guess Ah's got de big neck, Ah is, Mistah Boyce," the Negro says hoarsely.

"Salts. Return to work. Next!"

"A one-twenty-six!"

A young man with parchment-like face, sere and yellow, walks painfully from the line.

"Doctor, I seem to be gettin' worser, and I'm afraid——"

"What's the trouble?"

"Pains in the stomach. Gettin' so turrible, I——"

"Give him a plaster. Next!"

"Plaster hell!" the prisoner breaks out in a fury, his face growing livid. "Look at this, will you?" With a quick motion he pulls his shirt up to his head. His chest and back are entirely covered with porous plasters; not an inch of skin is visible. "Damn your plasters," he cries with sudden sobs, "I ain't got no more room for plasters. I'm putty near dyin', an' you won't do nothin' fer me."

The guards pounce upon the man, and drag him into the rotunda.

The Keepers

The comparative freedom of the range familiarizes me with the workings of the institution, and brings me in close contact with the authorities. The personnel of the guards is of very inferior character. I find their average intelligence considerably lower than that of the inmates. Especially does the element recruited from the police and the detective service lack sympathy with the unfortunates in their charge. They are mostly men discharged from city employment because of habitual drunkenness, or flagrant brutality and corruption. Their attitude toward the prisoners is summed up in coercion and suppression. They look upon the men as will-less objects of iron-handed discipline, exact unquestioning obedience and absolute submissiveness to peremptory whims, and harbor personal animosity toward the less pliant. The more intelligent among the officers scorn inferior duties, and crave advancement. The authority and remuneration of a Deputy Wardenship is alluring to them, and every keeper considers himself the fittest for the vacancy. But the coveted prize is awarded to the guard most feared by the inmates, and most subservient to the Warden,—a direct incitement to brutality on the one hand, to sycophancy on the other. . . .

Daily I behold the machinery at work, grinding and pulverizing, brutalizing the officers, dehumanizing the inmates. Far removed from the strife and struggle of the larger world, I yet witness its miniature replica, more agonizing and merciless within the walls. A perfected model it is, this prison life, with its apparent uniformity and dull passivity. But beneath the torpid surface smolder the fires of being, now crackling faintly under a dun smothering smoke, now blazing forth with the ruthlessness of despair. Hidden by the veil of discipline rages the struggle of fiercely contending wills, and intricate meshes are woven in the quagmire of darkness and suppression.

Intrigue and counter-plot, violence and corruption, are rampant in cell-house and shop. The prisoners spy upon each other, and in turn upon the officers. The latter encourage the trusties in unearthing the secret doings of the inmates, and the stools enviously compete with each other in supplying information to the keepers. Often they deliberately inveigle the trustful prisoner into a fake plot to escape, help and encourage him in the preparations, and at the critical moment denounce him to the authorities. The luckless man is severely punished, usually remaining in utter ignorance of the intrigue. The *provocateur* is rewarded with greater liberty and special privileges. Frequently his treachery proves the stepping-stone to freedom, aided by the Warden's official recommendation of the "model prisoner" to the State Board of Pardons.

By FREDERIC HARRISON

Society can overlook murder, adultery or swindling; it never forgives the preaching of a new gospel.

Woman in the 1905 Revolution, *Sakhnorskaya*

The Seven That Were Hanged

by Leonid Andreyev

One of the most famous of the Russian writer's stories, in which he describes the
execution of a group of terrorists, analyzing their sensations in their separate cells,
and on their journey together to the foot of the gallows.

The Unknown, surnamed Werner, was a man fatigued by
struggle. He had loved life, the theatre, society, art, literature,
passionately. Endowed with an excellent memory, he spoke several languages perfectly. He was fond of dress, and had excellent
manners. Of the whole group of terrorists he was the only one
who was able to appear in society without risk of recognition.

For a long time already, and without his comrades having
noticed it, he had entertained a profound contempt for men.
More of a mathematician than a poet, ecstasy and inspiration had
remained so far things unknown to him; at times he would look
upon himself as a madman seeking to square the circle in seas
of human blood. The enemy against which he daily struggled
could not inspire him with respect; it was nothing but a compact
network of stupidities, treasons, falsehoods, base deceits. . . .

Werner understood that the execution was not simply death,
but also something more. In any case, he was determined to meet
it calmly, to live until the end as if nothing had happened or
would happen. Only in this way could he repress the profoundest
contempt for the execution and preserve his liberty of mind.
His comrades, although knowing well his cold and haughty intre-
pidity, would perhaps not have believed it themselves; but in the
courtroom he thought not of life or of death: he played in his
mind a difficult game of chess, giving it his deepest and quietest
attention. An excellent player, he had begun this game on the
very day of his imprisonment, and he had kept it up continually.
And the verdict that condemned him did not displace a single
piece on the invisible board.

Now he was shrugging his shoulders and feeling his pulse.
His heart beat fast, but tranquilly and regularly, with a sonorous
force. Like a novice thrown into prison for the first time, he
examined attentively the cell, the bolts, the chair screwed to the
wall, and said to himself:

"Why have I such a sensation of joy, of liberty? Yes, of liberty;
I think of tomorrow's execution, and it seems to me it does not
exist. I look at the walls, and they seem to me not to exist either.
And I feel as free as if, instead of being in prison, I had just

come out of another cell in which I had been confined all my life."

Werner's hands began to tremble, a thing unknown to him. His thought became more and more vibrant. It seemed to him that tongues of fire were moving in his head, trying to escape from his brain to lighten the still obscure distance. Finally the flame darted forth, and the horizon was brilliantly illuminated.

The vague lassitude that had tortured Werner during the last two years had disappeared at sight of death; his beautiful youth came back. It was even something more than beautiful youth. With the astonishing clearness of mind that sometimes lifts man to the supreme heights of meditation, Werner saw suddenly both life and death; and the majesty of this new spectacle struck him. He seemed to be following a path as narrow as the edge of a blade, on the crest of the loftiest mountain. On one side he saw life, and on the other he saw death; and they were like two seas, sparkling and beautiful, melting into each other at the horizon in a single infinite extension.

"What is this, then? What a divine spectacle!" said he slowly.

He arose involuntarily and straightened up, as if in presence of the Supreme Being. And, annihilating the walls, annihilating space and time, by the force of his all-penetrating look, he cast his eyes into the depths of the life that he had quitted.

And life took on a new aspect. He no longer tried, as of old, to translate into words that he was; moreover, in the whole range of human language, still so poor and miserly, he found no words adequate. The paltry, dirty and evil things that suggested to him contempt and sometimes even disgust at the sight of men had completely disappeared, just as, to people rising in a balloon, the mud and filth of the narrow streets become invisible, and ugliness changes into beauty.

With an unconscious movement Werner walked toward the table and leaned upon it with his right arm. Haughty and authoritative by nature, he had never been seen in a prouder, freer, and more imperious attitude; never had his face worn such a look, never had he so lifted up his head, for at no previous time had he been as free and powerful as now, in this prison, on the eve of execution, at the threshold of death.

In his illuminated eyes men wore a new aspect, an unknown beauty and charm. He hovered above time, and never had this humanity, which only the night before was howling like a wild beast in the forest, appeared to him so young. What had heretofore seemed to him terrible, unpardonable and base, became suddenly touching and naïve, just as we cherish in the child the awkwardness of its behavior, the incoherent stammerings in which its unconscious genius glimmers, its laughable errors and blunders, its cruel bruises.

"My dear friends!" . . .

What mysterious path had he followed to pass from a feeling of unlimited and haughty liberty to this passionate and moving pity? He did not know. Did he really pity his comrades, or did his tears hide something more passionate, something really greater? His heart, which had suddenly revived and reblossomed, could not tell him. Werner wept, and whispered:

"My dear comrades! My dear comrades!"

And in this man who wept, and who smiled through his tears, no one—not the judges, or his comrades, or himself—would have recognized the cold and haughty Werner, sceptical and insolent.

By THOMAS JEFFERSON

The tree of liberty must be refreshed from time to time with the blood of patriots and tyrants. It is its natural manure.

Chillon

by LORD BYRON

Eternal Spirit of the chainless Mind!
   Brightest in dungeons, Liberty, thou art—
   For there thy habitation is the heart—
The heart which love of thee alone can bind;

And when thy sons to fetters are consign'd—
   To fetters, and the damp vault's dayless gloom—
   Their country conquers with their martyrdom,
And Freedom's fame finds wings on every wind.

Chillon! thy prison is a holy place,
   And thy sad floor an altar; for 'twas trod
Until his very steps have left a trace
   Worn, as if thy cold pavement were a sod,
By Bonnivard! May none those marks efface!
   For they appeal from tyranny to God.

Assassination

by AUGUST VAILLANT

From the speech before the French Chamber of Deputies in 1894, prior to receiving
sentence of death for a political crime.

Ah, gentlemen, if the governing classes could go down among
the unfortunates! But no, they prefer to remain deaf to their
appeals. It seems that a fatality impels them, like the royalty of
the eighteenth century, toward the precipice which will engulf
them; for woe be to those who remain deaf to the cries of the
starving, woe to those who, believing themselves of superior
essence, assume the right to exploit those beneath them! There
comes a time when the people no longer reason; they rise like a
hurricane, and rush onward like a torrent. Then we see bleeding
heads impaled on pikes.

Among the exploited, gentlemen, there are two classes of individuals. Those of one class, not realizing what they are and what
they might be, take life as it comes, believe that they are born
to be slaves, and content themselves with the little that is given
them in exchange for their labor. But there are others, on the
contrary, who think, who study and, looking about them, discover social iniquities. Is it their fault if they see clearly and
suffer at seeing others suffer? Then they throw themselves into
the struggle, and make themselves the bearers of the popular
claims.

I know very well that I shall be told that I ought to have
confined myself to speech for the vindication of the people's
claims. But what can you expect! It takes a loud voice to make
the deaf hear. Too long have they answered our voices by imprisonment, the rope, and rifle-volleys. Make no mistake; the explosion of my bomb is not only the cry of the rebel Vaillant, but
the cry of an entire class which vindicates its rights, and which
will soon add acts to words. For, be sure of it, in vain will they
pass laws. The ideas of the thinkers will not halt!

By GEORGE WASHINGTON

First President of the United States, 1732-1799

Government is not reason, it is not eloquence—it is force!
Like fire it is a dangerous servant and a fearful master; never
for a moment should it be left to irresponsible action.

The Walker

by ARTURO GIOVANNITTI

Clergyman of Italian descent, who left the Church for the labor movement and was imprisoned on a charge of "constructive murder" during a strike at Lawrence, Massachusetts; 1888-1959.

I hear footsteps over my head all night.

They come and they go. Again they come and they go all night.

They come one eternity in four paces and they go one eternity in four paces, and between the coming and the going there is Silence and the Night and the Infinite.

For infinite are the nine feet of a prison cell, and endless is the march of him who walks between the yellow brick wall and the red iron gate, thinking things that cannot be chained and cannot be locked, but that wander far away in the sunlit world, each in a wild pilgrimage after a destined goal.

. . . . . .

Throughout the restless night I hear the footsteps over my head.

Who walks? I know not. It is the phantom of the jail, the sleepless brain, a man, the man, the Walker.

One—two—three—four: four paces and the wall.

One—two—three—four: four paces and the iron gate.

He has measured his space, he has measured it accurately, scrupulously, minutely, as the hangman measures the rope and the grave-digger the coffin—so many feet, so many inches, so many fractions of an inch for each of the four paces.

One—two—three—four. Each step sounds heavy and hollow over my head, and the echo of each step sounds hollow within my head as I count them in suspense and in dread that once, perhaps, in the endless walk, there may be five steps instead of four between the yellow brick wall and the red iron gate.

But he has measured the space so accurately, so scrupulously, so minutely that nothing breaks the grave rhythm of the slow, fantastic march. . . .

All the sounds of the living beings and inanimate things, and all the noises of the night I have heard in my wistful vigil.

I have heard the moans of him who bewails a thing that is dead and the sighs of him who tries to smother a thing that will not die;

I have heard the stifled sobs of the one who weeps with his
head under the coarse blanket, and the whisperings of the one
who prays with his forehead on the hard, cold stone of the floor;

I have heard him who laughs the shrill, sinister laugh of folly
at the horror rampant on the yellow wall and at the red eyes of
the nightmare glaring through the iron bars;

I have heard in the sudden icy silence him who coughs a dry,
ringing cough, and wished madly that his throat would not rattle
so and that he would not spit on the floor, for no sound was
more atrocious than that of his sputum upon the floor;

I have heard him who swears fearsome oaths which I listen to
in reverence and awe, for they are holier than the virgin's prayer;

And I have heard, most terrible of all, the silence of two hundred brains all possessed by one single, relentless, unforgiving,
desperate thought.

All this I have heard in the watchful night,

And the murmur of the wind beyond the walls,

And the tolls of a distant bell,

And the woeful dirge of the rain,

And the remotest echoes of the sorrowful city,

And the terrible beatings, wild beatings, mad beatings of the
One Heart which is nearest to my heart.

All this have I heard in the still night;

But nothing is louder, harder, drearier, mightier, more awful
than the footsteps I hear over my head all night. . . .

All through the night he walks and he thinks. Is it more
frightful because he walks and his footsteps sound hollow over
my head, or because he thinks and speaks not his thoughts?

But does he think? Why should he think? Do I think? I only
hear the footsteps and count them. Four steps and the wall. Four
steps and the gate. But beyond? Beyond? Where goes he beyond
the gate and the wall?

He does not go beyond. His thought breaks there on the iron
gate. Perhaps it breaks like a wave of rage, perhaps like a sudden
flow of hope, but it also returns to beat the wall like a billow of
helplessness and despair.

He walks to and fro within the narrow whirlpit of this ever
storming and furious thought. Only one thought—constant, fixed,
immovable, sinister, without power and without voice.

A thought of madness, frenzy, agony and despair, a hell-brewed thought, for it is a natural thought. All things natural are things impossible while there are jails in the world—bread, work, happiness, peace, love.

But he thinks not of this. As he walks he thinks of the most superhuman, the most unattainable, the most impossible thing in the world:

He thinks of a small brass key that turns just half around and throws open the red iron gate.

That is all the Walker thinks, as he walks throughout the night.

And that is what two hundred minds drowned in the darkness and the silence of the night think, and that is also what I think.

Wonderful is the supreme wisdom of the jail that makes all think the same thought. Marvelous is the providence of the law that equalizes all, even in mind and sentiment. Fallen is the last barrier of privilege, the aristocracy of the intellect. The democracy of reason has leveled all the two hundred minds to the common surface of the same thought.

I, who have never killed, think like the murderer;

I, who have never stolen, reason like the thief;

I think, reason, wish, hope, doubt, wait like the hired assassin, the embezzler, the forger, the counterfeiter, the incestuous, the raper, the drunkard, the prostitute, the pimp, I, I who used to think of love and life and flowers and song and beauty and the ideal.

A little key, a little key as little as my little finger, a little key of shining brass.

All my ideas, my thoughts, my dreams are congealed in a little key of shiny brass.

All my brain, all my soul, all the suddenly surging latent powers of my deepest life are in the pocket of a white-haired man dressed in blue.

He is great, powerful, formidable, the man with the white hair, for he has in his pocket the mighty talisman which makes one man cry, and one man pray, and one laugh, and one cough, and one walk, and all keep awake and listen and think the same maddening thought.

Greater than all men is the man with the white hair and the small brass key, for no other man in the world could compel two hundred men to think for so long the same thought. Surely when the light breaks I will write a hymn unto him which shall hail him greater than Mohammed and Arbues and Torquemada and Mesmer, and all the other masters of other men's thoughts. I shall call him Almighty, for he holds everything of all and of me in a little brass key in his pocket.

Everything of me he holds but the branding iron of contempt and the claymore of hatred for the monstrous cabala that can make the apostle and the murderer, the poet and the procurer, think of the same gate, the same key and the same exit on the different sunlit highways of life.

My brother, do not walk any more.

It is wrong to walk on a grave. It is a sacrilege to walk four steps from the headstone to the foot and four steps from the foot to the headstone.

If you stop walking, my brother, no longer will this be a grave, for you will give me back that mind that is chained to your feet and the right to think my own thoughts.

I implore you, my brother, for I am weary of the long vigil, weary of counting your steps, and heavy with sleep.

Stop, rest, sleep, my brother, for the dawn is well nigh and it is not the key alone that can throw open the gate.

That Agony Is Our Triumph
by BARTOLOMEO VANZETTI

Anarchist immigrant who, along with Nicola Sacco, was executed for alleged murder after worldwide protests against the legal conduct of their prosecutors and the evidence submitted; 1888-1927; this extract is from a letter written shortly before his death.

If it had not been for these thing, I might have live out my life talking at street corners to scorning men. I might have die, unmarked, unknown, a failure. Now we are not a failure. Never in our full life could we hope to do so much work for tolerance, for Justice, for man's understanding of man, as now we do by accident. Our words—our lives—our pain—nothing! The taking of our lives—the lives of a good shoe-maker and a poor fish-peddler —all! That last moment belongs to us, that agony is our triumph!

The Eagle That Is Forgotten

by VACHEL LINDSAY

American poet, 1879-1931. This poem is addressed to John P. Altgeld, once Governor of Illinois, who sacrificed his career by pardoning labor leaders he considered innocent of the charges made against them.

Sleep softly . . . eagle forgotten . . . under the stone.
Time has its way with you there, and the clay has its own.
"We have buried him now," thought your foes, and in secret rejoiced.
They made a brave show of their mourning, their hatred unvoiced.
They had snarled at you, barked at you, foamed at you, day after day,
Now you were ended. They praised you . . . and laid you away.
The others, that mourned you in silence and terror and truth,
The widow bereft of her crust, and the boy without youth,
The mocked and the scorned and the wounded, the lame and the poor,
That should have remembered forever . . . remember no more.
Where are those lovers of yours, on what name do they call,
The lost, that in armies wept over your funeral pall?
They call on the names of a hundred high-valiant ones,
A hundred white eagles have risen, the sons of your sons.
The zeal in their wings is a zeal that your dreaming began,
The valor that wore out your soul in the service, of man.
Sleep softly . . . eagle forgotten . . . under the stone.
Time has its way with you there, and the clay has its own.
Sleep on, O brave-hearted, O wise man that kindled the flame—
To live in mankind is far more than to live in a name,
To live in mankind, far, far more . . . than to live in a name.

Johnny Comes Home
(From "Johnny Get Your Gun")

by DALTON TRUMBO

American screenwriter and novelist, 1905–1976

Take me into the places where men work and make things. Take me there and say boys here is a cheap way to get by. Maybe times are bad and your salaries are low. Don't worry boys because there is always a way to cure things like that. Have a war and then prices go up and wages go up and everybody makes a hell of a lot of money. There'll be one along pretty soon boys so don't get impatient. It'll come and then you'll have your chance.

Either way you win. If you don't have to fight why you stay at home and make sixteen bucks a day working in the shipyards. And if they draft you why you've got a good chance of coming back without so many needs. Maybe you'll need only one shoe instead of two that's saving money. Maybe you'll be blind and if you are why then you never need worry about the expense of glasses. Maybe you'll be lucky like me. Look at me close boys I don't need anything. A little broth or something three times a day and that's all. No shoes no socks no underwear no shirt no gloves no hat no necktie no collar-buttons no vest no coat no movies no vaudeville no football not even a shave. Look at me boys I have no expenses at all. You're suckers boys. Get on the gravy train. I know what I'm talking about. I used to need all the things that you need right now. I used to be a consumer. I've consumed a lot in my time. I've consumed more shrapnel and gunpowder than any living man. So don't get blue boys because you'll have your chance there'll be another war along pretty soon and then maybe you'll be lucky like me.

Take me into the schoolhouses all the schoolhouses in the world. Suffer little children to come unto me isn't that right? They may scream at first and have nightmares at night but they'll get used to it because they've got to get used to it and it's best to start them young. Gather them around my case and say here little girl here little boy come and take a look at your daddy. Come and look at yourself. You'll be like that when you grow up to be great big strong men and women. You'll have a chance to die for your country. And you may not die you may come back like this. Not everybody dies little kiddies.

Closer please. You over there against the blackboard what's the matter with you? Quit crying you silly little girl come over here and look at the nice man the nice man who was a soldier boy. You remember him don't you? Don't you remember little crybaby how you waved flags and saved tinfoil and put your savings in thrift stamps? Of course you do silly. Well here's the soldier you did it for.

Come on youngsters take a nice look and then we'll go into our nursery rhymes. New nursery rhymes for new times. Hickory dickory dock my daddy's nuts from shellshock. Humpty dumpty thought he was wise till gas came along and burned out his eyes. A diller a dollar a ten o'clock scholar blow off his legs and then watch him holler. Rockabye baby in the treetop don't stop a bomb or you'll probably flop. Now I lay me down to sleep my bombproof cellar's good and deep but if I'm killed before I wake remember god it's for your sake amen.

Take me into the colleges and universities and academies and convents. Call the girls together all the healthy beautiful young girls. Point down to me and say here girls is your father. Here is that boy who was strong last night. Here is your little son your baby son the fruit of your love the hope of your future. Look down on him girls so you won't forget him. See that red gash there with mucus hanging to it? That was his face girls. Here girls touch it don't be afraid. Bend down and kiss it. You'll have to wipe your lips afterward because they will have a strange rotten stuff on them but that's all right because a lover is a lover and here is your lover.

Call all the young men together and say here is your brother here is your best friend here you are young men. This is a very interesting case young men because we know there is a mind buried down there. Technically this thing is living meat like that tissue we kept alive all last summer in the lab. But this is a different cut of meat because it also contains a brain. Now listen to me closely young gentlemen. That brain is thinking. Maybe it's thinking about music. Maybe it has a great symphony all thought out or a mathematical formula that would change the world or a book that would make people kinder or the germ of an idea that would save a hundred million people from cancer. This is a very interesting problem young gentlemen because if this brain does hold such secrets how in the world are we ever going to find out? In any event there you are young gentlemen breathing and thinking and dead like a frog under chloroform with its stomach laid open so that its heartbeat may be seen so quiet so helpless but yet alive. There is your future and your sweet wild dreams there is the thing your sweethearts loved and there is the thing your leaders urged it to be. Think well young gentlemen. Think sharply young gentlemen and then we will go back to our studies of the barbarians who sacked Rome.

Take me wherever there are parliaments and diets and congresses and chambers of statesmen. I want to be there when they talk about honor and justice and making the world

safe for democracy and fourteen points and the self determination of peoples. I want to be there to remind them I
haven't got a tongue to stick into the cheek I haven't got
either. But the statesmen have tongues. The statesmen have cheek.
Put my glass case upon the speaker's desk and every time the
gavel descends let me feel its vibration through my little jewel
case. Then let them speak of trade policies and embargoes and
new colonies and old grudges. Let them debate the menace of
the yellow race and the white man's burden and the course of
empire and why should we take all this crap off Germany or
whoever the next Germany is. Let them talk about the South
American market and why so-and-so is beating us out of it and
why our merchant marine can't compete and oh what the hell
let's send a good stiff note. Let them talk more munitions and
airplanes and battleships and tanks and gases why of course we've
got to have them we can't get along without them how in the
world could we protect the peace if we didn't have them? Let
them form blocs and alliances and mutual assistance pacts and
guarantees of neutrality. Let them draft notes and ultimatums
and protests and accusations.

But before they vote on them before they give the order for
all the little guys to start killing each other let the main guy rap
his gavel on my case and point down at me and say here
gentlemen is the only issue before this house and that is are you
for this thing here or are you against it. And if they are against
it why goddam them let them stand up like men and vote. And
if they are for it let them be hanged and drawn and quartered
and paraded through the streets in small chopped up little bits
and thrown out into the fields where no clean animal will touch
them and let their chunks rot there and may no green thing ever
grow where they rot.

Take me into your churches your great towering cathedrals
that have to be rebuilt every fifty years because they are destroyed
by war. Carry me in my glass box down the aisles where kings
and priests and brides and children at their confirmation have
gone so many times before to kiss a splinter of wood from a true
cross on which was nailed the body of a man who was lucky
enough to die. Set me high on your altars and call on god to look
down upon his murderous little children his dearly beloved little
children. Wave over me the incense I can't smell. Swill down the
sacramental wine I can't taste. Drone out the prayers I can't hear.

Go through the old old holy gestures for which I have no legs and no arms. Chorus out the hallelujas I can't sing. Bring them out loud and strong for me your hallelujas all of them for me because I know the truth and you don't you fools. You fools you fools you fools...

MARTIN LUTHER KING, JR.
American civil rights leader, 1929-1968

If a man hasn't discovered something that he will die for, he isn't fit to live.

On Difficult Times and Violence

(From a speech given to a black audience shortly
after the assassination of the Reverend Martin Luther King, Jr)
BY ROBERT F. KENNEDY
U.S. Attorney General and U.S. Senator from New York

I have bad news for you, for all of our fellow citizens, and people who love peace all over the world, and that is that Martin Luther King was shot and killed tonight.

Martin Luther King dedicated his life to love and to justice for his fellow human beings, and he died because of that effort.

In this difficult day, in this difficult time for the United States, it is perhaps well to ask what kind of a nation we are and what direction we want to move in. For those of you who are black—considering the evidence there evidently is that there were white people who were responsible—you can be filled with bitterness, with hatred, and a desire for revenge. We can move in that direction as a country, in great polarization—black people amongst black, white people amongst white, filled with hatred toward one another.

Or we can make an effort, as Martin Luther King did, to understand with compassion and love.

For those of you who are black and are tempted to be filled with hatred and distrust at the injustice of such an act, against all white people, I can only say that I feel in my own heart the same kind of feeling. I had a member of my family killed, but he was killed by a white man. But we have to make an effort in the United States, we have to make an effort to understand, to go beyond these rather difficult times.

My favorite poet was Aeschylus. He wrote, "In our sleep, pain which cannot forget falls drop by drop upon the heart until, in our own despair, against our will, comes wisdom through the awful grace of God."

What we need in the United States is not division; what we need in the United States is not hatred; what we need in the United States is not violence or lawlessness but love and wisdom, and compassion toward one another, and a feeling of justice towards those who still suffer within our country, whether they be white or they be black.

So I shall ask you tonight to return home, to say a prayer for the family of Martin Luther King, that's true, but more importantly to say a prayer for our own country, which all of us love—a prayer for understanding and that compassion of which I spoke.

We can do well in this country. We will have difficult times. We've had difficult times in the past. We will have difficult times in the future. It is not the end of violence; it is not the end of disorder.

But the vast majority of white people and the vast majority of black people in this country want to live together, want to improve the quality of our life, and want justice for all human beings who abide in our land.

Let us dedicate ourselves to what the Greeks wrote so many years ago: to tame the savageness of man to make gentle the life of this world.

Let us dedicate ourselves to that, and say a prayer for our country and for our people.

On Going Underground

BY NELSON MANDELA

I am informed that a warrant for my arrest has been issued, and that the police are looking for me. The National Actions Committee has given full and serious consideration to this question, and has sought the advice of many trusted friends ... and they have advised me not to surrender myself. I have accepted this advice, and will not give myself up to a government I do not recognize. Any ... politician will realise that under present-day conditions in this country, to go for cheap martyrdom by handing myself to the police is naive and criminal. We have an important programme before us and it is important to carry it out very seriously and without delay.

I have chosen this latter course, which is more difficult and which

entails more toil and hardship than sitting in gaol. I have had to separate myself from my dear wife and children, from my mother and
sisters, to live as an outlaw in my own land. I have had to close my
business, to abandon my profession, and live in poverty and misery,
as many of my people are doing. I will continue to act as the
spokesman of the National Action Council during the phase that is
unfolding and in the tough struggles that lie ahead. I shall fight the
government side by side with you, inch by inch, and mile by mile,
and until victory is won. What are you going to do? Will you come
along with us, or are you going to co-operate with the government in
its efforts to suppress the claims and aspirations of your own people?
Or are you going to remain silent and neutral in a matter of life and
death to my people, to our people? For my own part I have made my
choice. I will not leave South Africa, nor will I surrender. Only
through hardship, sacrifice and militant action can freedom be won.
The struggle is my life. I will continue fighting for freedom until the
end of my days.

BOOK VII

Jesus and the Church

"The martyred Christ of the working class, the inspired evangel of the downtrodden masses, the world's supreme revolutionary leader, whose love for the poor and the children of the poor hallowed all the days of his consecrated life, lighted up and made forever holy the dark tragedy of his death, and gave to the ages his divine inspiration and his deathless name."—Debs.

Crusaders

by ELIZABETH WADDELL
Twentieth-century American writer

They have taken the tomb of our Comrade Christ—
  Infidel hordes that believe not in Man;
Stable and stall for his birth sufficed,
  But his tomb is built on a kingly plan.
They have hedged him round with pomp and parade,
  They have buried him deep under steel and stone—
But we come leading the great Crusade
  To give our Comrade back to his own.

Life of Jesus

by ERNEST RENAN
French philosopher and historian, 1823-1892

The chosen flock presented in fact a very mixed character, and one likely to astonish rigorous moralists. It counted in its fold men with whom a Jew, respecting himself, would not have associated. Perhaps Jesus found in this society, unrestrained by ordinary rules, more mind and heart than in a pedantic and formal middle class, proud of its apparent morality. . . . He appreciated conditions of soul only in proportion to the love mingled therein. Women with tearful hearts, and disposed through their sins to feelings of humanity, were nearer to his kingdom than ordinary natures, who often have little merit in not having fallen. We may conceive on the other hand that these tender souls, finding in their conversion to the sect an easy means of restoration, would passionately attach themselves to Him. Far from seeking to soothe the murmurs stirred up by his disdain for the social susceptibilities of the time, He seemed to take pleasure in exciting them. Never did anyone avow more loftily this contempt for the "world," which is the essential condition of great things and great originality. He pardoned a rich man, but only when the rich man, in consequence of some prejudice, was disliked by society. He greatly preferred men of equivocal life and of small consideration in the eyes of the orthodox leaders. "The publicans and the harlots go into the kingdom of God before you. For John came unto you and ye believed him not: but the publicans and the harlots believed him." We can understand how galling the reproach of not having followed the good example set by prostitutes must have been to men making a profession of seriousness and rigid morality.

237

Christ Mocked by Soldiers, *Georges Rouault*

Jesus the Revolutionist

by WALTER RAUSCHENBUSCH
American theologian, 1861-1918

There was a revolutionary consciousness in Jesus; not, of course, in the common use of the word "revolutionary," which connects it with violence and bloodshed. But Jesus knew that he had come to kindle a fire on earth. Much as he loved peace, he knew that the actual result of his work would be not peace but the sword. His mother in her song had recognized in her own experience the settled custom of God to "put down the proud and exalt them of low degree," to "fill the hungry with good things and to send the rich empty away." King Robert of Sicily recognized the revolutionary ring in those phrases, and thought it well that the Magnificat was sung only in Latin. The son of Mary expected a great reversal of values. The first would be last and the last would be first. He saw that what was exalted among man was an abomination before God, and therefore these exalted things had no glamor for his eye. This revolutionary note runs even through the beatitudes, where we should least expect it. The point of them is that henceforth those were to be blessed whom the world had not blessed, for the kingdom of God would reverse their relative standing. Now the poor and the hungry and sad were to be satisfied and comforted; the meek who had been shouldered aside by the ruthless would get their chance to inherit the earth, and conflict and persecution would be inevitable in the process.

We are apt to forget that his attack on the religious leaders and authorities of his day was of revolutionary boldness and thoroughness. He called the ecclesiastical leaders hypocrites, blind leaders who fumbled in their casuistry, and everywhere missed the decisive facts in teaching right and wrong. Their piety was no piety; their law was inadequate; they harmed the men whom they wanted to convert. Even the publicans and harlots had a truer piety than theirs. If we remember that religion was still the foundation of the Jewish State, and that the religious authorities were the pillars of existing society, much as in medieval Catholic Europe, we shall realize how revolutionary were his invectives. It was like Luther anathematizing the Catholic hierarchy.

His mind was similarly liberated from spiritual subjection to the existing civil powers. He called Herod, his own liege sovereign, "that fox." When the mother of James and John tried to steal a march on the others and secure for her sons a pledge of the highest places in the Messianic kingdom, Jesus felt that this was a backsliding into the scrambling methods of the present social order, in which each tries to make the others serve him, and he is greatest who can compel service from most. In the new social order, which was expressed in his own life, each must seek to give the maximum of service, and he would be greatest who would serve utterly. In that connection he sketched with a few strokes the pseudo-greatness of the present aristocracy: "Ye know that they which are supposed to rule over the nations lord it over them, and their great ones tyrannize over them. Thus shall it not be among you." The monarchies and aristocracies have always lived on the fiction that they exist for the good of the people, and yet it is an appalling fact how few kings have loved their people and have lived to serve. Usually the great ones have regarded the people as their oyster. In a similar saying reported by Luke, Jesus wittily adds that these selfish exploiters of the people graciously allow themselves to be called "Benefactors." His eyes were open to the unintentional irony of the titles in which the "majesties," "excellencies," and "holinesses" of the world have always decked themselves. Every time the inbred instinct to seek precedence cropped up among his disciples he sternly suppressed it. They must not allow themselves to be called Rabbi or Father or Master, "for all ye are brothers." Christ's ideal of society involved the abolition of rank and the extinction of those badges of rank in which former inequality was incrusted. The only title to greatness was to be distinguished service at cost to self. All this shows the keenest insight into the masked selfishness of those who hold power, and involves a revolutionary consciousness, emancipated from reverence for things as they are.

To the "Christians"
by FRANCIS W. L. ADAMS

Take, then, your paltry Christ,
    Your gentleman God.
We want the carpenter's son,
    With his saw and hod.

We want the man who loved
    The poor and the oppressed,

Who hated the Rich man and King
And the Scribe and the Priest.

We want the Galilean
Who knew cross and rod.
It's your "good taste" that prefers
A bastard "God!"

FROM THE GOSPEL ACCORDING TO LUKE

And as he spake, a certain Pharisee besought him to dine with him: and he went in, and sat down to meat. And when the Pharisee saw it, he marvelled that he had not first washed before dinner.

And the Lord said unto him, "Now do ye Pharisees make clean the outside of the cup and the platter; but your inward part is full of ravening and wickedness. Ye fools, did not he, that made that which is without, make that which is within also? But rather give alms of such things as ye have; and, behold, all things are clean unto you. But woe unto you, Pharisees! for ye tithe mint and rue and all manner of herbs, and pass over judgment and the love of God; these ought ye to have done, and not to leave the other undone. Woe unto you, Pharisees! for ye love the uppermost seats in the synagogues, and greetings in the markets. Woe unto you, scribes and Pharisees, hypocrites! for ye are as graves which appear not, and the men that walk over them are not aware of them."

Then answered one of the lawyers, and said unto him, "Master, thus saying thou reproachest us also."

And he said, "Woe unto you, also, ye lawyers, for ye lade men with burdens grievous to be borne, and ye yourselves touch not the burdens with one of your fingers. Woe unto you! for ye build the sepulchres of the prophets, and your fathers killed them.... Woe unto you, lawyers! for ye have taken away the key of knowledge; ye entered not in yourselves, and them that were entering in ye hindered."

And as he said these things unto them, the scribes and the Pharisees began to urge him vehemently, and to provoke him to speak of many things: laying wait for him, and seeking to catch something out of his mouth, that they might accuse him.

The Call of the Carpenter
by Bouck White
American clergyman, imprisoned for protesting in church against Colorado
massacres; born 1874

Jesus held that self-respect required of the rich young man that
he refuse to accept too long a handicap over his fellows in the
race of life, and start as near as may be from the same mark with
them. But he went also a step further. He exacted of the young
man that he de-class himself. "Come, follow me." This was the
staggerer. To stay in his own set and invest his fortune in works
of charity, would have been comparatively easy. Philanthropy
has been fashionable in every age. Charity takes the insurrectionary edge off of poverty. Therefore the philanthropic rich man
is a benefactor to his fellow magnates, and is made to feel their
gratitude; to him all doors of fashion swing. But Jesus issued a
veto. He denied the legitimacy of alms-giving as a plaster for the
deep-lying sore in the social tissue. Neighborly help, man to man,
was acceptable to him, and he commended it. But philanthropy
as a substitute for justice—he would have none of it. Charity is
twice cursed—it hardens him that gives and softens him that takes.
It does more harm to the poor than exploitation, because it makes
them willing to be exploited. It breeds slavishness, which is moral
suicide. The only thing Jesus would permit a swollen fortune to
do was to give itself to revolutionary propaganda, in order that
swollen fortunes might be forever after impossible. Patchwork
reformers are but hewing at a hydra. Confronted with this imperative, the rich young ruler made the great refusal. To give up his
fashionable set and join himself to this company of working-class
Galileans, was a moral heroism to which he was unequal. Therefore he was sorrowful; he went away, for he had a great social
standing.

Something of the same brand of atonement was evidently in
the mind of Dives when he awoke to the mistake he had made—
desirous to send from hell and tell his five brothers to use the
family fortune in erecting a "Dives Home for the Hungry," belike
with the family name and coat of arms over the front portal. Jesus
would concede no such privilege. He referred those "five
brethren" to "Moses and the prophets; let them hear them"—
Moses being the leader of the labor movement which had given
to the slaves in the Goshen brickyards their long-deferred rights;
and the prophets being those ardent Old Testament tribunes of

the people who had so hotly contended for the family idea of society against the exploiters and graspers at the top. Dante's idea that each sin on earth fashions its own proper punishment in hell receives confirmation in this parable. "The great gulf fixed," which constituted Dives's hell, was the gulf which he himself had brought about. For the private fortune he amassed had broken up the solidarity of society—had introduced into it a chasm both broad and deep. The gulf between him and Lazarus in this world exists in the world to come to plague him. The thirst which parched Dives's tongue, "being in torments," was the thirst for companionship, the healing contact once more with his fellows, from whom his fortune had sundered him like a butcher's cleaver. Jesus had so exalted a notion of the working class, their absence of cant, their rugged facing of the facts, their elemental simplicities, their first-hand contact with the realities of life, that he regarded any man who should draw himself off from them in a fancied superiority, as immeasurably the loser thereby, and as putting himself "in torments."

A Parable
by JAMES RUSSELL LOWELL

Said Christ our Lord, "I will go and see
How the men, my brethren, believe in me."
He passed not again through the gate of birth,
But made himself known to the children of earth.

Then said the chief priests, and rulers, and kings,
"Behold, now, the Giver of all good things;
Go to, let us welcome with pomp and state
Him who alone is mighty and great."

With carpets of gold the ground they spread
Wherever the Son of Man should tread,
And in palace chambers lofty and rare
They lodged him, and served him with kingly fare.

Great organs surged through arches dim
Their jubilant floods in praise of him;
And in church and palace, and judgment-hall,
He saw his image high over all.

But still, wherever his steps they led,
The Lord in sorrow bent down his head,
And from under the heavy foundation-stones
The son of Mary heard bitter groans.

And in church, and palace, and judgment-hall,
He marked great fissures that rent the wall,
And opened wider and yet more wide
As the living foundation heaved and sighed.

"Have ye founded your thrones and altars, then,
On the bodies and souls of living men?
And think ye that building shall endure,
Which shelters the noble and crushes the poor?

"With gates of silver and bars of gold
Ye have fenced my sheep from their Father's fold;
I have heard the dropping of their tears
In heaven these eighteen hundred years."

"O Lord and Master, not ours the guilt,
We built but as our fathers built;
Behold thine images, how they stand,
Sovereign and sole, through all our land.

"Our task is hard,—with sword and flame
To hold thine earth forever the same,
And with sharp crooks of steel to keep
Still, as thou leftest them, thy sheep."

Then Christ sought out an artisan,
A low-browed, stunted, haggard man,
And a motherless girl, whose fingers thin
Pushed from her faintly want and sin.

These set he in the midst of them,
And as they drew back their garment-hem,
For fear of defilement, "Lo, here," said he,
"The images ye have made of me!"

A Tramp's Confession
by HARRY KEMP
American working-class poet, 1883–1960

We huddled in the mission
   Fer it was cold outside,
An' listened to the preacher
   Tell of the Crucified;

Without, a sleety drizzle
   Cut deep each ragged form—
An' so we stood the talkin'
   Fer shelter from the storm

Fer I was cold an' hungry!
   They gave me grub an' bed
After I kneeled there with them
   An' many prayers was said.

An' so fergive me, Jesus,
   I didn't mean no harm—
An' outside it was zero,
   An' inside it was warm. . . .

Yes, I was cold an' hungry—
   An', O Thou Crucified,
Thou friend of all the Lowly,
   Fergive the lie I lied!

By ALFRED NORTH WHITEHEAD
English philosopher, 1861-1947

I consider Christian theology to be one of the great disasters of the human race. . . . It would be impossible to imagine anything more un-Christlike than Christian theology. Christ probably couldn't have understood it.

From the Gospel According to Matthew

Then shall the King say unto them on his right hand, "Come, ye blessed of my Father, inherit the kingdom prepared for you from the foundation of the world: For I was a hungered, and ye gave me meat; I was thirsty, and ye gave me drink; I was a stranger, and ye took me in; naked, and ye clothed me; I was sick, and ye visited me; I was in prison, and ye came unto me."

Then shall the righteous answer him, saying, "Lord, when saw we thee a hungered, and fed thee? or thirsty, and gave thee drink? when saw we thee a stranger, and took thee in? or naked, and clothed thee? or when saw we thee sick or in prison, and came unto thee?"

And the King shall answer and say unto them, "Verily I say unto you, inasmuch as ye have done it unto one of the least of these my brethren, ye have done it unto me."

Then shall he say also unto them on the left hand, "Depart from me, ye cursed, into everlasting fire, prepared for the devil and his angels: for I was a hungered, and ye gave me no meat; I was thirsty, and ye gave me no drink; I was a stranger, and ye took me not in; naked, and ye clothed me not; sick, and in prison, and ye visited me not."

Then shall they also answer him, saying, "Lord, when saw we thee a hungered, or athirst, or a stranger, or naked, or sick, or in prison, and did not minister unto thee?"

Then shall he answer them, saying, "Verily I say unto you, inasmuch as ye did it not to one of the least of these, ye did it not to me."

The Prince
by Niccolo Machiavelli
Italian courtier, author of a famous treatise on statecraft; 1469-1527

A Prince has to have particular care that, to see and to hear him, he appears all goodness, integrity, humanity and religion, which last he ought to pretend to more than ordinarily. For everybody sees, but few understand; everybody sees how you appear, but few know what in reality you are, and those few dare not oppose the opinion of the multitude, who have the majesty of their prince to defend them.

The Image in the Forum

by ROBERT BUCHANAN

English novelist and dramatist, 1814-1901

Not Baal, but Christus-Jingo! Heir
   Of him who once was crucified!
The red stigmata still are there,
   The crimson spear-wounds in the side;
But raised aloft as God and Lord,
He holds the Money-bag and Sword.

See, underneath the Crown of Thorn,
   The eye-balls fierce, the features grim!
And merrily from night to morn
   We chaunt his praise and worship him
Great Christus-Jingo, at whose feet
Christian and Jew and Atheist meet!

A wondrous god! most fit for those
   Who cheat on 'Change, then creep to prayer;
Blood on his heavenly altar flows,
   Hell's burning incense fills the air,
And Death attests in street and lane
The hideous glory of his reign.

O gentle Jew, from age to age
   Walking the waves thou could'st not tame,
This god hath ta'en thy heritage,
   And stolen thy sweet and stainless Name!
To him we crawl and bend the knee,
Naming thy Name, but scorning Thee!

The Swordless Christ

by PERCY ADAMS HUTCHISON

American poet, 1875-1952

"Vicisti Galilaee"

Ay, down the years behold he rides,
   The lowly Christ, upon an ass;
But conquering? Ten shall heed the call,
   A thousand idly watch him pass:

They watch him pass, or lightly hold
In mock lip-loyalty his name:
A thousand—were they his to lead!
But meek, without a sword, he came.

A myriad horsemen swept the field
With Attila, the whirlwind Hun;
A myriad cannon spake for him,
The silent, dread Napoleon.

For these had ready spoil to give,
Had reeking spoil for savage hands;
Slaves, and fair wives, and pillage rare:
The wealth of cities: teeming lands.

And if the world, once drunk with blood,
Sated, has turned from arms to peace,
Man hath not lost his ancient lusts;
The weapons change; war doth not cease.

The mother in the stifling den,
The brain-dulled child beside the loom,
The hordes that swarm and toil and starve—
We laugh, and tread them to their doom.

They shriek, and cry their prayers to Christ;
And lift wan faces, hands that bleed:
In vain they pray, for what is Christ?
A leader—without men to lead.

Ah, piteous Christ afar he rides!
We see him, but the face is dim;
We that would leap at crash of drums
Are slow to rise and follow him.

By HARRY A. OVERSTREET
American writer, 1875–1970

Exactly as in the great humanistic religions of Lao-tse, Buddha,
Isaiah, Jesus, so in psychoanalysis, the aim is to free the individual
from his various enslavements so that he is able "to see the truth,
to love, to become free and responsible, and to be sensitive to the
voice of his conscience."

In a Siberian Prison Church
(From "Resurrection")
by LEO TOLSTOY

The service began.

It consisted of the following. The priest, having dressed himself up in a strange and very inconvenient garb of gold cloth, cut and arranged little bits of bread on a saucer and then put most of them in a cup with wine, repeating at the same time different names and prayers. Meanwhile the deacon first read Slavonic prayers, difficult to understand in themselves, and rendered still more incomprehensible by being read very fast; he then sang them turn and turn about with the convicts.

The essence of the service consisted in the supposition that the bits of bread cut up by the priest and put into the wine, when manipulated and prayed over in a certain way, turned into the flesh and blood of God.

These manipulations consisted in the priest, hampered by the gold cloth sack he had on, regularly lifting and holding up his arms and then sinking to his knees and kissing the table and all that was on it; but chiefly in his taking a cloth by two of its corners and waving it rhythmically and softly over the silver saucer and the golden cup. It was supposed that at this point the bread and the wine turned into flesh and blood; therefore this part of the service was performed with the utmost solemnity. And the convicts made the sign of the cross, and bowed, first at each sentence, then after every two, and then after three; and all were very glad when the glorification ended and the priest shut the book with a sigh of relief and retired behind the partition. One last act remained. The priest took from a table a large gilt cross with enamel medallions at the ends, and came out into the center of the church with it. First the inspector came up and kissed the cross, then the jailers, and then the convicts, pushing and jostling, and abusing each other in whispers. The priest, talking to the inspector, pushed the cross and his hand, now against the mouths and now against the noses of the convicts, who were trying to kiss both the cross and the hand of the priest. And thus ended the Christian service, intended for the comfort and edification of these brothers who had gone astray.

And none of these present, from the inspector down, seemed conscious of the fact that this Jesus, whose name the priest re-

To Sustain the Body of the Church, If You Please,
Denis Auguste Marie Raffet

peated such a great number of times, whom he praised with all these curious expressions, had forbidden the very things that were being done there; that he had not only prohibited this meaningless much-speaking and the blasphemous incantation over the bread and wine, but had also, in the clearest words, forbidden men to call other men their master or to pray in temples; had taught that every one should pray in solitude; had forbidden to erect temples, saying that he had come to destroy them, and that one should worship not in a temple, but in spirit and in truth; and, above all, that not only had he forbidden to judge, to imprison, to torment, to execute men, as was done here, but had even prohibited any kind of violence, saying that he had come to give freedom to the captives.

No one present seemed conscious that all that was going on here was the greatest blasphemy, and a mockery of the same Christ in whose name it was being done. No one seemed to realize that the gilt cross with the enamel medallions at the ends, which the priest held out to the people to be kissed, was nothing but the emblem of that gallows on which Christ had been executed for denouncing just what was going on here. That these priests, who imagined they were eating and drinking the body and blood of Christ in the form of bread and wine, did in reality eat and drink his flesh and his blood, only not as wine and bits of bread, but by ensnaring "these little ones" with whom he identified himself, by depriving them of the greatest blessings and submitting them to most cruel torments, and by hiding from men the tidings of great joy which he had brought—that thought did not enter the mind of any one present.

Before a Crucifix

by ALGERNON CHARLES SWINBURNE
English poet, 1837-1909

Here, down between the dusty trees,
　At this lank edge of haggard wood,
Women with labor-loosened knees,
　With gaunt backs bowed by servitude,
Stop, shift their loads, and pray, and fare
Forth with souls easier for the prayer.

The suns have branded black, the rains
   Striped gray this piteous God of theirs;
The face is full of prayers and pains,
   To which they bring their pains and prayers;
Lean limbs that shew the laboring bones,
And ghastly mouth that gapes and groans.

God of this grievous people, wrought
   After the likeness of their race,
By faces like thine own besought,
   Thine own blind helpless, eyeless face,
I too, that have nor tongue nor knee
For prayer, I have a word to thee.

It was for this then, that thy speech
   Was blown about the world in flame
And men's souls shot up out of reach
   Of fear or lust or thwarting shame—
That thy faith over souls should pass
As sea-winds burning the grey grass?

It was for this, that prayers like these
   Should spend themselves about thy feet,
And with hard overlabored knees
   Kneeling, these slaves of men should beat
Bosoms too lean to suckle sons
And fruitless as their orisons?

It was for this, that men should make
   Thy name a fetter on men's necks,
Poor men made poorer for thy sake,
   And women withered out of sex?
It was for this, that slaves should be,
Thy word was passed to set men free?

The nineteenth wave of the ages rolls
   Now deathward since thy death and birth.
Hast thou fed full men's starved-out souls?
   Hast thou brought freedom upon earth?
Or are there less oppressions done
In this wild world under the sun?

Nay, if indeed thou be not dead,
  Before thy terrene shrine be shaken,
Look down, turn usward, bow thine head;
  O thou that wast of God forsaken,
Look on thine household here, and see
These that have not forsaken thee.

Thy faith is fire upon their lips,
  Thy kingdom golden in their hands;
They scourge us with thy words for whips,
  They brand us with thy words for brands;
The thirst that made thy dry throat shrink
To their moist mouths commends the drink. . . .

O sacred head, O desecrate,
  O labor-wounded feet and hands,
O blood poured forth in pledge to fate
  Of nameless lives in divers lands,
O slain and spent and sacrificed
People, the grey-grown speechless Christ!

Is there a gospel in the red
  Old witness of thy wide-mouthed wounds?
From thy blind stricken tongueless head
  What desolate evangel sounds
A hopeless note of hope deferred?
What word, if there be any word?

O son of man, beneath man's feet
  Cast down, O common face of man
Whereon all blows and buffets meet,
  O royal, O republican
Face of the people bruised and dumb
And longing till thy kingdom come! . . .

The tree of faith ingraft by priests
  Puts its foul foliage out above thee,
And round it feed man-eating beasts
  Because of whom we dare not love thee;
Though hearts reach back and memories ache,
We cannot praise thee for their sake. . . .

Nay, if their God and thou be one,
   If thou and this thing be the same,
Thou shouldst not look upon the sun;
   The sun grows haggard at thy name.
Come down, be done with, cease, give o'er;
Hide thyself, strive not, be no more.

From the Bottom Up

by ALEXANDER IRVINE
Slum missionary and socialist agitator, 1863-1941

After some years' experience in missions and mission churches,
I would find it very hard if I were a workingman living in a tenement not to be antagonistic to them; for, in large measure, such
work is done on the assumption that people are poor and degraded
through laxity in morals. The scheme of salvation is a salvation
for the individual; social salvation is out of the question. Social
conditions cannot be touched, because in all rotten social conditions, there is a thin red line which always leads to the rich man
or woman who is responsible for them.

Coming in contact with these ugly social facts continuously,
led me to this belief. It came very slowly; as did also the opinion
that the missionary himself or the pastor, be he as wise as Solomon, as eloquent as Demosthenes, as virtuous as St. Francis, has
no social standing whatever among the people whose alms support
the institutions, religious and philanthropic, of which he is the
executive head. The fellowship of the saints is a pure fiction, has
absolutely no foundation in fact in a city like New York except
as the poor saints have it by themselves.

Tainted Wealth

by JOHANN WOLFGANG VON GOETHE

Capacious is the Church's belly;
Whole nations it has swallowed down,
Yet no dyspepsia 'neath its gown;
The Church alone, in jewels drest,
Your "tainted wealth" can quite digest.

The Collection

by ERNEST HOWARD CROSBY
American writer and social reformer, 1856-1907

I passed the plate in church.

There was little silver, but the crisp bank-notes heaped themselves up high before me;

And ever as the pile grew, the plate became warmer and warmer until it burned my fingers, and a smell of scorching flesh rose from it, and I perceived that some of the notes were beginning to smoulder and curl, half-browned, at the edges.

And then I saw thru the smoke into the very substance of the money, and I beheld what it really was;

I saw the stolen earnings of the poor, the wide margins of wages pared down to starvation;

I saw the underpaid factory girl eking out her living on the street, and the overworked child, and the suicide of the discharged miner;

I saw poisonous gases from great manufactories spreading disease and death; . . .

I saw hideousness extending itself from coal mine and foundry over forest and river and field;

I saw money grabbed from fellow grabbers and swindlers, and underneath them the workman forever spinning it out of his vitals. . . .

I saw all this, and the plate burned my fingers so that I had to hold it first in one hand and then in the other; and I was glad when the parson in his white robes took the smoking pile from me on the chancel steps and, turning about, lifted it up and laid it on the altar.

It was an old-time altar indeed, for it bore a burnt offering of flesh and blood—a sweet savor unto the Moloch whom these people worship with their daily round of human sacrifices.

The shambles are in the temple as of yore, and the tables of the money-changers, waiting to be overturned.

By EMILE DE LAVALAYE
Belgian economist, 1822-1892

If Christianity were taught and understood conformably to the spirit of its Founder, the existing social organism could not last a day.

The Voice of the Early Church

by CLEMENT OF ALEXANDRIA
Greek Church; 150-215

I know that God has given us the use of goods, but only as far as is necessary; and He has determined that the use be common. It is absurd and disgraceful for one to live magnificently and luxuriously when so many are hungry.

By TERTULLIAN
Earliest of the Latin fathers; 155-222

All is common with us except women. Jesus was our man, God and brother. He restored unto all men what cruel murderers took from them by the sword. Christians have no master and no Christian shall be bound for bread and raiment. The land is no man's inheritance; none shall possess it as property.

By ST. CYPRIAN
Latin; 200-258

No man shall be received into our commune who sayeth that the land may be sold. God's footstool is not property.

By ST. BASIL
Greek Church; 329-379

Which things, tell me, are yours? Whence have you brought your goods into life? You are like one occupying a place in a theatre, who should prohibit others from entering, treating that as his own which was designed for the common use of all. Such are the rich. Because they preoccupy common goods, they take these goods as their own. If each one would take that which is sufficient for his needs, leaving what is superfluous to those in distress, no one would be rich, no one poor. . . . The rich man is a thief.

By ST. AMBROSE
Latin; 340-397

How far, O rich, do you extend your senseless avarice? Do you intend to be the sole inhabitants of the earth? Why do you drive out the fellow sharers of nature, and claim it all for yourselves? The earth was made for all, rich and poor, in common. Why do you rich claim it as your exclusive right? The soil was given to the rich and poor in common—wherefore, oh, ye rich, do you unjustly claim it for yourselves alone? Nature gave all things in common for the use of all; usurpation created private rights. Property hath no rights. The earth is the Lord's, and we are his offspring. The pagans hold earth as property. They do blaspheme God.

By St. Jerome
Latin; 340-420

All riches come from iniquity, and unless one has lost, another cannot gain. Hence that common opinion seems to me to be very true, "the rich man is unjust, or the heir an unjust one." Opulence is always the result of theft, if not committed by the actual possessor, then by his predecessor.

By St. John Chrysostom
Greek Church; 347-407

Tell me, whence are you rich? From whom have you received? From your grandfather, you say; from your father. Are you able to show, ascending in the order of generation, that that possession is just throughout the whole series of preceding generations? Its beginning and root grew necessarily out of injustice. Why? Because God did not make this man rich and that man poor from the beginning. Nor, when He created the world, did He allot much treasure to one man, and forbid another to seek any. He gave the same earth to be cultivated by all. Since, therefore, His bounty is common, how comes it that you have so many fields, and your neighbor not even a clod of earth? . . . The idea we should have of the rich and covetous—they are truly as robbers, who, standing in the public highway, despoil the passers.

By St. Augustine
Latin; 354-430

The superfluities of the rich are the necessaries of the poor. They who possess superfluities, possess the goods of others.

By St. Gregory the Great
Latin; 540-604

They must be admonished who do not seek another's goods, yet do not give of their own, that they may know that the earth from which they have received is common to all men, and therefore its products are given in common to all. They, therefore, wrongly think they are innocent who claim for themselves the common gift of God. When they do not give what they have received, they assist in the death of neighbors, because daily almost as many of the poor perish as have been deprived of means which the rich have kept to themselves. When we give necessaries to the needy we do not bestow upon them our goods; we return to them their own; we pay a debt of justice rather than fulfill a work of mercy.

Preface to "Major Barbara"
by George Bernard Shaw

Churches are suffered to exist only on condition that they preach submission to the State as at present capitalistically organized. The Church of England itself is compelled to add to the thirty-six articles in which it formulates its religious tenets, three more in which it apologetically protests that the moment any of these articles comes in conflict with the State it is to be entirely renounced, abjured, violated, abrogated and abhorred, the policeman being a much more important person than any of the Persons of the Trinity. And this is why no tolerated Church nor Salvation Army can ever win the entire confidence of the poor. It must be on the side of the police and the military, no matter what it believes or disbelieves; and as the police and the military are the instruments by which the rich rob and oppress the poor (on legal and moral principles made for the purpose), it is not possible to be on the side of the poor and of the police at the same time. Indeed the religious bodies, as the almoners of the rich, become a sort of auxiliary police, taking off the insurrectionary edge of poverty with coals and blankets, bread and treacle, and soothing and cheering the victims with hopes of immense and inexpensive happiness in another world, when the process of working them to premature death in the service of the rich is complete in this.

Prince Hagen

by UPTON SINCLAIR

Prince Hagen, ruler of the Nibelungs, a race of gold-hoarding gnomes, comes up
to visit the land of the earth-men, and study Christian civilization.

Prince Hagen paused for a moment and puffed in silence; then
suddenly he remarked: "Do you know that it is a very wonderful
idea—that immortality? Did you ever think about it?"

"Yes," I said, "a little."

"I tell you, the man who got that up was a world-genius. When
I saw how it worked, it was something almost too much for me
to believe; and still I find myself wondering if it can last. For
you know if you can once get a man believing in immortality,
there is no more left for you to desire; you can take everything in
the world he owns—you can skin him alive if it pleases you—and
he will bear it all with perfect good humor. I tell you what, I lie
awake at night and dream about the chances of getting the Nibelungs to believe in immortality; I don't think I can manage it, but
it is a stake worth playing for. I say the phrases over to myself—
you know them all—'It is better to give than to receive'—'Lay not
up for yourself treasures on earth'—'Take no heed, saying what
shall ye eat!' As a matter of fact, I fancy the Nibelungs will prove
pretty tough at reforming, but it is worth any amount of labor.
Suppose I could ever get them to the self-renouncing point! Just
fancy the self-renunciation of a man with a seventy-mile tunnel
full of gold!"

Prince Hagen's eyes danced; his face was a study. I watched
him wonderingly. "Why do you go to all that bother?" I demanded,
suddenly. "If you want the gold, why don't you simply kill the
Nibelungs and take it?"

"I have thought of that," he replied; "I might easily manage it
all with a single revolver. But why should I kill the geese that lay
me golden eggs? I want not only the gold they have, but the gold
that they will dig through the centuries that are to come; for I
know that the resources of Nibelheim, if they could only be properly developed, would be simply infinite. So I have made up my
mind to civilize the people and develop their souls."

"Explain to me just how you expect to get their gold," I said.

"Just as the capitalist is getting it in New York," was the response. "At present the Nibelungs hide their wealth; I mean to
broaden their minds, and establish a system of credit. I mean to
teach them ideals of usefulness and service, to establish the arts

and sciences, to introduce machinery and all the modern improvements that tend to increase the centralization of power; I shall be master—just as I am here—because I am the strongest, and because I am not a dupe."

"I see," I said; "but all this will take a long time."

"Yes," said he, "I know; it is the whole course of history to be lived over again. But there will be no mistakes and no groping in this case, for I know the way, and I am king. It will be a sort of benevolent despotism—the ideal form of government, as I believe."

"And you are sure there is no chance of your plans failing?"

"Failing!" he laughed. "You should have seen how they have worked so far."

"You have begun applying them?"

"I have been down to Nibelheim twice since the death of dear grandpa," said the prince. "The first time, as you imagine, there was tremendous excitement, for all Nibelheim knew what a bad person I had been, and stood in terror of my return. I got them all together and told them the truth—that I had become wise and virtuous, that I meant to respect every man's property, and that I meant to consecrate my whole endeavor to the developing of the resources of my native land. And then you should have witnessed the scene! They went half wild with rejoicing; they fell down on their knees and thanked me with tears in their eyes: I played the *pater patriae* in a fashion to take away your breath. And afterwards I went on to explain to them that I had discovered very many wonderful things up on the earth; that I was going to make a law forbidding any of them to go there, because it was so dangerous, but that I myself was going to brave all the perils for their sakes. I told them about a wonderful animal that was called a steam-drill, and that ate fire, and dug out gold with swiftness beyond anything they could imagine. I said that I was going to empty all my royal treasure caves, and take my fortune and some of theirs to the earth to buy a few thousand of these wonderful creatures; and I promised them that I would give them to the Nibelungs to use, and they might have twice as much gold as they would have dug with their hands, provided they would give me the balance. Of course they agreed to it with shouts of delight, and the contracts were signed then and there. They helped me get out all my gold, and I took them down the steam-drills, and showed them how to manage them; so before very long I expect to have quite a snug little income."

Children of the Dead End
by PATRICK MACGILL

Nearly every second year the potatoes went bad; then we were always hungry, although Farley McKeown, a rich merchant in the neighboring village, let my father have a great many bags of Indian meal on credit. A bag contained sixteen stone of meal and cost a shilling a stone. On the bag of meal Farley McKeown charged sixpence a month interest; and fourpence a month on a sack of flour which cost twelve shillings. All the people round about were very honest, and paid up their debts when they were able. Usually when the young went off to Scotland or England they sent home money to their fathers and mothers, and with this money the parents paid for the meal to Farley McKeown. "What doesn't go to the landlord goes to Farley McKeown," was a Glenmornan saying.

The merchant was a great friend of the parish priest, who always told the people if they did not pay their debts they would burn for ever and ever in hell. "The fires of eternity will make you sorry for the debts that you did not pay," said the priest. "What is eternity?" he would ask in a solemn voice from the altar steps. "If a man tried to count the sands on the seashore and took a million years to count every single grain, how long would it take him to count them all? A long time, you'll say. But that time is nothing to eternity. Just think of it! Burning in hell while a man, taking a million years to count a grain of sand, counts all the sand on the seashore. And this because you did not pay Farley McKeown his lawful debts, his lawful debts within the letter of the law." That concluding phrase, "within the letter of the law," struck terror into all who listened, and no one, maybe not even the priest himself, knew what it meant.

The Priest and the Devil
by FEODOR DOSTOYEVSKY
Russian novelist who wrote this brief story upon the wall of his Siberian prison; 1821-1881

"Hello, you little fat father!" the devil said to the priest. "What made you lie so to those poor, misled people? What tortures of hell did you depict? Don't you know they are already suffering the tortures of hell in their earthly lives? Don't you know that you and the authorities of the State are my representatives on earth? It is you that make them suffer the pains of hell with which you threaten them. Don't you know this? Well, then, come with me!"

The devil grabbed the priest by the collar, lifted him high in the air, and carried him to a factory, to an iron foundry. He saw the workmen there running and hurrying to and fro, and toiling in the scorching heat. Very soon the thick, heavy air and the heat are too much for the priest. With tears in his eyes, he pleads with the devil: "Let me go! Let me leave this hell!"

"Oh, my dear friend, I must show you many more places." The devil gets hold of him again and drags him off to a farm. There he sees workmen threshing the grain. The dust and heat are insufferable. The overseer carries a knout, and unmercifully beats anyone who falls to the ground overcome by hard toil or hunger.

Next the priest is taken to the huts where these same workers live with their families—dirty, cold, smoky, ill-smelling holes. The devil grins. He points out the poverty and hardships which are at home here.

"Well, isn't this enough?" he asks. And it seems as if even he, the devil, pities the people. The pious servant of God can hardly bear it. With uplifted hands he begs: "Let me go away from here. Yes, yes! This is hell on earth!"

"Well, then, you see. And you still promise them another hell. You torment them, torture them to death mentally when they are already all but dead physically. Come on! I will show you one more hell—one more, the very worst."

He took him to a prison and showed him a dungeon, with its foul air and the many human forms, robbed of all health and energy, lying on the floor, covered with vermin that were devouring their poor, naked, emaciated bodies.

"Take off your silken clothes," said the devil to the priest, "put on your ankles heavy chains such as these poor unfortunates wear; lie down on the cold and filthy floor—and then talk to them about a hell that still awaits them!"

"No, no!" answered the priest, "I cannot think of anything more dreadful than this. I entreat you, let me go away from here!"

"Yes, this is hell. There can be no worse hell than this. Did you not know it? Did you not know that these men and women whom you are frightening with the picture of a hell hereafter—did you not know that they are in hell right here, before they die?"

Exit Salvatore

by CLEMENT WOOD
American writer, 1888-1950

Salvatore's dead—a gap
   Where he worked in the ditch-edge, shovelling mud;
Slanting brow; a head mayhap
   Rather small, like a bullet; hot southern blood;
Surly now, now riotous
   With the flow of his joy; and his hovel bare,
As his whole life is to us—
   A stone in his belly the whole of his share.

Body starved, but the soul secure,
   Masses to save it from Purgatory,
And to dwell with the Son and the Virgin pure—
      Lucky Salvatore!

Salvatore's glad, for see
   On the hearse and the coffin, purple and black,
Tassels, ribbons, broidery
   Fit for the Priest's or the Pope's own back;
Flowers costly, waxen gay,
   And the mates from the ditch-edge, pair after pair;
Dirging band, and the Priest to pray,
   And the soul of the dead one pleasuring there.

Body starved, and the mind as well.
   Peace—let him rot in his costly glory,
Cheated no more with a Heaven or Hell—
      Exit Salvatore.

FROM MICAH

Hear this, I pray you, ye heads of the house of Jacob, and rulers of the house of Israel, that abhor judgment, and pervert all equity. They build up Zion with blood, and Jerusalem with iniquity. The heads thereof judge for reward, and the priests thereof teach for hire, and the prophets divine for money. . . . Therefore shall Zion for your sake be plowed as a field, and Jerusalem shall become heaps, and the mountain of the house as the high places of a forest.

Work According to the Bible
by T. M. BONDAREFF
From a pamphlet written by T. M. Bondareff, a Siberian peasant and ex-serf, at
the age of sixty-seven

They often arrest thieves in the world; but these culprits are
rather rogues than thieves. I have laid hands on the real thief, who
has robbed God and the church. He has stolen the primal commandment which belongs to us who till the fields. I will point him
out. It is he who does not produce his bread with his own hands,
but eats the fruit of others' toil. Seize him and lead him away to
judgment. All crimes such as robberies, murders, frauds and the
like arise from the fact that this commandment is hidden from
man. The rich do all they can to avoid working with their hands,
and the poor to rid themselves of the necessity. The poor man says,
"There are people who can live on others' labor; why should not
I?" and he kills, steals and cheats in consequence. Behold now
what harm can be done by white hands, more than all that good
grimy hands can repair upon the earth! You spread out before
the laborer the idleness of your life, and thus take away the force
from his hands. Your way of living is for us the most cruel of
offenses, and a shame withal. You are a hundredfold more wise
and learned than I am, and for that reason you take my bread.
But because you are wise you ought rather to have pity on me who
am weak. It is said, "Love thy neighbor as thyself." I am your
neighbor, and you are mine. Why are we coarse and untaught?
Because we produce our own bread, and yours too! Have we any
time to study and educate ourselves? You have stolen our brains
as well as our bread by trickery and violence.

How blind thou art, O wise man; thou that readest the scrip-
tures, and seest not the way in which thou mightest free thyself,
and the flock committed to thee, from the burden of sin! Thy
blindness is like unto that of Balaam, who, astride his ass, saw
not the angel of God armed with a sword of fire standing in the
way before him. Thou art Balaam, I am the ass, and thou hast
ridden upon my back from childhood!

BY SAVONAROLA
Italian religious reformer, 1452-1498; hanged and burned by his enemies

But dost thou know what I would tell thee? In the primitive
church, the chalices were of wood, the prelates of gold. In these
days the church hath chalices of gold and prelates of wood.

Resurrection

by Leo Tolstoy

In this novel the greatest of modern religious teachers presented his indictment of the government and church of his country. The hero is a Russian prince who in early youth seduces a peasant girl, and in after life meets her, a prostitute on trial for murder. He follows her to Siberia, in an effort to reclaim her. Near the end of his story Tolstoy introduces this scene. The Englishman may be said to represent modern science, which asks questions and accumulates futile statistics; while the old man voices the peculiar Christian Anarchism of the author, who at the age of eighty-two left his home and wandered out into the steppes to die.

In one of the exiles' wards, Nehlúdof [the prince] recognized the strange old man he had seen crossing the ferry that morning. This tattered and wrinkled old man was sitting on the floor by the beds, barefooted, wearing only a dirty cinder-colored shirt, torn on one shoulder, and similar trousers. He looked severely and inquiringly at the newcomers. His emaciated body, visible through the holes in his dirty shirt, looked miserably weak, but in his face was more concentrated seriousness and animation than even when Nehlúdof saw him crossing the ferry. As in all the other wards, so here also the prisoners jumped up and stood erect when the official entered; but the old man remained sitting. His eyes glittered and his brow frowned wrathfully.

"Get up!" the inspector called out to him.

The old man did not rise, but only smiled contemptuously.

"Thy servants are standing before thee, I am not thy servant. Thou bearest the seal. . . ." said the old man, pointing to the inspector's forehead.

"Wha—a—t?" said the inspector threateningly, and made a step towards him.

"I know this man," said Nehlúdof. "What is he imprisoned for?"

"The police have sent him here because he has no passport. We ask them not to send such, but they will do it," said the inspector, casting an angry side glance at the old man.

"And so it seems thou, too, art one of Antichrist's army?" said the old man to Nehlúdof.

"No, I am a visitor," said Nehlúdof.

"What, hast thou come to see how Antichrist tortures men? Here, see. He has locked them up in a cage, a whole army of them. Men should eat bread in the sweat of their brow. But He has locked them up with no work to do, and feeds them like swine, so that they should turn into beasts."

"What is he saying?" asked the Englishman.

Nehlúdof told him the old man was blaming the inspector for keeping men imprisoned.

"Ask him how he thinks one should treat those who do not keep the laws," said the Englishman.

Nehlúdof translated the question.

The old man laughed strangely, showing his regular teeth.

"The laws?" he repeated with contempt. "First Antichrist robbed everybody, took all the earth, and all rights away from them—took them all for himself—killed all those who were against him—and then He wrote laws forbidding to rob and to kill. He should have written those laws sooner."

Nehlúdof translated. The Englishman smiled.

"Well, anyhow, ask him how one should treat thieves and murderers now?"

Nehlúdof again translated the question.

"Tell him he should take the seal of Antichrist off from himself," the old man said, frowning severely; "then he will know neither thieves nor murderers. Tell him so."

"He is crazy," said the Englishman, when Nehlúdof had translated the old man's words; and shrugging his shoulders he left the cell.

"Do thine own task and leave others alone. Every one for himself. God knows whom to execute, whom to pardon, but we do not know," said the old man. "Be your own chief, then chiefs will not be wanted. Go, go," he added, frowning angrily, and looking with glittering eyes at Nehlúdof, who lingered in the ward. "Hast thou not gazed enough on how the servants of Antichrist feed lice on men? Go! Go!"

By Isaiah

Hear the word of the Lord, ye rulers of Sodom; give ear unto the law of our God, ye people of Gomorrah. To what purpose is the multitude of your sacrifices unto me? saith the Lord.... Bring no more vain oblations.... When ye spread forth your hands, I will hide mine eyes from you; yea when ye make many prayers I will not hear; your hands are full of blood.

Sunday

by LOUIS UNTERMEYER
American poet and anthologist, 1885–1977

It was Sunday—
Eleven in the morning; people were at church—
Prayers were in the making; God was near at hand—
Down the cramped and narrow streets of quiet Lawrence
Came the tramp of workers marching in their hundreds;
Marching in the morning, marching to the graveyard,
Where, no longer fiery, underneath the grasses,
Callous and uncaring, lay their friend and sister.
In their hands they carried wreaths and drooping flowers,
Overhead their banners dipped and soared like eagles—
Aye, but eagles bleeding, stained with their own heart's blood—
Red, but not for glory—red, with wounds and travail,
Red, the buoyant symbol of the blood of all the world.
So they bore their banners, singing toward the graveyard,
So they marched and chanted, mingling tears and tributes,
So, with flowers, the dying went to deck the dead.

> Within the churches people heard
>   The sound, and much concern was theirs—
> God might not hear the Sacred Word—
>   God might not hear their prayers!

> *Should such things be allowed these slaves—*
>   *To vex the Sabbath peace with Song,*
> *To come with chants, like marching waves,*
>   *That proudly swept along.*

> *Suppose God turned to these—and heard!*
>   *Suppose He listened unawares—*
> *God might forget the Sacred Word,*
>   *God might forget their prayers!*

> And so (the tragic irony)
>   The blue-clad Guardians of the Peace
> Were sent to sweep them back—to see
>   The ribald Song should cease;

To scatter those who came and vexed
  God with their troubled cries and cares.
Quiet—so God might hear the text;
  The sleek and unctuous prayers!

Up the rapt and singing streets of little Lawrence
Came the stolid soldiers; and, behind the bluecoats,
Grinning and invisible, bearing unseen torches,
Rode red hordes of anger, sweeping all before them.
Lust and Evil joined them—Terror rode among them;
Fury fired its pistols; Madness stabbed and yelled.
Through the wild and bleeding streets of shuddering Lawrence,
Raged the heedless panic, hour-long and bitter.
Passion tore and trampled; men once mild and peaceful,
Fought with savage hatred in the name of Law and Order.
And, below the outcry, like the sea beneath the breakers,
Mingled with the anguish, rolled the solemn organ. . . .

Eleven in the morning—people were at church—
Prayers were in the making—God was near at hand—
It was Sunday!

The Preacher
(From "The Canterbury Tales")

by GEOFFREY CHAUCER
Early English poet, c. 1345-1400

Than peyne I me to strecche forth my necke,
And est and west upon the people I bekke,
As doth a pigeon, syttyng on a loft;
Myn hondes and my tonge move so oft,
That it is joye to see my busynesse.
Of avarice and of suche cursedness
Is al my preching, for to make hem free
To give their pence, and namely unto me. . . .

Therfor my theem is yit, and ever was,
The root of evils is cupidity.
Thus can I preche agayn the same vice
Which that I use, and that is avarice.
But though myself be gilty in the same,
Yit can I maken other folks to blame.

The Reluctant Briber

by LINCOLN STEFFENS

American journalist and reformer, 1866-1936. The president of a powerful public corporation has become disturbed in conscience, and calls in a student of social conditions.

"You're unhappy because you are bribing and corrupting, and you ask my advice. Why? I'm no ethical teacher. You're a churchman. Why don't you go to your pastor?"

"Pastor!" he exclaimed, and he laughed. The scorn of that laugh! "Pastor!"

He turned and walked away, to get control, no doubt. I kept after him.

"Yes," I insisted, "you should go to the head of your church for moral counsel, and—for economic advice you should go to the professor of economics in—"

He stopped me, facing about. "Professor!" he echoed, and he didn't reflect my tone.

I was serious. I wanted to get something from him. I wanted to know why our practical men do not go to these professions for help, as they go to lawyers and engineers. And this man had given time and money to the university in his town and to his church, as I reminded him.

"You support colleges and churches, you and your kind do," I said. "What for?"

"For women and children," he snapped from his distance.

Twentieth Century Socialism

by EDMOND KELLY

American lawyer and socialist, 1851-1909

It is inconceivable that the same civilization should include two bodies of men living in apparent harmony and yet holding such opposite and inconsistent views of man as economists on the one hand and theologians on the other. To these last, man has no economic needs; this world does not count; it is merely a place of probation, mitigated sometimes, it is true, by ecclesiastical pomp and episcopal palaces; but serving for the most part as a mere preparation for a future existence which will satisfy the aspirations of the human soul—the only thing that does count, in this world or the next. So while to the economist man is all hog, to the theologian he is all soul; and between the two the devil secures the vast majority.

The True Faith

by RABINDRANATH TAGORE

Hindu poet, Nobel Prize for Literature 1913; 1861-1941

Leave this chanting and singing and telling of beads! Whom dost thou worship in this lonely dark corner of a temple with doors all shut? Open thine eyes and see thy God is not before thee!

He is there where the tiller is tilling the hard ground and where the pathmaker is breaking stones. He is with them in sun and in shower, and his garment is covered with dust. Put off thy holy mantle and even like him come down on the dusty soil!

Deliverance? Where is this deliverance to be found? Our master himself has joyfully taken upon him the bonds of creation; he is bound with us all for ever.

Come out of thy meditations and leave aside thy flowers and incense! What harm is there if thy clothes become tattered and stained? Meet him and stand by him in toil and in sweat of thy brow.

Brotherhood

by ROBERT DE LAMMENAIS

French priest-philosopher, driven from Church position for his liberal views; 1782-1854

Your task is to form the universal family, to build the City of God, and by a continuous labor gradually to translate His work in Humanity into fact.

When you love one another as brothers, and treat each other reciprocally as such; when each one, seeking his own good in the good of all, shall identify his own life with the life of all, his own interests with the interests of all, and shall be always ready to sacrifice himself for all the members of the common family— then most of the ills which weigh upon the human race will vanish, as thick mists gathered upon the horizon vanish at the rising of the sun.

Priests

by James Oppenheim

Priests are in bad odor,
And yet there shall be no lack of them.
The skies shall not lack a spokesman,
Nor the spirit of man a voice and a gesture.

Not garbed nor churched,
Yet, as of old, in loneliness and anguish,
They shall come eating and drinking among us,
With scourge, pity, and prayer.

BOOK VIII

The Voice of the Ages

Records from all the past history of mankind, from twenty-five different societies, the earliest being about 3500 B.C.

The Temperate Soul
by PLATO

If the temperate soul is the good soul, the soul, which is in the opposite condition, that is, the foolish and intemperate, is the bad soul. And will not the temperate man do what is proper, both in relation to the gods and to men; for he would not be temperate if he did not? Certainly he will do what is proper.

In his relation to other men he will do what is just; and in his relation to the gods he will do what is holy; and he who does what is just and holy must be just and holy? Very true. And must he not be courageous? For the duty of a temperate man is not to follow or to avoid what he ought not, but what he ought, whether things or men or pleasures or pains, and patiently to endure when he ought; and therefore the temperate man, being, as we have described, also just and courageous and holy, cannot be other than a perfectly good man, nor can the good man do otherwise than well and perfectly whatever he does.

He who does well must of necessity be happy and blessed, and the evil man who does evil, miserable. And he who desires to be happy must pursue and practice temperance and run away from intemperance as fast as his legs will carry him: he had better order his life so as not to need punishment. If he or any of his friends, whether private individual or city, are in need of punishment, then justice must be done and he must suffer punishment, if he would be happy. This appears to me to be the aim which a man ought to have, and toward which he ought to direct all the energies both of himself and of the state, acting so that he may have temperance and justice present with him and be happy.

The Suppressions of History
by C. OSBORNE WARD
American historian, 1831-1903

The great strikes and uprisings of the working people of the ancient world are almost unknown to the living age. It matters little how accounts of five immense strike-wars, involving destruction of property and mutual slaughter of millions of people, have been suppressed, or have otherwise failed to reach us; the fact remains that people are absolutely ignorant of these great events. A meager sketch of Spartacus may be seen in the encyclopedias, but it is always ruined and its interest pinched and blighted by being classed with crime, its heroes with criminals, its theme with desecration. Yet Spartacus was one of the great generals of history; fully equal to Hannibal and Napoleon, while his cause was much more just and infinitely nobler, his life a model of the beautiful and virtuous, his death an episode of surpassing grandeur.

Still more strange is it, that the great ten-years' war of Eunus should be unknown. He marshalled at one time an army of two hundred thousand soldiers. He maneuvered them and fought for ten full years for liberty, defeating army after army of Rome. Why is the world ignorant of this fierce, epochal rebellion? Almost the whole matter is passed over in silence by our histories of Rome. In these pages it will be read as news, yet should a similar war rage in our day, against a similar condition of slavery, its cause would not only be considered just, but the combatants would have the sympathy and support of the civilized world.

The great system of labor organization explained in these pages must likewise be regarded as a chapter of news. The portentous fact has lain in abeyance century after century, with the human family in profound ignorance of an organization of trades and other labor unions so powerful that for hundreds of years they undertook and successfully conducted the business of manufacture, of distribution, of purveying provisions to armies, of feeding the inhabitants of the largest cities in the world, of inventing, supplying and working the huge engines of war, and of collecting customs and taxes—tasks confided to their care by the state.

Our civilization has a blushingly poor excuse for its profound ignorance of these facts; for the evidences have existed from much before the beginning of our era. . . . They are growing fewer and dimmer as their value rises higher in the estimation of a thinking, appreciative, gradually awakening world.

Agis

by PLUTARCH
Greek historian, A.D. 50-120

When the love of gold and silver had once gained admittance into the Lacedæmonian commonwealth, it was quickly followed by avarice and baseness of spirit in the pursuit of it, and by luxury, effeminacy and prodigality in the use. Then Sparta fell from almost all her former virtue and repute....

For the rich men without scruple drew the estate into their own hands, excluding the rightful heirs from their succession; and all the wealth being centered upon the few, the generality were poor and miserable. Honorable pursuits, for which there was no longer leisure, were neglected; the state was filled with sordid business, and with hatred and envy of the rich....

Agis, therefore, believing it a glorious action, as in truth it was, to equalize and repeople the state, began to sound the inclinations of the citizens. He found the young men disposed beyond his expectation; they were eager to enter with him upon the contest in the cause of virtue, and to fling aside, for freedom's sake, their old manner of life, as readily as the wrestler does his garment. But the old men, habituated and confirmed in their vices, were most of them alarmed. These men could not endure to hear Agis continually deploring the present state of Sparta, and wishing she might be restored to her ancient glory....

Agis, nevertheless, little regarding these rumors, took the first occasion of proposing his measure to the council, the chief articles of which were these: That every one should be free from their debts; all the lands to be divided into equal portions....

The people were transported with admiration of the young man's generosity, and with joy that, after three hundred years' interval, at last there had appeared a king worthy of Sparta. But, on the other side, Leonidas was now more than ever averse, being sensible that he and his friends would be obliged to contribute with their riches, and yet all the honor and obligation would redound to Agis. [Sparta had two kings, Leonidas and Agis.]

From this time forward, as the common people followed Agis, so the rich men adhered to Leonidas. They besought him not to forsake their cause; and with persuasions and entreaties so far prevailed with the council of Elders, whose power consisted in preparing all laws before they were proposed to the people, that the designed measure was rejected, though but by one vote.

[Attacked by his enemies, Agis sought refuge in a temple.] Leonidas proceeded also to displace the ephors, and to choose others in their stead; then he began to consider how he might entrap Agis. At first, he endeavored by fair means to persuade him to leave the sanctuary, and partake with him in the kingdom. The people, he said, would easily pardon the errors of a young man, ambitious of glory. But finding Agis was suspicious, and not to be prevailed with to quit his sanctuary, he gave up that design; yet what could not then be effected by the dissimulation of an enemy, was soon after brought to pass by the treachery of friends.

Amphares, Damochares, and Arcesilaus often visited Agis, and he was so confident of their fidelity that after a while he was prevailed on to accompany them to the baths, which were not far distant, they constantly returning to see him safe again in the temple. They were all three his familiars; and Amphares had borrowed a great deal of plate and rich household stuff from the mother of Agis, and hoped if he could destroy her and the whole family, he might peaceably enjoy those goods. And he, it is said, was the readiest of all to serve the purposes of Leonidas, and being one of the ephors, did all he could to incense the rest of his colleagues against Agis. These men, therefore, finding that Agis would not quit his sanctuary, but on occasion would venture from it to go to the bath, resolved to seize him on the opportunity thus given them. And one day as he was returning, they met and saluted him as formerly, conversing pleasantly by the way, and jesting, as youthful friends might, till coming to the turning of the street which led to the prison, Amphares, by virtue of his office, laid his hand on Agis, and told him, "You must go with me, Agis, before the other ephors, to answer for your misdemeanors." At the same time Damochares, who was a tall, strong man, drew his cloak tight around his neck, and dragged him after by it, whilst the others went behind to thrust him on. So that none of Agis' friends being near to assist him, nor any one by, they easily got him into the prison, where Leonidas was already arrived, with a company of soldiers, who strongly guarded all the avenues; the ephors also came in, with as many of the Elders as they knew to be true to their party, being desirous to proceed with some semblance of justice. And thus they bade him give an account of his actions. To which Agis, smiling at their dissimulation, answered not a word. Amphares told him it was more seasonable for him to weep, for now the time was come in which he should be punished for his presumption. Another of the ephors, as though he would be more favorable, and offering as it were an excuse, asked him whether he was not forced to what he did by Agesilaus and Lysander. But Agis answered, he had not been constrained by any man, nor had any other intent in what he did but to follow the example of Lycurgus, and to govern conformably to his laws. The same ephor asked him whether now at least he did not repent his rashness. To which the young man answered that though he were to suffer the extremest penalty for it, yet he could never repent of so just and glorious a design. Upon this they passed sentence of death on him, and bade the officers carry him to the Dechas, as it is called, a place in the prison where they strangle malefactors. And when the officers would not venture to lay hands on him, and the very mercenary soldiers declined it, believing it an illegal and a wicked act to lay violent hands on a king, Damochares, threatening and reviling them for it, himself thrust him into the room.

For by this time the news of his being seized had reached many parts of the city, and there was a concourse of people with lights and torches about the prison gates, and in the midst of them the mother and the grandmother of Agis, crying out with a loud voice that their king ought to appear, and to be heard and judged by the people. But this clamor, instead of preventing, hastened his death; his enemies fearing, if the tumult should increase, he might be rescued during the night out of their hands.

Agis, being now at the point to die, perceived one of the officers bitterly bewailing his misfortune. "Weep not, friend," said he, "for me, who die innocent, by the lawless act of wicked men. My condition is much better than theirs." As soon as he had spoken these words, not showing the least sign of fear, he offered his neck to the noose.

The Labor Problem in Egypt
(*From the Book of Exodus*)

Pharaoh said, "Who is the Lord, that I should hearken unto his voice to let Israel go? I know not the Lord, and moreover I will not let Israel go.... Wherefore do ye, Moses and Aaron, loose the people from their work? get you unto your burdens. ... Let heavier work be laid upon the men, that they may labor therein; and let them not regard lying words.... Ye are idle, ye are idle; therefore ye say, Let us go and sacrifice to the Lord. Go therefore now, and work; for there shall no straw be given you, yet shall ye deliver the tale of bricks."

And the officers of the children of Israel did see that they were in evil case, when it was said, "Ye shall not minish aught from your bricks, your daily task."

And they met Moses and Aaron, who stood in the way, as they came forth from Pharaoh: and they said unto them, "The Lord look upon you and judge; because you have made our savour to be abhorred in the eyes of Pharaoh, and in the eyes of his servants, to put a sword in their hand to slay us."

And Moses returned unto the Lord, and said, "Lord, wherefore hast thou evil entreated this people? Why is it that thou hast sent me? For since I came to Pharaoh to speak in thy name, he hath evil entreated this people; neither hast thou delivered thy people at all."

Then the Lord said unto Moses, "Now shalt thou see what I will do to Pharaoh: for with a strong hand shall he let them go, and with a strong hand shall he drive them out of his land."

The People

by TOMMASO CAMPANELLA
Italian philosopher, 1568-1639; translation by John Addington Symonds

The people is a beast of muddy brain
That knows not its own strength, and therefore stands
Loaded with wood and stone; the powerless hands
Of a mere child guide it with bit and rein;
One kick would be enough to break the chain,
But the beast fears, and what the child demands
It does; nor its own terror understands,
Confused and stupefied by bugbears vain.
Most wonderful! With its own hand it ties
And gags itself—gives itself death and war
For pence doled out by kings from its own store.
Its own are all things between earth and heaven;
But this it knows not; and if one arise
To tell this truth, it kills him unforgiven.

Tiberius Gracchus
by PLUTARCH

Tiberius, maintaining an honorable and just cause, and possessed of eloquence sufficient to have made a less creditable action appear plausible, was no safe or easy antagonist, when, with the people crowding around the hustings, he took his place and spoke in behalf of the poor. "The savage beasts," said he, "in Italy, have their particular dens, they have their places of repose and refuge; but the men who bear arms, and expose their lives for the safety of their country, enjoy in the meantime nothing in it but the air and light; and, having no houses or settlements of their own, are constrained to wander from place to place with their wives and children." He told them that the commanders were guilty of a ridiculous error, when, at the head of their armies, they exhorted the common soldiers to fight for their sepulchers and altars; when not any amongst so many Romans is possessed of either altar or monument, neither have they any houses of their own, or hearths of their ancestors to defend. They fought indeed and were slain, but it was to maintain the luxury and the wealth of other men. They were styled the masters of the world, but had not one foot of ground they could call their own.

Seeking Causes
by PLATO
Greek philosopher, c.427-347 B.C.

Neither drugs nor charms nor burnings will touch a deep-lying political sore any more than a deep bodily one; but only right and utter change of constitution; and they do but lose their labor who think that by any tricks of law they can get the better of those mischiefs of commerce, and see not that they hew at a hydra.

The Promise
From the Psalms

The Lord shall deliver the needy when he crieth; the poor also, and him that hath no helper. He shall spare the poor and needy, and shall save the souls of the needy. He shall redeem their soul from deceit and violence; and precious shall their blood be in his sight.

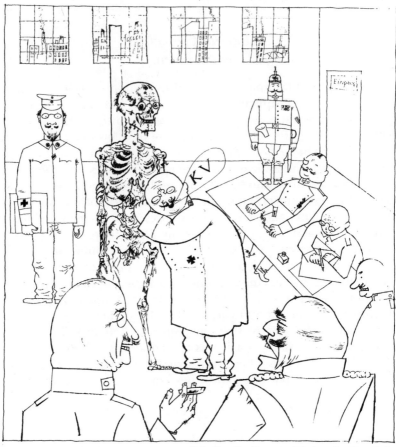

Fit for Active Service, *George Grosz*

Captive Good Attending Captain Ill
by EURIPIDES
Athenian tragic poet and dramatist, c.484-407 B.C.

Doth some one say that there be gods above?
There are not; no, there are not. Let no fool,
Led by the old false fable, thus deceive you.
Look at the facts themselves, yielding my words
No undue credence; for I say that kings
Kill, rob, break oaths, lay cities waste by fraud,
And doing thus are happier than those
Who live calm pious lives day after day.
How many little states that serve the gods
Are subject to the godless but more strong,
Made slaves by might of a superior army!

The Co-operative Commonwealth
by ISAIAH II
Prophet of the Exile, 550 B.C.

And they shall build houses, and inhabit them; and they shall plant vineyards, and eat the fruit of them. They shall not build, and another inhabit; they shall not plant, and another eat; for as the days of a tree are the days of my people, and mine elect shall long enjoy the work of their hands.

Poverty
by ALCAEUS
Greek lyric poet, 611-580 B.C.

The worst of ills, and hardest to endure,
　　Past hope, past cure,
Is Penury, who, with her sister-mate
Disorder, soon brings down the loftiest state,
　　And makes it desolate.
This truth the sage of Sparta told,
　　Aristodemus old,—
"Wealth makes the man." On him that's poor
Proud Worth looks down, and Honor shuts the door.

The Beggar's Complaint
Ancient Japanese classic

The heaven and earth they call so great,
    For me are very small;
The sun and moon they call so bright,
    For me ne'er shine at all.

Are all men sad, or only I?
    And what have I obtained—
What good the gift of mortal life,
    That prize so rarely gained—

If nought my chilly back protects
    But one thin grass-cloth coat,
In tatters hanging like the weeds
    That on the billows float?

If here in smoke-stained, darksome hut,
    Upon the bare cold ground,
I make my wretched bed of straw,
    And hear the mournful sound—

Hear how mine aged parents groan,
    And wife and children cry,
Father and mother, children, wife,
    Huddling in misery—

If in the rice-pan, nigh forgot,
    The spider hangs its nest,
And from the hearth no smoke goes up
    Where all is so unblest?

Shame and despair are mine from day to day,
But, being no bird, I cannot fly away.

Free Labor
by HAGGAI
Hebrew prophet, 515 B.C.

He that earneth wages earneth wages to put it into a bag
with holes.

The Lawyer and the Farmer

Egyptian; 1400 B.C. or earlier. A letter from a father to his son, exhorting him to stick to the study of his profession.

It is told to me that thou has cast aside learning, and givest thyself to dancing; thou turnest thy face to the work in the fields, and castest the divine words behind thee.

Behold, thou rememberest not the condition of the fellah (farmer) when the harvest is taken over. The worms carry off half the corn, and the hippopotamus devours the rest; mice abound in the fields, and locusts arrive; the cattle devour, the sparrows steal. How miserable is the lot of the fellah! What remains on the threshing-floor, robbers finish it it up. The bronzes ...are worn out, the horses die with threshing and plowing. Then the scribe (lawyer) moors at the bank, who is to take over the harvest for the government; the attendants bear staves, the Negroes carry palm sticks. They say, "Give corn!" But there is none. They beat the fellah prostrate;. they bind him and cast him into the canal, throwing him headlong. His wife is bound before him, his children are swung off; his neighbors let them go, and flee to look after their corn.

But the scribe is the leader of labor for all; he reckons to himself the produce in winter, and there is none that appoints him his tale of produce. Behold, now thou knowest!

Farmer and Lawyer Again

by WILLIAM LANGLAND

English poet, c.1332-c.1400. This work, generally attributed in its entirety to Langland, is one of the earliest of English social protests in literary form.

Some were for ploughing, and played full seldom,
Set their seed and sowed their seed and sweated hard,
To win what wastrels with gluttony destroy....
There wandered a hundred in hoods of silk,
Serjeants they seemed, and served at the Bar,
Pleading the Law for pennies and for pounds,
Unlocking their lips never for love of our Lord.
Thou mightest better mete the mist on Malvern hills
Than get a mutter from their mouths—save thou show thy
    money!

Plutus

by ARISTOPHANES

Greek writer of satiric comedy, c.448-385 B.C. In this scene Chremylus and
Blepsidemus, two citizens, have taken in charge Plutus, the god of wealth,
who is blind. They have undertaken to cure him of his blindness; but
Poverty, an old hag, appears, protesting their success would be a calamity
for humanity.

CHREMYLUS: As matters now stand (who will dare contradict it?)
the life of us men is compos'd

Of a system where folly, absurdity, madness, ay, raving down-
right is disclosed;

Since, how many a knave we see revel in wealth—the rich heap
of his ill-gotten store—

And how many a good man, by fortune unblest, with thee
begging bread at the door! (*Turns to Poverty.*)

I say, then, there is but one thing to be done, and if we succeed, what a prize

Will we bring to mankind! That thing it will be—to give
Plutus the use of his eyes.

POVERTY: A pest on your prate, and palavering stuff! back! begone
with ye, blockheads, to school!

You pair of old dotards, you drivelling comrades in trifling
and playing the fool!

If the plan ye propose be accomplish'd at last nothing worse
could mankind e'er befall,

Than that Plutus should have the full use of his eyes, and
bestow himself equal on all!

See you not, that at once, to all arts there would be, to each
craft that you reckon, an end?

If these were exploded (so much to your joy), say who *then*
should there be, who would lend

To the forge, to the hammer, the adze or the loom—to the
rule or the mallet—his hand?

Not a soul! The mechanic, the carpenter, shipwright—would
all be expelled from the land.

Where would tailor, or cobbler, or dyer of leather, or brick-
lay'r, or tanner be found?

Who would e'er condescend in this golden vacation, to till for
his bread's sake, the ground?

BLEPSIDEMUS: Hold, hold, jade! Whatever essentials of life in your catalogue's column you string,
Our servants, of course, shall provide us.

POVERTY: Your servants? and whence do you think *they* shall spring?

BLEPSIDEMUS: We shall buy them with cash—

POVERTY: But with cash all the world as well as yourself is supplied!
Who will care about selling?

BLEPSIDEMUS: Some dealer, no doubt, coming down from the Thessaly side,
(A rare kidnapping nest) who may wish to secure a good bargain to profit the trade.

POVERTY (*impatiently*): You will not understand! In the lots of mankind when this grand revolution is made
'Twill at once put an end to all wants—and of course then, the kidnapper's business will cease:
For who will court danger, and hazard his life, when, grown rich, he may live at his ease?
Thus each for himself will be forced to turn plowman, to dig and to delve and to sweat;
Wearing out an existence more grievous by far than he ever experienced yet.

CHREMYLUS: Curses on you!

POVERTY: You'll not have a bed to lie down on—no goods of the sort will be seen!
Not a carpet to tread on—for who, pray, will weave one, when well stock'd his coffers have been?
Farewell to your essences, perfumes, pastilles! When you lead to the altar your bride
Farewell to your roseate veil's drooping folds, the bright hues of its glittering pride!
Yet forsooth "to be rich"—say what is it, without all these gewgaws to swell the detail?
Now with me, every item that wish can suggest springs abundant and never can fail;

For who, but myself, urges on to his toil, like a mistress, and
    drives the mechanic?
If he flags, I but show him my face at the door, and he hies to
    his work in a panic!

CHREMYLUS: Pshaw! What good can *you* bring but sores, blisters
    and blains, on the wretch as he shivering goes
From the baths' genial clime driv'n forth to the cold, at the
    certain expense of his toes?
What, but poor little urchins, whose stomachs are craving,
    and little old beldames in shoals;
And lice by the thousand, mosquitoes and flies? (I can't count
    you the cloud as it rolls!)
Which keep humming and buzzing about one, a language
    denying the respite of sleep,
In a strain thus consoling—"Poor starveling, awake, tho to
    hunger!"—yet up you must leap!
Add to this, that you treat us with rags to our backs and a
    bundle of straw for a bed
(Woe betide the poor wretch on whose carcass the bugs of
    that ravenous pallet have fed!)
For a carpet, a rotten old mat—for a pillow, a great stone
    picked out of the street—
And for porridge, or bread, a mere leaf of radish, or stem of
    a mallow, to eat.
The head that remains of some wreck of a pitcher, by way of
    a seat you provide;
For the trough we make use of in kneading, we're driven to
    shift with a wine barrel's side,—
And this, too, all broken and split:—in a word, your magnifi-
    cent gifts to conclude,
(*Ironically*) To mankind you indeed are a blessed dispenser
    of mighty and manifold good!...
On my word, dame, your fav'rites are happily off, after striving
    and toiling to save,
If at last they are able to levy enough to procure them a
    cheque to the grave!

The Muckraker in Persia
by NIZAMI
Persian poet, A.D. 1200

There was a king who oppressed his subjects. An informer came to him, and said, "A certain old man has in private called thee a tyrant, a disturber, and bloodthirsty." The king, enraged, said, "Even now I put him to death." While the king made preparations for the execution, a youth ran to the old man, and said, "The king is ill-disposed to thee; hasten to assuage his wrath." The sage performed his ablutions, took his shroud, and went to the king. The tyrant, seeing him, clapped his hands together, and with eye hungry for revenge, cried, "I hear thou hast given loose to thy speech; thou hast called me revengeful, an oppressive demon." The sage replied, "I have said worse of thee than what thou repeatest. Old and young are in peril from thy action; town and village are injured by thy ministry. Apply thy understanding, and see if it be true; if it be not, slay me on a gibbet. I am holding a mirror before thee; when it shows thy blemishes truly, it is a folly to break the mirror. Break thyself!"

The king saw the rectitude of the sage, and his own crookedness. He said, "Remove his burial spices, and his shroud; bring to him sweet perfumes, and the robe of honor." He became a just prince, cherishing his subjects. Bring forward thy rough truth; truth from thee is victory; it shall shine as a pearl.

The System
by JEREMIAH
Hebrew prophet, 630 B.C.

For among my people are found wicked men; they lay wait, as he that setteth snares; they set a trap, they catch men. As a cage is full of birds, so are their houses full of deceit; therefore they are become great, and waxen rich. They are waxen fat, they shine; yea, they overpass the deeds of the wicked; they judge not the cause, the cause of the fatherless, yet they prosper; and the right of the needy do they not judge. Shall I not visit them for these things? saith the Lord; shall not my soul be avenged on such a nation as this? A wonderful and horrible thing is committed in the land; the prophets prophesy falsely, and the priests bear rule by their means; and my people love to have it so; and what will ye do in the end thereof?

Ladies of Fashion
by ISAIAH

The Lord standeth up to plead, and standeth to judge the people. The Lord will enter into judgment with the ancients of his people, and the princes thereof; for ye have eaten up the vineyard; the spoil of the poor is in your houses. What mean ye that ye beat my people to pieces, and grind the faces of the poor? saith the Lord God of Hosts. Moreover the Lord saith, Because the daughters of Zion are haughty, and walk with stretched forth necks and wanton eyes, walking and mincing as they go, and making a tinkling with their feet; therefore the Lord will smite with a scab the crown of the head of the daughters of Zion, and the Lord will discover their secret parts. In that day the Lord will take away the bravery of their tinkling ornaments about their feet, and their cauls, and their round tires like the moon, the chains, and the bracelets, and the mufflers, the bonnets, and the ornaments of the legs, and the headbands, and the tablets, and the earrings, the rings, and nose jewels, the changeable suits of apparel, and the mantles, and the wimples, and the crisping pins, the glasses, and the fine linen, and the hoods, and the veils. And it shall come to pass that instead of sweet smell there shall be stink; and instead of a girdle a rent; and instead of well set hair, baldness; and instead of a stomacher a girding of sackcloth; and burning instead of beauty. Thy men shall fall by the sword, and thy mighty in the war. And her gates shall lament and mourn; and she being desolate shall sit upon the ground.

By JEAN-JACQUES ROUSSEAU
French philosopher and novelist, 1712-1778

The first man who, having enclosed a piece of ground, bethought himself of saying, *This is mine,* and found people simple enough to believe him, was the real founder of civil society. From how many crimes, wars and murders, from how many horrors and misfortunes might not any one have saved mankind, by pulling up the stakes, or filling up the ditch, and crying to his fellows, "Beware of listening to this impostor; you are undone if you once forget that the fruits of the earth belong to us all, and the earth itself to nobody."

Grafters in Athens
by ARISTOPHANES

Keep silence—keep peace—and let all the profane
  From our holy solemnity duly refrain;
Whose souls unenlightened by taste, are obscure;
Whose poetical notions are dark and impure;
  Whose theatrical conscience
  Is sullied by nonsense;
Who never were train'd by the mighty Cratinus
In mystical orgies poetic and vinous;
Who delight in buffooning and jests out of season;
Who promote the designs of oppression and treason;
Who foster sedition, and strife, and debate;
All traitors, in short, to the stage and the state;
Who surrender a fort, or in private, export
To places and harbors of hostile resort,
Clandestine consignments of cables and pitch;
In the way the Thorycion grew to be rich
From a scoundrelly dirty collector of tribute!
All such we reject and severely prohibit:
All statesmen retrenching the fees and the salaries
Of theatrical bards, in revenge for the railleries,
And jests, and lampoons, of this holy solemnity,
Profanely pursuing their personal enmity,
For having been flouted, and scoff'd, and scorn'd,
All such are admonish'd and heartily warn'd!
  We warn them once,
  We warn them twice,
  We warn and admonish—we warn them thrice,
To conform to the law,
To retire and withdraw—
While the Chorus again with the formal saw
(Fixt and assign'd to the festive day)
Move to the measure and march away!

Pure Food Agitation
by Martin Luther
German religious reformer, 1483-1564

They have learned the trick of placing such commodities as pepper, ginger, saffron, in damp vaults or cellars in order to increase the weight. . . . Nor is there a single article of trade whatever out of which they cannot make unfair profit by false measuring, counting or weighing. They produce artificial colors, or they put the pretty things at the top and bottom and the ugly ones in the middle; and indeed there is no end to their trickery, and no one tradesman will trust another, for they know each other's ways.

The Agitator
by Isaiah
Hebrew prophet, c.740 B.C.

For Zion's sake will I not hold my peace,
And for Jerusalem's sake will I not rest,
Until the righteousness thereof go forth as brightness,
And the salvation thereof as a lamp that burneth.
Upon thy walls, O Jerusalem, have I set watchmen,
Who shall never hold their peace, day and night.
Go through, go through the gates;
Prepare ye the way of the people!
Lift up a standard to the peoples!

Wall Street
by Habakkuk
Hebrew prophet, 600 B.C.

They take up all of them with the angle, they catch them in their net, and gather them in their drag; therefore they sacrifice unto their nets, and burn incense unto their drags; because by them their portion is fat, and their meat plenteous.

By Martial
Latin poet, A.D. 43-104

If you are a poor man now, Aemilianus, a poor man you will always be. Nowadays, riches are bestowed on no one but the rich.

By Cato, the Censor
Latin, 234-149 B.C.

Small thieves lie in towers fastened to wooden blocks; big ones strut about in gold and silver.

Prosperity
(From the Book of Job)

Thou hast taken pledges of thy brother for nought, and stripped the naked of their clothing. Thou hast not given water to the weary to drink, and thou hast withholden bread from the hungry. But as for the mighty man, he had the earth; and the honourable man, he dwelt in it. Thou hast sent widows away empty, and the arms of the fatherless have been broken.

The Leading Citizen
by Horace
Latin poet, 65-8 B.C.: translation by John Milton

Whom do we count a good man? Whom but he
Who keeps the laws and statutes of the senate,
Who judges in great suits and controversies,
Whose witness and opinion wins the cause?
But his own house, and the whole neighborhood,
Sees his foul inside through his whited skin.

Hong's Experiences in Hades
by Im Bang
Korean poet, 1640-1722

The next hell had inscribed on it, "Deceivers." I saw in it many scores of people, with ogres that cut the flesh from their bodies, and fed it to starving demons. These ate and ate, and the flesh was cut and cut till only the bones remained. When the winds of hell blew, then flesh returned to them; then metal snakes and copper dogs crowded in to bite them and suck their blood. Their screams of pain made the earth tremble. The guides said to me, "When these offenders were on earth they held high office, and while they pretended to be true and good they received bribes in secret and were doers of all evil. As Ministers of State they ate the fat of the land and sucked the blood of the people, and yet advertised themselves as benefactors and were highly applauded. While in reality they lived as thieves, they pretended to be holy, as Confucius and Mencius were holy. They were deceivers of the world, and robbers, and so are punished thus."

Monopolies
by MARTIN LUTHER

Before all, if the princes and lords wish to fulfill the duties of their office they must prohibit and banish the vicious system of monopolies, which is altogether unendurable in town or country. As for the trading companies, they are thoroughly corrupt and made up of great injustices. They have every sort of commodity in their own power and they do with them just as they please, raise or lower the prices at their own convenience and crush and ruin all the small shop people—just as the pike does with the small fish in the water—as if they were lords over God's creatures and exempt from all laws of authority and religion. . . . How can it be godly and just that in so short a time a man should grow so rich that he can outbid kings and emperors? They have brought things to such a pass that all the rest of the world must carry on business with risk and damage, gaining today, losing tomorrow, while they continually grow richer and richer, and make up for their losses by higher profits; so it is no wonder that they are appropriating to themselves the riches of the whole world.

Intemperate Speech
(From the Epistle of James)
A.D. 100-120

Go to now, ye rich men, weep and howl for your miseries that shall come upon you. Your riches are corrupted, and your garments are moth-eaten. Your gold and silver are cankered; and the rust of them shall be a witness against you, and shall eat your flesh as it were fire. Ye have heaped treasures together for the last days. Behold, the hire of the laborers who have reaped down your fields, which is of you kept back by fraud, crieth: and the cries of them which have reaped are entered into the ears of the Lord of Sabaoth. Ye have lived in pleasure on the earth, and been wanton; ye have nourished your hearts, as in a day of slaughter. Ye have condemned and killed the just: and he doth not resist you. Be patient, therefore, brethren, unto the coming of the Lord. Behold, the husbandman waiteth for the precious fruit of the earth, and hath long patience for it, until he receive the early and latter rain. Be ye also patient; stablish your hearts; for the coming of the Lord draweth nigh.

Government
by MARCUS AURELIUS
Roman emperor and philosopher, A.D. 121-180

And these your professed politicians, the only true practical philosophers of the world (as they think themselves) so full of affected gravity, or such professed lovers of virtue and honesty, what wretches be they in very deed; how vile and contemptible in themselves! O man, what ado dost thou make!

The Parable of the Hungry Dog
(From the Gospel of Buddha)
Hindu Bible, 600 B.C.

There was a wicked tyrant; and the god Indra, assuming the shape of a hunter, came down upon earth with the demon Matali, the latter appearing as a dog of enormous size. Hunter and dog entered the palace, and the dog howled so woefully that the royal buildings shook with the sound to their very foundations. The tyrant had the awe-inspiring hunter brought before his throne and inquired after the cause of the terrible bark. The hunter said, "The dog is hungry," whereupon the frightened king ordered food for him. All the food prepared at the royal banquet disappeared rapidly in the dog's jaws, and still he howled with portentous significance. More food was sent for, and the royal storehouses were emptied, but in vain. Then the tyrant grew desperate and asked: "Will nothing satisfy the cravings of that woeful beast?" "Nothing," replied the hunter, "nothing except perhaps the flesh of all his enemies." "And who are his enemies?" anxiously asked the tyrant. The hunter replied: "The dog will howl as long as there are people hungry in the kingdom, and his enemies are those that practice injustice and oppress the poor." The oppressor of the people, remembering his evil deeds, was seized with remorse, and for the first time in his life he began to listen to the teachings of righteousness.

Murder by Statute
(From "The Sayings of Mencius")
Chinese classic, 300 B.C.

King Hwuy of Leang said, "I wish quietly to receive your instructions." Mencius replied, "Is there any difference between killing a man with a stick, and with a sword?" "There is not," was the answer.

Mencius continued, "Is there any difference between doing it with a sword and with government measures?" "There is not," was the answer again.

Mencius then said, "In your stalls there are fat beasts; in your stables there are fat horses. But your people have the look of hunger, and in the fields are those who have died of famine. This is leading on beasts to devour men. Beasts devour one another, and men hate them for doing so. When he who is called the parent of the people conducts his government so as to be chargeable with leading on beasts to devour men, where is that parental relation to the people?"

Rebuking a Tyrant
by SADI
Persian poet, c.1184-1291

In a certain year I was sitting retired in the great mosque at Damascus, at the head of the tomb of Yahiya the prophet (on whom be peace!). One of the kings of Arabia, who was notorious for his injustice, happened to come on a pilgrimage, and having performed his devotions, he uttered the following words: "The poor and the rich are servants of this earth, and those who are richest have the greatest wants." He then looked towards me, and said, "Because dervishes are strenuous and sincere in their commerce with heaven, unite your prayers with mine, for I am in dread of a powerful enemy."

I replied, "Show mercy to the weak peasant, that you may not experience difficulty from a strong enemy. It is criminal to crush the poor and defenceless subjects with the arm of power. He liveth in dread who befriendeth not the poor; for should his foot slip, no one layeth hold of his hand. Whosoever soweth bad seed, and looketh for good fruit, tortureth his imagination in vain, making a false judgment of things. Take the cotton out of thine ear, and distribute justice to mankind; for if thou refusest justice, there will be a day of retribution.

"The children of Adam are limbs of one another, and are all produced from the same substance; when the world gives pain to one member, the others also suffer uneasiness. Thou who are indifferent to the sufferings of others deservest not to be called a man."

The Eloquent Peasant
Egyptian, 2000 B.C. or earlier

An interesting primitive protest against injustice is the story of the Eloquent Peasant, which was one of the most popular of ancient Egyptian tales, and is found in scores of different papyri. The story narrates how a peasant named Rensi was robbed of his asses by the henchmen of a certain grand steward. In spite of all threats the peasant persisted in appealing against the robber to the grand steward himself. The scene is described in "Social Forces and Religion in Ancient Egypt," by James Henry Breasted, as follows:

"It is a tableau which epitomizes ages of social history in the East: on the one hand, the brilliant group of the great man's sleek and subservient suite, the universal type of the official class; and, on the other, the friendless and forlorn figure of the despoiled peasant, the pathetic personification of the cry for social justice. This scene is one of the earliest examples of that Oriental skill in setting forth abstract principles, so wonderfully illustrated later in the parables of Jesus. Seeing that the grand steward makes no reply, the peasant makes another effort to save his family and himself from the starvation which threatens them. He steps forward and with amazing eloquence addresses the great man in whose hands his case now rests, promising him a fair voyage as he embarks on the canal, and voicing the fame of the grand steward's benevolence, on which he had reckoned. 'For thou art the father of the orphan, the husband of the widow, the brother of the forsaken, the kilt of the motherless. Let me put thy name in this land above every good law, O leader free from avarice, great man free from littleness, who destroys falsehood and brings about truth. Respond to the cry which my mouth utters; when I speak, hear thou. Do justice, thou who art praised, whom the praised praise. Relieve my misery. Behold me, I am heavy laden; prove me, lo I am in sorrow.' "

To follow the account of the incident in other records, the grand steward is so much pleased with the peasant's eloquence that he goes to the king and tells him about it. "My Lord, I have found one of these peasants, excellent of speech, in very truth; stolen are his goods, and he has come to complain to me of the matter."

His majesty says, "As thou wishest that I may see health, lengthen out his complaint, without reply to any of his speeches! He who desireth him to continue speaking should be silent; behold, bring us his words in writing that we may listen to them."

So he keeps the peasant pleading for many days. The story quotes nine separate speeches, of constantly increasing bitterness and pathos. The peasant is beaten by the servants of the grand steward, but still he comes. "Thou art appointed to hear causes, to judge two litigants, to ward off the robber. But thou makest common cause with the thief. . . . Thou art instructed, thou art educated, thou art taught—but not for robbery. Thou art accustomed to do like all men, and thy kin are likewise ensnared. Thou the rectitude of all men, art the chief transgressor of the whole land. The gardener of evil waters his domain with iniquity that his domain may bring forth falsehood, in order to flood the estate with wickedness."

In spite of his eloquence, the grand steward remains unmoved. The peasant appeals to the gods of Justice; and in the ninth address he threatens to make his plea to the god Anubis, who is the god of the dead—meaning thereby that he will commit suicide. None of the extant papyri informs us as to the outcome of the whole proceedings.

Prayers Without Answer
(From "The Iliad")
by HOMER
Greek epic poet, c.850 B.C.

Prayers are Jove's daughters of celestial race,
Lame are their feet, and wrinkled is their face;
With homely mien and with dejected eyes,
Constant they follow where injustice flies.
Injustice, suave, erect, and unconfined,
Sweeps the wide earth, and tramples o'er mankind—
While prayers to heal her wrongs move slow behind.

The Suffering of Women
by HERBERT SPENCER
British philosopher, 1820-1903

In the history of humanity as written, the saddest part concerns the treatment of women; and had we before us its unwritten history we should find this part still sadder. I say the saddest part because there have been many things more conspicuously dreadful—cannibalism, the torturing of prisoners, the sacrifice of victims to ghosts and gods—these have been but occasionally; whereas the brutal treatment of woman has been universal and constant. If looking first at their state of subjection among the semi-civilized we pass to the uncivilized, and observe the lives of hardship borne by nearly all of them; if we then think what must have gone on among those still ruder peoples who, for so many thousands of years roamed over the uncultivated earth; we shall infer that the amount of suffering which has been and is borne by women is utterly beyond imagination.

The Nature of Kings
(From the First Book of Samuel)
Hebrew, eleventh century B.C.

And Samuel told all the words of the Lord unto the people that asked of him a king. And he said: "This will be the manner of the king that shall reign over you; he will take your sons, and appoint them for himself, for his chariots, and to be his horsemen; and some shall run before his chariots. And he will appoint him captains over thousands, and captains over fifties; and will set them to ear his ground, and to reap his harvest, and to make his instruments of war, and instruments of his chariots. And he will take your daughters to be confectionaries, and to be cooks, and to be bakers. And he will take your fields, and your vineyards, and your oliveyards, even the best of them, and give them to his servants. And he will take the tenth of your seed, and of your vineyards, and give to his officers, and to his servants. And he will take your menservants, and your maidservants, and your goodliest young men, and your asses, and put them to his work. He will take the tenth of your sheep; and ye shall be his servants. And ye shall cry out in that day because of your king which ye shall have chosen you; and the Lord will not hear you in that day."

Social Conflict, *José Orozco*

Divorce in Ancient Babylon
(From the Code of Hammurabi, 2250 B.C.)

Anu and Baal called me, Hammurabi, the exalted prince, the worshipper of the gods, to cause justice to prevail in the land, to destroy the wicked and evil, to prevent the strong from oppressing the weak, to enlighten the land and to further the welfare of the people. Hammurabi, the governor named by Baal am I, who brought about plenty and abundance.

§ 142: If a woman shall hate her husband and say: "Thou shalt not have me," they shall inquire into her antecedents for her defects. . . . If she have not been a careful mistress, have gadded about, have neglected her house and have belittled her husband, they shall throw that woman into the water.

King Yu's Misgovernment
(From the She-ching)
Chinese classic, 1000 B.C.

A fish in some translucent lake
Must ever live to fear a prey
He cannot hide himself away
From those who come the fish to take.
I, too, may not escape the eyes
Of those who cause these miseries;
My sorrowing heart must grieve to know
My country's deep distress and woe.

The Power of Justice
by MANU
Hindu poet, c.1200 B.C.

Iniquity, committed in this world, produces not fruit immediately, but, like the earth, in due season, and advancing by little and little, it eradicates the man who committed it.

He grows rich for a while through unrighteousness; then he beholds good things; then it is that he vanquishes his foes; but he perishes at length from his whole root upwards.

Justice, being destroyed, will destroy; being preserved, will preserve; it must never therefore be violated. Beware, O judge! lest justice, being overturned, overturn both us and thyself.

Slavery
(From the Edda)

King Frothi called his slaves renowned for strength, Fenia and Menia, and bade them grind for gold. The maidens ground through many years, they ground endless treasures; but at last they grew weary. Then Frothi said, "Grind on! Rest ye not, sleep ye not, longer than the cuckoo is silent, or a verse can be sung." The weary slaves ground on, till lo! from the mighty mill is poured forth an army of men. Now lies Frothi slain amid his gold. Now is Frothi's peace forever ended.

Legislators
by Isaiah

Woe unto them that decree unrighteous decrees, and that write grievousness which they have prescribed; to turn aside the needy from judgment, and to take away the right from the poor of my people, that widows may be their prey, and that they may rob the fatherless! And what will ye do in the day of visitation, and in the desolation which shall come from far? to whom will ye flee for help? and where will ye leave your glory? Without me they shall bow down under the prisoners, and they shall fall under the slain. For all this his anger is not turned away, but his hand is stretched out still.

By Virgil
Latin epic poet, 70-19 B.C.

Curst greed of gold, what crimes thy tyrant power has caused!

By Sophocles
Greek tragic poet, 495-406 B.C.

No such ill device
Ever appeared, as money to mankind:
This is it that sacks cities, this routs out
Men from their homes, and trains and turns astray
The minds of honest mortals, setting them
Upon base actions; this revealed to men
Habits of all misdoing, and cognizance
Of every work of wickedness.

Concerning Wealth
by HESIOD
Greek poet; 650 B.C.

Who, or by open force, or secret stealth,
Or perjured wiles, amasses wealth,
(Such many are, whom thirst of gain betrays)
The gods, all seeing, shall o'ercloud his days;
His wife, his children, and his friends shall die,
And, like a dream, his ill-got riches fly.

From the Instructions of Ptah-Hotep
Egyptian, 3550 B.C.

If thou be great, after being of no account, and hast gotten riches after squalor, being foremost in these in the city, and hast knowledge concerning useful matters, so that promotion is come unto thee; then swathe not thine heart in thine hoard, for thou art become a steward of the endowment of the God. Thou art not the last, others shall be thine equal, and to them shall come what has come to thee.

From the Icelandic, Eleventh Century

I saw the well-filled barns
Of the child of wealth;
Now leans he on the staff of the beggar.
Thus are riches,
As the glance of an eye,
They are an inconstant friend.

The Perfect City
by PLATO
Greek philosopher, 429-347 B.C.

We have, it seems, discovered other things, which our guardians must by all means watch against, that they may nowise escape their notice and steal into the city.

What kinds of things are these?

Riches, said I, and poverty.

From the Book of Good Counsels
Sanskrit, 300 B.C.

Wealth is friends, home, father, brother, title to respect, and
    fame;
Yea, and wealth is held for wisdom—that it should be so is
    shame.

From the "Medea" of Euripides

Speak not so hastily: the gods themselves
By gifts are swayed, as fame relates; and gold
Hath a far greater influence o'er the souls
Of mortals than the most persuasive words.

By DANTE ALIGHIERI
Italian epic poet, 1265-1321

I affirm that gain is precisely that which comes oftener to the
bad than to the good; for illegitimate gains never come to the
good at all, because they reject them. And lawful gains rarely
come to the good, because, since much anxious care is needful
thereto, and the anxious care of the good man is directed to
weightier matters, rarely does the good man give sufficient attention thereto. Wherefore it is clear that in every way the advent of
these riches is iniquitous. . . .

Let us give heed to the life of them who chase riches, and see
in what security they live when they have gathered of them, how
content they are, how reposeful! And what else, day by day, im-
perils and slays cities, countries and single persons so much as
the new amassing of wealth by anyone? Which amassing reveals
new longings, the goal of which may not be reached without
wrong to someone. . . .

Wherefore the baseness of riches is manifest enough by reason
of all their characteristics, and so a man of right appetite and of
true knowledge never loves them; and not loving them does not
unite himself to them, but ever wishes them to be far removed
from him, save as they be ordained to some necessary service.

Concerning Independence
by LUCRETIUS
Latin poet, 95-52 B.C.

But if men would live up to reason's rules,
They would not bow and scrape to wealthy fools.

From The Hitopadesa
Hindu religious work, 250 B.C.

It is better to abandon life than flatter the base. Impoverishment is better than luxury through another's wealth. Not to attend at the door of the wealthy, and not to use the voice of petition, these imply the best life of a man.

By XENOPHON
Greek historian, c.435-354 B.C.

If you perfume a slave and a freeman, the difference of their birth produces none in the smell; and the scent is perceived as soon in the one as the other; but the odor of honorable toil, as it is acquired with great pains and application, is ever sweet and worthy of a brave man.

By DANTE ALIGHIERI

What! You say a horse is noble because it is good in itself, and the same you say of a falcon or a pearl; but a man shall be called noble because his ancestors were so? Not with words, but with knives must one answer such a beastly notion.

A Home of Righteousness
Ancient Greek inscription

Piety has raised this house from the first foundation even to the lofty roof; for Macedonius fashioned not his wealth by heaping up from the possessions of others with plundering sword, nor has any poor man here wept over his vain and profitless toil, being robbed of just hire; and as rest from labor is kept inviolate by the just man, so let the works of pious mortals endure.

By Omar Khayyam
Persian poet, eleventh century

In this world he who possesses a morsel of bread, and some nest in which to shelter himself, who is master or slave of no man, tell that man to live content; he possesses a very sweet existence.

Palaces
(*From the Book of Enoch*)
Hebrew work of the second century B.C., preserved only in the Ethiopic tongue

Woe unto you who despise the humble dwelling and inheritance of your fathers! Woe unto you who build your palaces with the sweat of others! Each stone, each brick of which it is built, is a sin!

Pride in Poverty
by Confucius
Chinese philosopher, 550-479 B.C.

Riches and honor are what men desire; but if they attain to them by improper ways, they should not continue to hold them. Poverty and low estate are what men dislike; but if they are brought to such condition by improper ways, they should not feel shame for it.

Millionaires in Rome
by Cicero
Latin statesman and orator, 106-43 B.C.

As to their money, and their splendid mansions, and their wealth, and their lordship, and the delights by which they are chiefly attracted, never in truth have I ranked them amongst things good or desirable; inasmuch as I saw for a certainty that in the abundance of these things men longed most for the very things wherein they abounded. For never is the thirst of cupidity filled nor sated. And not only are they tortured by the longing to increase their possessions, but they are also tortured by fear of losing them.

The Ruling Classes
by EZEKIEL
Hebrew prophet, 600 B.C.

The word of the Lord came unto me, saying, Son of man, prophesy against the shepherds of Israel, prophesy and say unto them, Thus saith the Lord God unto the shepherds: Woe be to the shepherds of Israel that do feed themselves! Should not the shepherds feed the flocks? Ye eat the fat, and ye clothe you with the wool, ye kill them that are fed: but ye feed not the flock. The diseased have ye not strengthened, neither have ye bound up that which was broken, neither have ye brought again that which was driven away, neither have ye sought that which was lost; but with force and with cruelty have ye ruled them. And they were scattered, because there is no shepherd. . . . My sheep wandered through all the mountains, and upon every high hill; yea, my flock was scattered upon all the face of the earth, and none did search or seek after them. Therefore ye shepherds, hear the word of the Lord; as I live, saith the Lord God, . . . Behold, I am against the shepherds; and I will require my flock at their hand. . . . I will feed their flock, and I will cause them to lie down. . . . And they shall no more be a prey to the heathen, neither shall the beast of the land devour them; but they shall dwell safely, and none shall make them afraid. And ye my flock, the flock of my pasture, are men, and I am your God, saith the Lord God.

Concerning Justice
Ancient Hindu proverb

Justice is so dear to the heart of Nature, that if in the last day one atom of injustice were found, the universe would shrivel like a snakeskin to cast it off forever.

By SADI

Take heed that he weep not; for the throne of the Almighty is shaken to and fro when the orphan sets a-crying. Beware of the groans of the wounded souls, since the hidden sore will at length break out; oppress not to the utmost a single heart, for a single sigh has power to overset a whole world.

By Marcus Aurelius

In the whole constitution of man, I see not any virtue contrary
to justice, whereby it may be resisted and opposed.

From "The Koran"
Bible of Mohammedanism; Arabic, A.D. 600

Justice is an unassailable fortress, built on the brow of a mountain which cannot be overthrown by the violence of torrents, nor
demolished by the force of armies.

"Do you desire," said Abdallah, "to bring the praise of mankind upon your action? Then desire not unjustly, or even by
your right, to grasp that which belongs to another."

Arabian proverb, Sixteenth Century

The exercise of equity for one day is equal to sixty years spent
in prayer.

By Nintoku
Japanese emperor, Fourth Century

If the people are poor, I am the poorest.

Solon
by Plutarch

The Athenians fell into their old quarrels about the government, there being as many different parties as there were diversi-
ties in the country. The Hill quarter favored democracy, the
Plain, oligarchy, and those that lived by the Seaside stood for a
mixed sort of government, and so hindered either of the other
parties from prevailing. And the disparity of fortune between
the rich and the poor at that time also reached its height; so that
the city seemed to be in a truly dangerous condition, and there
appeared no other means for freeing it from disturbances and
settling it but a despotic power. All the people were indebted to
the rich; and either they tilled their land for their creditors, paying them a sixth part of the increase, or else they engaged their
body for the debt, and might be seized, and either sent into
slavery at home, or sold to strangers; some (for no law forbade

it) were forced to sell their children, or fly their country to avoid the cruelty of their creditors; but the most part and the bravest of them began to combine together and encourage one another to stand it, to choose a leader, to liberate the condemned debtors, divide the land, and change the government.

Then the wisest of the Athenians, perceiving Solon was of all men the only one not implicated in the troubles, that he had not joined in the exactions of the rich, and was not involved in the necessities of the poor, pressed him to succor the commonwealth and compose the differences. . . .

The first thing which he settled was, that what debts remained should be forgiven, and no man, for the future, should engage the body of his debtor for security.

Concerning Land

by SOLON
Greek lawgiver, 639-559 B.C.

The mortgage stones that covered her, by me
Removed, the land that was a slave is free.

DEUTERONOMY
Hebrew, 700 B.C.?

These are the statutes and judgments, which ye shall observe to do in the land, which the Lord God of thy fathers giveth thee to possess it, all the days that ye live upon the earth. . . . At the end of every seven years thou shalt make a release. And this is the manner of the release: Every creditor that lendeth ought unto his neighbor shall release it, he shall not exact it of his neighbor, or of his brother; because it is called the Lord's release.

LEVITICUS
Hebrew law-book, 700 B.C.?

And the Lord spake unto Moses in Mount Sinai, saying: . . . "The land shall not be sold for ever; for the land is mine; for ye are strangers and sojourners with me."

Concerning Usury

From "The Koran"

To him who is of kin to thee give his due, and to the poor and to the wayfarer: this will be best for those who seek the face of God; and with them it shall be well.

Whatever ye put out at usury to increase it with the substance of others shall have no increase from God: but whatever ye shall give in alms, as seeking the face of God, shall be doubled to you.

From the Psalms

Lord, who shall abide in thy tabernacle? Who shall dwell in thy holy hill?

He that walketh uprightly, and worketh righteousness, and speaketh the truth in his heart. . . .

He that putteth his money not out to usury, nor taketh reward against the innocent. He that doeth these things shall never be moved.

By ARISTOTLE
Greek philosopher, Fourth Century B.C.

Usury is the most reasonably detested of all forms of money-making; it is most against nature.

By FRANCIS BACON, LORD VERULAM
English philosopher and statesman, 1561-1626

The ways to enrich are many, and most of them foul. . . .

Usury is the certainest means of gain, though one of the worst; as that whereby a man doth eat his bread with sweat of another's face, and besides, doth plough upon Sundays.

Socialism
by WANG-AN-SHIH
Chinese statesman, Eleventh Century

The State should take the entire management of commerce, industry, and agriculture into its own hands, with a view to succoring the working classes and preventing their being ground to the dust by the rich.

BOOK IX

Mammon

Wealth, and the crimes that are committed in its name, and the protests of the spirit of humanity against its power in society.

Paradise Lost

by John Milton

English lyric and epic poet, 1608-1674

Mammon led them on—
Mammon, the least erected spirit that fell
From Heaven; for even in Heaven his looks and thoughts
Were always downward bent, admiring more
The riches of Heaven's pavement, trodden gold,
Than aught divine or holy else enjoyed
In vision beatific. By him first
Men also, and by his suggestion taught,
Ransacked the centre, and with impious hands
Rifled the bowels of their mother earth
For treasures better hid. Soon had his crew
Opened into the hill a spacious wound,
And digged out ribs of gold. Let none admire
That riches grow in Hell; that soil may best
Deserve the precious bane.

Miss Kilmansegg: Her Moral

by Thomas Hood

Gold! Gold! Gold! Gold!
Bright and yellow, hard and cold,
Molten, graven, hammer'd, and roll'd;
Heavy to get, and light to hold;
Hoarded, barter'd, bought, and sold,
Stolen, borrow'd, squander'd, doled;
Spurn'd by the young but hugg'd by the old
To the very verge of the churchyard mould;
Price of many a crime untold:
Gold! Gold! Gold! Gold!
Good or bad a thousand-fold!
How widely its agencies vary—
To save—to ruin—to curse—to bless—
As even its minted coins express,
Now stamp'd with the image of Good Queen Bess,
And now of a bloody Mary.

313

Northern Farmer: New Style
by ALFRED, LORD TENNYSON

Dosn't thou 'ear my 'erse's legs, as they canters awaäy,
Proputty, proputty, proputty—that's what I 'ears 'em saäy.
Proputty, proputty, proputty—Sam, thou's an ass for thy paäins,
Theer's moor sense i' one o' 'is legs nor in all thy braäins.

Me an' thy muther, Sammy, 'as beän a-talkin' o' thee;
Thou's beän talkin' to muther, an' she beän a tellin' it me.
Thou'll not marry for munny—thou's sweet upo' parson's lass—
Noä—thou'll marry for luvv—an' we boäth on us thinks tha an ass.
Seeä'd her todaäy goä by—Saäint's daäy—they was ringing the
        bells.
She's a beauty thou thinks—an' soä is scoors o' gells,
Them as 'as munny an' all—wot's a beauty?—the flower as blaws.
But proputty, proputty sticks, an' proputty, proputty graws.
Doänt't be stunt: taäke time: I knaws what maäkes tha sa mad.
Warn't I craäzed fur the lasses mysén when I wur a lad?
But I knaw'd a Quaäker feller as often 'as towd ma this:
"Doän't thou marry for munny, but goä wheer munny is!"

Now I Lay Me Down to Sleep
by JOHN D. ROCKEFELLER, SR.
American capitalist, 1839-1937

Then, and indeed for many years after, it seemed as though
there was no end to the money needed to carry on and develop
the business. As our successes began to come, I seldom put my
head upon the pillow at night without speaking a few words to
myself in this wise:

"Now a little success, soon you will fall down, soon you will
be overthrown. Because you have got a start, you think you are
quite a merchant; look out, or you will lose your head—go steady."
These intimate conversations with myself, I am sure, had a great
influence on my life.

FROM ECCLESIASTICUS

A merchant shall hardly keep himself from wrong-doing; and
a huckster shall not be acquitted of sin.

Dipsychus
by Arthur Hugh Clough
English poet and scholar, 1819-1861

As I sat at the café, I said to myself,
They may talk as they please about what they call pelf,
They may sneer as they like about eating and drinking,
But help it I cannot, I cannot help thinking,
   How pleasant it is to have money, heigh ho!
   How pleasant it is to have money.

I sit at my table *en grand seigneur,*
And when I have done, throw a crust to the poor;
Not only the pleasure, one's self, of good living,
But also the pleasure of now and then giving.
   So pleasant it is to have money, heigh ho!
   So pleasant it is to have money. . . .

I drive through the streets, and I care not a d—n;
The people they stare, and they ask who I am;
And if I should chance to run over a cad,
I can pay for the damage if ever so bad.
   So pleasant it is to have money, heigh ho!
   So pleasant it is to have money.

We stroll to our box and look down on the pit,
And if it weren't low should be tempted to spit;
We loll and we talk until people look up,
And when it's half over we go out to sup.
   So pleasant it is to have money, heigh ho!
   So pleasant it is to have money.

The best of the tables and best of the fare—
And as for the others, the devil may care;
It isn't our fault if they dare not afford
To sup like a prince and be drunk as a lord.
   So pleasant it is to have money, heigh ho!
   So pleasant it is to have money.

Mammon, *George Frederick Watts*

Past and Present
by THOMAS CARLYLE

What is it, if you pierce through his Cants, his oft-repeated Hearsays, what he calls his Worships and so forth,—what is it that the modern English soul does, in very truth, dread infinitely, and contemplate with entire despair? What *is* his Hell, after all these reputable, oft-repeated Hearsays, what is it? With hesitation, with astonishment, I pronounce it to be: The terror of "Not succeeding"; of not making money, fame, or some other figure in the world,—chiefly of not making money! Is not that a somewhat singular Hell?

Utopia
by SIR THOMAS MORE

They marveile also that golde, whych of the owne nature is a thinge so unprofytable, is nowe amonge all people in so hyghe estimation, that man him selfe, by whome, yea and for the use of whome it is so much set by, is in muche lesse estimation, then the golde it selfe. In so muche that a lumpyshe blockehedded churle, and whyche hathe no more wytte then an asse, yea and as ful of noughtynes as of follye, shall have nevertheless manye wyse and good men in subjectyon and bondage, only for this, bycause he hath a greate heape of golde. Whyche yf it shoulde be taken from hym by anye fortune, or by some subtyll wyle and cautele of the lawe (whyche no lesse then fortune dothe bothe raise up the lowe, and plucke downe the highe) and be geven to the moste vile slave and abject dryvell of all his housholde, then shortely after he shal goo into the service of his servaunt, as an augmentation or overplus beside his money. But they muche more marvell at and detest the madnes of them, whyche to those riche men, in whose debte and daunger they be not, do give almost divine honoures, for none other consideration, but bicause they be riche: and yet knowing them to bee suche nigeshe penny fathers, that they be sure as longe as they live, not the worthe of one farthinge of that heape of gold shall come to them. These and such like opinions have they conceaved, partly by education, beinge brought up in that common wealthe, whose lawes and customes be farre different from these kindes of folly, and partly by good litterature and learning.

Don Juan
by Lord Byron

Oh, Gold! Why call we misers miserable?
   Theirs is the pleasure that can never pall;
Theirs is the best bower-anchor, the chain-cable
   Which holds fast other pleasures great and small.
Ye who but see the saving man at table
   And scorn his temperate board, as none at all,
And wonder how the wealthy can be sparing,
Know not what visions spring from each cheese-paring. . . .

Perhaps he hath great projects in his mind
   To build a college, or to found a race,
An hospital, a church—and leave behind
   Some dome surmounted by his meagre face;
Perhaps he fain would liberate mankind,
   Even with the very ore that makes them base;
Perhaps he would be wealthiest of his nation,
Or revel in the joys of calculation. . . .

"Love rules the camp, the court, the grove—for love
   Is heaven, and heaven is love:" so sings the bard;
Which it were rather difficult to prove
   (A thing with poetry in general hard).
Perhaps there may be something in "the grove,"
   At least it rhymes to "love"; but I'm prepared
To doubt (no less than landlords of their rental)
If "courts" and "camps" be quite so sentimental.

But if Love don't, *Cash* does, and Cash alone:
   Cash rules the grove, and fells it too besides;
Without cash, camps were thin, and courts were none;
   Without cash, Malthus tells you, "take no brides."
So Cash rules Love the ruler, on his own
   High ground, as virgin Cynthia sways the tides:
And as for "Heaven being Love," why not say honey
Is wax? Heaven is not Love, 'tis Matrimony.

The Cave of Mammon
(From "The Faerie Queene")

by EDMUND SPENSER
English poet, 1552-1599

At last he came unto a gloomy glade
  Cover'd with boughs and shrubs from heavens light,
Whereas he sitting found in secret shade
  An uncouth, salvage, and uncivile wight,
  Of griesly hew and fowle ill-favour'd sight;
His face with smoke was tand, and eies were bleard,
  His head and beard with sout were ill bedight,
His cole-blacke hands did seem to have ben seard
In smythes fire-spitting forge, and nayles like clawes appeard. . . .

And round about him lay on every side
  Great heapes of gold that never could be spent;
Of which some were rude owre, not purifide,
  Of Mulcibers devouring element;
  Some others were new driven, and distent
Into great ingowes and to wedges square;
  Some in round plates withouten moniment;
But most were stampt, and in their metal bare
The antique shapes of kings and kesars straung and rare. . . .

"What secret place," quoth he, "can safely hold
  So huge a mass, and hide from heavens eie?
Or where hast thou thy wonne, that so much gold
  Thou canst preserve from wrong and robbery?"
  "Come thou," quoth he, "and see." So by and by
Through that black covert he him led, and fownd
  A darksome way, which no man could descry,
That deep descended through the hollow grownd,
And was with dread and horror compassèd arownd. . . .

So soon as Mammon there arrived, the dore
  To him did open and affoorded way:
Him followed eke Sir Guyon evermore,
  Ne darknesse him ne daunger might dismay.
  Soone as he entred was, the dore streightway
Did shutt, and from behind it forth there lept
  An ugly feend, more fowle then dismall day:

The which with monstrous stalke behind him stept,
And ever as he went dew watch upon him kept.

Well hopèd hee, ere long that hardy guest,
    If ever covetous hand, or lustfull eye,
Or lips he layd on thing that likte him best,
    Or ever sleepe his eie-strings did untye,
    Should be his pray: and therefore still on hye
He over him did hold his cruell clawes,
    Threatning with greedy gripe to doe him dye,
And rend in peeces with his ravenous pawes,
If ever he transgrest the fatall Stygian lawes.

In all that rowme was nothing to be seene
    But huge great yron chests, and coffers strong,
All bard with double bends, that none could weene
    Them to efforce by violence or wrong;
    On every side they placèd were along.
But all the grownd with sculs was scattered
    And dead mens bones, which round about were flong;
Whose lives, it seemed, whilome there was shed,
And their vile carcases now left unburièd.

Snobs and Marriage
by WILLIAM MAKEPEACE THACKERAY
English novelist, 1811-1863

People dare not be happy for fear of Snobs. People dare not love for fear of Snobs. People pine away lonely under the tyranny of Snobs. Honest kindly hearts dry up and die. Gallant generous lads, blooming with hearty youth, swell into bloated old bachelorhood, and burst and tumble over. Tender girls wither into shrunken decay, and perish solitary, from whom Snobbishness has cut off the common claim to happiness and affection with which Nature endowed us all. My heart grows sad as I see the blundering tyrant's handiwork. As I behold it I swell with cheap rage, and glow with fury against the Snob. Come down, I say, thou skulking dullness. Come down, thou stupid bully, and give up thy brutal ghost! And I arm myself with the sword and spear, and taking leave of my family, go forth to do battle with that hideous ogre and giant, that brutal despot in Snob Castle, who holds so many gentle hearts in torture and thrall.

Vanity Fair
(From "The Pilgrim's Progress")

by JOHN BUNYAN
English tinker and religious rebel who wrote one of the world's greatest
allegories while in prison; 1628-1688

Then I saw in my dream, that when they were got out of the
wilderness, they presently saw a town before them, and the name
of that town is Vanity; and at the town there is a fair kept, called
Vanity Fair. It is kept all the year long. . . . At this fair are all
such merchandise sold as houses, lands, trades, places, honors,
preferments, titles, countries, kingdoms, lusts, pleasures; and delights of all sorts, such as harlots, wives, husbands, children, masters, servants, lives, blood, bodies, souls, silver, gold, precious
stones, and what not.

And moreover, at this fair there are at all times to be seen
jugglings, cheats, games, plays, fools, apes, knaves, and rogues
and that of every kind.

Here are to be seen, too, and that for nothing, thefts, murders,
adulteries, false-swearers, and that of a blood-red color.

This Yellow Slave
by WILLIAM SHAKESPEARE

Gold? yellow, glittering, precious gold? . . .
 This yellow slave
Will knit and break religions; bless the accursed;
Make the hoar leprosy adored; place thieves,
And give them title, knee and approbation
With senators on the bench.

The Crown of Wild Olive
by JOHN RUSKIN

It is physically impossible for a well-educated, intellectual, or
brave man to make money the chief object of his thoughts; as
physically impossible as it is for him to make his dinner the principal object of them. All healthy people like their dinners, but
their dinner is not the main object of their lives. So all healthily
minded people like making money—ought to like it, and to enjoy
the sensation of winning it: but the main object of their life is
not money; it is something better than money.

Hotel Life
(From "The House of Mirth")

by EDITH WHARTON
American novelist, 1862-1937

The environment in which Lily found herself was as strange to her as its inhabitants. She was unacquainted with the world of the fashionable New York hotel—a world over-heated, over-upholstered, and over-fitted with mechanical appliances for the gratification of fantastic requirements, while the comforts of a civilized life were as unattainable as in a desert. Through this atmosphere of torrid splendor moved wan beings as richly upholstered as the furniture, beings without definite pursuits or permanent relations, who drifted on a languid tide of curiosity from restaurant to concert-hall, from palm-garden to music-room, from "art-exhibit" to dressmaker's opening. High-stepping horses or elaborately equipped motors waited to carry these ladies into vague metropolitan distances, whence they returned, still more wan from the weight of their sables, to be sucked back into the stifling inertia of the hotel routine. Somewhere behind them in the background of their lives, there was doubtless a real past, peopled by real human activities: they themselves were probably the product of strong ambitions, persistent energies, diversified contacts with the wholesome roughness of life; yet they had no more real existence than the poet's shades in limbo.

Lily had not been long in this pallid world without discovering that Mrs. Hatch was its most substantial figure. . . . The daily details of her existence were as strange to Lily as its general tenor. The lady's habits were marked by an oriental indolence and disorder peculiarly trying to her companion. Mrs. Hatch and her friends seemed to float together outside the bounds of time and space. No definite hours were kept; no fixed obligations existed: night and day floated into one another in a blur of confused and retarded engagements, so that one had the impression of lunching at the tea-hour, while dinner was often merged in the noisy after-theatre supper which prolonged Mrs. Hatch's vigil until daylight. Through this jumble of futile activities came and went a strange throng of hangers-on—manicures, beauty-doctors, hair-dressers, teachers of bridge, of French, of "physical development." . . . Mrs. Hatch swam in a haze of indeterminate enthusiasms, of aspirations culled from the stage, the newspapers, the fashion-journals, and a gaudy world of sport.

The Parasitic Female
by OLIVE SCHREINER

In place of the active laboring woman, upholding society by her toil, had come the effete wife, concubine or prostitute, clad in fine raiment, the work of others' fingers; fed on luxurious viands, the result of others' toil, waited on and tended by the labor of others. The need for her physical labor having gone, and mental industry not having taken its place, she bedecked and scented her person, or had it bedecked and scented for her, she lay upon her sofa, or drove or was carried out in her vehicle, and loaded with jewels, she sought by dissipations and amusements to fill up the inordinate blank left by the lack of productive activity. And the hand whitened and the frame softened, till at last, the very duties of motherhood, which were all the constitution of her life left her, became distasteful, and, from the instant when her infant came damp from her womb, it passed into the hands of others, to be tended and reared by them; and from youth to age her offspring often owed nothing to her personal toil. In many cases so complete was her enervation, that at last the very joy of giving life, the glory and beatitude of a virile womanhood, became distasteful; and she sought to evade it, not because of its interference with more imperious duties to those already born of her, or to her society, but because her existence of inactivity had robbed her of all joy in strenuous exertion and endurance in any form. Finely clad, tenderly housed, life became for her merely the gratification of her own physical and sexual appetites, and the appetites of the male, through the stimulation of which she could maintain herself. And, whether as kept wife, kept mistress, or prostitute, she contributed nothing to the active and sustaining labors of her society. She had attained to the full development of that type which, whether in modern Paris or New York or London, or in ancient Greece, Assyria, or Rome, is essentially one in its features, its nature, and its results. She was the "fine lady," the human female parasite—the most deadly microbe which can make its appearance on the surface of any social organism.

Wherever in the history of the past this type has reached its full development and has comprised the bulk of the females belonging to any dominant class or race, it has heralded its decay. In Assyria, Greece, Rome, Persia, as in Turkey today, the same

material conditions have produced the same social disease among
the wealthy and dominant races; and again and again when the
nation so affected has come into contact with nations more healthily constituted, this diseased condition has contributed to its
destruction.

Evils of Gold
by WILLIAM SHAKESPEARE

O thou sweet king killer, and dear divorce
'Twixt natural son and sire! thou bright defiler
Of Hymen's purest bed! thou valiant Mars;
Thou ever young, fresh, loved, and delicate wooer,
Whose blush doth thaw the consecrated snow
That lies on Dian's lap! thou visible god,
That solder'st close impossibilities,
And mak'st them kiss; that speak'st with every tongue,
To every purpose! O thou touch of hearts!
Think, thy slave, man, rebels; and by thy virtue
Set them into confounding odds, that beasts
May have the world in empire.

Fifth Avenue, 1915
by HERMANN HAGEDORN
American poet, 1882–1964

The motor cars go up and down,
    The painted ladies sit and smile.
    Along the sidewalks, mile on mile,
Parade the dandies of the town.

The latest hat, the latest gown,
    The tedium of their souls beguile.
The motor cars go up and down,
    The painted ladies sit and smile.

In wild and icy waters drown
    A thousand for a rock-bound isle.
    Ten thousand in a black defile
Perish for justice or a crown.
The motor cars go up and down. . . .

The Theory of the Leisure Class
by THORSTEIN VEBLEN
American political economist, 1857-1929

The function of dress as an evidence of ability to pay does not end with simply showing that the wearer consumes valuable goods in excess of what is required for physical comfort. Simple conspicuous waste of goods is effective and gratifying as far as it goes; it is good *prima facie* evidence of pecuniary success, and consequently *prima facie* evidence of social worth. But dress has subtler and more far-reaching possibilities than this crude, first-hand evidence of wasteful consumption only. If, in addition to showing that the wearer can afford to consume freely and uneconomically, it can also be shown in the same stroke that he or she is not under the necessity of earning a livelihood, the evidence of social worth is enhanced in a very considerable degree. Our dress, therefore, in order to serve its purpose effectually, should not only be expensive, but it should also make plain to all observers that the wearer is not engaged in any kind of productive labor. In the evolutionary process by which our system of dress has been elaborated into its present admirably perfect adaptation to its purpose, this subsidiary line of evidence has received due attention. A detailed examination of what passes in popular apprehension for elegant apparel will show that it is contrived at every point to convey the impression that the wearer does not habitually put forth any useful effort. It goes without saying that no apparel can be considered elegant, or even decent, if it shows the effect of manual labor on the part of the wearer, in the way of soil or wear. The pleasing effect of neat and spotless garments is chiefly, if not altogether, due to their carrying the suggestion of leisure—exemption from personal contact with industrial processes of any kind. Much of the charm that invests the patent-leather shoe, the stainless linen, the lustrous cylindrical hat, and the walking-stick, which so greatly enhance the native dignity of a gentleman, comes of their pointedly suggesting that the wearer cannot when so attired bear a hand in any employment that is directly and immediately of any human use....

The dress of women goes even farther than that of men in the way of demonstrating the wearer's abstinence from productive employment. It needs no argument to enforce the generalization that the more elegant styles of feminine bonnets go even farther towards making work impossible than does the man's high hat. The woman's shoe adds the so-called French heel to the evidence of enforced leisure afforded by its polish; because this high heel obviously makes any, even the simplest and most necessary manual work extremely difficult. The like is true even in a higher degree of the skirt and the rest of the drapery which characterizes woman's dress. The substantial reason for our tenacious attachment to the skirt is just this: it is expensive and it hampers the wearer at every turn and incapacitates her for all useful exertion. The like is true of the feminine custom of wearing the hair excessively long.

But the woman's apparel not only goes beyond that of the modern man in the degree in which it argues exemption from labor; it also adds a peculiar and highly characteristic feature which differs in kind from anything habitually practiced by the men. This feature is the class of contrivances of which the corset is the typical example. The corset is, in economic theory, substantially a mutilation, undergone for the purpose of lowering the subject's vitality and rendering her permanently and obviously unfit for work. It is true, the corset impairs the personal attractions of the wearer, but the loss suffered on that score is offset by the gain in reputability which comes of her visibly increased expensiveness and infirmity. It may broadly be set down that the womanliness of woman's apparel resolves itself, in point of substantial fact, into the more effective hindrance to useful exertion offered by the garments peculiar to women.

In Bohemia

by JOHN BOYLE O'REILLY
Irish-born American journalist, 1844-1890

The thirsty of soul soon learn to know
The moistureless froth of the social show,
The vulgar sham of the pompous feast
Where the heaviest purse is the highest priest;
The organized charity, scrimped and iced,
In the name of a cautious, statistical Christ.

Co-operation and Nationality
by GEORGE W. RUSSELL ("A.E.")

When steam first began to puff and wheels go round at so many revolutions per minute, the wild child humanity, who had hitherto developed his civilization in picturesque unconsciousness of where he was going, and without any set plan, was caught and put in harness. What are called business habits were invented to make the life of man run in harmony with the steam engine, and his movements rival the train in punctuality. The factory system was invented, and it was an instantaneous success. Men were clothed with cheapness and uniformity. Their minds grew numerously alike, cheap and uniform also. They were at their desks at nine o'clock, or at their looms at six. They adjusted themselves to the punctual wheels. The rapid piston acted as pacemaker, and in England, which started first in the modern race for wealth, it was an enormous advantage to have tireless machines of superhuman activity to make the pace, and nerve men, women and children to the fullest activity possible. Business methods had a long start in England, and irregularity and want of uniformity became after a while such exceptions that they were regarded as deadly sins. The grocer whose supplies of butter did not arrive week after week by the same train, at the same hour, and of the same quality, of the same color, the same saltness, and in the same kind of box, quarrelled with the wholesaler, who in his turn quarrelled with the producer. Only the most machine-like race could win custom. After a while every country felt it had to be drilled or become extinct. Some made themselves into machines to enter the English market, some to preserve their own markets. Even the indolent Oriental is getting keyed up, and in another fifty years the Bedouin of the desert will be at his desk and the wild horseman of Tartary will be oiling his engines.

Man the Reformer
by RALPH WALDO EMERSON

It is only necessary to ask a few questions as to the progress of the articles of commerce from the fields where they grew, to our houses, to become aware that we eat and drink and wear perjury and fraud in a hundred commodities. We are all implicated in this charge. The sins of our trade belong to no class, to no indi-

Marriage à la Mode, *William Hogarth*

vidual. Everybody partakes, everybody confesses, yet none feels himself accountable. The trail of the serpent reaches into all the lucrative professions and practices of man. Nay, the evil custom reaches into the whole institution of property, until our laws which establish and protect it seem not to be the issue of love and reason, but of selfishness.

The Communist Manifesto
by KARL MARX AND FREDERICK ENGELS

Karl Marx: founder of modern revolutionary socialism, 1818-1883. Frederick Engels: the most important associate of Marx in the development of dialectical materialism, 1820-1896.

The bourgeoisie, wherever it has got the upper hand, has put an end to all feudal, patriarchal, idyllic relations. It has pitilessly torn asunder the motley feudal ties that bound man to his "natural superiors," and has left remaining no other nexus between man and man than naked self-interest, than callous "cash payment." It has drowned the most heavenly ecstasies of religious fervor, of chivalrous enthusiasm, of philistine sentimentalism, in the icy water of egotistical calculation. It has resolved personal worth into exchange value, and in place of the numberless indefeasible chartered freedoms, has set up that single, unconscionable freedom—Free Trade.

Portrait of an American
by LOUIS UNTERMEYER

He slobbers over sentimental plays
   And sniffles over sentimental songs.
   He tells you often how he sadly longs
For the ideals of the dear old days.
In gatherings he is the first to raise
   His voice against "our country's shameful wrongs."
   He storms at greed. His hard, flat tone prolongs
The hymns and mumbled platitudes of praise.

I heard him in his office Friday past.
   "Look here," he said, "their talk is all a bluff;
You mark my words, this thing will never last.
   Let them walk out—they'll come back quick enough.
We'll have all hands at work—and working fast!
   How do they think we're running this—for *love?*"

Tono-Bungay
by H. G. WELLS
English novelist and historian, 1866-1946

It was my uncle's genius that did it. No doubt he needed me—
I was, I will admit, his indispensable right hand; but his was
the brain to conceive. He wrote every advertisement; some of
them even he sketched. You must remember that his were the
days before the *Times* took to enterprise and the vociferous
hawking of that antiquated *Encyclopaedia.* That alluring, button-
holing, let-me-just-tell-you-quite-soberly-something-you-ought-to-
know style of newspaper advertisement, with every now and then
a convulsive jump of some attractive phrase into capitals, was
then almost a novelty. "Many people who are MODERATELY
well think they are QUITE well," was one of his early efforts.
The jerks in capitals were, "DO NOT NEED DRUGS OR
MEDICINE," and "SIMPLY A PROPER REGIMEN TO GET
YOU IŃ TONE." One was warned against the chemist or drug-
gist who pushed "much-advertised nostrums" on one's attention.
That trash did more harm than good. The thing needed was
regimen—and Tono-Bungay!

Very early, too, was that bright little quarter column, at least
it was usually a quarter column in the evening papers:
"HILARITY—TONO-BUNGAY. Like Mountain Air in the
Veins." The penetrating trio of questions: "Are you bored with
your Business? Are you bored with your Dinner? Are you bored
with your Wife?"—that, too, was in our Gower Street days. Both
these we had in our first campaign when we worked London
south, central, and west; and then, too, we had our first poster,—
the HEALTH, BEAUTY AND STRENGTH one. That was
his design; I happen still to have got by me the first sketch he
made for it....

By all modern standards the business was, as my uncle would
say, "absolutely *bona fide.*" We sold our stuff and got the money,
and spent the money honestly in lies and clamor to sell more
stuff. Section by section we spread it over the whole of the British
Isles; first working the middle-class London suburbs, then the
outer suburbs, then the home counties, then going (with new
bills and a more pious style of "ad") into Wales, a great field
always for a new patent-medicine, and then into Lancashire. My
uncle had in his inner office a big map of England, and as we

took up fresh sections of the local press and our consignments invaded new areas, flags for advertisements and pink underlines for orders showed our progress.

"The romance of modern commerce, George!" my uncle would say, rubbing his hands together and drawing in air through his teeth. "The romance of modern commerce, eh? Conquest. Province by Province. Like sogers."

We subjugated England and Wales; we rolled over the Cheviots with a special adaptation containing eleven per cent. of absolute alcohol; "Tono-Bungay: Thistle Brand." We also had the Fog poster adapted to a kilted Briton in a misty Highland scene. . . .

As I look back at them now, those energetic years seem all compacted to a year or so; from the days of our first hazardous beginning in Farrington Street with barely a thousand pounds' worth of stuff or credit all told—and that got by something perilously like snatching—to the days when my uncle went to the public on behalf of himself and me (one-tenth share) and our silent partners, the drug wholesalers and the printing people and the owner of that group of magazines and newspapers, to ask with honest confidence for £150,000. Those silent partners were remarkably sorry, I know, that they had not taken larger shares and given us longer credit when the subscriptions came pouring in. My uncle had a clear half to play with (including the one-tenth understood to be mine).

£150,000—think of it!—for the goodwill in a string of lies and a trade in bottles of mitigated water! Do you realize the madness of the world that sanctions such a thing? Perhaps you don't. At times use and wont certainly blinded me. If it had not been for Ewart, I don't think I should have had an inkling of the wonderfulness of this development of my fortunes; I should have grown accustomed to it, fallen in with all its delusions as completely as my uncle presently did. He was immensely proud of the flotation. "They've never been given such value," he said, "for a dozen years." But Ewart, with his gesticulating hairy hands and bony wrists, is single-handed chorus to all this as it plays itself over again in my memory, and he kept my fundamental absurdity illuminated for me during all this astonishing time.

"It's just on all fours with the rest of things," he remarked; "only more so. You needn't think you're anything out of the way."

To a Certain Rich Young Ruler
A sonnet which was widely circulated at the time of the Colorado coal-strike
of 1913-14

by CLEMENT WOOD

White-fingered lord of murderous events,
   Well are you guarding what your father gained;
   With torch and rifle you have well maintained
The lot to which a heavenly providence
Has called you; laborers, risen in defense
   Of liberty and life, lie charred and brained
   About your mines, whose gutted hills are stained
With slaughter of these newer innocents.

Ah, but your bloody fingers clenched in prayer!
   Your piety, which all the world has seen!
The godly odor spreading through the air
   From your efficient charity machine!
Thus you rehearse for your high rôle up there,
   Ruling beside the lowly Nazarene!

Crowds
by GERALD STANLEY LEE
American author and lecturer, 1862-1944

As I have watched my fellow human beings, what I have come
to want most of all in this world is the inspired employer—or
what I have called the inspired millionaire or organizer; the man
who can take the machines off the backs of the people, and take
the machines out of their wits, and make the machines free their
bodies and serve their souls.

If we ever have the inspired employer, he will have to be made
by the social imagination of the people, by creating the spirit of
expectation and challenge toward the rich among the masses of
the people....

Nothing is more visionary than trying to run a world without
dreams, especially an economic world. It is because even bad
dreams are better in this world than having no dreams at all that
bad people so-called are so largely allowed to run it.

In the final and practical sense, the one factor in economics to
be reckoned with is Desire.

Concerning Charity

by JOHN R. LAWSON

Representative of striking Colorado miners who went to work as a pit-boy at
the age of eight; died 1945

There is another cause of industrial discontent. This is the skillful attempt that is being made to substitute Philanthropy for Justice. There is not one of these foundations, now spreading their millions over the world in showy generosity, that does not draw those millions from some form of industrial injustice. It is not *their* money that these lords of commercialized virtue are spending, but the withheld wages of the American working-class.

I sat in this room and heard a great philanthropist read the list of activities of his Foundation "to promote the well-being of mankind." An international health commission to extend to foreign countries and peoples the work of eradicating the hookworm; the promotion of medical education and health in China; the investigation of vice conditions in Europe; one hundred thousand dollars for the American Academy in Rome, twenty thousand a year for widows' pensions in New York, one million for the relief of Belgians, thirty-four millions for the University of Chicago, thirty-four millions for a General Education Board. A wave of horror swept over me during that reading, and I say to you that that same wave is now rushing over the entire working-class of the United States. Health for China, a refuge for birds in Louisiana, food for the Belgians, pensions for New York widows, university training for the elect—and never a thought or a dollar for the many thousands of men, women and children who starved in Colorado, for the widows robbed of husbands and children of their fathers, by law-violating conditions in the mines. There are thousands of this great philanthropist's former employees in Colorado today who wish to God that they were in Belgium to be fed, or birds to be cared for tenderly.

By ARISTOTLE

A tyrant must put on the appearance of uncommon devotion to religion. Subjects are less apprehensive of illegal treatment from a ruler whom they consider godfearing and pious. On the other hand, they do less easily move against him, believing that he has the gods on his side.

The Dying Boss
by LINCOLN STEFFENS

A story of the political leader of a corrupt city, who lies upon his death-bed, and has asked to have the meaning of his own career made plain to him.

"What kind of a kid were you, Boss?" I began.

"Pretty tough, I guess," he answered.

"Born here?"

"Yes; in the Third Ward."

"Tough then as it is now?"

"Tougher," he said.

"Produces toughness the way Kansas produces corn," I remarked. "Father?" I asked.

"Kept a saloon; a driver before that."

"Mother a girl of the ward?"

"Yes," he said. "She was brought up there; but she came to this country with her father from England, as a baby."

"What sort of woman was she?"

"Quiet," he said; "always still; silent-like; a worker. Kept the old man straight—some; and me too—'s well as she could. She's th' one that got him off th' wagon and started in th' liquor business."

"You were poor people?"

"Yes."

"And common?"

"Y-yes-s."

"A child of the people," I commented; "the common people."

He nodded, wondering.

"One of the great, friendless mass of helpless humanity?"

He nodded.

"That wasn't your fault, was it?" I said. "Not to blame for that? That's not your sin, is it?"

He shook his head, staring, and he was so mystified that I said that most people were "pretty terribly punished for being born poor and common." He nodded, but he wasn't interested or enlightened, apparently. "And you learned, somehow, that the thing to do was to get yourself on, get up out of it, make a success of your life?"

"Yes," he said slowly. "I don't know how, but I did get that, somehow."

"That was the ideal they taught you," I said. "Never heard of getting everybody on and making a success of society; of the city and State?"

But this line of questioning was beyond him. I changed my tack. . . .

"In that first interview we had," I said, "you insisted that, while the business boss was the real boss, the sovereign, you had some power of your own. And you described it today as the backing of your own ward, which, you said, you had in your pocket. When you became boss, you got the backing, the personal support, of other wards, didn't you?"

"Seven of 'em," he counted. "Made th' leaders myself."

"And you developed a big personal following in other wards, too?"

"Sure," he said; "in every one of them. I was a popular leader; not only a boss, but a friend with friends, lots of 'em. The people liked me."

"That's the point," I said. "The people liked you."

He nodded warmly.

"The common people," I went on, and he was about to nod, but he didn't. And his fingers became still. "Your own people—the great helpless mass of the friendless mob—liked you." His eyes were fixed on mine. "They followed you; they trusted you."

I paused a moment. Then I asked: "Didn't they, Boss?"

"Yes," he said with his lips alone.

"They didn't set a watch on you, did they?" I continued. "They voted as you bade them vote, elected the fellows you put on the tickets of their party for them. And, after they elected them, they left it to them, and to you, to be true to them; to stick to them; to be loyal."

His eyes fell to his fingers, and his fingers began again to pick.

"And when your enemies got after you and accused you," I said, "the people stuck by you?"

No answer; only the fingers picked.

"The great, friendless mass—the hopeful, hopeless majority—they were true to you and the party, and they re-elected you."

His eyes were on mine again, and there was light in them; but it was the reflected light of fire, and it burned.

"And you—you betrayed them," I said; and I hurried on, piling on the fuel, all I had. "They have power, the people have, and they have needs, great common needs; and they have great common wealth. All your fat, rich franchises, all your great social values, the values added to land and franchise by the presence of the great, common, numerous mass, all the city's public property —all are theirs, their common property. They own enough in common to meet all their great common needs, and they have an organization to keep for them and to develop for their use and profit all these great needed social values. It is the city; the city government; city, State, and national. And they have, they breed in their own ranks, men like you, natural political leaders, to go into public life and lead them, teach them, represent them. And they leave it all to you, trusting you. And you, all of you—not you alone, Boss, but all of you: ward leaders; State leaders; all the national political bosses—you all betray them. You receive from them their votes, so faithfully given, and you transform them into office-holders whom you teach or corrupt and compel to obey you. So you reorganize the city government. You, not the Mayor, are the head of it; you, not the council, are its legislature; you, not the heads of departments, are the administrators of the property and the powers of the people of your city; the common, helpless, friendless people. And, having thus organized and taken over all this power and property and—this beautiful faith, you do not protect their rights and their property. What do you do with it, Boss?"

He started. He could not answer. I answered for him:

"You sell 'em out; you turn over the whole thing—the city, its property, and its people—to Business, to the big fellows; to the business leaders of the people. You deliver, not only franchises, privileges, private rights and public properties, and values, Boss: you—all of you together—have delivered the government itself to these men, so that today this city, this State, and the national government represent, normally, not the people, not the great mass of common folk, who need protection, but—Business; preferably bad business; privileged business; a class; a privileged class."

He had sunk back among the pillows, his eyes closed, his fingers still. I sounded him.

"That's the system," I repeated. "It's an organization of social treason, and the political boss is the chief traitor. It couldn't stand without the submission of the people; the real bosses have to get that. They can't buy the people—too many of them; so they buy the people's leaders, and the disloyalty of the political boss is the key to the whole thing."

There was no response. I plumbed him again.

"And you—you believe in loyalty, Boss," I said—"in being true to your own." His eyes opened. "That's your virtue, you say, and you said, too, that you have practiced it."

"Don't," he murmured.

The Psychological Misery
(From "Civilization and Its Discontents")
by SIGMUND FREUD

The liberty of the individual is not a benefit of culture. It was greatest before any culture, though indeed it had little value at that time, because the individual was hardly in a position to defend it. Liberty has undergone restrictions through the evolution of civilization, and justice demands that these restrictions shall apply to all. The desire for freedom that makes itself felt in a human community may be a revolt against some existing injustice and so may prove favorable to a further development of civilization and remain compatible with it. But it may also have its origin in the primitive roots of the personality, still unfettered by civilizing influences, and so become a source of antagonism to culture. Thus the cry for freedom is directed either against particular forms or demands of culture or else against culture itself. It does not seem as if man could be brought by any sort of influence to change his nature into that of the ants; he will always, one imagines, defend his claim to individual freedom against the will of the multitude. A great part of the struggles of mankind centers round the single task of finding some expedient (*i.e.* satisfying) solution between these individual claims and those of the civilized community; it is one of the problems of man's fate whether this solution can be arrived at some particular form of culture or whether the conflict will prove irreconcilable.

The Communists believe they have found a way of delivering us from this evil. Man is wholeheartedly good and friendly to his neighbor, they say, but the system of private property has corrupted his nature. The possession of private property gives power to the individual and thence the temptation arises to ill-treat his neighbor; the man who is excluded from the possession of property is obliged to rebel in hostility against the oppressor. If private property were abolished, all valuables held in common and all allowed to share in the enjoyment of them, ill will and enmity would disappear from among men. Since all needs would be satisfied, none would have any reason to regard another as an enemy; all would willingly undertake the work which is necessary. I have no concern with any economic criticisms of the communistic system; I cannot enquire into whether the abolition of private property is advantageous and expedient.* But I am able to recognize that psychologically it is founded on an untenable illusion. By abolishing private property one deprives the human love of aggression of one of its instruments, a strong one undoubtedly, but assuredly not the strongest. It in no way alters the individual differences in power and influence which are turned by aggressiveness to its own use, nor does it change the nature of the instinct in any way. The instinct does not arise as the result of property; it reigned almost supreme in primitive times when possessions were still extremely scanty; it shows itself already in the nursery when possessions have hardly grown out of their original anal shape; it is at the bottom of all the relations of affection and love between human beings—possibly with the single exception of that of a mother to her male child. Suppose that personal rights to material goods are done away with, there still remain prerogatives in sexual relationships, which must arouse the strongest rancour and most violent enmity among men and women who are otherwise equal. Let us suppose this were also to be removed by instituting complete liberty in sexual life, so that the family, the germcell of culture, ceased to exist; one could now, it is true, foresee the new paths on which cultural development might then proceed, but one thing one would be bound to expect, and that is that the ineffaceable feature of human nature would follow wherever it led.

Men clearly do not find it easy to do without satisfaction of this tendency to aggression that is in them; when deprived of satisfaction of it they are ill at ease. There is an advantage, not to be undervalued, in the existence of smaller communities, through which the aggressive instinct can find an outlet in enmity towards those outside the group. It is always possible to unite considerable

* Anyone who has been through the misery of poverty in his youth, and has endured the indifference and arrogance of those who have possessions, should be exempt from the suspicion that he has no understanding of or goodwill towards the endeavors made to fight the economic inequality of men and all that it leads to. To be sure, if an attempt is made to base this fight upon an abstract demand for equality for all in the name of justice, there is a very obvious objection to be made, namely, that nature began the injustice by the highly unequal way in which she endows individuals physically and mentally, for which there is no help.

numbers of men in love towards one another, so long as there are still some remaining as objects for aggressive manifestations....

In rightly finding fault, as we thus do, with our present state of civilization for so inadequately providing us with what we require to make us happy in life, and for the amount of suffering of a probably avoidable nature it lays us open to—in doing our utmost to lay bare the roots of its deficiencies by our unsparing criticisms, we are undoubtedly exercising our just rights and not showing ourselves enemies of culture. We may expect that in the course of time changes will be carried out in our civilization so that it becomes more satisfying to our needs and no longer open to the reproaches we have made against it. But perhaps we shall also accustom ourselves to the idea that there are certain difficulties inherent in the very nature of culture which will not yield to any efforts at reform. Over and above the obligations of putting restrictions upon our instincts, which we see to be inevitable, we are imminently threatened with the dangers of a state one may call *"la misère psychologique"* of groups. This danger is most menacing where the social forces of cohesion consist predominantly of identifications of the individuals in the group with one another, whilst leading personalities fail to acquire the significance that should fall to them in the process of group-formation. The state of civilization in America at the present day offers a good opportunity for studying this injurious effect of civilization which we have reason to dread. But I will resist the temptation to enter upon a criticism of American culture; I have no desire to give the impression that I would employ American methods myself.

A Ballad of Dead Girls

by DANA BURNET
American poet, born 1888

Scarce had they brought the bodies down
    Across the withered floor,
Than Max Rogosky thundered at
    The District Leader's door.

Scarce had the white-lipped mothers come
    To search the fearful noon,
Than little Max stood shivering
    In Tom McTodd's saloon!

In Tom McTodd's saloon he stood,
  Beside the silver bar,
Where any honest lad may stand,
  And sell his vote at par.

"Ten years I've paid the System's tax,"
  The words fell, quivering, raw;
"And now I want the thing I bought—
  Protection from the law!"

The Leader smiled a twisted smile:
  "Your doors were locked," he said.
"You've overstepped the limit, Max—
  A hundred women....dead!"

Then Max Rogosky gripped the bar
  And shivered where he stood.
"You listen now to me," he cried,
  "Like business fellers should!

"I've paid for all my hundred dead,
  I've paid, I've paid, I've paid."
His ragged laughter rang, and died—
  For he was sore afraid.

"I've paid for wooden hall and stair,
  I've paid to strain my floors,
I've paid for rotten fire-escapes,
  For all my bolted doors.

"Your fat inspectors came and came—
  I crossed their hands with gold.
And now I want the thing I bought,
  The thing the System sold."

The District Leader filled a glass
  With whiskey from the bar,
(The little silver counter where
  He bought men's souls at par.)

And well he knew that he must give
  The thing that he had sold,

Else men should doubt the System's word,
    Keep back the System's gold.

The whiskey burned beneath his tongue:
    "A hundred women dead!
I guess the Boss can fix it up,
    Go home—and hide," he said.

All day they brought the bodies down
    From Max Rogosky's place—
And oh, the fearful touch of flame
    On hand and breast and face!

All day the white-lipped mothers came
    To search the sheeted dead;
And Horror strode the blackened walls,
    Where Death had walked in red.

But Max Rogosky did not weep.
    (He knew that tears were vain.)
He paid the System's price, and lived
    To lock his doors again.

Romance

by SEYMOUR DEMING
Twentieth-century American writer

The old idea of romance: The country boy goes to the city, marries his employer's daughter, enslaves some hundreds of his fellow humans, gets rich, and leaves a public library to his home town.

The new idea of romance: To undo some of the mischief done by the old idea of romance.

A Living Wage

by J. PIERPONT MORGAN
American banker, 1837-1913; testimony before the United States Commission on Industrial Relations

QUESTION: Do you consider ten dollars a week enough for a longshoreman with a family to support?

ANSWER: If that's all he can get, and he takes it, I should say it's enough.

The Soul's Errand

by SIR WALTER RALEIGH

Written by the English soldier and statesman, 1552-1618, just before his execution

Go, Soul, the body's guest,
  Upon a thankless errand;
Fear not to touch the best;
  The truth shall be thy warrant:
    Go, since I needs must die,
    And give them all the lie.

Go tell the Court it glows
  And shines like rotten wood;
Go tell the Church it shows
  What's good, but does no good:
    If Court and Church reply
    Give Court and Church the lie.

Tell Potentates they live
  Acting, but oh! their actions;
Not loved, unless they give,
  Nor strong but by their factions:
    If Potentates reply,
    Give Potentates the lie.

Tell men of high condition,
  That rule affairs of state,
Their purpose is ambition;
  Their practice only hate:
    And if they do reply,
    Then give them all the lie....

Tell Physic of her boldness;
  Tell Skill it is pretension;
Tell Charity of coldness;
  Tell Law it is contention:
    And if they yield reply,
    Then give them all the lie....

So when thou hast, as I
  Commanded thee, done blabbing;
Although to give the lie
  Deserves no less than stabbing:
    Yet stab at thee who will,
    No stab the Soul can kill.

The Butcher's Stall
by EMILE VERHAEREN
Belgian poet, 1855-1916

Hard by the docks, soon as the shadows fold
The dizzy mansion-fronts that soar aloft,
When eyes of lamps are burning soft,
The shy, dark quarter lights again its old
Allurement of red vice and gold.

Women, blocks of heaped, blown meat,
Stand on low thresholds down the narrow street,
Calling to every man that passes;
Behind them, at the end of corridors,
Shine fires, a curtain stirs
And gives a glimpse of masses
Of mad and naked flesh in looking-glasses.
Hard by the docks
The street upon the left is ended by
A tangle of high masts and shrouds that blocks
A sheet of sky;
Upon the right a net of grovelling alleys
Falls from the town—and here the black crowd rallies
And reels to rotten revelry.

It is the flabby, fulsome butcher's stall of luxury,
Time out of mind erected on the frontiers
Of the city and the sea.

Far-sailing melancholy mariners
Who, wet with spray, thru grey mists peer,
Cabin-boys cradled among the rigging, and they who steer
Hallucinated by the blue eyes of the vast sea-spaces,
All dream of it, evoke it when the evening falls;
Their raw desire to madness galls;
The wind's soft kisses hover on their faces;
The wave awakens rolling images of soft embraces;
And their two arms implore
Stretched in a frantic cry towards the shore.

And they of offices and shops, the city tribes,
Merchants precise, keen reckoners, haggard scribes,

Who sell their brains for hire, and tame their brows,
When the keys of desks are hanging on the wall,
Feel the same galling rut at even-fall,
And run like hunted dogs to the carouse.
Out of the depths of dusk come their dark flocks,
And in their hearts debauch so rudely shocks
Their ingrained greed and old accustomed care,
That they are racked and ruined by despair.

It is the flabby, fulsome butcher's stall of luxury,
Time out of mind erected on the frontiers
Of the city and the sea.

Come from what far sea-isles or pestilent parts?
Come from what feverish or methodic marts?
Their eyes are filled with bitter, cunning hate,
They fight their instincts that they cannot sate;
Around red females who befool them, they
Herd frenzied till the dawn of sober day.
The panelling is fiery with lewd art;
Out of the wall nitescent knick-knacks dart;
Fat Bacchuses and leaping satyrs in
Wan mirrors freeze an unremitting grin....

And women with spent loins and sleeping croups
Are piled on sofas and arm-chairs in groups,
With sodden flesh grown vague, and black and blue
With the first trampling of the evening's crew.
One of them slides a gold coin in her stocking;
Another yawns, and some their knees are rocking;
Others by bacchanalia worn out,
Feeling old age, and, sniffing them, Death's snout,
Stare with wide-open eyes, torches extinct,
And smooth their legs with hands together linked....

It is the flabby, fulsome butcher's stall of luxury,
Wherein Crime plants his knives that bleed,
Where lightning madness stains
Foreheads with rotting pains,
Time out of mind erected on frontiers that feed
The city and the sea.

BY WILLIAM SHAKESPEARE

The strongest castle, tower and town,
The golden bullet beats it down.

The Selling of Love
(From "Love's Coming of Age")
by EDWARD CARPENTER

The commercial prostitution of love is the last outcome of our
whole social system, and its most clear condemnation. It flaunts
in our streets, it hides itself in the garment of respectability under
the name of matrimony, it eats in actual physical disease and
death right through our midst; it is fed by the oppression and the
ignorance of women, by their poverty and denied means of livelihood, and by the hypocritical puritanism which forbids them by
millions not only to gratify but even to speak of their natural
desires; and it is encouraged by the callousness of an age which
has accustomed men to buy and sell for money every most precious
thing—even the life-long labor of their brothers, therefore why
not also the very bodies of their sisters?

Nothing to Fear but Fear
by FRANKLIN D. ROOSEVELT

Four times President of the United States, responsible for the New Deal, America's
Chief Executive in World War II; 1882-1945. The following is his First Inaugural
Address, March 4, 1933, given in full.

I am certain that my fellow Americans expect that on my
induction into the Presidency I will address them with a candor
and a decision which the present situation of our Nation impels.
This is preeminently the time to speak the truth, the whole truth,
frankly and boldly. Nor need we shrink from honestly facing conditions in our country today. This great Nation will endure as it
has endured, will revive and prosper. So, first of all, let me assert
my firm belief that the only thing we have to fear is fear itself—
nameless, unreasoning, unjustified terror which paralyzes needed
efforts to convert retreat into advance. In every dark hour of our
national life a leadership of frankness and vigor has met with that
understanding and support of the people themselves which is

essential to victory. I am convinced that you will again give that
support to leadership in these critical days.

In such a spirit on my part and on yours we face our common
difficulties. They concern, thank God, only material things. Values
have shrunken to fantastic levels; taxes have risen; our ability to
pay has fallen; government of all kinds is faced by serious curtail-
ment of income; the means of exchange are frozen in the currents
of trade; the withered leaves of industrial enterprise lie on every
side; farmers find no markets for their produce; the savings of
many years in thousands of families are gone.

More important, a host of unemployed citizens face the grim
problem of existence, and an equally great number toil with little
return. Only a foolish optimist can deny the dark realities of the
moment.

Yet our failure comes from no failure of substance. We are
stricken by no plague of locusts. Compared with the perils which
our forefathers conquered because they believed and were not
afraid, we have still much to be thankful for. Nature still offers
her bounty and human efforts have multiplied it. Plenty is at our
doorstep, but a generous use of it languishes in the very sight of
the supply. Primarily this is because the rulers of the exchange
of mankind's goods have failed through their own stubbornness
and their own incompetence, have admitted their failure, and
have abdicated. Practices of the unscrupulous moneychangers
stand indicted in the court of public opinion, rejected by the
hearts and minds of men.

True they have tried, but their efforts have been cast in the
pattern of an outworn tradition. Faced by failure of credit they
have proposed only the lending of more money. Stripped of the
lure of profit by which to induce our people to follow their false
leadership, they have resorted to exhortations, pleading tearfully
for restored confidence. They know only the rules of a generation
of self-seekers. They have no vision, and when there is no vision
the people perish.

The money changers have fled from their high seats in the temple of our civilization. We may now restore that temple to the
ancient truths. The measure of the restoration lies in the extent
to which we apply social values more noble than mere monetary
profit.

Happiness lies not in the mere possession of money; it lies in
the joy of achievement, in the thrill of creative effort. The joy

and moral stimulation of work no longer must be forgotten in the mad chase of evanescent profits. These dark days will be worth all they cost us if they teach us that our true destiny is not to be ministered unto but to minister to ourselves and to our fellow men.

Recognition of the falsity of material wealth as the standard of success goes hand in hand with the abandonment of the false belief that public office and high political position are to be valued only by the standards of pride of place and personal profit; and there must be an end to a conduct in banking and in business which too often has given to a sacred trust the likeness of callous and selfish wrongdoing. Small wonder that confidence languishes, for it thrives only on honesty, on honor, on the sacredness of obligations, on faithful protection, on unselfish performance; without them it cannot live.

Restoration calls, however, not for changes in ethics alone. This Nation asks for action, and action now.

Our greatest primary task is to put people to work. This is no unsolvable problem if we face it wisely and courageously. It can be accomplished in part by direct recruiting by the Government itself, treating the task as we would treat the emergency of a war, but at the same time, through this employment, accomplishing greatly needed projects to stimulate and reorganize the use of our natural resources.

Hand in hand with this we must frankly recognize the overbalance of population in our industrial centers and, by engaging on a national scale in a redistribution, endeavor to provide a better use of the land for those best fitted for the land. The task can be helped by definite efforts to raise the values of agricultural products and, with this, the power to purchase the output of our cities. It can be helped by preventing realistically the tragedy of the growing loss through foreclosure of our small homes and our farms. It can be helped by insistence that the Federal, State, and local governments act forthwith on the demand that their cost be drastically reduced. It can be helped by the unifying of relief activities which today are often scattered, uneconomical, and unequal. It can be helped by national planning for and supervision of all forms of transportation and of communications and other utilities which have a definite public character. There are many ways in which it can be helped, but it can never be helped merely by talking about it. We must act and act quickly.

Finally, in our progress toward a resumption of work we require two safeguards against a return of the evils of the old order; there must be a strict supervision of all banking and credits and investments, so that there will be an end to speculation with other people's money; and there must be provisions for an adequate but sound currency.

These are the lines of attack. I shall presently urge upon a new Congress, in special session, detailed measures for their fulfillment, and I shall seek the immediate assistance of the several States.

Through this program of action we address ourselves to putting our own national house in order and making income balance outgo. Our international trade relations, though vastly important, are in point of time and necessity secondary to the establishment of a sound national economy. I favor as a practical policy the putting of first things first. I shall spare no effort to restore world trade by international economic readjustment, but the emergency at home cannot wait on that accomplishment.

The basic thought that guides these specific means of national recovery is not narrowly nationalistic. It is the insistence, as a first consideration, upon the interdependence of the various elements in and parts of the United States—a recognition of the old and permanently important manifestation of the American spirit of the pioneer. It is the way to recovery. It is the immediate way. It is the strongest assurance that the recovery will endure.

In the field of world policy I would dedicate this Nation to the policy of the good neighbor—the neighbor who resolutely respects himself and because he does so, respects the rights of others—the neighbor who respects his obligations and respects the sanctity of his agreements in and with a world of neighbors.

If I read the temper of our people correctly, we now realize as we have never realized before our interdependence on each other; that we cannot merely take but we must give as well; that if we are to go forward, we must move as a trained and loyal army willing to sacrifice for the good of a common discipline, because without such discipline no progress is made, no leadership becomes effective. We are, I know, ready and willing to submit our lives and property to such discipline, because it makes possible a leadership which aims at a larger good. This I propose to offer, pledging that the larger purposes will bind upon us all as a sacred obligation with a unity of duty hitherto evoked only in time of armed strife.

With this pledge taken, I assume unhesitatingly the leadership of this great army of our people dedicated to a disciplined attack upon our common problems.

Action in this image and to this end is feasible under the form of government which we have inherited from our ancestors. Our Constitution is so simple and practical that it is possible always to meet extraordinary needs by changes in emphasis and arrangements without loss of essential form. That is why our constitutional system has proved itself the most superbly enduring political mechanism the modern world has produced. It has met every stress of vast expansion of territory, of foreign wars, of bitter internal strife, of world relations.

It is to be hoped that the normal balance of Executive and legislative authority may be wholly adequate to meet the unprecedented task before us. But it may be that an unprecedented demand and need for undelayed action may call for temporary departure from that normal balance of public procedure.

I am prepared under my constitutional duty to recommend the measures that a stricken Nation in the midst of a stricken world may require. These measures, or such other measures as the Congress may build out of its experience and wisdom, I shall seek, within my constitutional authority, to bring to speedy adoption.

But in the event that the Congress shall fail to take one of these two courses, and in the event that the national emergency is still critical, I shall not evade the clear course of duty that will then confront me. I shall ask the Congress for the one remaining instrument to meet the crisis—broad Executive power to wage a war against the emergency, as great as the power that would be given to me if we were in fact invaded by a foreign foe.

For the trust reposed in me I will return the courage and the devotion that befit the time. I can do no less.

We face the arduous days that lie before us in the warm courage of national unity; with the clear consciousness of seeking old and precious moral values; with the clear satisfaction that comes from the stern performance of duty by old and young alike. We aim at the assurance of a rounded and permanent national life.

We do not distrust the future of essential democracy. The people of the United States have not failed. In their need they have registered a mandate that they want direct, vigorous action. They have asked for discipline and direction under leadership. They have made me the present instrument of their wishes. In the spirit of the gift I take it.

In this dedication of a Nation we humbly ask the blessing of God. May He protect each and every one of us. May He guide me in the days to come.

Commanders of Power
(From "The Power Elite")
by C. Wright Mills
American sociologist and educator, 1916-1962

In none of the last three generations has a majority of the very rich been composed of men who have risen.

During the course of American history since the Civil War, the proportion of the very rich whose fathers worked as small farmers or storekeepers, as white-collar employees or wage workers has steadily decreased. Only 9 per cent of the very rich of our time originated in lower-class families—in families with only enough money to provide essential needs and sometimes minor comforts.

The history of the middle-class contribution to the very rich is a fairly stable one: in the 1900 generation, it provided two out of ten; in 1925, three; and in 1950 again two. But the upper-class and the lower-class contributions have quite steadily reversed themselves. Even in the famous nineteenth-century generation which scholarly historians usually discuss with the anecdotal details of the self-making myth, as many of the very rich derived from the upper class (39 per cent) as from the lower. Still, it is a fact that in that generation, 39 per cent of the very rich were sons of lower-class people. In the 1925 generation, the proportion had shrunk to 12 per cent, and by 1950, as we have seen, to 9 per cent. The upper classes, on the other hand, contributed 56 per cent in 1926; and in 1950, 68 per cent.

The reality and the trend are clearly the upper-class recruitment of the truly upper class of propertied wealth. Wealth not only tends to perpetuate itself, but as we shall see, tends also to monopolize new opportunities for getting "great wealth." Seven out of ten of the very rich among us today were born into distinctly upper-class homes, two out of ten on the level of middle-class comfort, and only one in lower-class milieu. . . .

The very rich do not reign alone on top of visible and simple hierarchies. But that they have been supplemented by agents and by hierarchies in the corporate structure of the economy and of the state does not mean that they have been displaced. Economically and socially, the very rich have not declined. After the crash and after the New Deal, the very rich have had to operate with skilled, legal technicians (both in and out of governments) whose services are essential in the fields of taxes and government regulations, corporate reorganization and merger, war contracts and public relations. They have also adopted every conceivable type of protective coloration for the essentially irresponsible nature of their power, creating the image of the small-town boy who made good, the "industrial statesman," the great inventor who "provides jobs," but who, withal, remains just an average guy.

What has happened is that the very rich are not so visible as they once seemed, to observers of the muckraker age, for example —who provided the last really public view of the top of American society. The absence of systematic information and the distraction of "human-interest" trivia tend to make us suppose that they do not really exist. But they are still very much among us—even though many are hidden, as it were, in the impersonal organizations in which their power, their wealth, and their privileges are anchored. . . .

The higher circles in America today contain, on the one hand, the laughing, erotic, dazzling glamor of the professional celebrity, and, on the other, the prestige aura of power, of authority, of might and wealth. These two pinnacles are not unrelated. The power elite is not so noticeable as the celebrities, and often does not want to be; the "power" of the professional celebrity is the power of distraction. America as a national public is indeed possessed of a strange set of idols. The professionals, in the main, are either glossy little animals or frivolous clowns; the men of power, in the main, rarely seem to be models of representative men.

Such moral uneasiness as prevails among the American elite themselves is accordingly quite understandable. Its existence is amply confirmed by the more serious among those who have come to feel that they represent America abroad. There, the double-faced character of the American celebrity is reflected both by the types of Americans who travel to play or to work, and in the images many literate and articulate Europeans hold of "Americans." Public honor in America tends now to be either frivolous or grim; either altogether trivial or portentous of a greatly tightened-up system of prestige.

The American elite is not composed of representative men whose conduct and character constitute models for American imitation and aspiration. There is no set of men with whom members of the mass public can rightfully and gladly identify. In this fundamental sense, America is indeed without leaders. Yet such is the nature of the mass public's morally cynical and politically unspecified distrust that it is readily drained off without real political effect. That this is so, after the men and events of the last thirty years, is further proof of the extreme difficulty of finding and using in America today the political means of sanity for morally sane objectives.

America—a conservative country without any conservative ideology—appears now before the world a naked and arbitrary power, as, in the name of realism, its men of decision enforce their often crackpot definitions upon world reality. The second-rate mind is in command of the ponderously spoken platitude. In the liberal rhetoric, vagueness, and in the conservative mood, irrationality, are raised to principle. Public relations and the official secret, the trivializing campaign and the terrible fact clumsily accomplished, are replacing the reasoned debate of political ideas in the privately incorporated economy, the military ascendancy, and the political vacuum of modern America.

The men of the higher circles are not representative men; their high position is not a result of moral virtue; their fabulous success is not firmly connected with meritorious ability. Those who sit in the seats of the high and mighty are selected and formed by the means of power, the sources of wealth, the mechanics of celebrity, which prevail in their society. They are not men selected and formed by a civil service that is linked with the world of knowledge and sensibility. They are not men shaped by nationally responsible parties that debate openly and clearly the issues this nation now so unintelligently confronts. They are not men held in responsible check by a plurality of voluntary associations which connect debating publics with the pinnacles of decision. Commanders of power unequaled in human history, they have succeeded within the American system of organized irresponsibility.

The Amorality of Money

(From "Money and Class in America")
BY LEWIS H. LAPHAM
American editor and essayist, born 1935

Money is like fire, an element as little troubled by moralizing as earth, air and water. Men can employ it as a tool or they can dance around it as if it were the incarnation of a god. Money votes socialist or monarchist, finds a profit in pornography or translations from the Bible, commissions Rembrandt and underwrites the technology of Auschwitz. It acquires its meaning from the uses to which it is put.

BY ANDREA DWORKIN
American feminist, born 1946

Money speaks, but it speaks with a male voice.

The Ambivalence of Money

(From the "Age of Uncertainty")
BY JOHN KENNETH GALBRAITH
American Keynesian economist, born 1908

Money is a singular thing. It ranks with love as man's greatest source of joy. And with death as his greatest source of anxiety. Over all history it has oppressed nearly all people in one of two ways: either it has been abundant and very unreliable, or reliable and very scarce.

BOOK X

War and Dictatorship

Two terrible evils and denunciations of them, which will be found timely in the era of the nuclear bomb and of the totalitarian threat to freedom.

I Sing the Battle
by HARRY KEMP

I sing the song of the great clean guns that belch forth death at
    will.
Ah, but the wailing mothers, the lifeless forms and still!

I sing the songs of the billowing flags, the bugles that cry before.
Ah, but the skeletons flapping rags, the lips that speak no more!

I sing the clash of bayonets and sabres that flash and cleave.
And wilt thou sing the maimed ones, too, that go with pinned-up
    sleeve?

I sing acclaimèd generals that bring the victory home.
Ah, but the broken bodies that drip like honey-comb!

I sing of hearts triumphant, long ranks of marching men.
And wilt thou sing the shadowy hosts that never march again?

Sartor Resartus
by THOMAS CARLYLE

What, speaking in quite unofficial language, is the net-purport
and upshot of war? To my own knowledge, for example, there
dwell and toil, in the British village of Dumdrudge, usually some
five hundred souls. From these, by certain "Natural Enemies" of
the French, there are successfully selected, during the French war,
say thirty able-bodied men: Dumdrudge, at her own expense, has
suckled and nursed them: she has, not without difficulty and
sorrow, fed them up to manhood, and even trained them to crafts,
so that one can weave, another build, another hammer and the
weakest can stand under thirty stone avoirdupois. Nevertheless,
amid much weeping and swearing, they are selected; all dressed
in red, and shipped away, at the public charges, some two thousand miles, or say only to the south of Spain; and fed there till
wanted. And now to that same spot, in the south of Spain, are
thirty similar French artisans, from a French Dumdrudge, in like
manner wending; till at length, after infinite effort, the two parties
come into actual juxtaposition, and Thirty stands fronting Thirty,
each with a gun in his hand. Straightway the word "Fire!" is given
and they blow the souls out of one another, and in place of sixty

brisk useful craftsmen, the world has sixty dead carcasses, which it must bury, and anew shed tears for. Had these men any quarrel? Busy as the Devil is, not the smallest! They lived far enough apart; were the entirest strangers; nay, in so wide a Universe, there was even, unconsciously, by Commerce, some mutual helpfulness between them. How then? Simpleton! their Governors had fallen out; and, instead of shooting one another, had the cunning to make these poor blockheads shoot.—Alas, so is it in Deutschland, and hitherto in all other lands; still as of old, "what devilry soever Kings do, the Greeks must pay the piper!"—In that fiction of the English Smollett, it is true, the final Cessation of War is perhaps prophetically shadowed forth; where the two Natural Enemies, in person, take each a Tobacco-pipe, filled with Brimstone; light the same, and smoke in one another's faces, till the weaker gives in: but from such predicted Peace-Era, what blood-filled trenches, and contentious centuries, may still divide us!

The Coming of War
by LEO TOLSTOY

The bells will peal, long-haired men will dress in golden sacks to pray for successful slaughter. And the old story will begin again, the awful customary acts.

The editors of the daily Press will begin virulently to stir men up to hatred and manslaughter in the name of patriotism, happy in the receipt of an increased income. Manufacturers, merchants, contractors for military stores, will hurry joyously about their business, in the hope of double receipts.

All sorts of Government officials will buzz about, foreseeing a possibility of purloining something more than usual. The military authorities will hurry hither and thither, drawing double pay and rations, and with the expectation of receiving for the slaughter of other men various silly little ornaments which they so highly prize, as ribbons, crosses, orders, and stars. Idle ladies and gentlemen will make a great fuss, entering their names in advance for the Red Cross Society, and ready to bind up the wounds of those whom their husbands and brothers will mutilate; and they will imagine that in so doing they are performing a most Christian work.

And, smothering despair within their souls by songs, licentiousness, and wine, men will trail along, torn from peaceful labor, from their wives, mothers and children—hundreds of thousands of simple-minded, good-natured men with murderous weapons in their hands—anywhere they may be driven.

They will march, freeze, hunger, suffer sickness, and die from it, or finally come to some place where they will be slain by thousands or kill thousands themselves with no reason—men whom they have never seen before, and who neither have done nor could do them any mischief.

And when the number of sick, wounded, and killed becomes so great that there are not hands enough left to pick them up, and when the air is so infected with the putrefying scent of the "food for powder" that even the authorities find it disagreeable, a truce will be made, the wounded will be picked up anyhow, the sick will be brought in and huddled together in heaps, the killed will be covered with earth and lime, and once more all the crowd of deluded men will be led on and on till those who have devised the project, weary of it, or till those who thought to find it profitable receive their spoil.

And so once more men will be made savage, fierce, and brutal, and love will wane in the world, and the Christianizing of mankind, which has already begun, will lapse for scores and hundreds of years. And so once more the men who reaped profit from it all, will assert with assurance that since there has been a war there must needs have been one, and that other wars must follow, and they will again prepare future generations for a continuance of slaughter, depraving them from their birth.

The Soldier's Oath
by Kaiser Wilhelm II
German emperor, 1859-1941

Recruits! Before the altar and the servant of God you have given me the oath of allegiance. You are too young to know the full meaning of what you have said, but your first care must be to obey implicitly all orders and directions. You have sworn fidelity to me, you are the children of my guard, you are my soldiers, you have surrendered yourselves to me, body and soul. Only one enemy can exist for you—my enemy. With the present Socialist machinations, it may happen that I shall order you to shoot your own relatives, your brothers, or even your parents—which God forbid—and then you are bound in duty implicitly to obey my orders.

Slavery
by WILLIAM COWPER
English poet, 1731-1800

O for a lodge in some vast wilderness,
Some boundless contiguity of shade,
Where rumor of oppression and deceit,
Of unsuccessful or successful war,
Might never reach me more. My ear is pained,
My soul is sick, with every day's report
Of wrong and outrage with which earth is filled.
There is no flesh in man's obdurate heart,
It does not feel for man; the natural bond
Of brotherhood is severed as the flax
That falls asunder at the touch of fire.
He finds his fellow guilty of a skin
Not colored like his own; and having power
To enforce the wrong, for such a worthy cause
Dooms and devotes him as his lawful prey.
Lands intersected by a narrow frith
Abhor each other. Mountains interposed
Make enemies of nations, who had else
Like kindred drops been mingled into one.
Thus man devotes his brother, and destroys;
And, worse than all, and most to be deplored,
As human nature's broadest, foulest blot,
Chains him, and tasks him, and exacts his sweat
With stripes, that Mercy, with a bleeding heart,
Weeps when she sees inflicted on a beast.

The Biglow Papers
by JAMES RUSSELL LOWELL
These poems, first published in the *Atlantic Monthly* in 1846, voiced the bitter
opposition of New England to the Mexican war as a slaveholders' enterprise.

Thrash away, you'll *hev* to rattle
  On them kittle-drums o' yourn,—
'Tain't a knowin' kind o' cattle
  Thet is ketched with mouldy corn;
Put in stiff, you fifer feller,
  Let folks see how spry you be,—
Guess you'll toot till you are yeller
  'Fore you git ahold o' me! . . .

Ez fer war, I call it murder,—
　　There you hev it plain an' flat;
I don't want to go no furder
　　Than my Testyment fer that;
God hez sed so plump an' fairly,
　　It's ez long ez it is broad,
An' you've got to git up airly
　　Ef you want to take in God.

'Tain't your eppyletts an' feathers
　　Make the thing a grain more right;
'Tain't afollerin' your bell-wethers
　　Will excuse ye in His sight;
Ef you take a sword an' dror it,
　　An' go stick a feller thru,
Guv'mint ain't to answer for it,
　　God'll send the bill to you.

Wut's the use o' meetin'-goin'
　　Every Sabbath, wet or dry,
Ef it's right to go amowin'
　　Feller-men like oats an' rye?
I dunno but wut it's pooty
　　Trainin' round in bobtail coats,—
But it's curus Christian dooty
　　This 'ere cuttin' folks's throats. . . .

Tell ye jest the end I've come to
　　Arter cipherin' plaguey smart,
An' it makes a handy sum, tu,
　　Any gump could larn by heart;
Laborin' man an' laborin' woman
　　Hev one glory an' one shame.
Ev'y thin' thet's done inhuman
　　Injers all on 'em the same.

'Tain't by turnin' out to hack folks
　　You're agoin' to git your right,
Nor by lookin' down on black folks
　　Coz you're put upon by white;
Slavery ain't o' nary color,
　　'Tain't the hide thet makes it wus,
All it keers fer in a feller
　　'S jest to make him fill its pus.

To a Nine-inch Gun
by P. F. McCarthy
This poem came to the New York *World* office on a crumpled piece of soiled
paper. The author's address was given as Fourth Bench, City Hall Park.

Whether your shell hits the target or not,
Your cost is Five Hundred Dollars a Shot.
You thing of noise and flame and power,
We feed you a hundred barrels of flour
Each time you roar. Your flame is fed
With twenty thousand loaves of bread.
Silence! A million hungry men
Seek bread to fill their mouths again.

Kruppism
by Percy Mackaye
American poet and dramatist, 1875-1956

Crowned on the twilight battlefield, there bends
   A crooked iron dwarf, and delves for gold,
   Chuckling: "One hundred thousand gatlings—sold!"
And the moon rises, and a moaning rends
The mangled living, and the dead distends,
   And a child cowers on the chartless wold,
   Where, searching in his safety vault of mold,
The kobold kaiser cuts his dividends.

We, who still wage his battles, are his thralls,
   And dying do him homage; yea, and give
   Daily our living souls to be enticed
Into his power. So long as on war's walls
   We build engines of death that he may live,
So long shall we serve Krupp instead of Christ.

By The Empress Catherine II of Russia
1729-1796

The only way to save our empires from the encroachment of
the people is to engage in war, and thus substitute national
passions for social aspirations.

The War Prayer

by Mark Twain

This "War Prayer," withheld from publication until after Mark Twain's death, pictures the assembling of soldiers in church, and the prayer of the chaplain for victory. In answer to the prayer, God sends down a white-robed messenger, who voices the unspoken meaning of the prayer.

"O Lord our God, help us to tear their soldiers to bloody shreds with our shells; help us to cover their smiling fields with the pale forms of their patriot dead; help us to drown the thunder of the guns with the wounded, writhing in pain; help us to lay waste their humble homes with a hurricane of fire; help us to wring the hearts of their unoffending widows with unavailing grief; help us to turn them out roofless with their little children to wander unfriended through wastes of their desolated land in rags and hunger and thirst, sport of the sun-flames of summer and the icy winds of winter, broken in spirit, worn with travail, imploring Thee for the refuge of the grave and denied it—for our sakes, who adore Thee, Lord, blast their hopes, blight their lives, protract their bitter pilgrimage, make heavy their steps, water their way with their tears, stain the white snow with the blood of their wounded feet! We ask of one who is the Spirit of love and who is the ever-faithful refuge and friend of all that are sore beset, and seek His aid with humble and contrite hearts. Grant our prayer, O Lord, and Thine shall be the praise and honor and glory now and ever, Amen."

(After a pause.) "Ye have prayed it; if ye still desire it, speak! —the messenger of the Most High waits."

Song of the Exposition

by Walt Whitman

Away with themes of war! away with War itself!
Hence from my shuddering sight, to never more return, that
    show of blacken'd, mutilated corpses!
That hell unpent, and raid of blood—fit for wild tigers, or for
    lop-tongued wolves—not reasoning men!
And in its stead speed Industry's campaigns!
With thy undaunted armies, Engineering!
Thy pennants, Labor, loosen'd to the breeze!
Thy bugles sounding loud and clear!

The Illusion of War
by RICHARD LeGALLIENNE
British-American poet, 1866-1947

War I abhor, and yet how sweet
The sound along the marching street
Of drum and fife, and I forget
Wet eyes of widows, and forget
Broken old mothers, and the whole
Dark butchery without a soul.

Without a soul, save this bright drink
Of heady music, sweet as hell;
And even my peace-abiding feet
Go marching with the marching street—
For yonder, yonder goes the fife,
And what care I for human life!

The tears fill my astonished eyes,
    And my full heart is like to break;
And yet 'tis all embannered lies,
    A dream those little drummers make.

O, it is wickedness to clothe
    Yon hideous grinning thing that stalks,
Hidden in music, like a queen,
    That in a garden of glory walks,
Till good men love the thing they loathe.

Art, thou hast many infamies,
    But not an infamy like this—
Oh, snap the fife, and still the drum,
    And show the monster as she is!

Buttons
by CARL SANDBURG
American poet, 1878–1967

I have been watching the war map slammed up for advertising
    in front of the newspaper office.
Buttons—red and yellow buttons—blue and black buttons—are
    shoved back and forth across the map.

A laughing young man, sunny with freckles,
Climbs a ladder, yells a joke to somebody in the crowd,
And then fixes a yellow button one inch west
And follows the yellow button with a black button one inch
  west.

(Ten thousand men and boys twist on their bodies in a red soak
  along a river edge,
Gasping of wounds, calling for water, some rattling death in
  their throats.)
Who by Christ would guess what it cost to move two buttons
  one inch on the war map here in front of the newspaper
  office where the freckle-faced young man is laughing to us?

The Wine Press
by ALFRED NOYES
English poet, 1880-1958

A murdered man, ten miles away,
  Will hardly shake your peace,
Like one red stain upon your hand;
And a tortured child in a distant land
Will never check one smile to-day,
  Or bid one fiddle cease.

The News

It comes along a little wire,
  Sunk in a deep sea;
It thins in the clubs to a little smoke
Between one joke and another joke,
For a city in flames is less than the fire
  That comforts you and me.

The Diplomats

Each was honest after his way,
  Lukewarm in faith, and old;
And blood, to them, was only a word,
And the point of a phrase their only sword,
And the cost of war, they reckoned it
  In little disks of gold.

They were cleanly groomed.
           They were not to be bought.
  And their cigars were good.
But they had pulled so many strings
In the tinselled puppet-show of kings
That, when they talked of war, they thought
  Of sawdust, not of blood;

Not of the crimson tempest
  Where the shattered city falls:
They thought, behind their varnished doors,
Of diplomats, ambassadors,
Budgets, and loans and boundary lines,
  Coercions and re-calls.

The Charge

Slaughter! Slaughter! Slaughter!
  The cold machines whirred on.
And strange things crawled amongst the wheat
With entrails dragging round their feet,
And over the foul red shambles
  A fearful sunlight shone. . . .

The maxims cracked like cattle-whips
  Above the struggling hordes.
They rolled and plunged and writhed like snakes
In the trampled wheat and the blackthorn brakes,
And the lightnings leapt among them
  Like clashing crimson swords.

The rifles flogged their wallowing herds,
  Flogged them down to die.
Down on their slain the slayers lay,
And the shrapnel thrashed them into the clay,
And tossed their limbs like tattered birds
  Thro' a red volcanic sky.

By FREDERICK THE GREAT OF PRUSSIA
1712-1786

If my soldiers were to begin to reflect, not one of them would remain in the ranks.

War

by WILLIAM H. DAVIES
English poet who spent many years as a tramp, 1871-1940

Ye Liberals and Conservatives,
Have pity on our human lives,
  Waste not more blood on human strife;
Until we know some way to use
This human blood we take or lose,
  'Tis sin to sacrifice our life.

When pigs are stuck we save their blood
And make puddings for our food,
  The sweetest and the cheapest meat;
And many a woman, man and boy
Have ate those puddings with great joy,
  And oft-times in the open street.

Let's not have war till we can make,
Of this sweet life we lose or take,
  Some kind of pudding of man's gore;
So that the clergy in each parish
May save the lives of those that famish
  Because meat's dear and times are poor.

In Praise of the Warrior
(From "Don Quixote")
by MIGUEL DE CERVANTES
Greatest of Spanish novelists, 1547-1616

I am not a barbarian, and I love letters, but let us beware of according them pre-eminence over arms, or even an equality with arms. The man of letters, it is very true, instructs and illuminates his fellows, softens manners, elevates minds, and teaches us justice, a beautiful and sublime science. But the warrior makes us observe justice. His object is to procure us the first and sweetest of blessings, peace, gentlest peace, so necessary to human happiness. This peace, adorable blessing, gift divine, source of happiness, this peace is the object of war. The warrior labors to procure it for us, and the warrior therefore performs the most useful labor in the world.

The Arsenal at Springfield

by HENRY WADSWORTH LONGFELLOW
American poet, 1807-1882

This is the Arsenal. From floor to ceiling,
  Like a huge organ, rise the burnished arms;
But from their silent pipes no anthem pealing
  Startles the villages with strange alarms.

Ah! what a sound will rise—how wild and dreary—
  When the death-angel touches those swift keys!
What loud lament and dismal Miserere
  Will mingle with their awful symphonies!

I hear even now the infinite fierce chorus—
  The cries of agony, the endless groan,
Which, through the ages that have gone before us,
  In long reverberations reach our own. . . .

Is it, O man, with such discordant noises,
  With such accursed instruments as these,
Thou drownest Nature's sweet and kindly voices,
  And jarrest the celestial harmonies?

Were half the power that fills the world with terror,
  Were half the wealth bestowed on camps and courts,
Given to redeem the human mind from error,
  There were no need of arsenals or forts.

War

by CHIEF JOSEPH
Indian chief, c.1840-1904

Hear me, my warriors; my heart is sick and sad;
Our chiefs are killed,
The old men are all dead,
It is cold and we have no blankets;
The little children are freezing to death.
Hear me, my warriors; my heart is sick and sad;
From where the sun now stands I will fight no more forever!

A Project for a Perpetual Peace

by JEAN JACQUES ROUSSEAU
French novelist and philosopher, 1712-1788

As a more noble, useful, and delightful Project never engaged the human mind, than that of establishing a perpetual peace among the contending nations of Europe, never did a writer lay a better claim to the attention of the public than he who points out the means to carry such a design into execution. It is indeed very difficult for a man of probity and sensibility, not to be fired with a kind of enthusiasm on such a subject; nay, I am not clear that the very illusions of a heart truly humane, whose warmth makes everything easily surmountable, are not in this case more eligible than that rigid and forbidding prudence, which finds in its own indifference and want of public spirit, the chief obstacle to everything that tends to promote the public good.

I doubt not that many of my readers will be forearmed with incredulity, to withstand the pleasing temptation of being persuaded; and indeed I sincerely lament their dullness in mistaking obstinacy for wisdom. But I flatter myself, that many an honest mind will sympathize with me in that delightful emotion, with which I take up the pen to treat of a subject so greatly interesting to the world. I am going to take a view, at least in imagination, of mankind united by love and friendship: I am going to take a contemplative prospect of an agreeable and peaceful society of brethren, living in constant harmony, directed by the same maxims, and joint sharers of one common felicity; while, realizing to myself so affecting a picture, the representation of such imaginary happiness will give me the momentary enjoyment of a pleasure actually present.

By MICAH

Hebrew prophet, 700 B.C.

He shall judge among many people, and rebuke strong nations afar off: and they shall beat their swords into plowshares, and their spears into pruninghooks: nation shall not lift up a sword against nation, neither shall they learn war any more. But they shall sit every man under his vine and under his fig tree; and none shall make them afraid; for the mouth of the Lord of hosts hath spoken it.

Guernica, *Pablo Picasso*

A Prayer of the Peoples
by PERCY MACKAYE

God of us who kill our kind!
Master of this blood-tracked Mind
Which from wolf and Caliban
Staggers toward the star of Man—
Now, on Thy cathedral stair,
God, we cry to Thee in prayer!

Where our stifled anguish bleeds
Strangling through Thine organ reeds,
Where our voiceless songs suspire
From the corpses in Thy choir—
Through Thy charred and shattered nave,
God, we cry on Thee to save!

Save us from our tribal gods!
From the racial powers, whose rods—
Wreathed with stinging serpents—stir
Odin and old Jupiter
From their ancient hells of hate
To invade Thy dawning state....

Lord, our God! to whom, from clay,
Blood and mire, Thy peoples pray—
Not from Thy cathedral's stair
Thou hearest:—Thou criest *through* our prayer
For our prayer is but the gate:
We, who pray, ourselves are fate.

War and Peace
by BENJAMIN FRANKLIN
American statesman and scientist, 1706-1790

I join with you most cordially in rejoicing at the return of
peace. I hope it will be lasting, and that mankind will at length,
as they call themselves reasonable creatures, have reason enough
to settle their differences without cutting throats; for, in my
opinion, there never was a good war or a bad peace. What vast
additions to the conveniences and comforts of life might man-

kind have acquired, if the money spent in wars had been employed in works of utility! What an extension of agriculture, even to the tops of the mountains; what rivers rendered navigable, or joined by canals; what bridges, aqueducts, new roads, and other public works, edifices and improvements, rendering England a complete paradise, might not have been obtained by spending those millions in doing good, which in the last war have been spent in doing mischief—in bringing misery into thousands of families, and destroying the lives of so many working people, who might have performed the useful labors.

"I Am Prepared to Receive Your Sentence"
(From statement to court, September, 1918, before being sentenced for violation of Espionage Act)
by EUGENE V. DEBS
Most popular of all socialist leaders, three times candidate for President, 1855-1926

Your Honor, I have stated in this court that I am opposed to the form of our present Government; that I am opposed to the social system in which we live; that I believe in the change of both—but by perfectly peaceable and orderly means.

I believe, Your Honor, in common with all Socialists, that this nation ought to own and control its industries. I believe, as all Socialists do, that all things that are jointly needed and used ought to be jointly owned—that industry, the basis of life, instead of being the private property of the few and operated for their enrichment, ought to be the common property of all, democratically administered in the interest of all.

I have been accused, Your Honor, of being an enemy of the soldier. I hope I am laying no flattering unction to my soul when I say that I don't believe the soldier has a more sympathetic friend than I am. If I had my way there would be no soldiers. But I realize the sacrifice they are making. Your Honor, I can think of them. I can feel for them. I can sympathize with them. That is one of the reasons why I have been doing what little has been in my power to bring about a condition of affairs in this country worthy of the sacrifices they have made and that they are now making in its behalf.

Your Honor, I wish to make acknowledgement of my thanks to the counsel for the defense. They have not only defended me with exceptional legal ability, but with a personal attachment and devotion of which I am deeply sensible, and which I can never forget.

Your Honor, I ask no mercy. I plead for no immunity. I realize that finally the right must prevail. I never more clearly comprehended than now the great struggle between the powers of greed on the one hand and upon the other the rising hosts of freedom.

I can see the dawn of a better day of humanity. The people are awakening. In due course of time they will come to their own.

When the mariner, sailing over tropic seas, looks for release from his weary watch, he turns his eyes toward the Southern Cross, burning luridly above the tempest-tossed ocean. As the midnight approaches, the Southern Cross begins to bend, and the whirling worlds change their places, and with starry finger-points the Almighty marks the passage of time upon the dial of the universe, and though no bell may beat the glad tidings, the lookout knows that the midnight is passing—that relief and rest are close at hand.

Let the people take heart and hope everywhere, for the cross is bending, the midnight is passing, and joy cometh with the morning.

Your Honor, I thank you, and I thank all of this court for their courtesy, for their kindness, which I shall remember always.

I am prepared to receive your sentence.

The End of Isolation
by WOODROW WILSON
President of the United States during World War I, 1856-1924

The United States enjoyed the spiritual leadership of the world until the Senate of the United States failed to ratify the treaty by which the belligerent nations sought to effect the settlements by which they had fought throughout the war.

It is inconceivable that at this supreme crisis and final turning point in the international relations of the whole world, when the results of the Great War are by no means determined and are still questionable and dependent upon events which no man can foresee or count upon, the United States should withdraw from the congress of progressive and enlightened nations by which Germany was defeated, and all similar Governments (if the world be so unhappy as to contain any) warned of the consequences of any attempt at a like iniquity, and yet that is the effect of the course which the United States has taken with regard to the Treaty of Versailles.

Germany is beaten, but we are still at war with her, and the old stage is reset for a repetition of the whole plot. It is now ready for a resumption of the old offensive and defensive alliances which made settled peace impossible. It is now open again to every sort of intrigue.

The old spies are free to resume their former abominable activities. They are again at liberty to make it impossible for Governments to be sure what mischief is being worked among their own people, what internal disorders are being fomented.

Without the Covenant of the League of Nations there may be as many secret treaties as ever, to destroy the confidence of Governments in each other, and their validity cannot be questioned.

None of the objects we professed to be fighting for has been secured, or can be made certain of, without this Nation's ratification of the treaty and its entry into the Covenant. This Nation entered the Great War to vindicate its own rights and to protect and preserve free government. It went into the war to see it through to the end, and the end has not yet come. It went into the war to make an end of militarism, to furnish guarantees to weak nations, and to make a just and lasting peace. It entered it with noble enthusiasm. Five of the leading belligerents have accepted the treaty and formal ratifications soon will be exchanged. The question is whether this country will enter and enter wholeheartedly. If it does not do so, the United States and Germany will play a lone hand in the world.

The maintenance of the peace of the world and the effective execution of the treaty depend upon the whole-hearted participation of the United States. I am not stating it as a matter of power. The point is that the United States is the only Nation which has sufficient moral force with the rest of the world to guarantee the substitution of discussion for war. If we keep out of this agreement, if we do not give our guarantees, then another attempt will be made to crush the new nations of Europe.

The Revolution Betrayed
by LEON TROTSKY
Russian Bolshevik, assassinated in exile by an agent of Stalin's secret police,
1877-1940

The social meaning of the Soviet Thermidor now begins to take form before us. The poverty and cultural backwardness of the masses has again become incarnate in the malignant figure of the ruler with a great club in his hand. The deposed and abused bureaucracy, from being a servant of society, has again become its lord. On this road it has attained such a degree of social and moral alienation from the popular masses, that it cannot now permit any control over either its activities or its income.

The bureaucracy's seemingly mystic fear of "petty speculators, grafters, and gossips" thus finds a wholly natural explanation. Not yet able to satisfy the elementary needs of the population, the Soviet economy creates and resurrects at every step tendencies to graft and speculation. On the other side, the privileges of the new aristocracy awaken in the masses of the population a tendency to listen to anti-Soviet "gossips"—that is, to anyone who, albeit in a whisper, criticizes the greedy and capricious bosses. It is a question, therefore, not of specters of the past, not of the remnants of what no longer exists, not, in short, of the snows of yesteryear, but of new, mighty and continually reborn tendencies to personal accumulation. The first still very meager wave of prosperity in the country, just because of its meagerness, has not weakened, but strengthened, these centrifugal tendencies. On the other hand, there has developed simultaneously a desire of the under-privileged to slap the grasping hands of the new gentry. The social struggle again grows sharp. Such are the sources of the power of the bureaucracy. But from these same sources comes also a threat to its power.

Tyranny: U.S.A.
(From "It Can't Happen Here")
by SINCLAIR LEWIS
American novelist, Nobel Prize for Literature 1930; 1885-1951

Doremus went on: "If Bishop Prang, our Savonarola in a Cadillac 16, swings his radio audience and his League of Forgotten Men to Buzz Windrip, Buzz will win. People will think they're electing him to create more economic security. Then watch the Terror! God knows there's been enough indication that we *can* have tyranny in America—the fix of the Southern share-croppers, the working conditions of the miners and garment-makers, and our keeping Mooney in prison so many years. But wait till Windrip shows us how to say it with machine guns! Democracy—here and in Britain and France, it hasn't been so universal a sniveling slavery as Naziism in Germany, such an imagination-hating, pharisaic materialism as Russia—even if it has produced industrialists like you, Frank, and bankers like you, R. C., and given you altogether too much power and money. On the whole, with scandalous exceptions, Democracy's given the ordinary worker more dignity than he ever had. That may be menaced now by Windrip—all the Windrips. All right! Maybe we'll have to fight paternal dictatorship with a little sound patricide—fight machine guns with machine guns. Wait till Buzz takes charge of us. A real Fascist dictatorship!"

"Nonsense! Nonsense!" snorted Tasbrough. "That couldn't happen here in America, not possibly! We're a country of freemen."

"The answer to that," suggested Doremus Jessup, "if Mr. Falck will forgive me, is 'the hell it can't!' Why, there's no country in the world that can get more hysterical—yes, or more obsequious!—than America. Look how Huey Long became absolute monarch over Louisiana, and how the Right Honorable Mr. Senator Berzelius Windrip owns *his* state. Listen to Bishop Prang and Father Coughlin on the radio—divine oracles, to millions. Remember how casually most Americans have accepted Tammany grafting and Chicago gangs and the crookedness of so many of President Harding's appointees? Could Hitler's bunch, or Windrip's, be worse? Remember the Ku Klux Klan? Remember our war hysteria, when we called sauerkraut 'Liberty cabbage' and somebody actually proposed calling German measles 'Liberty measles'? And wartime censorship of honest papers? Bad as Russia! Remember our kissing the—well, the feet of Billy Sunday, the million-dollar evangelist, and of Aimee McPherson, who swam from the Pacific Ocean clear into the Arizona desert, and got away with it? Remember Voliva and Mother Eddy? . . . Remember our Red scares and our Catholic scares, when all well-informed people knew that the O. G. P. U. were hiding out in Osklaloosa, and the Republicans campaigning against Al Smith told the Carolina mountaineers that if Al won the Pope would illegitimatize their children? Remember Tom Heflin and Tom Dixon? Remember when the hick legislators in certain states, in obedience to William Jennings Bryan, who learned his biology from his pious old grandma, set up shop as scientific experts and made the whole world laugh itself sick by forbidding the teaching of evolution? . . . Remember the Kentucky night-riders? Remember how trainloads of people have gone to enjoy lynchings? Not happen here? Prohibition—shooting down people just because they *might* be transporting liquor—no, that couldn't happen in A erica! Why, where in all history has there ever been a people so ripe for dictatorship as ours! We're ready to start on a Children's Crusade—only of adults—right now, and the Right Reverend Abbots, Windrip and Prang are all ready to lead it!"

"Well, what if they are?" protested R. C. Crowley. "It might not be so bad. I don't like all these irresponsible attacks on us bankers all the time. Of course, Senator Windrip has to pretend publicly to bawl the banks out, but once he gets into power he'll give the banks their proper influence in the administration and take our expert financial advice. Yes. Why are you so afraid of the word 'Fascism,' Doremus? Just a word—just a word! And might not be so bad, with all the lazy bums we got panhandling relief nowadays, and living on my income tax and yours—not so worse to have a Strong Man, like Hitler or Mussolini—like Napoleon and Bismarck in the good old days—and have 'em really *run* the country and make it efficient and prosperous again. 'Nother words, have a doctor who won't take any back-chat, but really boss the patient and make him get well whether he likes it or not!"

"Yes!" said Emil Staubmeyer. "Didn't Hitler save Germany from the Red Plague of Marxism? I got cousins there. I *know!*"

"Hm," said Doremus, as often Doremus did say it. "Cure the evils of Democracy by the evils of Fascism! Funny therapeutics. I've heard of their curing syphilis by giving the patient malaria, but I've never heard of their curing malaria by giving the patient syphilis!"

"Think that's nice language to use in the presence of the Reverend Falck?" raged Tasbrough.

Mr. Falck piped up. "I think it's quite nice language, and an interesting suggestion, Brother Jessup!"

"Besides," said Tasbrough, "this chewing the rag is all nonsense, anyway. As Crowley says, might be a good thing to have a strong man in the saddle, but—it just can't happen here in America."

And it seemed to Doremus that the softly moving lips of the Reverend Mr. Falck were framing, "The hell it can't!"

Fascism in Italy
(From "Sawdust Caesar")
by GEORGE SELDES
American journalist, 1890–1995

We have passed slowly through the centuries of village economy, serfdom, and the feudal overlords; very quickly through the era of industrial and commercial expansion, the era of colonization, the opening of world markets, the exploitation of "inferior" peoples, and we have arrived at the most magnificent smash-up in history in the decade and a half of the World War and the economic debacle of 1929.

The rule of capital, big business, commercial penetration, and colonial expansion has been a time of democracy and social reform. But apparently, as Mussolini himself claims, liberalism is dead and the Goddess of Liberty is a rotten carcass: the ruling class can no longer make their profits and afford to grant democracy and social reforms. The various imperialisms which have divided the world have left no new markets to conquer, no inferior people to make into slaves and serfs to produce wealth and absorb the production of the superior people.

In this world emergency Fascism arose to perpetuate the system of exploitation of its own people as well as those which it could conquer. The Authoritarian State is also the Helot State, the Serf State, for the vast majority outside the reigning hierarchy. Year by year Italy has been returning to the time of serfdom and the feudal overlords . . .

Those opponents of Fascism who have always maintained that it presented no new philosophy, no new ideology, but was merely a restatement of a medieval system and that every step taken by Mussolini was a step backwards into a dead civilization, had proof of their view in the official reasons Italy gave to the League of Nations for war in Ethiopia.

The massacre of Val-Val was the first excuse given. But it was dropped even before the League's commission absolved both countries of guilt. Then came two new reasons: imperialism, or the necessity of expansion by powerful nations, and *Kultur*, or the right of a civilized country to take over a barbaric country where slavery still flourished.

Both reasons date from the eighteenth and nineteenth centuries; it is true they were used by Britain in building her empire, and were advanced by Wilhelm in an attempt to rule the world, but no nation has been hypocritical enough to use them again in our own time. As for slavery in Ethiopia, the League has taken actions, the Emperor of Ethiopia has done his best, considering the fact the country is a loose confederation in which tribal chiefs frequently refuse to. listen to Addis Ababa, but the hypocrisy of the whole matter is best shown in the fact that Fascist Italy has herself admitted slavery in the form of economic servitude still flourishes in her African colony of Libya.

The road to war has been inevitable. Even before John Strachey wrote that "Fascism means war," an Italian writer, Mario Carli, predicted that "Fascism issued from the war and in war it must find its outlet." Fascism means war because imperialism means war, and no has ever denied that Fascism is imperialistic.

"Imperialism is at the base of the life of every people which desires economic and spiritual expansion," Mussolini once wrote, and again, "We must have the courage to say that Italy cannot remain forever penned up in one sea, even if it is the Adriatic," while in the famous June 5, 1923, speech against Yugoslavia, he said that "all Italians of my generation understand the lack of territory. It is not surprising, therefore, that our spirit is frequently excited as it turns towards imperialistic aspirations. This is an expression of immanent historic reality, because people who are progressing have their rights against people who are declining. These rights are marked with letters of fire in the pages of our destiny."

The Peat-Bog Soldiers
(Song of the Nazi Concentration Camps)

Far and wide as the eye can wander,
Heath and bog are everywhere.
Not a bird sings out to cheer us,
Oaks are standing gaunt and bare.

    We are the peat-bog soldiers,
    We're marching with our spades to the bog.

Up and down the guards are pacing,
No one, no one can get through.
Flight would mean a sure death-facing,
Guns and barbed wire greet our view.

We are the peat-bog soldiers,
We're marching with our spades to the bog.

But for us there is no complaining,
Winter will in time be past.
One day we shall cry rejoicing:
Homeland dear, you're mine at last!

Then will the peat-bog soldiers
March no more with their spades to the bog.

Song of the International Brigades
by ERICH WEINERT

From far-off fatherlands we've come here,
We took nothing with us but our hate;
Yet we haven't ever lost a homeland,
For our homeland is now outside Madrid,
Yet we haven't ever lost a homeland,
For our homeland is now outside Madrid.
With our Spanish brothers in the trenches,
Fighting in the hot Castilian sun—

REFRAIN:
Forward, International Brigaders, forward!
Raise the banner of solidarity.
Forward, International Brigaders, forward!
Raise the banner of solidarity.

Spanish freedom now is in our keeping,
To defend it we came across the seas;
Devil take the hated Foreign Legion,
Drive the bandit general to the sea.
Devil take the hated Foreign Legion,
Drive the bandit general to the sea.
Dreamed he'd be in Madrid for the parade soon;
We came first, Franco's army was too late—

REFRAIN

With rifle, bomb, and our machine guns
We'll exterminate the fascist plague,
Free all Spain of plunderers and pirates—
Spanish brothers, Spain belongs to you.
Free all Spain of plunderers and pirates—
Spanish brothers, Spain belongs to you.
Show no mercy to the fascist rebels,
Nor to any traitor in our ranks—

REFRAIN

The Dead Don't Count
(From "Stalingrad")
by THEODORE PLIEVIER

German novelist, refugee from Nazis in Soviet Union who later fled East German
Communist regime also; 1892-1955

Private Widomec recalled the starving Greeks, Roumanians,
Poles and Slovaks in the streets of Vienna and thought: "This
had to happen to us!"

But there were few who thought like this or indeed thought
at all. The mass trudged on at the speed of one kilometer an hour.
The army had been an elite army and had been mostly recruited
not in towns but from country districts. The peasant lads had
already been torn from their soil by "Arbeitsdienst" and pre-
military training, and those who were infantrymen had a march
of more than two thousand kilometers behind them. Their in-
testines, as later post-mortems showed, were without windings and
flat as tape; the men were outwardly and inwardly deformed.
They found themselves now in the bottomless pit, and with the
last roar of their cannon their souls seemed to have fluttered away;
the silence they were going through was already like the land of
death. They trudged on, with frozen feet or frozen toes, faces
gnawed by frost, some without ears, some without noses. To them
the chevrons of lance-corporal and sergeant had been the rank-
badges of the only conceivable order, and with the vanished
importance of these badges their world of order had collapsed.
They drifted on, and it was an exception when a hand was held
out to one of them; it was scarcely thinkable for a last crust of
bread to be shared. The whole organism was sick, the cell was
sick, and each man was alone. The organism was dissolved into
blood and mucus and yellow and black bile. The individual found

"Bury Them and Be Silent," *F. Goya*

himself on the brink of dissolution. Only a step separated him from it, with only one hand he was holding on to the ship of life. Many let go, their will power used up on the endless road and in the thunder of battle from the Carpathians to the Volga.

The chaos had been ordered and there it was.

The grey procession reached the plain of the Don and streamed on by the railway-tracks towards Kotuban. At villages, at stud farms, at tractor stations, stood wagons; the wagons took up the flood of men, and on they rolled on railway-axles. The excreta that poured out of the closets of the wagons and froze in thick lumps of bloody red on axles and wheels betrayed the passenger that travelled with the afflicted multitude.

Like a plague-ship this procession on the march through the white land and rolling onward on railway-axles, left dead in its wake—those who died of their wounds, of white and red dysentery, of sheer paralysis of the spirit. These dead don't count; their name was written in snow. But there are graves of Russian military doctors and of male and female nurses who accompanied the procession and found death in the journey. These graves count; they are written in the book of humanity. On the first stage, to the first assembly-camp, there are forty-two of them.

Human beings misled and scattered, striding over all the drawn frontiers, following the unfurled banners of insanity, spreading over the map of Europe—and in this inhuman enterprise ground to refuse, ground to dust.

The Nazi War Criminals
by ROBERT H. JACKSON

Supreme Court Justice and Chief Prosecutor for the United States at the Nuremberg War Crimes Trials; 1892-1954. The following is from the opening statement for the U.S.A. at the trials.

I am too well aware of the weakness of juridical action alone to contend that in itself your decision under this Charter can prevent future wars. Judicial action always comes after the event. Wars are started only on the theory and in the confidence that they can be won. Personal punishment, to be suffered only in the event the war is lost, will probably not be a sufficient deterrent to prevent a war where the war-makers feel the chances of defeat to be negligible.

But the ultimate step in avoiding periodic wars, which are inevitable in a system of international lawlessness, is to make statesmen responsible to law. And let me make clear that while this law is first applied against German aggressors, the law includes, and if it is to serve a useful purpose it must condemn, aggression by any other nations, including those which sit here now in judgment. We are able to do away with domestic tyranny and violence and aggression by those in power against the rights of their own people only when we make all men answerable to the law. This trial represents mankind's desperate effort to apply the discipline of the law to statesmen who have used their powers of state to attack the foundations of the world's peace and to commit aggressions against the rights of their neighbors.

The usefulness of this effort to do justice is not to be measured by considering the law or your judgment in isolation. This trial is part of the great effort to make the peace more secure. One step in this direction is the United Nations organization, which may take joint political action to prevent war if possible, and joint military action to insure that any nation which starts a war will lose it. This Charter and this trial, implementing the Kellogg-Briand Pact, constitute another step in the same direction —juridical action of a kind to ensure that those who start a war will pay for it personally.

While the defendants and the prosecutors stand before you as individuals, it is not the triumph of either group alone that is committed to your judgment. Above all personalities there are anonymous and impersonal forces whose conflict makes up much of human history. It is yours to throw the strength of the law back of either the one or the other of these forces for at least another generation. What are the real forces that are contending before you?

No charity can disguise the fact that the forces which these defendants represent, the forces that would advantage and delight in their acquittal, are the darkest and most sinister forces in society—dictatorship and oppression, malevolence and passion, militarism and lawlessness. By their fruits we best know them. Their acts have bathed the world in blood and set civilization back a century. They have subjected their European neighbors to every outrage and torture, every spoliation and deprivation that insolence, cruelty, and greed could inflict. They have brought the German people to the lowest pitch of wretchedness, from which they can entertain no hope of early deliverance. They have stirred hatreds and incited domestic violence on every continent. These are the things that stand in the dock shoulder to shoulder with these prisoners.

The real complaining party at your bar is Civilization. In all our countries it is still a struggling and imperfect thing. It does not plead that the United States, or any other country, has been blameless of the conditions which made the German people easy victims to the blandishments and intimidations of the Nazi conspirators.

But it points to the dreadful sequence of aggressions and crimes I have recited, it points to the weariness of flesh, the exhaustion of resources, and the destruction of all that was beautiful or useful in so much of the world, and to greater potentialities for destruction in the days to come. It is not necessary among the ruins of this ancient and beautiful city, with untold members of its civilian inhabitants still buried in its rubble, to argue the proposition that to start or wage an aggressive war has the moral qualities of the worst of crimes. The refuge of the defendants can be only their hope that International Law will lag so far behind the moral sense of mankind that conduct which is crime in the moral sense must be regarded as innocent in law.

Civilization asks whether law is so laggard as to be utterly helpless to deal with crimes of this magnitude by criminals of this order of importance. It does not expect that you can make war impossible. It does expect that your juridical action will put the forces of International Law, its precepts, its prohibitions and, most of all, its sanctions, on the side of peace, so that men and women of good will in all countries may have "leave to live by no man's leave, underneath the law."

Stalin and Mass Terror
by NIKITA S. KHRUSHCHEV
President of the Soviet Union, 1894–1991

Stalin put the Party and the NKVD up to the use of mass terror when the exploiting classes had been liquidated in our country and when there were no serious reasons for the use of extraordinary mass terror.

This terror was actually directed not at the remnants of the defeated exploiting classes but against the honest workers of the Party and of the Soviet State; against them were made lying, slanderous and absurd accusations concerning "two-facedness," "espionage," "sabotage," preparation of fictitious "plots," etc.

At the February-March Central Committee Plenum in 1937 many members actually questioned the rightness of the established course regarding mass repressions under the pretext of combating "two-facedness."

Comrade Postyshev most ably expressed these doubts. He said:

"I have philosophized that the severe years of fighting have passed, Party members who have lost their backbones have broken down or have joined the camp of the enemy; healthy elements have fought for the Party. These were the years of industrialization and collectivization. I never thought it possible that after this severe era had passed Karpov and people like him would find themselves in the camp of the enemy. (Karpov was a worker in the Ukrainian Central Committee whom Postyshev knew well.) And now, according to the testimony, it appears that Karpov was recruited in 1934 by the Trotskyites. I personally do not believe that in 1934 an honest Party member who had trod the long road of unrelenting fight against enemies for the Party and for Socialism, would now be in the camp of the enemies. I do not believe it . . . I cannot imagine how it would be possible to travel with the Party during the difficult years and then, in 1934, join the Trotskyites. It is an odd thing . . ."

Using Stalin's formulation, namely that the closer we are to Socialism the more enemies we will have, and using the resolution of the February-March Central Committee Plenum passed on the basis of Yezhov's report—the provocateurs who had infiltrated the state security organs together with conscienceless careerists began to protect with the Party name the mass terror against Party cadres, cadres of the Soviet State and the ordinary Soviet citizens. It should suffice to say that the number of arrests based on charges of counter-revolutionary crimes had grown ten times between 1936 and 1937.

It is known that brutal willfulness was practiced against leading Party workers. The Party Statute approved at the XVIIth Party Congress was based on Leninist principles expressed at the Xth Party Congress. It stated that in order to apply an extreme method such as exclusion from the Party against a Central Committee member, against a Central Committee candidate, and against a member of the Party Control Commission, "it is necessary to call a Central Committee Plenum and to invite to the Plenum all Central Committee candidate members and all members of the Party Control Commission"; only if two thirds of the members of such a general assembly of responsible Party leaders find it necessary, only then can a Central Committee member or candidate be expelled.

The majority of the Central Committee members and candidates elected at the XVIIth Congress and arrested in 1937-1938 were expelled from the Party illegally through the brutal abuse of the Party Statute, because the question of their expulsion was never studied at the Central Committee Plenum.

Now when the cases of some of these so-called "spies" and "saboteurs" were examined it was found that all their cases were fabricated. Confessions of guilt of many arrested and charged with enemy activity were gained with the help of cruel and inhuman tortures.

At the same time Stalin, as we have been informed by members of the Political Bureau of that time, did not show them the statements of many accused political activists when they retracted their confessions before the military tribunal and asked for an objective examination of their cases. There were many such declarations, and Stalin doubtless knew of them.

The Central Committee considers it absolutely necessary to inform the Congress of many such fabricated "cases" against the members of the Party's Central Committee elected at the XVIIth Party Congress . . .

Many thousands of honest and innocent Communists have died as a result of this monstrous falsification of such "cases," as a result of the fact that all kinds of slanderous "confessions" were accepted, and as a result of the practice of forcing accusations against oneself and others. In the same manner were fabricated the "cases" against eminent Party and State workers—Kossior, Chubar, Postyshev, Kosaryev, and others.

In those years repressions on a mass scale were applied which were based on nothing tangible and which resulted in heavy cadre losses to the Party.

The vicious practice was condoned of having NKVD prepare lists of persons whose cases were under the jurisdiction of the Military Collegium and whose sentences were prepared in advance. Yezhov would send these lists to Stalin personally for his approval of the proposed punishment. In 1937-1938, 383 such lists contained the names of many thousands of Party, Soviet, Komsomol, Army and economic workers were sent to Stalin. He approved these lists.

A large part of these cases are being reviewed now and a great part of them are being voided because they were baseless and falsified. Suffice it to say that from 1954 to the present time the Military Collegium of the Supreme Court has rehabilitated 7,670 persons many of whom were rehabilitated posthumously.

Mass arrests of Party, Soviet, economic and military workers caused tremendous harm to our country and to the cause of Socialist advancement.

Mass repressions had a negative influence on the moral-political condition of the Party, created a situation of uncertainty, contributed to the spreading of unhealthy suspicion, and sowed distrust among Communists. All sorts of slanderers and careerists were active.

Butcher of Human-Kind
(From "The Murder of Lidice")
by EDNA ST. VINCENT MILLAY
American poet, 1892-1950

The women and children out to the square
They marched, that there they could plainly see
How mighty a state is Germany!—
That can drag from his bed unawake, unaware,
Unarmed, a man, to be murdered, where
His wife and children must watch and see;
Then carted them off in truck and cart
Into Germany, into Germany,—
The wives to be slaves of German men;
The children to start life over again,
In German schools, to German rules,
As butchers' apprentices;
And hail and salute the master-mind
Of Hitler, Butcher of Human-kind.

The whole world holds in its arms today
The murdered village of Lidice,
Like the murdered body of a little child,
Innocent, happy, surprised at play—
The murdered body, stained and defiled,
Tortured and mangled of a little child!

And moans of vengeance frightful to hear
From the throat of a whole world, reach his ear—
The maniac killer who still runs wild—
Where he sits, with his long and cruel thumbs,
Eating pastries, moulding the crumbs
Into bullets (for the day is always near
For another threat, another fear,
Another killing of the gentle and mild.)

But a moaning whine of vengeance comes—
Sacred vengeance awful and dear,
From the throat of a world that has been too near
And seen too much, at last too much—
Cries of vengeance sacred and dear,
For the murdered body of a helpless child—
And terrible sobs unreconciled.

The Supremacy of Conscience
by NORMAN THOMAS
American Socialist leader, several times candidate for President, 1884–1968

It is not likely that wars will be ended by the refusal of men to fight. Those who have resolved that there must be no more war should not forget that unless the causes of war are removed, well-founded fears and hatreds may submerge the popular desire for peace. But it is significant that in many countries today former soldiers and others are pledging themselves against participation in new international wars—some of the pledges extend to all war —and that labor organizations are disposed to indorse that idea. A small minority of determined objectors to conscription for the next war will give a definiteness and driving force to the amorphous peace movement which the old peace societies lacked. That minority, thanks to conscientious objectors in this war, ought to have a more definite understanding of the meaning of their struggle than those opponents of conscription who yielded to the herd instinct.

The example of the conscientious objectors in war time ought also to strengthen a wholesome iconoclasm in peace time directed against that extraordinary idol, the political state, which, in

Lord Acton's words, "suffers neither limit nor equality and is bound by no duty to nations or men, that thrives on destruction and sanctifies whatever things contribute to increase power." The cynic may argue that a people as proficient in the art of bootlegging as Americans scarcely needs encouragement in law-breaking or in contempt for the state. It is part of our shame that the right to drink is more highly prized than the right to think. The real test, however, of state worship in time of peace does not lie in man's attitude toward prohibition—the faithful have always been inclined to take minor liberties with their gods—but in their attitude to such autocracy as the misuse of injunctions in the name of the state but in the interests of the employing class. Labor might profitably reflect that its opposition to acts of tyranny like Mr. Palmer's injunction in the coal strike of 1919 and Mr. Daugherty's injunction in the railroad strike of 1922 might have taken on a more heroic quality if in the Great War the workers had not gone so far in acknowledging the supremacy of the state over conscience.

The Need to Be Pacifist
by ALBERT EINSTEIN

German-Swiss mathematician, creator of the theory of relativity which ushered in the atomic era, Nobel Prize for Physics 1921, and refugee from Nazi persecution; 1879-1955.

Wars are the most serious hindrance to the development of every striving for the cooperation of the peoples of all nations—especially cultural strivings. War deprives the intellectual worker of the inner and external conditions on which his exertions are based. If he happens to be strong and young enough, war makes him a slave of an organization directed toward destruction; if he is not, war at any rate surrounds him with an atmosphere of excitement and hatred. Moreover, war creates oppressive economic dependence of many years' duration because of consequent impoverishment. That is why a human being who considers spiritual values as supreme must be a pacifist.

Power
(From "The First Circle")
by ALEXANDER SOLZEHENITSYN

You only have power over people so long as you don't take *everything* away from them. But when you've robbed a man of *everything* he's no longer in your power—he's free again.

To Fight Against Dictatorship
(From "Summer Meditations")
by VACLAV HAVEL
Prominent Czech dramatist who attacked totalitarianism in his absurdist plays and in this piece. President of Czechoslovakia; born 1936

Neither I nor anyone else will ever win this war once and for all. At the very most, we can win a battle or two—and not even that is certain. Yet I still think it makes sense to wage this war persistent. It has been waged for centuries, and it will continue to be waged—we hope—for centuries to come. This must be done on principle because it is the right thing to do. Or, if you like, because God wants it that way. It is an eternal, never-ending struggle waged not just by good people (among whom I count myself, more or less) against evil people, by honourable people against dishonourable people, by people who think about the world and eternity against people who think only of themselves and the moment. It takes place inside everyone. It is what makes a person a person, and life, life.

So anyone who claims that I am a dreamer who expects to transform hell into heaven is wrong. I have few illusions. But I feel a responsibility to work towards the things I consider good and right. I don't know whether I'll be able to change certain things for the better, or not at all. Both outcomes are possible. There is only one thing I will not concede; that it might be meaningless to strive in a good cause.

By an Anonymous Belfast, Northern Ireland, resident

It's not the bullet with my name on it that worries me. It's the one that says "To Whom It May Concern."

by BERTRAND RUSSELL
English mathematician, philosopher
and pacifist, Nobel Prize for Literature 1950; 1872-1970

The idea of weapons of mass extermination is utterly horrible and is something which no one with one spark of humanity can tolerate. I will not pretend to obey a government which is organizing a mass massacre of mankind.

The Rescue Party

(From "Black Rain")

BY MASUJI IBUSE
Prominent Japanese writer who received the country's
celebrated Noma Prize after this novel was published, born 1898

(Young men from the village of Kobatake had been sent to Hiroshima to help in the demolition of damaged buildings. They were part of the Kōjin unit.)

Unfortunately, the members of the Kōjin unit and the Service Corps had barely got down to work, having arrived in Hiroshima only the day before, when the bomb fell. Those who were not killed outright were taken, their bodies burned raw all over, to reception centers at Miyoshi, Shōbara, Tōjō, and other places round about Hiroshima. The first party sent from Kobatake to the ruins of Hiroshima consisted of the village firemen, who went there in a charcoal-burning bus. They were followed, early on the morning of the day the war ended, by a party of volunteer workers from the Young Men's Association, who went to the temporary reception centers at Miyoshi, Tōjō and elsewhere to search for the injured from the village.

The members of the Young Men's Association who were offering their services were given an official send-off by the village headman, in the presence of the acting president of the Association.

"Gentlemen," he said, "you have our deepest gratitude for giving thus of your services in these busy wartime days. I scarcely need remind you that the injured you will be bringing back with you are blistered with burns over their entire bodies, and to request you, therefore, to take every care not to cause them yet further suffering. It is said the enemy used what is referred to as a 'new weapon' in his attack on Hiroshima, which instantly plunged hundreds of thousands of blameless residents of the city into a hell of unspeakable torments. A member of the Patriotic Service Corps who escaped with his life from Hiroshima has told me that at that moment when the new weapon wiped out the city he heard countless cries of succor—the voice of those hundreds of thousands of souls—seemingly welling up from beneath the earth. Even the Fukuyama district, which he passed through on his way back, was a burnt-out waste; the keep and the Summer Gallery of Fukuyama Castle had been destroyed in the flames. His heart was wrung, he told me, by the realization of the awfulness of war ..."

REST IN PEACE.
THE MISTAKE SHALL NOT BE REPEATED

Inscription on the cenotaph for Hiroshima

BOOK XI

Nations and Colonies

The duty of man to his country, as seen by those who would make the country the parent and friend of all who dwell in it; and the struggle of colonial peoples for their national liberation.

To the Goddess of Liberty
(New York Harbor)

by GEORGE STERLING
American poet, 1869-1926

Oh! is it bale-fire in thy brazen hand—
The traitor-light set on betraying coasts
To lure to doom the mariner? Art thou
Indeed that Freedom, gracious and supreme,
By France once sighted over seas of blood—
A beacon to the ages, and their hope,
A star against the midnight of the race,
A vision, an announcement? Art thou she
For whom our fathers fought at Lexington
And trod the ways of death at Gettysburg?
Thy torch is lit, thy steadfast hand upheld,
Before our ocean-portals. For a sign
Men set thee there to welcome—loving men,
With faith in man. Thou wast upraised to tell,
To simple souls that seek from over-seas
Our rumored liberty, that here no chains
Are on the people, here no kings can stand,
Nor the old tyranny confound mankind,
Sapping with craft the ramparts of the Law
For such, O high presentment of their dream!
Thy pathless sandals wait upon the stone,
Thy tranquil face looks evermore to sea:
Now turn, and know the treason at thy back!
Turn to the anarchs' turrets, and behold
The cunning ones that reap where others sow!

In those great strongholds lifted to the sun
They plot dominion. Thronèd greeds conspire,
Half allied in a brotherhood malign,
Against the throneless many. . . .
Would One might pour within thy Breast of bronze
Spirit and life! Then should thy loyal hand
Cast down its torch, and thy deep voice should cry:
"Turn back! Turn back, O liberative ships!

Be warned, ye voyagers! From tyranny
To vaster tyranny ye come! Ye come
From realms that in my morning twilight wait
My radiant invasion. But these shores
Have known me and renounced me. I am raised
In mockery, and here the forfeit day
Deepens to West, and my indignant Star
Would hide her shame with darkness and the sea—
A sun of doom forecasting on the Land
The shadow of the sceptre and the sword."

The Price of Liberty
by Thomas Jefferson

Cherish the spirit of our people and keep alive their attention. Do not be too severe upon their errors, but reclaim them by enlightening them. If once they become inattentive to public affairs, you and I, and Congress and Assemblies, judges and governors, shall all become wolves. It seems to be the law of our general nature, in spite of individual exceptions; and experience declares that man is the only animal which devours his own kind; for I can apply no milder term to the governments of Europe, and to the general prey of the rich on the poor.

To the United States Senate
by Vachel Lindsay
Upon the arrival of the news that the United States Senate had declared the
election of William Lorimer good and valid.

And must the Senator from Illinois
  Be this squat thing, with blinking, half-closed eyes?
This brazen gutter idol, reared to power
  Upon a leering pyramid of lies?

And must the Senator from Illinois
  Be the world's proverb of successful shame,
Dazzling all State house flies that steal and steal,
  Who, when the sad State spares them, count it fame?

If once or twice within his new won hall
  His vote had counted for the broken men;
If in his early days he wrought some good—
  We might a great soul's sins forgive him then.

But must the Senator from Illinois
  Be vindicated by fat kings of gold?
And must he be belauded by the smirched,
  The sleek, uncanny chiefs in lies grown old?

Be warned, O wanton ones, who shielded him—
  Black wrath awaits. You all shall eat the dust.
You dare not say: "Tomorrow will bring peace;
  Let us make merry, and go forth in lust."

What will you trading frogs do on a day
  When Armageddon thunders thro' the land;
When each sad patriot rises, mad with shame,
  His ballot or his musket in his hand?

A Prophecy
(Written during the Revolutionary War)
by THOMAS JEFFERSON

The spirit of the times may alter, will alter. Our rulers will become corrupt, our people careless. A single zealot may become persecutor, and better men be his victims. It can never be too often repeated that the time for fixing essential right, on a legal basis, is while our rulers are honest, ourselves united. *From the conclusion of this war we shall be going down hill.* It will not then be necessary to resort every moment to the people for support. They will be forgotten, therefore, and their rights disregarded. They will forget themselves in the sole faculty of making money, and will never think of uniting to effect a due respect for their rights. The shackles, therefore, which shall not be knocked off at the conclusion of this war, will be heavier and heavier, till our rights shall revive or expire in a convulsion.

An Election Campaign in New York
by REGINALD WRIGHT KAUFFMAN
American novelist, born 1877

For many days previously, any outsider, reading the newspapers or attending the mass-meetings in Cooper Union and Carnegie Hall, would have supposed that a prodigious battle was waging and that the result would be, until the last shot, in doubt. There were terrible scareheads, brutal cartoons, and extra editions. As the real problem was whether one organization of needy men should remain in control, or whether another should replace it, there were few matters of policy to be discussed; and so the speech-making and the printing resolved themselves into personal investigations, and attacks upon character. Private detectives were hired, records searched, neighbors questioned, old enemies sought out, and family feuds revived. Desks were broken open, letters bought, anonymous communications mailed, boyhood indiscretions unearthed, and women and men hired to wheedle, to commit perjury, to entrap. Whatever was discovered, forged, stolen, manufactured—whatever truth or falsehood could be seized by whatever means—was blazoned in the papers, shrieked by the newsboys, bawled from the cart-tails at the corners under the campaign banners, in the light of the torches and before the cheering crowds. It would be all over in a very short while; in a very short while there would pass one another, with pleasant smiles, in court, at church, and along Broadway, the distinguished gentlemen that were now, before big audiences, calling one another adulterers and thieves; but it is customary for distinguished gentlemen so to call one another during a manly campaign in this successful democracy of ours, and it seems to be an engrossing occupation while the chance endures.

The Doom of Empires
by ROBERT G. INGERSOLL
American lawyer and lecturer, 1833-1899

The traveler standing amid the ruins of ancient cities and empires, seeing on every side the fallen pillar and the prostrate wall, asks why did these cities fall, why did these empires crumble? And the Ghost of the Past, the wisdom of ages, answers: These temples, these palaces, these cities, the ruins of which you stand upon, were built by tyranny and injustice. The hands that built them were unpaid. The backs that bore the burdens also bore the marks of the lash. They were built by slaves to satisfy the vanity and ambition of thieves and robbers. For these reasons they are dust.

Their civilization was a lie. Their laws merely regulated robbery and established theft. They bought and sold the bodies and souls of men, and the mournful wind of desolation, sighing amid their crumbling ruins, is a voice of prophetic warning to those who would repeat the infamous experiment, uttering the great truth, that no nation founded upon slavery, either of body or mind, can stand.

By FRANCIS BACON
English philosopher and statesman, father of modern scientific thought; 1561-1626

Let states that aim at greatness take heed how their nobility and gentlemen do multiply too fast. For that maketh the common subject grow to be a peasant and base swain, driven out of heart, and in effect but the gentleman's laborer.

By DANIEL WEBSTER
American statesman, 1782-1852

The freest government cannot long endure when the tendency of the law is to create a rapid accumulation of property in the hands of a few, and to render the masses poor and dependent.

The Deserted Village
by OLIVER GOLDSMITH
English poet and novelist, 1728-1774

Sweet-smiling village, loveliest of the lawn!
Thy sports are fled, and all thy charms withdrawn;
Amidst thy bowers the tyrant's hand is seen,
And desolation saddens all thy green;
One only master grasps the whole domain,
And half a tillage stints thy smiling plain;
No more thy glassy brook reflects the day,
But, choked with sedges, works its weedy way;
Along thy glades, a solitary guest,

The hollow-sounding bittern guards its nest;
Amidst thy desert walks the lapwing flies,
And tires their echoes with unvaried cries;
Sunk are thy bowers in shapeless ruin all,
And the long grass o'ertops the mouldering wall;
And, trembling, shrinking from the spoiler's hand;
Far, far away thy children leave the land.

Ill fares the land, to hastening ills a prey,
Where wealth accumulates, and men decay:
Princes and lords may flourish, or may fade—
A breath can make them, as a breath has made:
But a bold peasantry, their country's pride,
When once destroyed, can never be supplied.
A time there was, ere England's griefs began,
When every rood of ground maintained its man;
For him light labor spread her wholesome store,
Just gave what life required, but gave no more:
His best companions, innocence and health;
And his best riches, ignorance of wealth.

But times are altered: trade's unfeeling train
Usurp the land, and dispossess the swain;
Along the lawn, where scattered hamlets rose,
Unwieldy wealth and cumbrous pomp repose;
And every want to luxury allied,
And every pang that folly pays to pride,
Those gentle hours that plenty bade to bloom,
Those calm desires that asked but little room,
Those healthful sports that graced the peaceful scene,
Lived in each look, and brightened all the green—
These, far departing, seek a kinder shore,
And rural mirth and manners are no more....

Ye friends to truth, ye statesmen, who survey
The rich man's joys increase, the poor's decay,
'Tis yours to judge how wide the limits stand
Between a splendid and a happy land.
Proud swells the tide with loads of freighted ore,
And shouting Folly hails them from her shore;
Hoards, e'en beyond the miser's wish, abound,

And rich men flock from all the world around.
Yet count our gains; this wealth is but a name,
That leaves our useful products still the same.

Not so the loss: the man of wealth and pride
Takes up a space that many poor supplied;
Space for his lake, his park's extended bounds,
Space for his horses, equipage, and hounds;
The robe that wraps his limbs in silken sloth,
Has robbed the neighboring fields of half their growth;
His seat, where solitary sports are seen,
Indignant spurns the cottage from the green;
Around the world each needful product flies,
For all the luxuries the world supplies;
While thus the land, adorned for pleasure all,
In barren splendor, feebly waits the fall....

Where then, ah! where, shall poverty reside,
To 'scape the pressure of contiguous pride?
If, to some common's fenceless limits strayed,
He drives his flock to pick the scanty blade,
Those fenceless fields the sons of wealth divide,
And even the bare-worn common is denied.
If to the city sped, what waits him there?
To see profusion that he must not share;
To see ten thousand baneful arts combined
To pamper luxury, and thin mankind;
To see each joy the sons of pleasure know
Extorted from his fellow-creatures' woe.
Here while the courtier glitters in brocade,
There the pale artist plies the sickly trade;
Here while the proud their long-drawn pomps display,
There the black gibbet glooms beside the way.
The dome where Pleasure holds her midnight reign,
Here, richly decked, admits the gorgeous train;
Tumultuous grandeur crowds the blazing square—
The rattling chariots clash, the torches glare.
Sure scenes like these no troubles e'er annoy!
Sure these denote one universal joy!
Are these thy serious thoughts? Ah! turn thine eyes
Where the poor, houseless, shivering female lies;

She once, perhaps, in village plenty blest,
Has wept at tales of innocence distrest;
Her modest looks the cottage might adorn,
Sweet as the primrose peeps beneath the thorn;
Now lost to all—her friends, her virtue fled—
Near her betrayer's door she lays her head;
And, pinched with cold, and shrinking from the shower,
With heavy heart deplores that luckless hour
When, idly first, ambitious of the town,
She left her wheel, and robes of country brown....

O luxury! thou curst by Heaven's decree,
How ill exchanged are things like these for thee!
How do thy potions, with insidious joy,
Diffuse their pleasures only to destroy!
Kingdoms by thee, to sickly greatness grown,
Boast of a florid vigor not their own.
At every draught more large and large they grow,
A bloated mass of rank unwieldy woe;
Till sapped their strength, and every part unsound,
Down, down they sink, and spread a ruin round.

By OTTO VON BISMARCK
German statesman, 1815-1898

I believe that those who profess horror at the intervention of the state for the protection of the weak lay themselves open to the suspicion that they are desirous of using their strength for the benefit of a portion, for the oppression of the rest.

By FERDINAND LASSALLE
German socialist leader, 1825-1864

It is the opposition of the personal interest of the higher classes to the development of the nation in culture, which causes the great and necessary immorality of the higher classes.

England in 1819
by PERCY BYSSHE SHELLEY

An old, mad, blind, despised, and dying king,—
   Princes, the dregs of their dull race, who flow
Through public scorn—mud from a muddy spring,—
   Rulers, who neither see, nor feel, nor know,
But leech-like to their fainting country cling,
   Till they drop, blind in blood, without a blow—
A people starved and stabbed in the untilled field,—
   An army, which liberticide and prey
Makes as a two-edged sword to all who wield,—
   Golden and sanguine laws which tempt and slay;
Religion Christless, Godless—a book sealed;
A Senate,—Time's worst statute unrepealed,—
Are graves, from which a glorious Phantom may
Burst, to illumine our tempestuous day.

Coronation Day
(From "The People of the Abyss")
by JACK LONDON

Vivat Rex Eduardus! They crowned a king this day, and there have been great rejoicing and elaborate tomfoolery, and I am perplexed and saddened. I never saw anything to compare with the pageant, except Yankee circuses and Alhambra ballets; nor did I ever see anything so hopeless and so tragic.

To have enjoyed the Coronation procession, I should have come straight from America to the Hotel Cecil, and straight from the Hotel Cecil to a five-guinea seat among the washed. My mistake was in coming from the unwashed of the East End. There were not many who came from that quarter. The East End, as a whole, remained in the East End and got drunk. The Socialists, Democrats, and Republicans went off to the country for a breath of fresh air, quite unaffected by the fact that four hundred millions of people were taking to themselves a crowned and anointed ruler. Six thousand five hundred prelates, priests, statesmen, princes and warriors beheld the crowning, and the rest of us the pageant as it passed.

I saw it at Trafalgar Square, "the most splendid site in Europe,"

and the very innermost heart of the empire. There were many
thousands of us, all checked and held in order by a superb display
of armed power. The line of march was double-walled with
soldiers. The base of the Nelson Column was triple-fringed with
bluejackets. Eastward, at the entrance to the square, stood the
Royal Marine Artillery. In the triangle of Pall Mall and Cockspur
Street, the statue of George III was buttressed on either side by
the Lancers and Hussars. To the west were the red-coats of the
Royal Marines, and from the Union Club to the embouchure of
Whitehall swept the glittering, massive curve of the First Life
Guards—gigantic men mounted on gigantic chargers, steel-
breastplated, steel-helmeted, steel-caparisoned, a great war-sword
of steel ready to the hand of the powers that be. And further,
throughout the crowd, were flung long lines of the Metropolitan
Constabulary, while in the rear were the reserves—tall, well-fed
men, with weapons to wield and muscles to wield them in case
of need.

And as it was thus at Trafalgar Square, so was it along the whole
line of march—force, overpowering force; myriads of men, splendid men, the pick of the people, whose sole function in life is
blindly to obey, and blindly to kill and destroy and stamp out
life. And that they should be well fed, well clothed, and well
armed, and have ships to hurl them to the ends of the earth, the
East End of London, and the "East End" of all England, toils and
rots and dies.

There is a Chinese proverb that if one man lives in laziness
another will die of hunger; and Montesquieu has said, "The fact
that many men are occupied in making clothes for one individual
is the cause of there being many people without clothes." We cannot understand the starved and runty toiler of the East End (living
with his family in a one-room den, and letting out the floor space
for lodgings to other starved and runty toilers) till we look at the
strapping Life Guardsmen of the West End, and come to know
that the one must feed and clothe and groom the other.. . .

In these latter days, five hundred hereditary peers own one-fifth
of England; and they, and the officers and servants under the
King, and those who go to compose the powers that be, yearly
spend in wasteful luxury $1,850,000,000, or £370,000,000, which
is thirty-two per cent of the total wealth produced by all the toilers
of the country.

At the Abbey, clad in wonderful golden raiment, amid fanfare of trumpets and throbbing of music, surrounded by a brilliant throng of masters, lords, and rulers, the King was being invested with the insignia of his sovereignty. The spurs were placed to his heels by the Lord Great Chamberlain, and a sword of state, in purple scabbard, was presented him by the Archbishop of Canterbury, with these words:—

"Receive this kingly sword brought now from the altar of God, and delivered to you by the hands of the bishops and servants of God, though unworthy."

Whereupon, being girded, he gave heed to the Archbishop's exhortation:—

"With this sword do justice, stop the growth of iniquity, protect the Holy Church of God, help and defend widows and orphans, restore the things that are gone to decay, maintain the things that are restored, punish and reform what is amiss, and confirm what is in good order...."

"And how did you like the procession, mate?" I asked an old man on a bench in Green Park.

"'Ow did I like it? A bloomin' good chawnce, sez I to myself, for a sleep, wi' all the coppers aw'y, so I turned into the corner there, along wi' fifty others. But I couldn't sleep, a-lyin' there 'ungry an' thinkin' 'ow I'd worked all the years o' my life, an' now 'ad no plyce to rest my 'ead; an' the music comin' to me, an' the cheers an' cannon, till I got almost a hanarchist an' wanted to blow out the brain o' the Lord Chamberlain."

Why the Lord Chamberlain I could not precisely see, nor could he, but that was the way he felt, he said conclusively, and there was no more discussion....

At three in the morning I strolled up the Embankment. It was a gala night for the homeless, for the police were elsewhere; and each bench was jammed with sleeping occupants. There were as many women as men, and the great majority of them, male and female, were old. Occasionally a boy was to be seen. On one bench I noticed a family, a man sitting upright with a sleeping babe in his arms, his wife asleep, her head on his shoulder, and in her lap the head of a sleeping youngster. The man's eyes were wide open. He was staring out over the water and thinking, which is not a good thing for a shelterless man with a family to do. It would not be a pleasant thing to speculate upon his thoughts; but this I know, and all London knows, that the cases of out-of-works killing their wives and babies is not an uncommon happening.

One cannot walk along the Thames Embankment, in the small hours of morning, from the Houses of Parliament, past Cleopatra's Needle, to Waterloo Bridge, without being reminded of the sufferings, seven and twenty centuries old, recited by the author of "Job":—

"There are that remove the landmarks; they violently take away flocks and feed them.

"They drive away the ass of the fatherless, they take the widow's ox for a pledge.

"They turn the needy out of the way; the poor of the earth hide themselves together.

"Behold, as wild asses in the desert they go forth to their work, seeking diligently for meat; the wilderness yieldeth them food for their children.

"They cut their provender in the field, and they glean the vintage of the wicked.

"They lie all night naked without clothing, and have no covering in the cold.

"They are wet with the showers of the mountains, and embrace the rock for want of a shelter.

"There are that pluck the fatherless from the breast, and take a pledge of the poor.

"So that they go about naked without clothing, and being an hungered they carry the sheaves."

Seven and twenty centuries agone! And it is all as true and apposite today in the innermost centre of this Christian civilization whereof Edward VII is king.

The Rights of Man
by THOMAS PAINE
English political philosopher, 1737-1809; came to the colonies and played an
important part in the American Revolution

The superstitious awe, the enslaving reverence, that formerly surrounded affluence, is passing away in all countries, and leaving the possessor of property to the convulsion of accidents. When wealth and splendor, instead of fascinating the multitude, excite emotions of disgust; when, instead of drawing forth admiration, it is beheld as an insult upon wretchedness; when the ostentatious appearance it makes serves to call the right of it in question, the case of property becomes critical, and it is only in a system of justice that the possessor can contemplate security.

The Demand of Labor
by ABRAHAM LINCOLN

Inasmuch as most good things are produced by labor, it follows that all such things ought to belong to those whose labor has produced them. But it has happened in all ages of the world that some have labored, and others, without labor, have enjoyed a large proportion of the fruits. This is wrong, and should not continue. To secure to each laborer the whole product of his labor as nearly as possible is a worthy object of any good government.

The Victorian Age
by EDWARD CARPENTER

I found myself—and without knowing where I was—in the middle of that strange period of human evolution, the Victorian Age, which in some respects, one now thinks, marked the lowest ebb of modern civilized society; a period in which not only commercialism in public life, but cant in religion, pure materialism in science, futility in social conventions, the worship of stocks and shares, the starving of the human heart, the denial of the human body and its needs, the huddling concealment of the body in clothes, the "impure hush" on matters of sex, class-division, contempt of manual labor, and the cruel barring of women from every natural and useful expression of their lives, were carried to an extremity of folly difficult for us now to realize.

Utopia
by SIR THOMAS MORE

When I consider and way in my mind all these common wealthes, which now a dayes any where do florish, so god helpe me, I can perceave nothing but a certain conspiracy of riche men procuringe theire owne commodities under the name and title of the commen wealth. They invent and devise all meanes and craftes, first how to kepe safely, without feare of losing, that they have unjustly gathered together, and next how to hire and abuse the worke and laboure of the poore for as litle money as may be. These devises, when the riche men have decreed to be kept and observed under coloure of the comminaltie, that is to saye, also of the pore people, then they be made lawes. But these most wicked and vicious men, when they have by their unsatiable covetousnes devided among them selves al those thinges, whiche woulde have sufficed all men, yet how farre be they from the welth and felicitie of the Utopian commen wealth?

The Rough Rider
by BLISS CARMAN
Canadian nature-poet, 1861-1929

Take up, who will, the challenge;
   Stand pat on graft and greed;
Grow sleek on others' labor,
   Surfeit on others' need;
Let paid and bloodless tricksters
   Devise a legal way
Our common right and justice
   "To sell, deny, delay."

Not yesterday nor lightly
   We came to know that breed;
Our quarrel with that cunning
   Is old as Runnymede.
We saw enfranchised insult
   Deploy in kingly line,
When broke our sullen fury
   On Rupert of the Rhine. . . .

Now, masking raid and rapine
   In debonair disguise,
The foe we thought defeated
   Deludes our careless eyes,
Entrenched in law and largess
   And the vested wrong of things,
Cloaking a fouler treason
   Than any faithless king's.

He takes our life for wages,
   He holds our land for rent,

He sweats our little children
   To swell his cent per cent;
With secret grip and levy
   On every crumb we eat,
He drives our sons to thieving,
   Our daughters to the street. . . .

Against the grim defenses
   Where might and murrain hide,
Unswerving to the issue
   Loose-reined and rough we ride
Full tardily, to rescue
   Our heritage from wrong,
And stablish it on manhood,
   A thousand times more strong.

By WILLIAM EWART GLADSTONE
English liberal statesman, 1809-1898

In almost every one, if not in every one, of the greatest political controversies of the last fifty years, whether they affected the franchise, whether they affected commerce, whether they affected religion, whether they affected the bad and abominable institution of slavery, or what subject they touched, these leisured classes, these educated classes, these titled classes, have been in the wrong.

The Cultured Classes
by JOHANN GOTTLIEB FICHTE
German philosopher, 1762-1814

It is particularly to the cultured classes that I wish to direct my remarks in the present address. I implore these classes to take the initiative in the work of reconstruction, to atone for their past deeds, and to earn the right to continue life in the future. It will appear in the course of this address that hitherto all the advance in the German nation has originated with the common people; that hitherto all the great national interests have, in the first instance, been the affair of the people, have been taken in hand and pushed forward by the body of the people.

The Happiness of Nations
by JAMES MACKAYE
American writer, born 1872

Everywhere we are taught that "life is sacred," that "liberty is sacred," that "property is sacred,"—but where are we taught that happiness is sacred? And yet it is only because of their relation to happiness that these other things have a trace of sacredness.

The Tragedy of China
by SUN YAT-SEN
Leader of the revolution that overthrew imperial rule and established the
Republic of China, 1867-1925

Considering the law of survival of ancient and modern races, if we want to save China and to preserve the Chinese race, we must certainly promote nationalism. To make this principle luminous for China's salvation, we must first understand it clearly. The Chinese race totals four hundred million people; of mingled races there are only a few million Mongolians, a million or so Manchus, a few million Tibetans, and over a million Mohammedan Turks. These alien races do not number altogether more than ten million, so that, for the most part, the Chinese people are of the Han or Chinese race with common blood, common language, common religion, and common customs—a single, pure race.

What is the standing of our nation in the world? In comparison with other nations we have the greatest population and the oldest culture, of four thousand years' duration. We ought to be advancing in line with the nations of Europe and America. But the Chinese people have only family and clan groups; there is no national spirit. Consequently, in spite of four hundred million people gathered together in one China, we are in fact but a sheet of loose sand. We are the poorest and weakest state in the world, occupying the lowest position in international affairs; the rest of mankind is the carving knife and the serving dish, while we are the fish and the meat. Our position now is extremely perilous; if we do not earnestly promote nationalism and weld together our four hundred millions into a strong nation, we face a tragedy —the loss of our country and the destruction of our race. To ward off this danger, we must espouse nationalism and employ the national spirit to save the country.

America the Beautiful
by KATHARINE LEE BATES
American educator, 1859-1929

O beautiful for spacious skies,
   For amber waves of grain,
For purple mountain majesties
   Above the fruited plain!
     America! America!
   God shed His grace on thee
And crown thy good with brotherhood
   From sea to shining sea!

O beautiful for pilgrim feet,
   Whose stern, impassioned stress
A thoroughfare for freedom beat
   Across the wilderness!
     America! America!
   God mend thine every flaw,
Confirm thy soul in self-control,
   Thy liberty in law!

O beautiful for heroes proved
   In liberating strife,
Who more than self their country loved,
   And mercy more than life!
     America! America!
   May God thy gold refine,
Till all success be nobleness,
   And every gain divine!

O beautiful for patriot dream
   That sees beyond the years
Thine alabaster cities gleam
   Undimmed by human tears!
     America! America!
   God shed His grace on thee
And crown thy good with brotherhood
   From sea to shining sea!

Paris
by Émile Zola

All boiled in the huge vat of Paris; the desires, the deeds of violence, the strivings of one and another man's will, the whole nameless medley of the bitterest ferments, whence, in all purity, the wine of the future would at last flow.

Then Pierre became conscious of the prodigious work which went on in the depths of the vat, beneath all the impurity and waste. What mattered the stains, the egotism and greed of politicians, if humanity were still on the march, ever slowly and stubbornly stepping forward! What mattered, too, that corrupt and emasculate *bourgeoisie,* nowadays as moribund as the aristocracy, whose place it took, if behind it there ever came the inexhaustible reserve of men who surged up from the masses of the countryside and the towns! . . . If in the depths of pestilential workshops and factories the slavery of ancient times subsisted in the wage-earning system, if men still died of want on their pallets like broken-down beasts of burden, it was nevertheless a fact that once already, on a memorable day of tempest, Liberty sprang forth from the vat to wing her flight throughout the world. And why in her turn should not Justice spring from it, proceeding from those troubled elements, freeing herself from all dross, ascending with dazzling splendor and regenerating the nations?

Monopoly Capitalism
by Lenin
Assumed name of Vladimir Ilyitch Ulianov, leader of Russia's Bolshevik Revolution; 1870-1924

Imperialism emerged as the development and direct continuation of the fundamental attributes of capitalism in general. But capitalism only became capitalist imperialism at a definite and very high stage of its development, when certain of its fundamental attributes began to be transformed into their opposites, when the features of a period of transition from capitalism to a higher social and economic system began to take shape and reveal themselves all along the line. Economically, the main thing in this process is the substitution of capitalist monopolies for capitalist free competition. Free competition is the fundamental attribute of capitalism, and of commodity production generally. Monopoly is exactly the opposite of free competition but we have seen the latter being transformed into monopoly before our eyes, creating large-scale industry and eliminating small industry, finally leading to such a concentration of production and capital that monopoly has been and is the result: cartels, syndicates and trusts, and merging with them, the capital of a dozen or so banks manipulating thousands of millions. At the same time monopoly, which has grown out of free competition, does not abolish the latter, but exists over it and alongside of it, and thereby gives rise to a number of very acute, intense antagonisms, friction and conflicts. Monopoly is the transition from capitalism to a higher system.

If it were necessary to give the briefest definition of imperialism we should have to say that imperialism is the monopoly stage of capitalism. Such a definition would include what is most important; for, on the one hand, finance capital is the bank capital of a few big monopolist banks, merged with the capital of the monopolist combines of manufacturers; and, on the other hand, the division of the world is the transition from a colonial policy which has expanded without hindrance to territories unoccupied by any capitalist power, to a colonial policy of monopolistic possession of the territory of the world which has been completely divided up.

America South
by CARLETON BEALS
World traveler and writer on social questions, 1893–1981

American initiative, ambition, greed, science and industry have been constant factors in the development, and often the harrassment, of our southern neighbors. But few persons have pointed out clearly the real meaning of our eager frontiersmen, our knights-errant of business, our sentimental sellers of chewing gum, our angels of efficiency.

Few such have worked there with truly noble resolve; practically none has caught the meaning or possibilities granted to us by the early founders of liberty in the Americas. Worshipers of material power never see such things. Most of what we have done in the past in Latin America—as a government, by social or

Somalia Celebrates Independence

medical institutions, as engineers, as individuals—has been opportunistic, at best fragmentary, unillumined. Our great engineering feats are strewn about like jig-saw puzzles which no one has thought to fit together to find their meaning in terms of abiding relationships between two great peoples. These deeds of mechanical achievement—many of them as magnificent as any works in the world—are like barren islands left behind a sunken continent that someone long ago dreamed about and made more real than the present scattered pieces.

Three decades ago, for instance, we robbed two continents of a dream of unity and of a strip of land to build a transoceanic canal, through which went, as the first cargo, nitrates for the World War. We have built fine roads for paupers and called ourselves civilizers. We have conceived of Uncle Sam as a divinely sublimated sewer-digger for the tropics, and some of us have made much 'money out of the good deeds. We stamp out yellow fever in the name of humanity—and who will deny that humanity is not served?—in order to pose our idealism and gain gold and rubber. We have tried to create democracy in the Caribbean by the use of force and marines and have left behind only worse tyrannies. Our great empire of investment in those lands—over six billion—has no true articulation with the various peoples nor has our export trade; a large portion represents Americans and American capital in Latin America, buying from Americans and American capital in the United States.

Justice for Hungary

Appeal of the Revolutionary Committee of the Hungarian Intellectuals.
October 28, 1956

Hungarians!

There may be differences of opinion among us but we agree on the main demands and we suggest to the Government that it should adopt the following as its programme:

1. The Government should regulate our relations with the Soviet Union, without delay and on the basis of equality. The Soviet forces should begin their withdrawal from the whole territory of the country.

2. The Government should abrogate all foreign trade agree-

ments which are disadvantageous to the country. It should make public all foreign trade agreements concluded in the past, including those relating to uranium ore and bauxite.

3. We demand general elections with secret ballot. The people should be able freely to nominate their candidates.

4. Factories and mines should really become the property of the workers. We shall not return the factories and the land to the capitalists and to the landowners. Our factories should be managed by freely elected workers' councils. The Government should guarantee the functioning of small-scale private industry and private trade.

5. The Government should abolish the exploiting "norm" scheme. The Government should raise low wages and pensions to the limit of economic possibilities.

6. The trade unions should become genuine workers' organizations representing the workers' interests, with their leaders freely elected. The working peasants should form their own organizations to safeguard their interests.

7. The Government should ensure the freedom and security of agricultural production by supporting individual farmers and voluntary farm co-operatives. The hated delivery system, by which the peasants have been robbed, should be abolished.

8. Justice should be done and material compensation paid to those peasants who were harmed by regrouping of plots of land and by other unlawful measures.

9. We demand complete freedom of speech, of the press and of the right of assembly.

10. The Government should declare October 23, the day when our national liberation fight began, a national holiday.

> On behalf of the Revolutionary
> Committee of the Hungarian
> Intellectuals

The Cause of Mexico
by LAZARO CARDENAS
President of Mexico and social reformer, 1895–1970

The organized Mexican workers are not indifferent to the serious conditions of disparity, both material and cultural, which prevent the assimilation of all popular groups into a coherent nation because of its ideological unity, into a strong nation by virtue of the vigor of its race, and into a satisfied nation through the well-being of all its components. Thus we have seen that the working class does not limit its objectives to the solution of its own problems, but feels intimately linked with the solution to the deep national problems, among which is that of liberating from their age-old dejection the Indian nuclei, who still live in various sections of the country in conditions of misery.

The factory workers will not consider their social aims fulfilled, as long as the farm labor classes have not succeeded in securing the transformation of the scheme of land exploitation, which will make the "ejido" the structural unit of an economy fully capable of meeting the needs of our population.

We also keep in mind that the educational program being directed towards the integral emancipation of the people, the activities of the educators are now being backed enthusiastically by family heads and workers' organizations. The interest of the farmer class in public education is becoming a general social sentiment as evidenced by the building of schools and their equipment, etc., for no matter how great the amounts appropriated in the official budgets for the expansion of education may be, they can never suffice for the needs of the nation.

Neither has the Army been alien to this enthusiastic revolutionary movement and its members, genuinely of popular extraction, who took up arms to establish institutions which safeguard the rights of the laboring classes, now after the period of violence is ended, and no conflict exists either in the Republic or abroad, have directed their social function toward the glorification of revolutionary aims now carried to the ranks of constitutional provisions.

And so in order that the march of the Revolution may proceed without pause in the execution of its eminently constructive purposes, it is necessary that at all times we be prepared to resist, even at the expense of serious economic sacrifice, the attacks of those who have failed to understand the justice of Mexico's cause and who persist in trying to defeat its purpose by the creation of a state of uncertainty and alarm.

For Passive Resistance
by MAHATMA GANDHI

Exponent of nonviolence, hero of India's struggle for independence, assassinated
by right-wing Hindu fanatic; 1869-1948

I came reluctantly to the conclusion that the British connection had made India more helpless than she ever was before, politically and economically. A disarmed India has no power of resistance against any aggressor if she wanted to engage in an armed conflict with him. So much is this the case that some of our best men consider that India must take generations before she can achieve the Dominion status. She has become so poor that she has little power of resisting famines.

Before the British advent, India spun and wove in her millions of cottages just the supplement she needed for adding to her meager agricultural resources. This cottage industry, so vital for India's existence, has been ruined by incredibly heartless and inhuman processes as described by the English witnesses. Little do town dwellers know how the semistarved masses of India are slowly sinking to lifelessness. Little do they know that their miserable comfort represents the brokerage they get for the work they do for the foreign exploiter, that the profits and the brokerage are sucked from the masses. Little do they realize that the government established by law in British India is carried on for this exploitation of the masses. No sophistry, no jugglery in figures can explain away the evidence that the skeletons in many villages present to the naked eye. I have no doubt whatsoever that both England and the town dwellers of India will have to answer, if there is a God above, for this crime against humanity which is perhaps unequaled in history.

The law itself in this country has been used to serve the foreign exploiter. My unbiased examination of the Punjab Martial Law cases has led me to believe that at least ninety-five per cent of convictions were wholly bad. My experience of political cases in India leads me to the conclusion that in nine out of every ten the condemned men were totally innocent. Their crime consisted in the love of their country. In ninety-nine cases out of a hundred justice has been denied to Indians as against Europeans in the courts of India. This is not an exaggerated picture. It is the experience of almost every Indian who has had anything to do with such cases. In my opinion, the administration of the law is thus prostituted consciously or unconsciously for the benefit of the exploiter.

The greatest misfortune is that Englishmen and their Indian associates in the administration of the country do not know that they are engaged in the crime I have attempted to describe. I am satisfied that many Englishmen and Indian officials honestly believe that they are administering one of the best systems devised in the world and that India is making steady though slow progress. They do not know that a subtle but effective system of terrorism and an organized display of force on the one hand, and the deprivation of all powers of retaliation or self-defense on the other, have emasculated the people and induced in them the habit of simulation.

This awful habit has added to the ignorance and the self-deception of the administrators. Section 124-A, under which I am happily charged, is perhaps the prince among the political sections of the Indian Penal Code designed to suppress the liberty of the citizen.

Affection cannot be manufactured or regulated by law. If one has an affection for a person or system, one should be free to give the fullest expression to his disaffection, as long as he does not contemplate, promote, or incite to violence. But the section under which Mr. Banker and I are charged is one under which mere promotion of disaffection is a crime. I have studied some of the cases tried under it, and I know that some of the most loved of India's patriots have been convicted under it. I consider it a privilege, therefore, to be charged under that section. I have endeavored to give in their briefest outline the reasons for my disaffection. I have no personal ill will against any single administrator, much less can I have any disaffection toward the King's person. But I hold it to be a virtue to be disaffected toward a government which in its totality has done more harm to India than any previous system. India is less manly under the British rule than she ever was before. Holding such a belief, I consider it to be a sin to have affection for the system. And it has been a precious privilege for me to be able to write what I have in various articles, tendered in evidence against me.

In fact, I believe that I have rendered a service to India and England by showing in non-co-operation the way out of the unnatural state in which both are living. In my humble opinion, non-co-operation with evil is as much a duty as is co-operation with good. But in the past, non-co-operation has been deliberately expressed in violence to the evildoer. I am endeavoring to show my countrymen that violent non-co-operation only multiplies evil and that as evil can only be sustained by violence, withdrawal of support of evil requires complete abstention from violence. Non-violence implies voluntary submission to the penalty for non-co-operation with evil.

I am here, therefore, to invite and submit cheerfully to the highest penalty that can be inflicted upon me for what in law is a deliberate crime and what appears to me to be the highest duty of a citizen. The only course open to you, the judge, is either to resign your post, and thus dissociate yourself from evil if you feel that the law you are called upon to administer is an evil and that in reality I am innocent, or to inflict on me the severest penalty if you believe that the system and the law you are assisting to administer are good for the people of this country and that my activity is therefore injurious to the public weal.

The Road to Freedom Is Via the Cross
by ALBERT LUTHULI
Black South African liberation leader, Nobel Prize for Peace, 1960, 1898–1967

I have been dismissed from the Chieftainship of the Abase-Makolweni Tribe in the Grouville Mission Reserve. I presume that this has been done by the Governor-General in his capacity as Supreme Chief of the "Native" people of the Union of South Africa save those of the Cape Province. I was democratically elected to this position in 1935 by the people of Grouville Mission Reserve and was duly approved and appointed by the Governor-General.

Previous to my being a chief I was a school teacher for about seventeen years. In these past thirty years or so I have striven with tremendous zeal and patience to work for the progress and welfare of my people and for their harmonious relations with other sections of our multi-racial society in the Union of South Africa. In this effort I have always pursued what liberal-minded people rightly regarded as the path of moderation. Over this great length of time I have, year after year, gladly spent hours of my time with such organizations as the Church and its various agencies such as the Christian Council of South Africa, the Joint Council of Europeans and Africans and the now defunct Native Representative Council.

In so far as gaining citizenship rights and opportunities for the unfettered development of the African people, who will deny that thirty years of my life have been spent knocking in vain, patiently, moderately and modestly at a closed and barred door?

What have been the fruits of my many years of moderation? Has there been any reciprocal tolerance or moderation from the Government, be it Nationalist or United Party? No! On the contrary, the past thirty years have seen the greatest number of Laws restricting our rights and progress until today we have reached a stage where we have almost no rights at all: no adequate land for our occupation, our only asset, cattle, dwindling, no security of homes, no decent and remunerative employment, more restrictions to freedom of movement through passes, curfew regulations, influx control measures; in short we have witnessed in these years an intensification of our subjection to ensure and protect white supremacy.

It is with this background and with a full sense of responsibility that, under the auspices of the African National Congress (Natal), I have joined my people in the new spirit that moves them today, the spirit that revolts openly and boldly against injustice and expresses itself in a determined and non-violent manner. Because of my association with the African National Congress in this new spirit which has found an effective and legitimate way of expression in the non-violent Passive Resistance Campaign, I was given a two-week-limit ultimatum by the Secretary for Native Affairs calling upon me to choose between the African National Congress and the chieftainship of the Grouville Mission Reserve. He alleged that my association with Congress in its non-violent Passive Resistance Campaign was an act of disloyalty to the State. I did not, and do not, agree with this view. Viewing non-violent Passive Resistance as a non-revolutionary and, therefore, a most legitimate and humane political pressure technique for a people denied all effective forms of constitutional striving, I saw no real conflict in my dual leadership of my people: leader of this tribe as chief and political leader in Congress.

I saw no cause to resign from either. This stand of mine which resulted in my being sacked from the chieftainship might seem foolish and disappointing to some liberal and moderate Europeans and non-Europeans with whom I have worked these many years and with whom I still hope to work. This is no parting of the ways but "a launching farther into the deep." I invite them to join us in our unequivocal pronouncement of all legitimate African aspirations and in our firm stand against injustice and oppression.

I do not wish to challenge my dismissal, but I would like to suggest that in the interest of the institution of chieftainship in these modern times of democracy, the Government should define more precisely and make more widely known the status, functions and privileges of chiefs.

My view has been, and still is, that a chief is primarily a servant of his people. He is the voice of his people. He is the voice of his people in local affairs. Unlike a Native Commissioner, he is part and parcel of the Tribe, and not a local agent of the Government. Within the bounds of loyalty it is conceivable that he may vote and press the claims of his people even if they should be unpalatable to the Government of the day. He may use all legitimate modern techniques to get these demands satisfied. It is inconceivable how chiefs could effectively serve the wider and common interest of their own tribe without co-operating with other leaders of the people, both the natural leaders (chiefs) and leaders elected democratically by the people themselves.

It was to allow for these wider associations intended to promote the common national interests of the people as against purely local interests that the Government in making rules governing chiefs did not debar them from joining political associations so long as those associations had not been declared "by the Minister to be subversive of or prejudicial to constituted Government." The African National Congress, its non-violent Passive Resistance Campaign, may be of nuisance value to the Government but it is not subversive since it does not seek to overthrow the form and machinery of the State but only urges for the inclusion of sections of the community in a partnership in the Government of the country on the basis of equality.

Laws and conditions that tend to debase human personality— a God-given force—be they brought about by the State or other individuals, must be relentlessly opposed in the spirit of defiance shown by St. Peter when he said to the rulers of his day: "Shall we obey God or man?" No one can deny that in so far as non-Whites are concerned in the Union of South Africa, laws and conditions that debase human personality abound. Any chief worthy of his position must fight fearlessly against such debasing conditions and laws. If the Government should resort to dismissing such chiefs, it may find itself dismissing many chiefs or causing people to dismiss from their hearts chiefs who are indifferent to the needs of the people through fear of dismissal by the Government. Surely the Government cannot place chiefs in such an uncomfortable and invidious position.

As for myself, with a full sense of responsibility and a clear conviction, I decided to remain in the struggle for extending democratic rights and responsibilities to all sections of the South African community. I have embraced the non-violent Passive Resistance technique in fighting for freedom because I am convinced it is the only non-revolutionary, legitimate and humane way that could be used by people denied, as we are, effective constitutional means to further aspirations.

The wisdom or foolishness of this decision I place in the hands of the Almighty.

What the future has in store for me I do not know. It might be ridicule, imprisonment, concentration camp, flogging, banishment and even death. I only pray to the Almighty to strengthen my resolve so that none of these grim possibilities may deter me from striving, for the sake of the good name of our beloved country, the Union of South Africa, to make it a true democracy and a true union in form and spirit of all the communities in the land.

My only painful concern at times is that of the welfare of my family but I try even in this regard, in a spirit of trust and surrender to God's will as I see it, to say: "God will provide."

It is inevitable that in working for Freedom some individuals and some families must take the lead and suffer: The Road to Freedom is via the CROSS.

MAYIBUYE!
AFRIKA!   AFRIKA!   AFRIKA!

The Truth Shall Be Known
by JOMO KENYATTA
Kenyan anti-colonist, 1893–1978

Testimony at trial which began November 17, 1952:

Defense Attorney D. N. Pritt: "You answered my friend—I think it was what purists call a responsive answer—that the Government is to blame for the present virulence of Mau Mau. Will you tell us why you think that, what is it the government has done wrong or omitted to do?

Kenyatta: I blame the Government because knowing that the Africans have grievances they did not go into these grievances such as shortage of houses in places like Nairobi, and land shortage, and many other things—poverty of the African people both in towns and the reserves—and I believe that if the Government had gone into the economic and social conditions of the people they should have done something good. Rather than that, the Government—instead of joining with us to fight Mau Mau, they arrested all the leading members of KAU, accusing them of being Mau Mau, whereas it would have been the Government's duty to co-operate with KAU to stamp out anything that was bad, such as Mau Mau. But instead of doing that they have arrested thousands of people who would have been useful in helping to put things right in the country, and it is on these points that I blame Government, that they did not tackle the business in the right way. They wanted to, I think, not to eliminate Mau Mau, sir, but what they wanted to eliminate is the only political organization—that is KAU —which fights constitutionally for the rights of the African people, just as the Electors' Union fights for the rights of the Europeans, and Indian National Congress for the rights of the Asians. And I think and believe that by the activity of Government in arresting all the leading members of KAU who are in concentration camps —I do not think that is the right way of combating Mau Mau because most of these people who are behind bars today are people who would be helping to adjust things and eliminate Mau Mau in the country. But instead of Government cooperating with these people they put false allegations on the Union that they were Mau Mau, whereas we do know pretty well that the reason for our arrest was not Mau Mau, but because they think we are going ahead uniting our people to demand our rights. The Government arrested us simply because when they saw we could have an organization of 30,000 or 40,000 or more Africans demanding their rights here, they say, "We've an excuse—Mau Mau."

Kenyatta's last speech to court:

May it please Your Honour. On behalf of my colleagues I wish to say that we are not guilty and we do not accept your findings, and that during the hearing of this trial which has been so arranged as to place us in difficulties and inconvenience in preparing our cases, we do not feel that we have received the justice of hearing which we would have liked.

I would like also to tell Your Honour that we feel that this case, from our point of view, has been so arranged as to make scapegoats of us in order to strangle the Kenya African Union, the only organization which fights for the rights of the African people. We wish to say that what we have done in our activities has been to try our level best to find ways and means by which the community in this country can live in harmony. But what we have objected to—and we shall continue to object—are the discriminations in the government of this country. We cannot accept that, whether we are in gaol or out of it, sir, because we find that this world has been made for human beings to live in happily, to enjoy the good things and the produce of the country equally, and to enjoy the opportunities that this country has to offer. Therefore, Your Honour, I will not say that you have been misled or influenced, but the point that you have made is that we have been against the Europeans, and, sir, you being a European, it is only natural that perhaps you should feel more that way. I am not accusing you of being prejudiced, but I feel that you should not stress so much the fact that we have been entirely motivated by hatred of Europeans.

We ask you to remove that from your mind and to take this line: that our activities have been against the injustices that have been suffered by the African people and if in trying to establish the rights of the African people we have turned, out to be what you say, Mau Mau, we are very sorry that you have been misled in that direction. What we have done, and what we shall continue to do, is to demand the rights of the African people as human beings that they may enjoy the facilities and privileges in the same way as other people.

We look forward to the day when peace shall come to this land, and that the truth shall be known that we, as African leaders, have stood for peace. None of us would be happy or would condone the mutilation of human beings. We are humans and we have families and none of us will ever condone such activities as arson, etc.

Without taking up much more of your time, I will tell Your Honour that we as political bodies or political leaders stand constitutionally by our demands which no doubt are known to you and the Government of this country, and in saying this I am ask-

ing for no mercy at all on behalf of my colleagues. We are asking
that justice may be done and that the injustices that exist may be
righted. No doubt we have grievances, and everybody in this country, high or low, knows perfectly well that there are such grievances, and it is those grievances which affect the African people
that we have been fighting for. We will not ask to be excused for
asking for those grievances to be righted.

BOOK XII

Children

Social injustice as it bears upon the future generation; pictures of child labor, and of the degradation of children in slums; also hopes for the future deliverance of the child.

The Children of the Poor
(Translated by Charles Algernon Swinburne)
by VICTOR HUGO

Take heed of this small child of earth;
    He is great: he hath in him God most high.
Children before their fleshly birth
    Are lights alive in the blue sky.

In our light bitter world of wrong
    They come; God gives us them awhile.
His speech is in their stammering tongue,
    And his forgiveness in their smile.

Their sweet light rests upon our eyes.
    Alas! their right to joy is plain.
If they are hungry, Paradise
    Weeps, and, if cold, Heaven thrills with pain.

The want that saps their sinless flower
    Speaks judgment on sin's ministers.
Man holds an angel in his power.
    Ah! deep in Heaven what thunder stirs,

When God seeks out these tender things
    Whom in the shadow where we sleep
He sends us clothed about with wings,
    And finds them ragged babes that weep!

In a Southern Cotton Mill
by ELBERT HUBBARD
American author and lecturer, 1859-1915

    I thought to lift one of the little toilers to ascertain his weight. Through his thirty-five pounds of skin and bone there ran a tremor of fear, and he struggled forward to tie a broken thread. I attracted his attention by a touch, and offered him a silver dime. He looked at me dumbly through a face that might have belonged to a man of sixty, so furrowed, tightly drawn, and full of pain it was. He did not reach for the money—he did not know what it

431

was. There were dozens of such children, in this particular mill. A physician who was with me said that they would all be dead probably in two years, and their places filled by others—there were plenty more. Pneumonia carries off most of them. Their systems are ripe for disease, and when it comes there is no rebound—no response. Medicine simply does not act—nature is whipped, beaten, discouraged, and the child sinks into a stupor and dies.

Past and Present
by THOMAS CARLYLE

Descend where you will into the lower class, in Town or Country, by what avenue you will, by Factory Inquiries, Agricultural Inquiries, by Revenue Returns, by Mining-Laborer Committees, by opening your own eyes and looking, the same sorrowful result discloses itself: you have to admit that the working body of this rich English Nation has sunk or is fast sinking into a state, to which, all sides of it considered, there was literally never any parallel. At Stockport Assizes, a Mother and a Father are arraigned and found guilty of poisoning three of their children, to defraud a "burial-society" of some £3 8s. due on the death of each child: they are arraigned, found guilty; and the official authorities, it is whispered, hint that perhaps the case is not solitary, that perhaps you had better not probe farther into that department of things. ...In the British land, a human Mother and Father, of white skin and professing the Christian religion, had done this thing; they, with their Irishism and necessity and savagery, had been driven to do it. Such instances are like the highest mountain apex emerged into view; under which lies a whole mountain region and land, not yet emerged. A human Mother and Father had said to themselves, what shall we do to escape starvation? We are deep sunk here, in our dark cellar; and help is far.—Yes, in the Ugolino Hungertower stern things happen; best-loved little Gaddo fallen dead on his father's knees!—The Stockport Mother and Father think and hint: Our poor little starveling Tom, who cries all day for victuals, who will see only evil and not good in this world: if he were out of misery at once; he well dead, and the rest of us perhaps kept alive? It is thought, and hinted; at last it is done. And now Tom being killed, and all spent and eaten, is it poor little starveling Jack that must go, or poor little starveling Will? —What a committee of ways and means!

The Flower Factory
by FLORENCE WILKINSON EVANS
Twentieth-century American poet

Lizabetta, Marianina, Fiametta, Teresina,
They are winding stems of roses, one by one, one by one,
Little children who have never learned to play;
Teresina softly crying that her fingers ache to-day;
Tiny Fiametta nodding, when the twilight slips in, gray.
High above the clattering street, ambulance and fire-gong beat,
They sit, curling crimson petals, one by one, one by one.

Lizabetta, Marianina, Fiametta, Teresina,
They have never seen a rose-bush nor a dew-drop in the sun.
They will dream of the vendetta, Teresina, Fiametta,
Of a Black Hand and a Face behind a grating;
They will dream of cotton petals, endless, crimson, suffocating,
Never of a wild rose thicket or the singing of a cricket,
But the ambulance will bellow through the wanness of their
     dreams,
And their tired lids will flutter with the street's hysteric screams.

Lizabetta, Marianina, Fiametta, Teresina,
They are winding stems of roses, one by one, one by one.
Let them have a long, long play-time, Lord of Toil, when toil
     is done,
Fill their baby hands with roses, joyous roses of the sun.

The Beast
by BEN B. LINDSEY AND HARVEY J. O'HIGGINS
Ben B. Lindsey: Jurist who founded America's first children's court, 1869-1943.
Harvey J. O'Higgins: American writer on social questions, 1876-1939. The following
extract tells what came of a newspaper interview the judge granted to publicize the
treatment of children in prison.

The result was an article that took even *my* breath away when
I read it next day on the front page of the newspaper. It was the
talk of the town. It was certainly the talk of the Police Board; and
Mr. Frank Adams talked to the reporters in a high voice, indis-
creetly. He declared that the boys were liars, that I was "crazy,"
and that conditions in the jails were as good as they could be.

This reply was exactly what we wished. I demanded an investigation. The Board professed to be willing, but set no date. We promptly set one *for* them—the following Thursday at two o'clock in my chambers at the Court House—and I invited to the hearing Governor Peabody, Mayor Wright, fifteen prominent ministers in the city, and the Police Board and some members of the City Council.

On Thursday morning—to my horror—I learned from a friendly Deputy Sheriff that the subpœnas I had ordered sent to a number of boys whom I knew as jail victims had not been served. I had no witnesses. And in three hours the hearing was to begin. I appealed to the Deputy Sheriff to help me. He admitted that he could not get the boys in less than two days. "Well then," I said, "for heaven's sake, get me Mickey."

And Mickey? Well, Mickey was known to fame as "the worst kid in town." As such, his portrait had been printed in the newspapers—posed with his shine-box over his shoulder, a cigarette in the corner of his grin, his thumbs under his suspenders at the shoulders, his feet crossed in an attitude of nonchalant youthful deviltry. He had been brought before me more than once on charges of truancy, and I had been using him in an attempt to organize a newsboys' association under the supervision of the court. Moreover, he had been one of the boys who had been beaten by the jailer, and I knew he would be grateful to me for defending him.

It was midday before the Sheriff brought him to me. "Mickey," I said, "I'm in trouble, and you've got to help me out of it. You know I helped *you*."

"Betcher life yuh did, Judge," he said. "I'm wit' yuh. W'at d'yuh want?"

I told him what I wanted—every boy that he could get, who had been in jail. "And they've got to be in this room by two o'clock. Can you do it?"

Mickey threw out his dirty little hand. "Sure I kin. Don't yuh worry, Judge. Get me a wheel—dhat's all."

I hurried out with him and got him a bicycle, and he flew off down Sixteenth Street on it, his legs so short that his feet could only follow the pedals half way round. I went back to my chambers to wait....

As two o'clock approached, the ministers began to come into my room, one by one, and take seats in readiness. Mr. Wilson of the

Police Board arrived to represent his fellow-commissioners. The Deputy District Attorney came, the president of the upper branch of the City Council came, Mayor Wright came, and even Governor Peabody came—but no boys! I felt like a man who had ordered a big dinner in a strange restaurant for a party of friends, and then found that he had not brought his purse. . . . I was just about to begin my apologies when I heard an excited patter of small feet on the stairs and the shuffle and crowding of Mickey's cohorts outside in the hall. I threw open the door. "I got 'em, Judge," Mickey cried.

He had them—to the number of about twenty. I shook him by the shoulder, speechless with relief. "I tol' yuh we'd stan' by yuh, Judge," he grinned.

He had the worst lot of little jailbirds that ever saw the inside of a county court, and he pointed out the gem of his collection proudly—"Skinny," a lad in his teens, who had been in jail twenty-two times! "All right, boys," I told them, "I don't know you all, but I'll take Mickey's word for you. You've all been in jail and you know what you do there—all the dirty things you hear and see and do yourselves. I want you to tell some gentlemen in here about it. Don't be scared. They're your friends the same as I am. The cops say you've been lying to me about the way things are down in the jails there, and I want you to tell the truth. Nothing but the truth, now. Mickey, you pick them out and send them in one by one—your best witnesses first."

I went back to my chambers. "Gentlemen," I said, "we're ready."

I sat down at the big table with the Governor at my right, the Mayor at my left and the president of the Board of Supervisors and Police Commissioner Wilson at either end of the table. The ministers seated themselves in the chairs about my room. (We allowed no newspaper reporters in, because I knew what sort of vile and unprintable testimony was coming.) Mickey sent in his first witness.

One by one, as the boys came, I impressed upon them the necessity of telling the truth, encouraged them to talk, and tried to put them at their ease. I started each by asking him how often he had been in jail, what he had seen there, and so forth. Then I sat back and let him tell his story.

And the things they told would raise your hair. I saw the blushes rise to the foreheads of some of the ministers at the first details. As we went on, the perspiration stood on their faces. Some sat pale, staring appalled at these freckled youngsters from whose little lips, in a sort of infantile eagerness to tell all they knew, there came stories of bestiality that were the more horrible because they were so innocently, so boldly given. It was enough to make a man weep; and indeed tears of compassionate shame came to the eyes of more than one father there, as he listened. One boy broke down and cried when he told of the vile indecencies that had been committed upon him by the older criminals; and I saw the muscles working in the clenched jaws of some of our "investigating committee"—saw them swallowing the lump in the throat —saw them looking down at the floor blinkingly, afraid of losing their self-control. The Police Commissioner made the mistake of cross-examining the first boy, but the frank answers he got only exposed worse matters. The boys came and came, till at last, a Catholic priest, Father O'Ryan, cried out: "My God! I have had enough!" Governor Peabody said hoarsely: "I never knew there was such immorality *in the world!*" Some one else put in, "It's awful,—awful!" in a half groan.

"Gentlemen," I said, "there have been over two thousand Denver boys put through those jails and those conditions, in the last five years. Do you think it should go on any longer?"

Governor Peabody arose. "No," he said; "no. Never in my life have I heard of so much rot—corruption—vileness—as I've heard today from the mouths of these babies. I want to tell you that nothing I can do in my administration can be of more importance —nothing I can do will I do more gladly than sign those bills that Judge Lindsey is trying to get through the Legislature to do away with these terrible conditions. And if," he said, turning to the Police Commissioner, "Judge Lindsey is '*crazy,*' I want my name written under his, among the *crazy* people. And if any one says these boys are 'liars,' that man is a liar himself!"

Phew! The "committee of investigation" dissolved, the boys trooped away noisily, and the ministers went back to their pulpits to voice the horror that had kept them silent in my small chamber of horrors for two hours. Their sermons went into the newspapers under large black headlines; and by the end of the next week our juvenile court bills were passed by the Legislature and made law in Colorado.

The Cry of the Children
by Elizabeth Barrett Browning

Do ye hear the children weeping, O my brothers,
    Ere the sorrow comes with years?
They are leaning their young heads against their mothers—
    And *that* cannot stop their tears.
The young lambs are bleating in the meadows;
    The young birds are chirping in the nest;
The young fawns are playing with the shadows;
    The young flowers are blowing toward the west—
But the young, young children, O my brothers,
    They are weeping bitterly!
They are weeping in the playtime of the others,
    In the country of the free.

Do you question the young children in the sorrow
    Why their tears are falling so?
The old man may weep for his tomorrow
    Which is lost in Long Ago;
The old tree is leafless in the forest,
    The old year is ending in the frost,
The old wound, if stricken, is the sorest,
    The old hope is hardest to be lost:
But the young, young children, O my brothers,
    Do you ask them why they stand
Weeping sore before the bosoms of their mothers,
    In our happy Fatherland?

They look up with their pale and sunken faces,
    And their looks are sad to see,
For the man's hoary anguish draws and presses
    Down the cheeks of infancy;
"Your old earth," they say, "is very dreary,
    Our young feet," they say, "are very weak;
Few paces have we taken, yet are weary—
    Our grave-rest is very far to seek.
Ask the old why they weep, and not the children,
    For the outside earth is cold,
And we young ones stand without, in our bewildering,
    And the graves are for the old.". . .

The Russian Revolution

"For oh," say the children, "we are weary,
　　And we cannot run or leap;
If we cared for any meadows, it were merely
　　To drop down in them and sleep.
Our knees tremble sorely in the stooping,
　　We fall upon our faces, trying to go;
And, underneath our heavy eyelids drooping,
　　The reddest flower would look as pale as snow.
For, all day, we drag our burden tiring
　　Through the coal-dark, underground,
Or, all day, we drive the wheels of iron
　　In the factories, round and round.

"For, all day, the wheels are droning, turning;
　　Their wind comes in our faces,
Till our hearts turn, our head, with pulses burning,
　　And the walls turn in their places:
Turns the sky in the high window blank and reeling,
　　Turns the long light that drops adown the wall,
Turn the black flies that crawl along the ceiling,
　　All are turning, all the day, and we with all.
And all day, the iron wheels are droning,
　　And sometimes we could pray,
'O ye wheels,' (breaking out in a mad moaning)
　　'Stop! be silent for to-day!' "...

They look up, with their pale and sunken faces,
　　And their look is dread to see,
For they mind you of the angels in their places,
　　With eyes turned on Deity.
"How long," they say, "how long, O cruel nation,
　　Will you stand, to move the world, on a child's heart,—
Stifle down with a mailed heel its palpitation,
　　And tread onward to your throne amid the mart?
Our blood splashes upward, O gold-heaper,
　　And your purple shows your path!
But the child's sob in the silence curses deeper
　　Than the strong man in his wrath."

Child Labor in England
by HENRY DE B. GIBBINS
American author, 1865-1907

Sometimes regular traffickers would take the place of the manufacturer, and transfer a number of children to a factory district, and there keep them, generally in some dark cellar, till they could hand them over to a mill owner in want of hands, who would come and examine their height, strength, and bodily capacities, exactly as did the slave owners in the American markets. After that the children were simply at the mercy of their owners, nominally as apprentices, but in reality as mere slaves, who got no wages, and whom it was not worth while even to feed and clothe properly, because they were so cheap and their places could be so easily supplied. It was often arranged by the parish authorities, in order to get rid of imbeciles, that one idiot should be taken by the mill owner with every twenty sane children. The fate of these unhappy idiots was even worse than that of the others. The secret of their final end has never been disclosed, but we can form some idea of their awful sufferings from the hardships of the other victims to capitalist greed and cruelty. The hours of their labor were only limited by exhaustion, after many modes of torture had been unavailingly applied to force continued work. Children were often worked sixteen hours a day, by day and by night.

In the Slums of London
by JACK LONDON

There is one beautiful sight in the East End, and only one, and it is the children dancing in the street when the organ-grinder goes his round. It is fascinating to watch them, the new-born, the next generation, swaying and stepping, with pretty little mimicries and graceful inventions all their own, with muscles that move swiftly and easily, and bodies that leap airily, weaving rhythms never taught in dancing school.

I have talked with these children, here, there, and everywhere, and they struck me as being bright as other children, and in many ways even brighter. They have most active little imaginations. Their capacity for projecting themselves into the realm of romance and fantasy is remarkable. A joyous life is romping in their blood. They delight in music, and motion, and color, and very often they betray a startling beauty of face and form under their filth and rags.

But there is a Pied Piper of London Town who steals them all away. They disappear. One never sees them again, or anything that suggests them. You may look for them in vain among the generation of grown-ups. Here you will find stunted forms, ugly faces, and blunt and stolid minds. Grace, beauty, imagination, all the resiliency of mind and muscle, are gone. Sometimes, however, you may see a woman, not necessarily old, but twisted and deformed out of all womanhood, bloated and drunken, lift her draggled skirts and execute a few grotesque and lumbering steps upon the pavement. It is a hint that she was once one of those children who danced to the organ-grinder. Those grotesque and lumbering steps are all that is left of the promise of childhood. In the befogged recesses of her brain has arisen a fleeting memory that she was once a girl. The crowd closes in. Little girls are dancing beside her, about her, with all the pretty graces she dimly recollects, but can no more than parody with her body. Then she pants for breath, exhausted, and stumbles out through the circle. But the little girls dance on.

The children of the Ghetto possess all the qualities which make for noble manhood and womanhood; but the Ghetto itself, like an infuriated tigress turning on its young, turns upon and destroys all these qualities, blots out the light and laughter, and moulds those it does not kill into sodden and forlorn creatures, uncouth, degraded, and wretched below the beasts of the field.

Locksley Hall Fifty Years After
by ALFRED, LORD TENNYSON

Is it well that while we range with Science, glorying in the time,
City children soak and blacken soul and sense in city slime?
There among the gloomy alleys Progress halts on palsied feet;
Crime and hunger cast out maidens by the thousand on the
     street;

There the master scrimps his haggard seamstress of her daily
     bread;
There the single sordid attic holds the living and the dead;
There the smouldering fire of fever creeps across the rotted floor,
And the crowded couch of incest, in the warrens of the poor.

Slum Children
by WILLIAM H. DAVIES

Your songs at night a drunkard sings,
    Stones, sticks and rags your daily flowers;
Like fishes' lips, a bluey white,
    Such lips, poor mites, are yours.

Poor little things, so sad and solemn,
    Whose lives are passed in human crowds—
When in the water I can see
    Heaven with a flock of clouds.

Poor little mites that breathe foul air,
    Where garbage chokes the sink and drain—
Now when the hawthorn smells so sweet,
    Wet with the summer rain.

But few of ye will live for long;
    Ye are but small new islands seen,
To disappear before your lives
    Can grow and be made green.

Child Labor
by CHARLOTTE PERKINS GILMAN
American poet and critic, 1860-1937

No fledgling feeds the father bird!
    No chicken feeds the hen!
No kitten mouses for the cat—
    This glory is for men:

We are the Wisest, Strongest Race—
    Loud may our praise be sung!
The only animal alive
    That lives upon its young!

Waifs and Strays

by ARTHUR RIMBAUD

French poet, all of whose great works were written by the age of nineteen, 1854-1891

Black in the fog and in the snow,
Where the great air-hole windows glow,
   With rounded rumps,

Upon their knees five urchins squat,
Looking down where the baker, hot,
   The thick dough thumps.

They watch his white arm turn the bread,
Ere through an opening flaming red
   The loaf he flings.

They smell the good bread baking, while
The chubby baker with a smile
   An old tune sings.

Breathing the warmth into their soul,
They squat around the red air-hole,
   As a breast warm;

And when, for feasters' midnight bout,
The ready bread is taken out,
   In a cake's form—

Sigh with low voices like a prayer,
Bending toward the light, down there
   Where heaven gleams

—So eager that they burst their breeches,
And in the winter wind that screeches
   Their linen streams!

The Children's Auction
by CHARLES MACKAY
English Chartist poet, 1814-1889

Who bids for the little children—
　　Body, and soul and brain?
Who bids for the little children—
　　Young and without a stain?
"Will no one bid," said England,
　　"For their souls so pure and white,
And fit for all good or evil
　　The world on their page may write?"

"We bid," said Pest and Famine;
　　"We bid for life and limb;
Fever and pain and squalor,
　　Their bright young eyes shall dim.
When the children grow too many,
　　We'll nurse them as our own,
And hide them in secret places
　　Where none may hear their moan."

"I bid," said Beggary, howling;
　　"I bid for them one and all!
I'll teach them a thousand lessons—
　　To lie, to skulk, to crawl!
They shall sleep in my lair like maggots,
　　They shall rot in the fair sunshine;
And if they serve my purpose
　　I hope they'll answer thine."

"I'll bid you higher and higher,"
　　Said Crime, with a wolfish grin;
"For I love to lead the children
　　Through the pleasant paths of sin.
They shall swarm in the streets to pilfer,
　　They shall plague the broad highway,
They shall grow too old for pity
　　And ripe for the law to slay.

> "Give me the little children,
>   Ye good, ye rich, ye wise,
> And let the busy world spin round
>   While ye shut your idle eyes;
> And your judges shall have work,
>   And your lawyers wag the tongue,
> And the jailers and policemen
>   Shall be fathers to the young!"

Oliver Twist
by CHARLES DICKENS

The room in which the boys were fed, was a large stone hall, with a copper at one end; out of which the master, dressed in an apron for the purpose, and assisted by one or two women, ladled the gruel at meal times. Of this festive composition each boy had one porringer, and no more—except on occasions of great public rejoicing, when he had two ounces and a quarter of bread besides. The bowls never wanted washing. The boys polished them with their spoons till they shone again; and when they had performed this operation (which never took very long, the spoons being nearly as long as the bowls) they would sit staring at the copper, with such eager eyes, as if they could have devoured the very bricks of which it was composed; employing themselves, meanwhile, in sucking their fingers most assiduously, with the view of catching up any stray splashes of gruel that might have been cast thereon. Boys have generally excellent appetites. Oliver Twist and his companions suffered the tortures of slow starvation for three months; at last they got so voracious and wild with hunger, that one boy, who was tall for his age, and hadn't been used to that sort of thing (for his father had kept a small cook-shop), hinted darkly to his companions, that unless he had another basin of gruel *per diem*, he was afraid he might some night happen to eat the boy who slept next to him, who happened to be a weakly youth of tender age. He had a wild, hungry eye; and they implicitly believed him. A council was held; lots were cast who should walk up to the master after supper that evening, and ask for more; and it fell to Oliver Twist.

This evening arrived; the boys took their places. The master, in his cook's uniform, stationed himself at the copper; his pauper assistants ranged themselves behind him; the gruel was served out; and a long grace was said over the short commons. The gruel disappeared; the boys whispered to each other, and winked at Oliver; while his next neighbors nudged him. Child as he was, he was desperate with hunger, and reckless with misery. He rose from the table; and advancing to the master, basin and spoon in hand, said, somewhat alarmed at his own temerity:

"Please, sir, I want some more."

The master was a fat, healthy man; but he turned very pale. He gazed in stupefied astonishment on the small rebel for some seconds, and then clung for support to the copper. The assistants were paralyzed with wonder; the boys with fear.

"What!" said the master at length, in a faint voice.

"Please, sir," replied Oliver, "I want some more."

The master aimed a blow at Oliver's head with the ladle; pinioned him in his arms; and shrieked aloud for the beadle.

The board were sitting in solemn conclave, when Mr. Bumble rushed into the room in great excitement, and addressing the gentleman in the high chair, said:

"Mr. Limbkins, I beg your pardon, sir! Oliver Twist has asked for more!"

There was a general start. Horror was depicted on every countenance.

"For *more!*" said Mr. Limbkins. "Compose yourself, Bumble, and answer me distinctly. Do I understand that he asked for more, after he had eaten the supper allotted by the dietary?"

"He did, sir," replied Bumble.

"That boy will be hung," said the gentleman in the white waistcoat. "I know that boy will be hung."

Nobody controverted the prophetic gentleman's opinion. An animated discussion took place. Oliver was ordered into instant confinement; and a bill was next morning pasted on the outside of the gate, offering a reward of five pounds to anybody who would take Oliver Twist off the hands of the parish. In other words, five pounds and Oliver Twist were offered to any man or woman who wanted an apprentice to any trade, business, or calling.

"I never was more convinced of anything in my life," said the gentleman in the white waistcoat, as he knocked at the gate and read the bill the next morning: "I never was more convinced of anything in my life, than I am that that boy will come to be hung."

A Modest Proposal

(From "A Modest Proposal for Preventing the Children of Poor People from Being a Burthen to their Parents or Country, and for making them Beneficial to the Public")

by JONATHAN SWIFT

British man of letters, master of the bitterest satiric pen in English literature, 1667-1745

It is a melancholy object to those, who walk through this great town, or travel in the country, when they see the streets, the roads, and cabin-doors, crowded with beggars of the female sex, followed by three, four or six children, *all in rags,* and importuning every passenger for an alms. These mothers instead of being able to work for their honest livelihood, are forced to employ all their time in strolling, to beg sustenance for their helpless infants, who, as they grow up, either turn thieves for want of work, or leave their dear Native Country to fight for the Pretender in Spain, or sell themselves to the Barbadoes.

I think it is agreed by all parties, that this prodigious number of children, in the arms, or on the backs, or at the heels of their mothers, and frequently of their fathers, is in the present deplorable state of the kingdom, a very great additional grievance; and therefore whoever could find out a fair, cheap and easy method of making these children sound, useful members of the commonwealth would deserve so well of the public, as to have his statue set up for a preserver of the nation.

But my intention is very far from being confined to provide only for the children of professed beggars, it is of much greater extent, and shall take in the whole numbers of infants at a certain age, who are born of parents in effect as little able to support them, as those who demand our charity in the streets. . . .

There is another great advantage in my scheme, that it will prevent those voluntary abortions, and that horrid practice of women murdering their bastard children, alas, too frequent among us, sacrificing the poor innocent babes, I doubt, more to avoid the expense, than the shame, which would move tears and pity in the most savage and inhuman breast. . . .

I have been assured by a very knowing American of my acquaintance in London that a young healthy child well nursed is at a year old a most delicious, nourishing, and wholesome food, whether stewed, roasted, baked, or boiled; and I make no doubt that it will equally serve in a fricassee, or a ragout.

I do therefore humbly offer it to public consideration, that of the hundred and twenty thousand children, already computed, twenty thousand may be reserved for breed, whereof only one fourth part to be males, which is more than we allow to sheep, black-cattle, or swine; and my reason is that these children are seldom the fruits of marriage, a circumstance not much regarded by our savages; therefore only one male will be sufficient to serve four females. That the remaining hundred thousand may at a year old be offered in sale to the persons of quality, and fortune, through the kingdom, always advising the mother to let them suck plentifully in the last month, so as to render them plump, and fat for a good table. . . .

I am not so violently bent upon my opinion, as to reject any offer, proposed by wise men, which shall be found equally innocent, cheap, easy, and effectual. But before something of that kind shall be advanced in contradiction to my scheme, and offering a better, I desire the author, or authors will be pleased maturely to consider two points. First, as things now stand, how they will be able to find food and raiment for an hundred thousand useless mouths and backs. And secondly, there being a round million of creatures in human figure, throughout this kingdom, whose whole subsistence put into a common stock, would leave them in debt two millions of pounds sterling, adding those, who are beggars by profession, to the bulk of farmers, cottagers and laborers with their wives and children, who are beggars in effect. I desire those politicians, who dislike my overture, and may perhaps be so bold to attempt an answer, that they will first ask the parents of these mortals, whether they would not at this day think it a great happiness to have been sold for food at a year old, in the manner I prescribe, and thereby have avoided such a perpetual scene of misfortunes, as they have since gone through, by the oppression of landlords, the impossibility of paying rent without money or trade, the want of common sustenance, with neither house nor clothes to cover them from the inclemencies of the weather, and the most inevitable prospect of entailing the like, or greater miseries upon their breed for ever.

I profess in the sincerity of my heart that I have not the least personal interest in endeavoring to promote this necessary work, having no other motive than the *public good of my country, by advancing our trade, providing for infants, relieving the poor, and giving some pleasure to the rich.* I have no children, by which I can propose to get a single penny; the youngest being nine years old, and my wife past child-bearing.

True Education

(From "Zadig")

by Voltaire

French philosopher and poet, one of the major intellectual forces preparing the
way for the French Revolution; 1694-1778

A widow, having a young son, and being possessed of a handsome fortune, had given a promise of marriage to two magi, who were both desirous of marrying her.

"I will take for my husband," said she, "the man who can give the best education to my beloved son."

The two magi contended who should bring him up, and the cause was carried before Zadig. Zadig summoned the two magi to attend him.

"What will you teach your pupil?" he said to the first.

"I will teach him," said the doctor, "the eight parts of speech, logic, astrology, pneumatics, what is meant by substance and accident, abstract and concrete, the doctrine of the monads, and the pre-established harmony."

"For my part," said the second, "I will endeavor to give him a sense of justice, and to make him worthy the friendship of good men."

Zadig then cried: "Whether thou art the child's favorite or not, thou shalt have his mother."

The Way to Freedom

by Francisco Ferrer

Spanish educator and radical, executed by a plot of his clerical enemies, 1859-1909

We must destroy all which in the present school answers to the organization of constraint, the artificial surroundings by which children are separated from nature and life, the intellectual and moral discipline made use of to impose ready-made ideas upon them, beliefs which deprave and annihilate natural bent. Without fear of deceiving ourselves, we can restore the child to the environment which entices it, the environment of nature in which he will be in contact with all that he loves, and in which impressions of life will replace fastidious book-learning. If we did no more than that, we should already have prepared in great part the deliverance of the child.

Water for the Gardens
by DANILO DOLCI
Contemporary Italian architect who has sacrificed his earning potential and private
comforts to share and publicize the grinding poverty of the Sicilian masses

The Capo is the section southeast of the Massimo Theatre and
some thirty yards behind it, in the very heart of Palermo. The
hundred families under consideration were picked at random;
thirty-one in Cortile Scalilla, nineteen in Vicolo Catar, twenty-
nine in Cartile degli Orfani, thirteen in Cortile Capellaio and
eight in Cortile Maestro Carlo.

The streets are narrow; in some places they are less than three
feet wide. In one alley, close to a second-hand-clothes stand, we
saw a naked child squat down to do his business and pass a tape-
worm, twenty-five inches long. The houses are high; some have as
many as four stories.

At night the floors of most of the rooms are strewn with mat-
tresses, rags and blankets. If a child gets up to do his business, he
has to fumble and grope every inch of the way in the dark to avoid
walking on the body of a sleeper. Families sleep on the table, as
well as under it; one old woman managed to bed down her ten
grandchildren, for whom there was no accommodation in their
own home, in this way. Another tiny room was shared by three
young married couples.

The hundred families number five hundred and seventy-six
persons, all of whom live in eighty homes, or ninety rooms. The
average number of persons to a room, then, is 6.33.

Only one family has a proper toilet; the other families do their
business in an open drain which is frequently situated just below
the kitchen. Fourteen families have water taps, but in summer
the water is cut off as it is needed for the plants in the public
gardens. The "Christians" can do without it!

Forty-nine families have electric light. Two rooms have floors
of packed dirt; seventy-nine, of broken tile; and one, of coarse
cement. The floors of the remaining rooms are fairly good.

There are two hundred and twenty-three places large enough
for one person to sleep. This means that the average number of
persons to one such place is 2.58.

Among the children three through six years old, four go to
kindergarten and fifty-three do not. Among those six through
thirteen, forty-nine go to school, fifty-eight do not. On the average,

the four hundred and forty-four persons over six years old have finished only a third of the second grade.

As for the occupations of the heads-of-family, twenty-eight are hawkers; nine are laborers; eight, shoemakers; four, bricklayers and carpenters; three, candy sellers; three, streetcleaners; one is a stevedore; one, a tailor; one, a plasterer; one, a painter; one, a craftsman who decorates carts; one, a chauffeur; one, a poolroom attendant; one, a barber's assistant; one, a mailman; one, a sawdust merchant; one, a moneychanger; one, a grocery assistant; and one, a cigarette seller. Four of the men are disabled, and ten have no trade or calling. Thirteen of the families are on relief.

As for the women, ten are chambermaids, two are dressmakers, one is a hawker, one is a beggar, one is a laundress. The other women do not go out to work, but help out by doing various jobs at home for the stores; for example, stringing string beans.

With few exceptions, the children follow the family calling.

Twenty persons have had typhus, from which there have been several deaths. Forty-one children have suffered from various chest diseases, nearly all of which were diagnosed as tubercular. Infant mortality is due largely to some form of blood poisoning.

The authorities frequently refuse to issue licenses to peddlers, hence they are forced into far less harmless "work." It is difficult to say how often these unfortunates have been fined. They cannot remember how many fines they have incurred, but can only give a rough monthly estimate. The twenty-eight hawkers interviewed in Capo have been fined approximately eight thousand times in the last ten years.

The Leaden-Eyed
(From "The Congo")
by Vachel Lindsay

Let not young souls be smothered out before
They do quaint deeds and fully flaunt their pride.
It is the world's one crime its babes grow dull,
Its poor are ox-like, limp and leaden-eyed.
Not that they starve, but starve so dreamlessly,
Not that they sow, but that they seldom reap,
Not that they serve, but have no gods to serve,
Not that they die, but that they die like sheep.

Children's Crusade

by CHRISTOPHER MORLEY

American poet, essayist and novelist, 1890-1957

Peter the
Hermit, in
horror of his
time, walks in
a forest of
young grow-
ing . . .

Peter the Hermit riddled the air,
He cursed himself in his despair,
He wondered how to put in words
The milk of the matter, churned to curds.

Peter the Hermit—half clown, half sage—
Walked the dark woods of his Middle Age
Mulling his tripes and simmering rage:
Saw young plantations, pine and fir,
Striplings growing, some *him,* some *her,*
And cried to the gods Oh Madam, Oh Sir,
Who cares what the roots and brambles were?
All make sense to the Forester.
He looks with charity on both,
Since Growth is God, and God is Growth.

Sees its swift
changes, and
perils of
chance . . .

The life so brief
From seed to leaf
Gropes and climbs and rearranges
In shapes and energies so sweet
No loving memory can repeat
Their gradual and subtle changes.
But woods, and men, can burn, who hinders
Idiots who scatter cinders?
Who appoints himself fire-warden
And makes all his plans accord'n?

A skyline of
strange shapes,
and "bright-
ness falls from
the air". . .

Peter saw T.V. antennae
Of many forms (and payments many)
Built like crowsnests rather skinny,
Patterns parallel or lopsides
Crowning second-mortgage topsides.
A fishrod this way baits for yammer,
A prong stuck that way pipes in glamor,
And how much codfish, how much crow
Comes scooping in by video!
Such juice of hebenon had been poured
(See "Hamlet") Pete went overboard.

Listen, children, and you shall hear
His midnight ride in ionosphere.

A vision of
children on bi-
cycles . . .

The trees grow, the winds blow,
Kids ride bicycles to and fro:
But listen, kids,
The time is near to open the bids.
Fear compounds and pyramids,
The world is lying in wait for you,
It might be even too late for you
In Nineteen-Fifty-X or so.

And those
children, not
long hence,
in the stress
of young
parents . . .

Maybe you're parents by then, poor apes?
Parents, you'll find, have no escapes.
Good-by bobbysocks, good-by comics,
Roll down jeans; Home Economics
Deals with actual human stummicks.
The stroller (be careful how you park it)
Goes only to the supermarket;
Bubble the diapers, hoist like a sack
The twenty-pound babe till your pelves crack;
Meet, six-thirty, your young-old man

A montage
of their
memories of
high school . . .

Who looks, by then, like Caliban.
Farewell teachers and teachers' pets,
Farewell white-ham majorettes,
Forgotten the halfback (second string)
Who made your high-school hormones sing.
Life was too smart to let you or me
Guess how tough it was going to be.
It'll bend your back and swell your girth—it
Is still unquestionably worth it.

But the Old
Folks are not
likely to have
any fresh
ideas, while
behind the
radish-shape
domes of the
Kremlin is the

And 'bye now old folks, 'bye grandparents
Full of I dassn'ts and We daren'ts:
They swinked their utmost, hither and yon,
But if men begin to throw chunks of sun
Yours is the chin they're taken on.
The Kremlin's heart is a cold red radish,
Reads no Bible, sings no Kaddish?
Yet maybe behind-the-curtain Russians
Are no keener than we on world-concussions?

riddle of an- Farewell lethargy and despair—
other world, Up with political fresh air.
where sickles
look like ques- United Nations dance dozy-doe:
tion marks . . . Set to partners, then back-to-backed
                  Politburo and Atlantic Pact
And two halves And thinking their prestige enhancing
of the world Cry to the world, Look Ma, we're dancing.
dance back-to- And the kids ride bicycles to and fro—
back . . . But listen, kids, they've got you cased:
                  Unless a few millions of you make haste
                  The future is aiming straight for you,
                  Planning a wholesale fate for you.
                  Drawing (your favor!) its big blank checks
                  On Nineteen-Hundred-and-Fifty-X.

                  Spring trees growing,
                  Spring winds blowing,
The youngest *Kids on bicycles to-and-froing,*
of all are al- *And smaller tykes, too small for bikes,*
ready out in *Too innocent to know or care*
scooters and *Or how or where*
strollers and *The Great Stupidity is flowing.*
baby-car- *My daughter's son, my daughter's daughter,*
riages . . . *Are they to be drowned in Heavy Water?*

                  Time and differentials vary,
                  Each human soul is momentary,
                  But its brief and craving fit
                  Is urgently, terribly, to it:
                  So what, cried Peter, is good intent's worth?
                  Let's put in our own three cents' worth:
A dream of How's about writing ten million letters
hands, writ- To your elders (not your betters) —
ing . . . World-revolution lilliputian
                  Might mean stay of execution?
                  Strong as a bomb of hydrogen
                  Could be the school-kids' ballpoint pen?
                  Click-clack-click on the typewriter platen
                  Probably won't outstupefy Satan,
                  But have we born a generation

Sterile for lack of imagination?
The Future is our own creation.

In a smell of
smoke the
whole world
needs a baby-
sitter . . .

Young parents woke
To a smell of smoke,
Saw, and stamped on, a burning ember
(Speech of a highrank Cabinet member).
Call the firehouse, ring from the steeple:
Talk about "licking hell out of people"
Is crude bravado, bunkum, pus—
Listen, you can't do that to Us.
Unless our nerves are mighty steady
Maybe we're in hell already.
You see, we're learning:
We'll stay awake
For Buster's sake
If his guts are churning—
We'll do our bit
And babysit
For a whole world, if it's burning.

Peter hears the
Forgotten
Voice, the
Voice that has
no audience,
and appeals for
a showman . . .

Said Peter: there are V. I. P.'s
(Too silent, most, in libraries)
And these, immortals who never died,
Might check our push for suicide:
Come in, come in, wherever you are,
From Germany, France, USSR,
Come before we get hysteric, a
Voice not just the Voice of America
But a Voice wherever said or sung
In comedy, cartoon, poem, ballet
To dance us out of our black blind alley—
The Forgotten Voice. The Voice of the Young.
We have chivvied the earth and strafed her
With prude, professor, gull and grafter:
We have tried everything but Laughter.
The Author of All is a showman, isn't he?
Come in, some supercosmic Disney.

I summon, said Peter, without schmoos
Uncle Remus and Mother Goose,

He calls on
Some Very
Important
People . . .

I call the spirits who understand:
Snow White, Alice in Wonderland,
Davy's Goblin, Beautiful Joe,
Little Boy Blue and Ivanhoe;
Sherlock Holmes and Little Red Hen,
Little Women, and Little Men.
I call Three Bears and Five Little Peppers,
Helen's Babies at their capers,
I am fed up with Mr. Bigs,
I call instead on Four Little Pigs,
Calling all ghosts that can rise above
This gumshoe death.
         Call those you love.
Call Fauntleroy in his velvet suits,
Or Peck's Bad Boy, or Puss-in-Boots,
Call Cinderella's midnight coach,
Mehitabel and Archy the Roach,
Bulldog Drummond, Christopher Robin,
Topsy (c/o Uncle Tom's Cabin),
The Robinsons (Swiss) or Robinson Crusoe,
Or Leatherstocking—and when you do so
Remember Krag the Kootenai Ram,
Mr. Pickwick, Penrod and Sam,
The Psammead and the Bandersnatch,
And Mrs. Wiggs of the Cabbage Patch.
Call for help, when the world looks ugly,
Mickey Mouse, Mother Wolf and Mowgli:
Broadcast any kindly parable
(Said Peter) that makes life look less horrible.
If I'm wrong, I won't be found
In dispersal underground.
I'm right here, where I always was,
With Huck Finn and the Wizard of Oz.

And even sug-
gests that
Laughter
might help . . .

So borrow, boxtop, beg or steal,
Thumb your way by automobile,
By flattery, impudence or stealth
To the jaded men of the commonwealth:
Cry from a hundred thousand schools
What do you think you're doing, fools?
The old folks are a bunch of shown-ups,
Life's too humorous for grown-ups,

All they can think of is to break it:
Their slumber is too deep to wake it—
Older people just can't take it.
When all the anger has been spent
Laughter is disarmament.

Trees were growing,
Fresh winds blowing,
Children getting a bit more knowing.
They scripted it, in ballpoint ink,
Now is later than you think.
The only language universal
Is laughter, which needs no rehearsal—
Laughter, which disarms and cures:
Make the world laugh and it is yours.
So Peter the Hermit spilled his soul.
They monitored him in the glass control,
But having no   *But he really called a spade a spade . . .*
Sponsor, is cut
off the air . . .   And that's what started the Kids' Crusade.

What to Do
by LEO TOLSTOY

It is very easy to take a child away from a prostitute, or from a
beggar. It is very easy, when one has money, to have him washed,
cleaned and dressed in good clothes, fed up, and even taught various sciences; but for us who do not earn our own bread, it is not
only difficult to teach him to earn his bread, it is impossible; because by our example, and even by those material improvements
of his life which cost us nothing, we teach the opposite.

Poor Black Girls Having Babies

(From "Facing Common Sense," an address made in 1987)

BY ANGELA DAVIS

American Black activist who went underground for two years
in 1970 after she was accused of abetting a botched courtroom
escape in which four people were killed, born 1944

Media mystification should not obfuscate a simple, perceivable fact; Black teenage girls do not create poverty by having babies. Quite the contrary, they have babies at such a young age precisely because they are poor—because they do not have the opportunity to acquire an education, because meaningful, well-paying jobs and creative forms of recreation are not accessible to them ... because safe, effective forms of contraception are not available to them.

BOOK XIII

Humor

Comedy of the social struggle; masterpieces from those who have had the courage to fight the battle for social progress with the weapons of laughter and satire.

The Reserved Section
by Wilbur Nesbit

American writer, 1871-1927. At the time of the great anthracite coal strike of 1902, George F. Baer, head of the coal trust was quoted as declaring: "The rights and interests of the laboring man will be protected and cared for, not by labor and agitation, but by the Christian men to whom God in his infinite wisdom has given control of the property interests of this country."

In the prehistoric ages, when the world was a ball of mist—
A seething swirl of something unknown in the planet list;
When the earth was vague with vapor, and formless and dark and
    void—
The sport of the wayward comet—the jibe of the asteroid—
Then the singing stars of morning chanted soft: "Keep out of
    there!
Keep off that spot which is sizzling hot—it is making coal for Baer!"

When the pterodactyl ambled, or fluttered, or swam, or jumped,
And the plesiosaurus rambled, all careless of what he bumped,
And the other old time monsters that thrived on the land and sea,
And did not know what their names were, any more than today
    do we—
Wherever they went they heard it: "You fellows keep out of
    there—
That place which shakes and quivers and quakes—it is making
    coal for Baer."

The carboniferous era consumed but a million years;
It started when earth was shedding the last of her baby tears,
When still she was swaddled softly in clumsily tied on clouds,
When stars from the shop of nature were being turned out in
    crowds;
But high o'er the favored section this sign said to all: "Beware!
Stay back of the ropes that surround these slopes—they are making
    coal for Baer!"

From Ecclesiasticus

A rich man speaketh, and all keep silence; and what he saith they extol to the clouds: A poor man speaketh, and they say, Who is this? and if he stumble, they will help to overthrow him.

461

Penguin Island
by ANATOLE FRANCE

French man of letters, 1844-1924. In this novel of social satire the aged and half-blind Saint Maël has by mistake baptized a flock of penguins. After a consultation of the heavenly powers, the penguins are turned into human beings.

Now one autumn morning, as the blessed Maël was walking in the valley of Clange in company with a monk of Yvern called Bulloch, he saw bands of fierce-looking men loaded with stones passing along the roads. At the same time he heard in all directions cries and complaints mounting up from the valley towards the tranquil sky.

And he said to Bulloch:

"I notice with sadness, my son, that since they became men the inhabitants of this island act with less wisdom than formerly. When they were birds they only quarrelled during the season of their love affairs. But now they dispute all the time; they pick quarrels with each other in summer as well as in winter. How greatly have they fallen from that peaceful majesty which made the assembly of the penguins look like the senate of a wise republic!

"Look towards Surelle, Bulloch, my son. In yonder pleasant valley a dozen men penguins are busy knocking each other down with the spades and picks that they might employ better in tilling the ground. The women, still more cruel than the men, are tearing their opponents' faces with their nails. Alas! Bulloch, my son, why are they murdering each other in this way?"

"From a spirit of fellowship, father, and through forethought for the future," answered Bulloch. "For man is essentially provident and sociable. Such is his character, and it is impossible to imagine it apart from a certain appropriation of things. Those penguins whom you see are dividing the ground among themselves."

"Could they not divide it with less violence?" asked the aged man. "As they fight they exchange invectives and threats. I do not distinguish their words, but they are angry ones, judging from the tone."

"They are accusing one another of theft and encroachment," answered Bulloch. "That is the general sense of their speech."

At that moment the holy Maël clasped his hands and sighed deeply.

"Do you see, my son," he exclaimed, "that madman who with his teeth is biting the nose of the adversary he has overthrown, and that other one who is pounding a woman's head with a huge stone?"

"I see them," said Bulloch. "They are creating law; they are founding property; they are establishing the principles of civilization, the basis of society, and the foundations of the State."

"How is that?" asked old Maël.

"By setting bounds to their fields. That is the origin of all government. Your penguins, O Master, are performing the most august of functions. Throughout the ages their work will be consecrated by lawyers, and magistrates will confirm it."

"Mr. Dooley" on Success
by FINLEY PETER DUNNE
American humorist and social commentator, 1867-1936

Th' millyionaire starts in as a foreman in a can facthry. By an' by, he larns that wan iv th' men wurrukin' f'r him has invinted a top that ye can opin with a pair iv scissors, an' he throws him down an' takes it away fr'm him. He's a robber, says ye? He is while he's got th' other man down. But whin he gets up he's a magnate.

The Leisure Classes
ANONYMOUS

There was a little beggar maid
  Who wed a king long, long ago;
Of course the taste that he displayed
  Was criticised by folks who know
Just what formalities and things
Are due to beggar maids and kings.

But straight the monarch made reply:
  "There is small difference, as I live,
Between our stations! She and I
  Subsist on what the people give.
We do not toil with strength and skill,
And, pleasing Heaven, never will."

The Pauper's Drive

by T. NOEL
English Chartist poet, 1834-1894

There's a grim one-horse hearse in a jolly round trot;
To the churchyard a pauper is going, I wot;
The road it is rough, and the hearse has no springs,
And hark to the dirge that the sad driver sings:—
    "Rattle his bones over the stones:
    He's only a pauper, whom nobody owns!"

Oh, where are the mourners? alas! there are none;
He has left not a gap in the world now he's gone,
Not a tear in the eye of child, woman, or man—
To the grave with his carcase as fast as you can.
    "Rattle his bones over the stones;
    He's only a pauper, whom nobody owns!"

What a jolting and creaking, and splashing and din;
The whip how it cracks! and the wheels how they spin!
How the dirt, right and left, o'er the hedges is hurled!
The pauper at length makes a noise in the world.
    "Rattle his bones over the stones;
    He's only a pauper, whom nobody owns!" . . .

You bumpkin, who stare at your brother conveyed;
Behold what respect to a cloddy is paid,
And be joyful to think, when by death you're laid low
You've a chance to the grave like a gemman to go.
    "Rattle his bones over the stones;
    He's only a pauper, whom nobody owns!"

But a truce to this strain—for my soul it is sad,
To think that a heart in humanity clad
Should make, like the brutes, such a desolate end,
And depart from the light without leaving a friend.
    Bear softly his bones over the stones;
    Though a pauper, he's one whom his Maker yet owns.

Song of the Lower Classes

by ERNEST JONES
Chartist leader and poet, 1819-1869

We plow and sow, we're so very, very low,
    That we delve in the dirty clay;
Till we bless the plain with the golden grain,
    And the vale with the fragrant hay.
Our place we know, we're so very, very low,
    'Tis down at the landlord's feet;
We're not too low the grain to grow,
    But too low the bread to eat.

Down, down we go, we're so very, very low,
    To the hell of the deep-sunk mines;
But we gather the proudest gems that glow,
    When the crown of the despot shines;
And when'er he lacks, upon our backs
    Fresh loads he deigns to lay;
We're far too low to vote the tax,
    But not too low to pay.

We're low, we're low—we're very, very low,—
    And yet from our fingers glide
The silken floss and the robes that glow
    Round the limbs of the sons of pride;
And what we get, and what we give,
    We know, and we know our share;
We're not too low the cloth to weave,
    But too low the cloth to wear.

We're low, we're low, we're very, very low,
    And yet when the trumpets ring,
The thrust of a poor man's arm will go
    Through the heart of the proudest king.
We're low, we're low—mere rabble, we know—
    We're only the rank and file;
We're not too low to kill the foe,
    But too low to share the spoil.

Zadig
by VOLTAIRE

The lord of the castle was one of those Arabians who are commonly called robbers; but he now and then performed some good actions amidst a multitude of bad ones. He robbed with furious rapacity, and granted favors with great generosity.

"May I take the liberty of asking thee," said Zadig, "how long thou hast followed this noble profession?"

"From my most tender youth," replied the lord. "I was servant to a petty, good-natured Arabian, but could not endure the hardships of my situation. I was vexed to find that fate had given me no share of the earth which equally belongs to all men. I imparted the cause of my uneasiness to an old Arabian, who said to me:

" 'My son, do not despair; there was once a grain of sand that lamented that it was no more than a neglected atom in the deserts; at the end of a few years it became a diamond, and it is now the brightest ornament in the crown of the king of the Indies.'

"This discourse made a deep impression on my mind. I was the grain of sand, and I resolved to become the diamond. I began by stealing two horses. I soon got a party of companions. I put myself in a condition to rob small caravans; and thus, by degrees, I destroyed the difference which had formerly subsisted between me and other men. I had my share of the good things of this world; and was even recompensed with usury for the hardships I had suffered. I was greatly respected, and became the captain of a band of robbers. I seized this castle by force. The satrap of Syria had a mind to dispossess me of it; but I was too rich to have anything to fear. I gave the satrap a handsome present, by which I preserved my castle, and increased my possessions. He even appointed me treasurer of the tributes which Arabia Petraea pays to the king of kings. I perform my office of receiver with great punctuality; but I take the freedom to dispense with that of paymaster."

Diomedes the Pirate to Alexander
by FRANÇOIS VILLON
French poet and vagabond, 1431-c.1463

The Emperor reasoned with him: "Why should you desire to be a pirate?" And the other replied: "Why call me a pirate? Because you see me going about in a little galley? If I could arm myself like you, like you I would be an emperor."

Lines
by Stephen Crane

"Have you ever made a just man?"
"Oh, I have made three," answered God,
"But two of them are dead,
And the third—
Listen! listen,
And you will hear the thud of his defeat. . . ."

Complaint to My Empty Purse
by Geoffrey Chaucer

To you, my purse, and to none other wight
   Complain I, for ye be my lady dear!
I am so sorry, now that ye be light;
   For certès, but ye make me heavy cheer,
   Me were as lief be laid upon my bier;
For which unto your mercy thus I cry:
Be heavy again, or elles might I die!

Now voucheth safe this day, or it be night,
   That I of you the blissful sound may hear,
Or see your colour like the sun bright
   That of yellowness had never a peer.
   Ye be my life, ye be my hertes stere,
Queen of comfort and of good company:
Be heavy again, or elles might I die!

For the Other 365 Days
by Franklin P. Adams
American columnist and author, 1881-1960

Christmas is over. Uncork your ambition!
Back to the battle! Come on, competition!
Down with all sentiment, can scrupulosity!
Commerce has nothing to gain by jocosity;
Money is all that is worth all your labors;
Crowd your competitors, nix on your neighbors!
Push 'em aside in a passionate hurry,
Argue and bustle and bargain and worry!
Frenzy yourself into sickness and dizziness—
Christmas is over and Business is Business.

Don Quixote

Sancho Panza, the servant of the half-crazed knight, has accompanied him upon the
promise of being promoted to a high station.

by MIGUEL DE CERVANTES

"Troth, wife," quoth Sancho, "were not I in hopes to see myself, ere it be long, governor of an island, on my conscience I
should drop down dead on the spot." "Not so, my chicken," quoth
the wife, " 'let the hen live, though it be with pip'; do thou live,
and let all the governments in the world go to the Devil. Thou
camest out of thy mother's belly without government, and thou
mayest be carried to thy long home without government, when
it shall please the Lord. How many people in this world live
without government yet do well enough, and are well looked
upon? There is no sauce in the world like hunger; and as the
poor never want that, they always eat with a good stomach."

The Freebooter's Prayer
Scotland, 1405

Thou that willed us naked-born,
Send us meat against the morn—
Got with right or got with wrong
So we fast not overlong.
Prosper "Snaffle, Spur and Spear!"
Grant us booty, horse and gear;
Save our necks from hempen thrall,
Bless the souls of them that fall.

A Modern Version
U.S.A., 1905
by ARTHUR GUITERMAN
American poet, 1871-1943

Thou, Whom rich and poor adore,
Grant me fifty millions more,
Earned or pilfered, foul or pure;
From man's law hold me secure.
So, when I have gained of gold
All my coffers well can hold,
I may give, O Lord, for Thee,
One-sixteenth in Charity.

The Latest Decalogue
by ARTHUR HUGH CLOUGH

Thou shalt have one God only; who
Would be at the expense of two?
No graven images may be
Worshipped, except the currency.
Swear not at all; for, for thy curse
Thine enemy is none the worse.
At church on Sunday to attend
Will serve to keep the world thy friend.
Honor thy parents; that is, all
From whom advancement may befall.
Thou shalt not kill; but need'st not strive
Officiously to keep alive.
Do not adultery commit;
Advantage rarely comes of it.
Thou shalt not steal; an empty feat,
When it's so lucrative to cheat.
Bear not false witness; let the lie
Have time on its own wings to fly.
Thou shalt not covet, but tradition
Approves all forms of competition.

The Road to Success
(From "Random Reminiscences of Men and Events")
by JOHN D. ROCKEFELLER, SR.

If I were to give advice to a young man starting out in life,
I should say to him: If you aim for a large broad-gauged success,
do not begin your business career, whether you sell your labor or
are an independent producer, with the idea of getting from the
world by hook or crook all you can. In the choice of your profession or your business employment, let your first thought be: Where
can I fit in so that I may be most effective in the work of the
world? Where can I lend a hand in a way most effective to advance
the general interests? Enter life in such a spirit, choose your voca-
tion in that way, and you have taken the first step on the highest
road to a large success. Investigation will show that the great fortunes which have been made in this country, and the same is prob-

ably true of other lands, have come to men who have performed great and far-reaching economic services—men who, with great faith in the future of their country, have done most for the development of its resources. The man will be most successful who confers the greatest service on the world.

"Mr. Dooley" on the Trusts
by FINLEY PETER DUNNE

"Mind ye, Jawn, I've no wurrud to say again thim that sets back in their own house an' lot an' makes th' food iv th' people dear. They're good men, good men. Whin they tilt the price iv beef to where wan pound iv it costs as much as many th' man in this Ar-rchey Road 'd wurruk from th' risin' to th' settin' iv th' sun to get, they have no thought iv th' likes iv you an' me. 'Tis aisy come, aisy go with thim; an' ivry cint a pound manes a new art musoom or a new church, to take th' edge off hunger. They're all right, thim la-ads with their own porkchops delivered free at th' door. 'Tis, 'Will ye have a new spring dress, me dear? Willum, ring thim up, an' tell thim to hist the price iv beef. If we had a few more pitchers an' statoos in th' musoom 'twud ilivate th' people a sthory or two. Willum, afther this steak 'll be twinty cints a pound.' Oh, they're all right, on'y I was thinkin' iv th' Connock man's fam'ly back iv th' dumps."

"For a man that was gay a little while ago, it looks to me as if you'd grown mighty solemn-like," said Mr. McKenna.

"Mebbe so," said Mr. Dooley. "Mebbe so. What th' 'ell, anny-how. Mebbe 'tis as bad to take champagne out iv wan man's mouth as round steak out iv another's. Lent is near over. I seen Doherty out shinin' up his pipe that's been behind th' clock since Ash Winsdah. Th' girls 'll be layin' lilies on th' altar in a day or two. The springs come on. Th' grass is growin' good; an', if th' Connock man's children back iv th' dumps can't get meat, they can eat hay."

Thinking
by ANATOLE FRANCE

'Tis a great infirmity to think. God preserve you from it, my son, as He has preserved His greatest saints, and the souls whom He loves with especial tenderness and destines to eternal felicity.

What the Moon Saw
by VACHEL LINDSAY

Two statesmen met by moonlight.
   Their ease was partly feigned.
They glanced about the prairie,
   Their faces were constrained.
In various ways aforetime
   They had misled the state,
Yet did it so politely
   Their henchmen thought them great.
They sat beneath a hedge and spake
   No word, but had a smoke.
A satchel passed from hand to hand.
   Next day the deadlock broke.

The Furred Law-Cats
(*From "Pantagruel"*)
by FRANÇOIS RABELAIS
French satirist of the late Middle Ages, 1483-1553

The Furred Law-Cats are most terrible and dreadful monsters; they devour little children, and trample over marble stones. Pray tell me, noble topers, do they not deserve to have their snouts slit? The hair of their hides doesn't lie outward, but inwards, and every mother's son of them for his device wears a gaping pouch, but not all in the same manner; for some wear it tied to their neck scarf-wise, others upon the breech, some on the side, and all for a cause, with reason and mystery. They have claws so very strong, long, and sharp that nothing can get from 'em what is once fast between their clutches. Sometimes they cover their heads with mortar-like caps, at other times with mortified caparisons.

Examine well the countenance of these stout props and pillars of this catch-coin law and iniquity; and pray observe, that if you live but six olympiads, and the age of two dogs more, you'll see these Furred Law-Cats lords of all Europe, and in peaceful possession of all the estates and domains belonging to it; unless, by divine providence, what's got over the devil's back is spent under his belly, or the goods which they unjustly get perish with their prodigal heirs. Take this from an honest beggar!

Among 'em reigns the sixth essence; by the means of which they gripe all, devour all, conskite all, burn all, draw all, hang all, quarter all, behead all, murder all, imprison all, waste all, and ruin all, without the least notice of right and wrong; for among them vice is called virtue; wickedness, piety; treason, loyalty; robbery, justice. Plunder is their motto, and when acted by them is approved by all men, except the heretics; and all this they do because they dare; their authority is sovereign and irrefragable. Should all their villainy be once displayed in its true colours and exposed to the people, there never was, is, nor will be any spokesman could save 'em; nor any magistrate so powerful as to hinder their being burnt alive in their coney-burrows without mercy. Even their own furred kittlings, friends and relations would abominate 'em.

The Gentleman Inside
by DAMON RUNYON
American short-story writer and journalist, 1884-1946

They's a banker that's a trusty workin' on the warden's books;
   I kin see him from the rock pile where I'm sittin',
An' on his case I'm basin' this advice to feller crooks:
   You'd better git a plenty while yer gittin'.
Now, this guy wrecked a county an' he copped his neighbor's dough;
He got six hundred thousand, which is some change, as you know;
They give him one or two years, an' the softest job here—Oh
   It pays to git a plenty while yer gittin'.

Wit' me little flask o' nitro an' me bar o' laundry soap,
   I blew a safe, an' then, as was befittin',
I took me ten years smilin', glad I didn't get the rope!—
   But the next time! Oh, a plenty while I'm gittin'!
For this guy tore off half a state an' shook the other half;
He robbed his friends an' neighbors an' he handed both the laugh—
But you oughta heard him holler at that one or two year gaff.
   You'd better git a plenty while yer gittin'!

An' so he's here a trusty, while I wear a ball an' chain—
  (They say he beat most every statoot written.)
He's got a fortune planted an' all I've got's a pain;
  You'd better git a plenty while yer gittin'!
He cost the state a million bucks before they put him here;
He had ten lawyers for his trial, w'ich lasted most a year;
An' the jedge who had to sentence him pronounced it wit' a
    tear—
  It pays to git a plenty while yer gittin'!

Penguin Island

by ANATOLE FRANCE

In the following passage one of the most learned of the penguins pays a visit to
America

After a voyage of fifteen days his steamer entered, during the night, the harbor of Titanport, where thousands of ships were anchored. An iron bridge thrown across the water and shining with lights, stretched between two piers so far apart that Professor Obnubile imagined he was sailing on the seas of Saturn, and that he saw the marvellous ring which girds the planet of the Old Man. And this immense conduit bore upon it more than a quarter of the wealth of the world. The learned Penguin, having disembarked, was waited on by automatons in a hotel forty-eight stories high. Then he took the great railway that led to Gigantopolis, the capital of New Atlantic. In the train there were restaurants, gaming-rooms, athletic arenas, telegraphic, commercial, and financial offices, a Protestant Church, and the printing-office of a great newspaper, which latter the doctor was unable to read, as he did not know the language of the New Atlantans. The train passed along the banks of great rivers, through manufacturing cities which concealed the sky with the smoke from their chimneys, towns black in the day, towns red at night, full of noise by day and full of noise also by night.

"Here," thought the doctor, "is a people far too much engaged in industry and trade to make war. I am already certain that the New Atlantans pursue a policy of peace. For it is an axiom admitted by all economists that peace without and peace within are necessary for the progress of commerce and industry."

As he surveyed Gigantopolis, he was confirmed in this opinion.

People went through the streets so swiftly propelled by hurry that they knocked down all who were in their way. Obnubile was thrown down several times, but soon succeeded in learning how to demean himself better; after an hour's walking he himself knocked down an Atlantan.

Having reached a great square he saw the portico of a palace in the classic style, whose Corinthian columns reared their capitals of arborescent acanthus seventy metres above the stylobate.

As he stood with his head thrown back admiring the building, a man of modest appearance approached him and said in Penguin:

"I see by your dress that you are from Penguinia. I know your language; I am a sworn interpreter. This is the Parliament palace. At the present moment the representatives of the States are in deliberation. Would you like to be present at the sitting?"

The doctor was brought into the hall and cast his looks upon the crowd of legislators who were sitting on cane chairs with their feet upon their desks.

The president arose, and, in the midst of general inattention, muttered rather than spoke the following formulas which the interpreter immediately translated to the doctor.

"The war for the opening of the Mongol markets being ended to the satisfaction of the States, I propose that the accounts be laid before the finance committee...."

"Is there any opposition?..."

"The proposal is carried."

"The war for the opening of the markets of Third-Zealand being ended to the satisfaction of the States, I propose that the accounts be laid before the finance committee...."

"Is there any opposition?..."

"The proposal is carried."

"Have I heard aright?" asked Professor Obnubile. "What? you an industrial people and engaged in all these wars!"

"Certainly," answered the interpreter, "these are industrial wars. Peoples who have neither commerce nor industry are not obliged to make war, but a business people is forced to adopt a policy of conquest. The number of wars necessarily increases with our productive capacity. As soon as one of our industries fails to find a market for its products a war is necessary to open new outlets. It is in this way we have had a coal war, a copper war, and a cotton war. In Third-Zealand we have killed two-thirds of the inhabitants in order to compel the remainder to buy our umbrellas and braces."

At that moment a fat man who was sitting in the middle of the assembly ascended the tribune.

"I claim," said he, "a war against the Emerald Republic, which insolently contends with our pigs for the hegemony of hams and sauces in all the markets of the universe."

"Who is that legislator?" asked Doctor Obnubile.

"He is a pig merchant."

"Is there any opposition?" said the President. "I put the proposition to the vote."

The war against the Emerald Republic was voted with uplifted hands by a very large majority.

"What?" said Obnubile to the interpreter; "you have voted a war with that rapidity and that indifference!"

"Oh! it is an unimportant war which will hardly cost eight million dollars."

"And men...."

"The men are included in the eight million dollars."

Then Doctor Obnubile bent his head in bitter reflection.

"Since wealth and civilization admit of as many causes of poverty as war and barbarism, since the folly and wickedness of men are incurable, there remains but one good action to be done. The wise man will collect enough dynamite to blow up this planet. When its fragments fly through space an imperceptible amelioration will be accomplished in the universe and a satisfaction will be given to the universal conscience. Moreover, this universal conscience does not exist."

Why the Socialist Party Is Growing
(Dedicated to the School of Journalism)
by FRANKLIN P. ADAMS

"A story," the reporter said, "about commercial crime.
A merchant's been convicted of selling phony stuff.
The sentence is a thousand meg and seven years of time—"
"A hundred words," the city Ed. replied, "will be enough."

"A story," the reporter said, "about a crimson dame
Just landed from the steamer, wearing slippers that are red.
She used to be the Dearest Friend of Emperor Wotsisname—"
"Three columns and a layout!" cried the eager city Ed.

The Preacher and the Slave
by Joe Hill

A sample of many parodies upon Christian hymns which were published by the
Industrial Workers of the Worlld and sung by migratory workers of the Far West
in their hobo jungles.

Long-haired preachers come out every night,
Try to tell you what's wrong and what's right;
But when asked how 'bout something to eat
They will answer with voices so sweet:

CHORUS

You will eat, bye and bye,
  In that glorious land above the sky;
Work and pray, live on hay,
  You'll get pie in the sky when you die.

And the Starvation Army they play,
And they sing and they clap and they pray,
Till they get all your coin on the drum,
Then they'll tell you when you're on the bum: (Chorus)

If you fight hard for children and wife—
Try to get something good in this life—
You're a sinner and bad man, they tell,
When you die you will sure go to hell. (Chorus)

Workingmen of all countries, unite,
Side by side we for freedom will fight;
When the world and its wealth we shall gain
To the grafters we'll sing this refrain:

CHORUS

You will eat, bye and bye,
  When you've learned how to cook and to fry;
Chop some wood, 'twill do you good,
  And you'll eat in the sweet bye and bye.

Lines to a Pomeranian Puppy Valued at $3,500
by Louis Untermeyer

Often as I strain and stew,
  Digging in these dirty ditches,
I have dared to think of you—
  You and all your riches.

Lackeys help you on and off;
  And the bed is silk you lie in;
You have doctors when you cough,
  Priests when you are dying.

Wrapt in soft and costly furs,
  All sewed up with careful stitches,
You consort with proper curs
  And with perfumed bitches....

You don't sweat to struggle free,
  Work in rags and rotting breeches—
Puppy, have a laugh at me
  Digging in the ditches!

"Mr. Dooley" on Prosperity
by Finley Peter Dunne

"Yes, Prosperity has come hollerin' an' screamin'. To read th' papers, it seems to be a kind iv a vagrancy law. No wan can loaf anny more. Th' end iv vacation has gone f'r manny a happy lad that has spint six months ridin' through th' counthry, dodgin' wurruk, or loafin' under his own vine or hat-three. Prosperity grabs ivry man be th' neck, an' sets him shovellin' slag or coke or runnin' up an' down a ladder with a hod iv mortar. It won't let th' wurruld rest....It goes around like a polisman givin' th' hot fut to happy people that are snoozin' in th' sun. 'Get up,' says Prosperity. 'Get up, an' hustle over to th' rollin' mills: there's a man over there wants ye to carry a ton iv coal on ye'er back.' 'But I don't want to wurruk,' says th' lad. 'I'm very comfortable th' way I am.' 'It makes no difference,' says Prosperity. 'Ye've got to do ye'er lick. Wurruk, f'r th' night is comin'. Get out, an' hustle. Wurruk, or ye can't be unhappy; an', if th' wurruld isn't unhappy, they'se no such a thing as Prosperity.'"

The Babble Machines

(From "When the Sleeper Wakes")

by H. G. WELLS

A science-fiction forecast of journalism under capitalism triumphant

Beyond this place they came into a closed hall, and Graham discovered the cause of the noise that had perplexed him. His attention was arrested by a violent, loud hoot, followed by a vast leathery voice. He stooped and, looking up, beheld a foolish trumpet face. This was the General Intelligence Machine. For a space it seemed to be gathering breath, and a regular throbbing from its cylindrical body was audible. Then it trumpeted "Galloop, Galloop," and broke out again.

"Paris is now pacified. All resistance is over. Galloop! The black police hold every position of importance in the city. They fought with great bravery, singing songs written in praise of their ancestors by the poet Kipling. Once or twice they got out of hand, and tortured and mutilated wounded and captured insurgents, men and women. Moral—don't go rebelling. Haha! Galloop, Galloop! They are lively fellows. Lively brave fellows. Let this be a lesson to the disorderly banderlog of this city. Yah! Banderlog! Filth of the earth! Galloop, Galloop!"

The voice ceased. There was a confused murmur of disapproval among the crowd. "Damned niggers." A man began to harangue near them. "Is this the Master's doing, brothers? Is this the Master's doing?"

"Black police!" said Graham. "What is that? You don't mean——"

His companion touched his arm and gave him a warning look, and forthwith another of these mechanisms screamed deafeningly and gave tongue in a shrill voice. "Yahaha! Yahah, Yap! Hear a live paper yelp! Live paper. Yaha! Shocking outrage in Paris. Yahahah! The Parisians exasperated by the black police to the pitch of assassination. Dreadful reprisals. Savage times come again. Blood! Blood! Yahah!" The nearer Babble Machine hooted stupendously, "Galloop, Galloop," drowned the end of the sentence, and proceeded in a rather flatter note than before with novel comments on the horrors of disorder. "Law and order must be maintained," said the nearer Babble Machine....

Militancy
by Israel Zangwill

Heckling became a fine art, and even a joyous: for, despite all the suffering it cost them, they carried it through with such inexhaustible spirit and invention as to restore a touch of chic and bravado to our drab life and add to the gaiety of nations. Miss Pankhurst even managed to badger Cabinet Ministers in the witness-box.... There was no meeting, however guarded, to which, by hook or crook, organ-pipe or drain-pipe, she did not gain admission, padlocking herself against easy expulsion; while, even were her bodily presence averted, always, like the horns of Elfland faintly blowing, came from some well-placed megaphone that inevitable and implacable slogan "Votes for Women." Chalked on pavement or scrawled on walls or blazoned on sky-signs, it became a universal, ubiquitous obsession. Streamers carried it under the terrace of Parliament or balloons suspended it from above. Cabinet Ministers were dogged to their privatest haunts, for the leakages of information were everywhere. Since Christianity no such force has arisen to divide families. No household, however Philistine, was safe from a jail-bird. If Lady Anon asked Lady Alamode when her daughter was coming out, it no longer referred to the young lady's début. The most obstinate autocrat since Pharaoh, Mr. Asquith, has been shown similar signs and wonders. "We are the appointed plagues," said Mrs. Pankhurst, with a rare touch of humor. And nothing has plagued British society more than that outbreak of religion which brought disgrace upon so many respectable homes. Incidentally, the prisons and the courts were improved by receiving critics instead of criminals. "We do not care for ourselves," cried Christabel Pankhurst at the London Police Court, "because prison is nothing to us. But the injustice done here to thousands of helpless creatures is too terrible to contemplate." Warders and wardresses, too, profited by the society of their new prisoners. It was like a rise in the social scale to them. Nor was even the Bench immune from education.

"Boyle!" called the magistrate. "*Miss* Boyle," corrected the prisoner. "We always call our prisoners by their surnames," explained the magistrate. "We are here to teach you better manners," said the Suffragette.

"Mr. Dooley" on Woman Suffrage
by FINLEY PETER DUNNE

Don't ask f'r rights. Take thim. An' don't let anny wan give thim to ye. A right that is handed to ye f'r nawthin' has somethin' the matther with it. It's more than likely it's on'y a wrong turned inside out.

What's In A Name?

(From a cartoon strip that appeared in 1964)
BY JULES FEIFFER
American cartoonist and social commentator, born 1929

I used to think I was poor. Then they told me I wasn't poor, I was needy. Then they told me it was self-defeating to think of myself as needy, I was deprived. Then they told me deprived was a bad image, I was underprivileged. Then they told me underprivileged was overused, I was disadvantaged. I still don't have a dime. But I sure have a great vocabulary.

BY ART BUCHWALD
American political humorist, born 1925

If you attack the establishment long enough and hard enough, they will make you a member of it.

Voting

(From "Jumpers")
BY TOM STOPPARD
British playwright, born 1937

It's not the voting that's democracy, it's the counting.

BOOK XIV

The Poet

Social injustice as it bears upon literature and the producers of literature; pictures of the life of the outcast poet, and of art in conflict with mammon.

Democratic Vistas
by WALT WHITMAN

Literature, strictly considered, has never recognized the people, and, whatever may be said, does not today. Speaking generally, the tendencies of literature, as hitherto pursued, have been to make mostly critical and querulous men. It seems as if, so far, there were some natural repugnance between a literary and professional life, and the rude rank spirit of the democracies. There is, in later literature, a treatment of benevolence, a charity business, rife enough it is true; but I know nothing more rare, even in this country, than a fit scientific estimate and reverent appreciation of the People—of their measureless wealth of latent worth and capacity, their vast, artistic contrasts of lights and shades—with, in America, their entire reliability in emergencies, and a certain breadth of historic grandeur, of peace or war, far surpassing all the vaunted samples of book-heroes, or any *haut ton* coteries, in all the records of the world. . . .

Dominion strong is the body's; dominion stronger is the mind's. What has filled, and fills today our intellect, our fancy, furnishing the standards therein, is yet foreign. The great poems, Shakespeare's included, are poisonous to the idea of the pride and dignity of the common people, the life-blood of democracy. The models of our literature, as we get it from other lands, ultramarine, have had their birth in courts, and basked and grown in castle sunshine; all smells of princes' favors. Of workers of a certain sort, we have, indeed, plenty, contributing after their kind; many elegant, many learned, all complacent. But touched by the national test, or tried by the standards of democratic personality, they wither to ashes. I say I have not seen a single writer, artist, lecturer, or what not, that has confronted the voiceless but ever erect and active, pervading, underlying will and typic inspiration of the land, in a spirit kindred to itself. Do you call these genteel little creatures American poets? Do you term that perpetual, pistareen, pastepot work, American art, American drama, taste, verse? I think I hear, echoed as from some mountain-top afar in the west, the scornful laugh of the Genius of these States. . . .

Did you, too, O friend, suppose democracy was only for elections, for politics, and for a party name? I say democracy is only of use there that it may pass on and come to its flower and fruit in manners, in the highest forms of interaction between men, and their beliefs—in religion, literature, colleges, and schools—democracy in all public and private life, and in the army and navy.

Fires

by WILFRID WILSON GIBSON
English poet of the lives of the poor, 1878–1962

Snug in my easy chair,
    I stirred the fire to flame.
Fantastically fair
    The flickering fancies came,
Born of heart's desire:
    Amber woodlands streaming;
    Topaz islands dreaming,
    Sunset-cities gleaming,
Spire on burning spire;
    Ruddy-windowed taverns;
Sunshine-spilling wines;
    Crystal-lighted caverns
Of Golconda's mines;
    Summers, unreturning;
    Passion's crater yearning;
    Troy, the ever-burning;
Shelley's lustral pyre;
    Dragon-eyes, unsleeping;
    Witches' cauldrons leaping;
    Golden galleys sweeping
Out from sea-walled Tyre:
    Fancies, fugitive and fair,
    Flashed with winging through the air;
    Till, dazzled by the drowsy glare,
I shut my eyes to heat and light;
And saw, in sudden night,
Crouched in the dripping dark,
With streaming shoulders stark,
The man who hews the coal to feed my fire.

What Is Art?

by Leo Tolstoy

Art of the future, that is to say, such part of art as will be chosen from among all the art diffused among mankind, will consist, not in transmitting feelings accessible only to members of the rich classes, as is the case today, but in transmitting such feelings as embody the highest religious perceptions of our times. Only those productions will be considered art which transmit feelings drawing men together in brotherly union, or such universal feelings as can unite all men. Art transmitting feelings flowing from antiquated, worn-out religious teachings—church art, patriotic art, voluptuous art, transmitting feelings of superstitious fear, of pride, of vanity, of ecstatic admiration for national heroes—art exciting exclusive love of one's own people, or sensuality, will be considered bad, harmful art, and will be censured and despised by public opinion. All the rest of art, transmitting feelings accessible only to a section of the people, will be considered unimportant, and will be neither blamed nor praised. And the appraisement of art in general will devolve, not, as is now the case, on a separate class of rich people, but on the whole people; so that for a work to be esteemed good, and to be approved of and diffused, it will have to satisfy the demands, not of a few people living in identical and often unnatural conditions, but it will have to satisfy the demands of all those great masses of people who are situated in the natural conditions of laborious life. And the artists producing art will not be, as now, merely a few people selected from a small section of the nation, members of the upper classes or their hangers-on, but will consist of all those gifted members of the whole people who prove capable of, and are inclined towards, artistic activity.

By Heinrich Heine

I know not if I deserve that a laurel-wreath should one day be laid on my coffin. Poetry, dearly as I have loved it, has always been to me but a divine plaything. I have never attached any great value to poetical fame; and I trouble myself very little whether people praise my verses or blame them. But lay on my coffin a *sword;* for I was a brave soldier in the Liberation War of humanity.

A Catechism for Workers
by August Strindberg
Swedish dramatist, 1849-1912

What is philosophy?
A seeking of the truth.
Then how can philosophy be the friend of the upper classes?
The upper classes pay the philosopher, in order that he may discover only such truths as are expedient in their eyes.
But suppose uncomfortable truths should be discovered?
They are called lies, and the philosopher gets no pay.
What is history?
The story of the past, presented in a light favorable to the interests of the upper classes.
Suppose the light is unfavorable?
That is scandalous.
What is a scandal?
Anything offending the upper classes.
What is esthetics?
The art of praising or belittling works of art.
What works of art must be praised?
Those that glorify the upper classes.
Therefore Raphael and Michaelangelo are the most famous artists, for they glorified the religious falsehoods of the upper classes. Shakespeare magnified kings, and Goethe magnified himself, the writer for the upper classes.
But how about other works of art?
There must not be others.

The Last Word
by Matthew Arnold

They out-talk'd thee, hiss'd thee, tore thee.
Better men fared thus before thee;
Fired their ringing shot and pass'd,
Hotly charged—and broke at last.

Charge once more, then, and be dumb!
Let the victors, when they come,
When the forts of folly fall,
Find thy body by the wall.

The Superior Classes
by GEORGE D. HERRON
American clergyman and socialist, 1862-1925

It is customary to speak of the unpreparedness of the proletary for Socialism. But I am sure that, even today, the working-class would give a vastly better organization of industrial forces, a profoundly nobler and freer society, than ever the world has had. The ignorance of the working-class and the superior intelligence of the privileged class are superstitions—are superstitions fostered by intellectual mercenaries, by universities and churches, and by all the centers of privilege. And the assumption of superior intelligence on the part of the privileged is not warranted by a single historical experience. The derangements and miseries of mankind are precisely due to the ignorant and arrogant rule of "superior" classes and persons. The mental and spiritual capacity of these classes is a myth; their so-called culture but thinly veneers their essential savagery, their social rapacity and impudence. . . .

The system that divides society into classes can bring forth no true knowledge, no living truth, no industrial competence, no fundamental social decency. It can only continue the desolation of labor and increase the blindness and depravity of the privileged. So long as some people own the tools upon which others depend for bread, so long as the few possess themselves of the fruits of the labor of the many, so long as the arts and the institutions and the sciences are built upon exploited workers, just so long will our so-called progress be through the perennial exhaustion of generations and races; just so long will successive civilizations be but voracious parasites upon the spirit and body of mankind.

What Life Means to Me
(From "Revolution")
by JACK LONDON

I was born into the working class. I early discovered enthusiasm, ambition, and ideas; and to satisfy these became the problem of my childlife. My environment was crude and rough and raw. I had no outlook, but an uplook rather. My place in society was at the bottom. Here life offered nothing but sordidness and wretchedness, both of the flesh and the spirit; for here flesh and spirit were alike starved and tormented.

Above me towered the colossal edifice of society, and to my mind the only way out was up. Into this edifice I early resolved to climb. Up above, men wore black clothes and boiled shirts, and women dressed in beautiful gowns. Also, there were good things to eat, and there was plenty to eat. This much for the flesh. Then there were the things of the spirit. Up above me, I knew, were unselfishness of the spirit, clean and noble thinking, keen intellectual living. I knew all this because I read "Seaside Library" novels, in which, with the exception of the villains and adventuresses, all men and women thought beautiful thoughts, spoke a beautiful tongue, and performed glorious deeds. In short, as I accepted the rising of the sun, I accepted that up above me was all that was fine and noble and gracious, all that gave decency and dignity to life, all that made life worth living and that remunerated one for his travail and misery.

But it is not particularly easy for one to climb up out of the working class—especially if he is handicapped by the possession of ideals and illusions. I lived on a ranch in California, and I was hard put to find the ladder whereby to climb. I early inquired the rate of interest on invested money, and worried my child's brain into an understanding of the virtues and excellences of that remarkable invention of man, compound interest. Further, I ascertained the current rates of wages for workers of all ages, and the cost of living. From all these data I concluded that if I began immediately and worked and saved until I was fifty years of age, I could then stop working and enter into participation in a fair portion of the delights and goodnesses that would then be open to me higher up in society. Of course, I resolutely determined not to marry, while I quite forgot to consider at all that great rock of disaster in the working class world—sickness.

But the life that was in me demanded more than a meager existence of scraping and scrimping. Also, at ten years of age, I became a newsboy on the streets of a city, and found myself with a changed uplook. All about me were still the same sordidness and wretchedness, and up above me was still the same paradise waiting to be gained; but the ladder whereby to climb was a different one. It was now the ladder of business. Why save my earnings and invest in government bonds, when by buying two newspapers for five cents, with a turn of the wrist I could sell them for ten cents and double my capital? The business ladder was the ladder for me, and I had a vision of myself becoming a baldheaded and successful merchant prince. . . .

[The author became the owner of an oyster-boat, and thereby a capitalist; but was ruined by the burning of his boat.]

From then on I was mercilessly exploited by other capitalists. I had the muscle, and they made money out of it while I made but a very indifferent living out of it. I was a sailor before the mast, a longshoreman, a roustabout; I worked in canneries, and factories, and laundries; I mowed lawns, and cleaned carpets, and washed windows. And I never got the full product of my toil. I looked at the daughter of the cannery owner, in her carriage, and knew that it was my muscle, in part, that helped drag along that carriage on its rubber tires. I looked at the son of the factory owner, going to college, and knew that it was my muscle that helped, in part, to pay for the wine and good-fellowship he enjoyed.

But I did not resent this. It was all in the game. They were the strong. Very well, I was strong. I would carve my way to a place among them, and make money out of the muscles of other men. I was not afraid of work. I loved hard work. I would pitch in and work harder than ever and eventually become a pillar of society.

And just then, as luck would have it, I found an employer that was of the same mind. I was willing to work, and he was more than willing that I should work. I thought I was learning a trade. In reality, I had displaced two men. I thought he was making an electrician out of me; as a matter of fact, he was making fifty dollars per month out of me. The two men I had displaced had received forty dollars each per month; I was doing the work of both for thirty dollars per month.

This employer worked me nearly to death. A man may love oysters, but too many oysters will disincline him toward that particular diet. And so with me. Too much work sickened me. I did not wish ever to see work again. I fled from work. I became a tramp, begging my way from door to door, wandering over the United States, and sweating bloody sweats in slums and prisons.

I had been born in the working class, and I was now, at the age of eighteen, beneath the point at which I had started. I was down in the cellar of society, down in the subterranean depths of misery about which it is neither nice nor proper to speak. I was in the pit, the abyss, the human cesspool, the shambles and the

charnel house of our civilization. This is the part of the edifice
of society that society chooses to ignore. Lack of space compels
me here to ignore it, and I shall say only that the things I there
saw gave me a terrible scare. . . .

[The author reflected, and decided that it was better to sell
brains than muscle.] Then began a frantic pursuit of knowledge.
I returned to California and opened the books. While thus
equipping myself to become a brain merchant, it was inevitable
that I should delve into sociology. There I found, in a certain
class of books, scientifically formulated, the simple sociological
concepts I had already worked out for myself. Other and greater
minds, before I was born, had worked out all that I had thought,
and a vast deal more. I discovered that I was a Socialist.

The Socialists were revolutionists, inasmuch as they struggled
to overthrow the society of the present, and out of the material
to build the society of the future. I, too, was a Socialist, and a
revolutionist. I joined the groups of working-class and intellectual revolutionists, and for the first time came into intelligent
living. Here I found keen-flashing intellects and brilliant wits;
for here I met strong and alert-brained, withal horny-handed,
members of the working class; unfrocked preachers too wide in
their Christianity for any congregation of Mammon-worshippers;
professors broken on the wheel of university subservience to the
ruling class and flung out because they were quick with knowledge which they strove to apply to the affairs of mankind.

Here I found, also, warm faith in the human, glowing idealism, sweetness of unselfishness, renunciation and martyrdom—all
the splendid, stinging things of the spirit. Here life was clean,
noble, and alive. Here life rehabilitated itself, became wonderful and glorious; and I was glad to be alive. I was in touch with
great souls who exalted flesh and spirit over dollars and cents;
and to whom the thin wail of the starved slum-child meant more
than all the pomp and circumstance of commercial expansion
and world-empire. All about me were nobleness of purpose and
heroism of effort, and my days and nights were sunshine and
starshine, all fire and dew, with before my eyes, ever burning
and blazing, the Holy Grail, Christ's own Grail, the warm human, long suffering and maltreated, but to be rescued and saved
at the last. . . .

As a brain merchant I was a success. Society opened its portals to me. I entered right in on the parlor floor, and my disillusionment proceeded rapidly. I sat down to dinner with the masters of society, and with the wives and daughters of the masters of society. The women were gowned beautifully, I admit; but to my naive surprise I discovered that they were of the same clay as all the rest of the women I had known down below in the cellar. "The colonel's lady and Judy O'Grady were sisters under their skins"—and gowns.

It was not this, however, so much as their materialism, that shocked me. It is true these beautifully gowned, beautiful women prattled sweet little ideals and dear little moralities; but in spite of their prattle the dominant key of the life they lived was materialistic. And they were so sentimentally selfish! They assisted in all kinds of sweet little charities, and informed one of the fact, while all the time the food they ate and the beautiful clothes they wore were bought out of dividends stained with the blood of child labor, and sweated labor, and of prostitution itself. When I mentioned such facts, expecting in my innocence that these sisters of Judy O'Grady would at once strip off their blood-dyed silks and jewels, they became excited and angry, and read me preachments about the lack of thrift, the drink, and the innate depravity that caused all the misery in society's cellar. When I mentioned that I couldn't quite see that it was the lack of thrift, the intemperance, and the depravity of a half-starved child of six that made it work twelve hours every night in a Southern cotton mill, these sisters of Judy O'Grady attacked my private life and called me an "agitator"—as though that, forsooth, settled the argument.

Nor did I fare better with the masters themselves. I had expected to find men who were clean, noble and alive, whose ideals were clean, noble and alive. I went out amongst the men who sat in the high places, the preachers, the politicians, the business men, the professors, and the editors. I ate meat with them, drank wine with them, automobiled with them, and studied them. It is true, I found many that were clean and noble; but, with rare exceptions, they were not alive. I do verily believe I could count the exceptions on the fingers of my two hands. Where they were not alive with rottenness, quick with unclean life, they were merely the unburied dead—clean and noble, like well-preserved mummies, but not alive. In this connection I may especially mention the professors I met, the men who live up to that decadent university ideal, "the passionless pursuit of passionless intelligence."

I met men who invoked the name of the Prince of Peace in their diatribes against war, and who put rifles in the hands of Pinkertons with which to shoot down strikers in their own factories. I met men incoherent with indignation at the brutality of prize-fighting, and who, at the same time, were parties to the adulteration of food that killed each year more babies than even red-handed Herod had killed. . . .

I discovered that I did not like to live on the parlor floor of society. Intellectually I was bored. Morally and spiritually I was sickened. I remembered my intellectuals and idealists, my unfrocked preachers, broken professors, and clean-minded, class-conscious workingmen. I remembered my days and nights of sunshine and starshine, where life was all a wild wonder, a spiritual paradise of unselfish adventure and ethical romance. And I saw before me, ever blazing and burning, the Holy Grail.

So I went back to the working-class, in which I had been born and where I belonged. I care no longer to climb. This imposing edifice of society above my head holds no delight for me. It is the foundation of the edifice that interests me. There I am content to labor, crowbar in hand, shoulder to shoulder with intellectuals, idealists, and class-conscious workingmen, getting a solid pry now and again and setting the whole edifice rocking. Some day, when we get a few more hands and crowbars to work, we'll topple it over, along with all its rotten life and unburied dead, its monstrous selfishness and sodden materialism. Then we'll cleanse the cellar and build a new habitation for mankind, in which there will be no parlor floor, in which all the rooms will be bright and airy, and where the air that is breathed will be clean, noble and alive.

Chants Communal
by HORACE TRAUBEL
American poet and editor, 1858-1919

What can I do? I can talk out when others are silent. I can say man when others say money. I can stay up when others are asleep. I can keep on working when others have stopped to play. I can give life big meanings when others give life little meanings. I can say love when others say hate. I can say every man when others say one man. I can try events by a hard test when others try it by an easy test.

What can I do? I can give myself to life when other men refuse themselves to life.

No Enemies
by Charles Mackay

You have no enemies, you say?
  Alas! my friend, the boast is poor;
He who has mingled in the fray
  Of duty, that the brave endure,
Must have made foes! If you have none,
Small is the work that you have done.
You've hit no traitor on the hip,
You've dashed no cup from perjured lip,
You've never turned the wrong to right,
You've been a coward in the fight.

An Appeal to the Young
by Peter Kropotkin

If your heart really beats in unison with that of humanity, if like a true poet you have an ear for Life, then, gazing out upon this sea of sorrow whose tide sweeps up around you, face to face with these people dying of hunger, in the presence of these corpses piled up in the mines, and these mutilated bodies lying in heaps on the barricades, looking on these long lines of exiles who are going to bury themselves in the snows of Siberia and in the marshes of tropical islands; in full view of this desperate battle which is being fought, amid the cries of pain from the conquered and the orgies of the victors, of heroism in conflict with cowardice, of noble determination face to face with contemptible cunning—you cannot remain neutral; you will come and take the side of the oppressed because you know that the beautiful, the sublime, the spirit of life itself is on the side of those who fight for light, for humanity, for justice!...

It rests with you either to palter continually with your conscience, and in the end to say, one fine day: "Perish humanity, provided I can have plenty of pleasures and enjoy them to the full, so long as the people are foolish enough to let me." Or, once more the inevitable alternative, to take part with the Socialists and work with them for the complete transformation of society. That is the logical conclusion which every intelligent man must perforce arrive at, provided that he reasons honestly about what passes around him, and discards the sophisms which his bourgeois education and the interested views of those about him whisper in his ear.

The Prophetic Book "Milton"
by WILLIAM BLAKE

And did those feet in ancient time
    Walk upon England's mountain green?
And was the holy Lamb of God
    On England's pleasant pastures seen?

And did the countenance divine
    Shine forth upon our clouded hills?
And was Jerusalem builded here
    Among these dark Satanic mills?

Bring me my bow of burning gold!
    Bring me my arrows of desire!
Bring me my spear: O clouds, unfold!
    Bring me my chariot of fire!

I will not cease from mental fight,
    Nor shall my sword sleep in my hand,
Till we have built Jerusalem
    In England's green and pleasant land.

The Revolution
by RICHARD WAGNER

Unhappy man! uplift thine eyes, look up to where a thousand thousand gather on the hills in joyous expectation of the dawn! Regard them, they are all thy brothers, sisters, the troops of those poor wights who hitherto knew naught of life but suffering, have been but strangers on this earth of Joy; they all are waiting for that Revolution which affrights thee, their redeemer from this world of sorrow, creator of a new world that blesses all! See there, there stream the legions from the factories; they have made and fashioned lordly stuffs,—themselves and children, they are naked, frozen, hungry; for not to them belongs the fruit of all their labor, but to the rich and mighty one who calls men and the earth his own! So, there they troop, from fields and farmyards; they have tilled the earth and turned it to a smiling garden, and fruits in plenty, enough for all who live, have paid their pains,—yet poor are they, and naked, starving; for not to them, nor to others who are needy, belongs earth's blessing, but solely to the rich and mighty one who calls men and the earth his own. They all, the hundred-thousands, millions, are camped upon the hills and gaze into the distance, where thickening clouds proclaim the advent of emancipating Revolution; they all, to whom nothing is left to grieve for, from whom men rob the sons to train them into sturdy gaolers of their fathers; whose daughters walk the city's streets with burden of their shame, an offering to the baser lusts of rich and mighty; they all, with the sallow, careworn faces, the limbs devoured by frost and hunger, they all who have never known joy, encamp there on the heights and strain their eyes in blissful expectation of its coming, and listen in rapt silence to the rustle of the rising storm, which fills their ears with Revolution's greeting.

The Lost Leader
by ROBERT BROWNING
English poet, 1812-1889. This poem has been generally thought to refer to Wordsworth who started life as a revolutionary liberal but ended it as conservative Poet Laureate of an equally conservative government.

> Just for a handful of silver he left us,
>   Just for a riband to stick in his coat—
> Found the one gift of which fortune bereft us,
>   Lost all the others she lets us devote;
> They, with the gold to give, doled him out silver,
>   So much was theirs who so little allowed:
> How all our copper had gone for his service!
>   Rags—were they purple, his heart had been proud!

We that had loved him so, followed him, honored him,
　　Lived in his mild and magnificent eye,
Learned his great language, caught his clear accents,
　　Made him our pattern to live and to die!
Shakespeare was of us, Milton was for us,
　　Burns, Shelley, were with us,—they watch from their graves!
He alone breaks from the van and the freemen,
　　He alone sinks to the rear and the slaves!

We shall march prospering,—not thro' his presence;
　　Songs may inspirit us,—not from his lyre;
Deeds will be done,—while he boasts his quiescence,
　　Still bidding crouch whom the rest bade aspire:
Blot out his name, then, record one lost soul more,
　　One task more declined, one more footpath untrod,
One more devil's-triumph and sorrow for angels,
　　One wrong more to man, one more insult to God!

Journalism

by JOHN SWINTON

American journalist, 1829-1901. One of America's oldest and most beloved
journalists was tendered a banquet by his fellow editors, and surprised his
hosts by the following words.

There is no such thing in America as an independent press,
unless it is in the country towns.

You know it and I know it. There is not one of you who dares
to write his honest opinions, and if you did you know beforehand
that it would never appear in print.

I am paid $150.00 a week for keeping my honest opinions out
of the paper I am connected with—others of you are paid similar
salaries for similar things—and any of you who would be so foolish
as to write his honest opinions would be out on the streets looking
for another job.

The business of the New York journalist is to destroy the truth,
to lie outright, to pervert, to vilify, to fawn at the feet of Mammon,
and to sell his race and his country for his daily bread.

You know this and I know it, and what folly is this to be toasting
an "Independent Press."

We are the tools and vassals of rich men behind the scenes. We
are the jumping-jacks; they pull the strings and we dance. Our
talents, our possibilities and our lives are all the property of other
men. We are intellectual prostitutes.

The Rebel

by HILAIRE BELLOC
English writer, 1870-1953

There is a wall of which the stones
Are lies and bribes and dead men's bones.
And wrongfully this evil wall
Denies what all men made for all,
And shamelessly this wall surrounds
Our homestead and our native grounds.

But I will gather and I will ride,
And I will summon a countryside,
And many a man shall hear my halloa
Who never had thought the horn to follow;
And many a man shall ride with me
Who never had thought on earth to see
High Justice in her armoury.

When we find them where they stand,
A mile of men on either hand,
I mean to charge from right away
And force the flanks of their array,
And press them inward from the plains,
And drive them clamoring down the lanes,
And gallop and harry and have them down,
And carry the gates and hold the town.
Then shall I rest me from my ride
With my great anger satisfied.

Only, before I eat and drink,
When I have killed them all, I think
That I will batter their carven names,
And slit the pictures in their frames,
And burn for scent their cedar door,
And melt the gold their women wore,
And hack their horses at the knees,
And hew to death their timber trees,
And plough their gardens deep and through—
And all these things I mean to do
For fear perhaps my little son
Should break his hands, as I have done.

The Death of Chatterton, *Henry Wallis*

Ad Valorem
by JOHN RUSKIN

In a community regulated by laws of demand and supply, but protected from open violence, the persons who become rich are, generally speaking, industrious, resolute, proud, covetous, prompt, methodical, sensible, unimaginative, insensitive, and ignorant. The persons who remain poor are the entirely foolish, the entirely wise, the idle, the reckless, the humble, the thoughtful, the dull, the imaginative, the sensitive, the well-informed, the improvident, the irregularly and impulsively wicked, the clumsy knave, the open thief, and the entirely merciful, just, and godly person.

For Hire
by MORRIS ROSENFELD
(Translated by Rose Pastor Stokes)

Work with might and main,
Or with hand or heart,
Work with soul and brain,
Or with holy art,
Thread, or genius' fire—
Make a vest, or verse—
If 'tis done for hire,
It is done the worse.

By JOHN RUSKIN

I feel the force of mechanism and the fury of avaricious commerce to be at present so irresistible, that I have seceded from the study not only of architecture, but nearly of all art; and have given myself, as I would in a besieged city, to seek the best modes of getting bread and water for its multitudes.

By O-SHI-O
Japanese scholar of the Eighteenth Century

I have a suit of new clothes in this happy new year;
Hot rice cake soup is excellent to my taste;
But when I think of the hungry people in this city,
I am ashamed of my fortune in the presence of God.

Jean-Christophe

by ROMAIN ROLLAND
French novelist, Nobel Prize for Literature 1915; 1866-1944

Christophe was dragged into the wake of force in the track of the army of the working-classes in revolt. But he was hardly aware that it was so; and he would tell his companions in the restaurant that he was not with them.

"As long as you are only out for material interests," he would say, "you don't interest me. The day when you march out for a belief, then I shall be with you. Otherwise, what have I to do with the conflict between one man's belly and another's? I am an artist; it is my duty to defend art; I have no right to enroll myself in the service of a party. I am perfectly aware that recently certain ambitious writers, impelled by a desire for an unwholesome popularity, have set a bad example. It seems to me that they have not rendered any great service to the cause which they defended in that way; but they have certainly betrayed art. It is our business —the artists'—to save the light of the intellect. We have no right to obscure it with your blind struggles. Who shall hold the light aloft if we let it fall? You will be glad enough to find it still intact after the battle. There must always be workers busy keeping up the fire in the engine, while there is fighting on the deck of the ship. To understand everything is to hate nothing. The artist is the compass which, through the raging of the storm, points steadily to the north."

They regarded him as a maker of phrases, and said that, if he were talking of compasses, it was very clear that he had lost his: and they gave themselves the pleasure of indulging in a little friendly contempt at his expense. In their eyes an artist was a shirker who contrived to work as little and as agreeably as possible.

He replied that he worked as hard as they did, even harder, and that he was not nearly so afraid of work. Nothing disgusted him so much as *sabotage*, the deliberate bungling of work, and skulking raised to the level of a principle.

"All these wretched people," he would say, "afraid for their own skins!...Good Lord! I've never stopped working since I was eight. You people don't love your work; at heart you're just common men.... If only you were capable of destroying the old world! But you can't do it. You don't even want to. No, you don't even want to. It is all very well for you to go about shrieking menace

and pretending you're going to exterminate the human race. You
have only one thought: to get the upper hand and lie snugly in
the warm beds of the middle classes...."

Thereupon they would all lose their tempers and all talk at
once. And in the heat of the argument it would often happen that
Christophe, whirled away by his passion, would become more
revolutionary than the others. In vain did he fight against it; his
intellectual pride, his complacent conception of a purely esthetic
world, made for the joy of the spirit, would sink deep into the
ground at the sight of injustice. Esthetic, a world in which eight
men out of ten live in nakedness and want, in physical and moral
wretchedness? Oh, come! A man must be an impudent creature
of privilege who would dare to claim as much. An artist like
Christophe, in his inmost conscience, could not but be on the side
of the working-classes. What man more than the spiritual worker
has to suffer from the immorality of social conditions, from the
scandalously unequal partition of wealth among men? The artist
dies of hunger or becomes a millionaire for no other reason than
the caprice of fashion and of those who speculate on fashion. A
society which suffers its best men to die or gives them extravagant
rewards is a monstrous society: it must be swept and put in order.
Every man, whether he works or no, has a right to a living minimum. Every kind of work, good or mediocre, should be rewarded,
not according to its real value— (who can be the infallible judge
of that?)—but according to the normal legitimate needs of the
worker. Society can and should assure the artist, the scientist, and
the inventor an income sufficient to guarantee that they have the
means and the time yet further to grace and honor it. Nothing
more. The *Gioconda* is not worth a million. There is no relation
between a sum of money and a work of art: a work of art is neither
above nor below money: it is outside it. It is not a question of
payment: it is a question of allowing the artist to live. Give him
enough to feed him, and allow him to work in peace. It is absurd
and horrible to try to make him a robber of another's property.
This thing must be put bluntly: every man who has more than
is necessary for his livelihood and that of his family, and for the
normal development of his intelligence, is a thief and a robber.
If he has too much, it means that others have too little. How often
have we smiled sadly to hear tell of the inexhaustible wealth of
France, and the number of great fortunes—we workers, and toilers,
and intellectuals, and men and women who from our very birth

have been given up to the wearying task of keeping ourselves from dying of hunger, often struggling in vain, often seeing the very best of us succumbing to the pain of it all,—we who are the moral and intellectual treasure of the nation! You who have more than your share of the wealth of the world are rich at the cost of our suffering and our poverty. That troubles you not at all; you have sophistries and to spare to reassure you: the sacred rights of property, the fair struggle for life, the supreme interests of that Moloch, the State, and Progress, that fabulous monster, that problematical Better to which men sacrifice the Good,—the Good of other men. But for all that, the fact remains, and all your sophistries will never manage to deny it: "You have too much to live on. We have not enough. And we are as good as you. And some of us are better than the whole lot of you put together."

The Problem Play
by George Bernard Shaw

When we succeed in adjusting our social structure in such a way as to enable us to solve social questions as fast as they become really pressing, they will no longer force their way into the theatre. Had Ibsen, for instance, had any reason to believe that the abuses to which he called attention in his prose plays would have been adequately attended to without his interference, he would no doubt have gladly left them alone. The same exigency drove William Morris in England from his tapestries, his epics, and his masterpieces of printing, to try and bring his fellow citizens to their senses by the summary process of shouting at them in the streets and in Trafalgar Square. John Ruskin's writing began with Modern Painters; Carlyle began with literary studies of German culture and the like; both were driven to become revolutionary pamphleteers. If people are rotting and starving in all directions, and nobody else has the heart or brains to make a disturbance about it, the great writers must.

From the Book of Proverbs

Open thy mouth, judge righteously, and plead the cause of the poor and needy.

To a Bourgeois Litterateur
(*Who referred to a group of agitators as "Professional Hoboes"*)
by MAX EASTMAN
American journalist, 1883–1969

How old, my friend, is that fine-pointed pen
Wherewith in smiling quietude you trace
The maiden maxims of your writing-place,
And o'er this gripped and mortal-sweating den
And battle-pit of hunger, now and then
Dip out, with nice and intellectual grace,
The faultless wisdoms of a nurtured race
Of pale-eyed, pink, and perfect gentlemen?

How long have art and wit and poetry,
With all their power, been content, like you,
To gild the smiling fineness of the few,
To filmy-curtain what they dare not see
In multitudinous reality—
The rough and bloody soul of what is true?

The Scholar as Revolutionist
by GEORG BRANDES
Danish critic, 1842-1925

What gives Anatole France his lasting hold over his hearers is not his cleverness, but himself—the fact that this savant who bears the heavy load of three cultures, nay, who is in himself a whole little culture—this sage, to whom the whole life of the earth is but an ephemeral eruption on its surface, and who consequently regards all human endeavor as finally vain—this thinker, who can see everything from innumerable sides and might have come to the conclusion that, things being bad at the best, the existing state of matters was probably as good as the untried: that this man should proclaim himself a son of the Revolution, side with the workingman, acknowledge his belief in liberty, throw away his load and draw his sword—that is what moves a popular audience, this is what plain people can understand and can prize. It has shown them that behind the author there dwells a man—behind the great author a brave man.

A Warning

by HEINRICH HEINE

(*Translated by Louis Untermeyer*)

You will print such books as these!
Then you're lost, my friend, that's certain.
If you wish for gold and honor,
Write more humbly—bend your knees!

Aye, you must have lost your senses
Thus to speak before the people;
Thus to dare to speak of Preachers
And of Potentates and Princes.

Friend, you're lost—so it appears—
For the Princes have long arms,
And the Preachers have long tongues,
—And the masses have long ears!

A Man of Genius

(*From "The New Grub Street"*)

by GEORGE GISSING

His name was Harold Biffen, and, to judge from his appearance, he did not belong to the race of common mortals. His excessive meagerness would all but have qualified him to enter an exhibition in the capacity of living skeleton, and the garments which hung upon this framework would perhaps have sold for three and sixpence at an old-clothes dealer's. But the man was superior to these accidents of flesh and raiment. He had a fine face: large, gentle eyes, nose slightly aquiline, small and delicate mouth. Thick black hair fell to his coat-collar; he wore a heavy moustache and a full beard. In his gait there was a singular dignity; only a man of cultivated mind and grateful character could move and stand as he did.

His first act on entering the room was to take from his pocket a pipe, a pouch, a little tobacco-stopper, and a box of matches, all of which he arranged carefully on a corner of the central table. Then he drew forward a chair and seated himself.

"Take your top-coat off," said Reardon.

"Thanks, not this evening."

"Why the deuce not?"

"Not this evening, thanks."

The reason, as soon as Reardon sought for it, was obvious. Biffen had no ordinary coat beneath the other. To have referred to this fact would have been indelicate; the novelist of course understood it, and smiled, but with no mirth.

"Let me have your Sophocles," were the visitor's next words.

Reardon offered him a volume of the Oxford Pocket Classics.

"I prefer the Wunder, please."

"It's gone, my boy."

"Gone?"

"Wanted a little cash."

Biffen uttered a sound in which remonstrance and sympathy were blended.

"I'm sorry to hear that; very sorry. Well, this must do. Now, I want to know how you scan this chorus in the 'Oedipus Rex.'"

Reardon took the volume, considered, and began to read aloud with metric emphasis.

"Choriambics, eh?" cried the other. "Possible, of course; but treat them as Ionics *a minore* with an anacrusis, and see if they don't go better."

He involved himself in terms of pedantry, and with such delight that his eyes gleamed. Having delivered a technical lecture, he began to read in illustration, producing quite a different effect from that of the rhythm as given by his friend. And the reading was by no means that of a pedant, rather of a poet.

For half an hour the two men talked Greek metres as if they lived in a world where the only hunger known could be satisfied by grand or sweet cadences....

Biffen was always in dire poverty, and lived in the oddest places; he had seen harder trials than even Reardon himself. The teaching by which he partly lived was of a kind quite unknown to the respectable tutorial world. In these days of examinations, numbers of men in a poor position—clerks chiefly—conceive a hope that by "passing" this, that, or the other formal test they may open for themselves a new career. Not a few such persons nourish preposterous ambitions; there are warehouse clerks privately preparing (without any means or prospect of them) for a call to the Bar, drapers' assistants who "go in" for the preliminary examination of the College of Surgeons, and untaught men innumerable, who desire to procure enough show of education to be eligible for a curacy. Candidates of this stamp frequently advertise in the newspapers for cheap tuition, or answer advertisements which are intended to appeal to them; they pay from sixpence to half a crown an hour—rarely as much as the latter sum. Occasionally it happened that Harold Biffen had three or four such pupils in hand, and extraordinary stories he could draw from his large experience in this sphere. . . .

Biffen Falls in Love

A fatal day. There was an end of all his peace, all his capacity for labor, his patient endurance of penury. Once, when he was about three and twenty, he had been in love with a girl of gentle nature and fair intelligence; on account of his poverty, he could not even hope that his love might be returned, and he went away to bear the misery as best he might. Since then the life he had led precluded the forming of such attachments; it would never have been possible for him to support a wife of however humble origin. At intervals he felt the full weight of his loneliness, but there were happily long periods during which his Greek studies and his efforts in realistic fiction made him indifferent to the curse laid upon him. But after that hour of intimate speech with Amy, he never again knew rest of mind or heart. . . .

He was not the kind of man that deceives himself as to his own aspect in the eyes of others. Be as kind as she might, Amy could not set him strutting Malvoliowise; she viewed him as a poor devil who often had to pound his coat—a man of parts who could never get on in the world—a friend to be thought of kindly because her dead husband had valued him. Nothing more than that; he understood perfectly the limits of her feeling. But this could not put restraint upon the emotion with which he received any trifling utterance of kindness from her. He did not think of what was, but of what, under changed circumstances, might be. To encourage such fantasy was the idlest self-torment, but he had gone too far in this form of indulgence. He became the slave of his inflamed imagination. . . .

Companionless, inert, he suffered the tortures which are so ludicrous and contemptible to the happily married. Life was barren to him, and would soon grow hateful; only in sleep could he cast off the unchanging thoughts and desires which made all else meaningless. And rightly meaningless; he revolted against the unnatural constraints forbidding him to complete his manhood. By what fatality was he alone of men withheld from the winning of a woman's love?

He could not bear to walk the streets where the faces of beautiful women would encounter him. When he must needs leave the house, he went about in the poor, narrow ways, where only spectacles of coarseness, and want, and toil would be presented to him. Yet even here he was too often reminded that the poverty-stricken of the class to which poverty is natural were not condemned to endure in solitude. Only he who belonged to no class, who was rejected alike by his fellows in privation and by his equals in intellect, must die without having known the touch of a loving woman's hand.

The summer went by, and he was unconscious of its warmth and light. How his days passed he could not have said....

One evening in early autumn, as he stood before the book-stall at the end of Goodge Street, a familiar voice accosted him. It was Whelpdale's. A month or two ago he had stubbornly refused an invitation to dine with Whelpdale and other acquaintances, and since then the prosperous young man had not crossed his path.

"I've something to tell you," said the assailer, taking hold of his arm. "I'm in a tremendous state of mind, and want someone to share my delight.... You know Dora Milvain; I have asked her to marry me, and, by the Powers! she has given me an encouraging answer! Not an actual yes, but encouraging! She's away in the Channel Islands, and I wrote——"

He talked on for a quarter of an hour. Then, with a sudden movement, the listener freed himself.

"I can't go any farther," he said hoarsely. "Good-bye!"

Whelpdale was disconcerted.

"I have been boring you. That's a confounded fault of mine; I know it."

Biffen had waved his hand, and was gone.

A week or two would see him at the end of his money. He had no lessons now, and could not write; from his novel nothing was to be expected. He might apply again to his brother, but such dependence was unjust and unworthy. And why should he struggle to preserve a life which had no prospect but of misery?...

It was in the hours following his encounter with Whelpdale that he first knew the actual desire of death, the simple longing for extinction. One must go far in suffering before the innate will-to-live is thus truly overcome; weariness of bodily anguish may induce this perversion of the instincts; less often, that despair of suppressed emotion which had fallen upon Harold. Through the night he kept his thoughts fixed on death in its aspect of repose, of eternal oblivion. And herein he found solace.

The next night it was the same. Moving among many common needs and occupations, he knew not a moment's cessation of heartache, but when he lay down in the darkness a hopeful summons whispered to him. Night, which had been the worst season of his pain, had now grown friendly; it came as an anticipation of the sleep that is everlasting.

A few more days, and he was possessed by a calm of spirit such as he had never known. His resolve was taken, not in a moment of supreme conflict, but as the result of a subtle process by which his imagination had become in love with death. Turning from contemplation of life's one rapture, he looked with the same intensity of desire to a state that had neither fear nor hope.

One afternoon he went to the Museum Reading Room, and was busy for a few minutes in consultation of a volume which he took from the shelves of medical literature. On his way homeward he entered two or three chemists' shops. Something of which he had need could be procured only in very small quantities; but repetition of his demand in different places supplied him sufficiently. When he reached his room, he emptied the contents of sundry little bottles into one larger, and put this in his pocket. Then he wrote rather a long letter, addressed to his brother in Liverpool....

"Really," said Jasper, "one can't grieve. There seemed no possibility of his ever earning enough to live decently upon. But why the deuce did he go all the way out there? Consideration for the people in whose house he lived, I dare say; Biffen had a good deal of native delicacy...."

"Was he still so very poor?" asked Amy, compassionately.

"I'm afraid so. His book failed utterly."

"Oh, if I had imagined him in such distress, surely I might have done something to help him!"—So often the regretful remark of one's friends, when one has been permitted to perish.

Letter to the Earl of Chesterfield
by SAMUEL JOHNSON
English author, lexicographer, 1709–1784

My Lord, I have been lately informed, by the proprietor of the World, that two papers, in which my Dictionary is recommended to the publick, were written by your Lordship. To be so distinguished, is an honour, which, being very little accustomed to favours from the great, I know not well how to receive, or in what terms to acknowledge.

When, upon some slight encouragement, I first visited your Lordship, I was overpowered, like the rest of mankind, by the enchantment of your address, and could not forbear to wish that I might boast myself *Le vainquer du vainqueur de la terre;*—that I might obtain that regard for which I saw the world contending; but I found my attendance so little encouraged, that neither pride nor modesty would suffer me to continue it. When I had once addressed your Lordship in publick, I had exhausted all the art of pleasing which a retired and uncourtly scholar can possess. I had done all that I could; and no man is well pleased to have his all neglected, be it ever so little.

Seven years, my Lord, have now past, since I waited in your outward rooms, or was repulsed from your door; during which time I have been pushing my work through difficulties, of which it is useless to complain, and have brought it, at last, to the verge of publication, without one act of assistance, one word of encouragement, or one smile of favour. Such treatment I did not expect, for I never had a Patron before.

The shepherd in Virgil grew at last acquainted with Love, and found him a native of the rocks.

Is not a Patron, my Lord, one who looks with unconcern on a man struggling for life in the water, and, when he has reached ground, encumbers him with help? The notice which you have been pleased to take of my labours, had it been early, had been kind; but it has been delayed till I am indifferent, and cannot enjoy it; till I am solitary, and cannot impart it; till I am known, and do not want it. I hope it is no very cynical asperity, not to confess obligations where no benefit has been received, or to be unwilling that the Publick should consider me as owing that to a Patron, which Providence has enabled me to do for myself.

Having carried my work thus far with so little obligation to any favourer of learning, I shall not be disappointed though I should conclude it, if less be possible, with less; for I have been long wakened from that dream of hope in which I once boasted myself with so much exultation,

> My Lord,
>> Your Lordship's most humble
>> Most obedient servant,

SAM. JOHNSON.

The "Pinch of Poverty"
by FRANCIS THOMPSON
English poet, 1859-1907

'Tis the convinced belief of mankind that to make a poet sing you must pinch his belly, as if the Almighty had constructed him like a certain rudimentary vocal doll.

Learning
(*From "Thus Spake Zarathustra"*)
by FRIEDRICH NIETZSCHE
German philosopher, 1844-1900

As I lay in sleep a sheep ate up the ivy crown of my head—ate then said: "Zarathustra is no more a scholar."

Said it and went strutting away, and proud. A child told it to me....

This is the truth. I am gone out of the house of the scholars, and have slammed to the door behind me....

I am too hot, and burning with my own thoughts; oft will it take away my breath. I must into the open and out of all dusty rooms.

But they sit cool in cool shadows; they wish in all things to be but spectators, and guard themselves lest they sit where the sun burn the steps.

Like those who stand upon the street and stare at the people who go by; so they wait also and stare at the thoughts that others have thought.

If one touches them with the hands, they make dust around them like meal-sacks, and involuntarily; but who could guess that their dust comes from corn and the golden rapture of the summer fields?

Last Verses

by THOMAS CHATTERTON

This boy, 1752-1770, committed suicide because of poverty and neglect, and has become the classic example of the world's mistreatment of its poets. Bristol was his native city.

Farewell, Bristolia's dingy piles of brick,
Lovers of mammon, worshippers of trick!
Ye spurned the boy who gave you antique lays,
And paid for learning with your empty praise.
Farewell, ye guzzling aldermanic fools,
By nature fitted for corruption's tools!
I go to where celestial anthems swell;
But you, when you depart, will sink to hell.
Farewell, my mother!—cease, my anguished soul,
Nor let distraction's billows o'er me roll!
Have mercy, Heaven! when here I cease to live,
And this last act of wretchedness forgive.

The Journal of Arthur Stirling

by UPTON SINCLAIR

A young poet, starving and about to commit suicide, leaves his farewell testament to the world.

The poet! He comes with a heart trembling with gladness; he comes with tears of rapture in his eyes. He comes with bosom heaving and throat choking and heart breaking. He comes with tenderness and with trust, with joy in the beauty that he beholds. He comes a minstrel, with a harp in his hand—and you set your dogs upon him, you drive him torn and bleeding from your gates!

The poet! You make him go out into the market and chaffer for his bread! You subject him to the same law to which you subject your loafers and your louts—that he who will not work cannot eat! Your drones and your drunkards—and your poets! Every man must earn for himself, every man must pay his way! No man must ask favors, no man must be helped, no man shall be different from other men! For shame! For shame!...

I am to die now, therefore let me write it: that I was a man of Genius. And that you have trodden me down in the struggle for existence. I saw things that no other man has ever seen, I would have written things that no other man can ever write. And you have trodden me down in the struggle for existence—you have trodden me down because I could not earn my bread!

This is what I tell you—this is what I cry out to you, that the man of Genius *cannot* earn his bread; that the work by which he develops his power is something absolutely and utterly different from the work by which he earns his bread; and that every hour which he gives to the one, he lessens his power and his capacity for the other. Every hour that he gives to the earning of his bread, he takes from his soul, he weakens his work, he destroys beauty which never again can he know or dream.

And this again is what I tell you, this again is what I cry out to you: that the power by which a man of Genius does his work, and the power by which he earns his bread, are things so entirely distinct that *they may not occur together at all!* The man may have both, but then again he may only have the former. And in that case he will die like a poisoned rat in a hole.

The Death of Tom Paine

by HOWARD FAST
American historical novelist, born 1914

There was nothing but pain now in his side where it had become infected during his stay in the Luxembourg, in his head, everywhere. A man dies so slowly. Madame Bonneville got him a nurse, but the nurse was a deeply religious woman and let it be known all about that Tom Paine was living his last hours. Thus began a pilgrimage; for what a splendid thing it would be to hear Paine denounce *The Age of Reason* on his deathbed!

One and all they came, Catholics, Methodists, Congregationalists, Lutherans, Quakers, Presbyterians—they had not read his book, yet they came to fight the book and the devil.

"Renounce it! Renounce God and goodness and hope, for you are dying! Renounce mankind!"

Ministers, priests, pastors, fathers, nuns—they crept into his room, aided by the nurse, who had been divinely placed in this holy position. The old warrior was dying, and what had they or anyone to fear! The horns of the angels had pealed over Concord and Lexington, but here was only the rustle of stiff, black garments. If he called weakly for aid, his comrades could not hear him, for they were dead or far away, crossing the mountains and the plains, driving their oxen and their covered wagons, going to make the land and the world that was the dream, the handiwork, and the suffering of Tom Paine. The ones in black crouched over him; they darkened and pushed away the little sunlight. They screamed, "Recant." Ladies came to do their bit of good, dressed in proper ebony. Even the doctor, bending low, prodded him: "Mr. Paine, do you hear me? There is still time, there is still hope. Do you wish to believe that Jesus Christ is the Son of God?"

"Do you wish to believe?"

"Do you recant?"

"Do you renounce?"

"You are a dirty old man, you are all alone. Give up, give up."

If there was a moment of peace, as there was bound to be, early in the morning and late at night, the nurse read in ringing tones from the Bible. This was a crusade; come, all ye faithful!

And then he no longer heard their voices, their prodding, their torments, their pleas that he should be weak, he whose strength was the strength of storied heroes, of the gods of old. He had peace; he had his comrades by his side; he stood among the men of good will, those who came before him and those who came after him.

Mother Hubbard's Tale
by Edmund Spenser

Full little knowest thou that hast not tride,
What hell it is in suing long to bide:
To loose good dayes, that might be better spent;
To waste long nights in pensive discontent;
To speed to-day, to be put back to-morrow;
To feed on hope, to pine with feare and sorrow;
To fret thy soule with crosses and with cares;
To eate thy heart through comfortlesse dispaires;
To fawne, to crowche, to waite, to ride, to ronne,
To spend, to give, to want, to be undonne.
Unhappie wight, borne to desastrous end,
That doth his life in so long tendence spend!

A Preface to Politics
by WALTER LIPPMANN
American journalist-commentator, ex-Socialist, 1889–1974

We have almost no spiritual weapons against classicalism: universities, churches, newspapers are by-products of a commercial success; we have no tradition of intellectual revolt. The American college student has the gravity and mental habits of a Supreme Court judge; his "wild oats" are rarely spiritual; the critical, analytical habit of mind is distrusted. We say that "knocking" is a sign of the "sorehead" and we sublimate criticism by saying that "every knock is a boost." America does not play with ideas; generous speculation is regarded as insincere, and shunned as if it might endanger the optimism which underlies success. All this becomes such an insulation against new ideas that when the Yankee goes abroad he takes his environment with him.

Off Maysi
by JOSÉ MARTÍ
Cuban patriot, 1853-1895
(Translated by Cecil Charles)

I slept to the waves' nocturne, in the light of a single star,
The splendid midnight god of the Southern heavens afar,
And the starshine bathed my brain with a vision of planets free
As the ship went sailing down on the breast of a sapphire sea.

I waked and the day had come, for land on the starboard grew
Till the cliffs of an island shone through langorous veils of blue;
And I knew the emerald sheen and the amethyst afterglow
On the breast of the lovely slave—the daughter of Spain and woe.

I gazed and the turquoise bowl of a marvelous sky was near
And closed with a rim of gold warm over the widening sphere,
And the sea was a blaze of fire with the scimitars of the sun
Flung forth in a burst of joy as the battle of dawn was won.

And the flame to the westward ran and shook in the breakers' rise
At the base of the island couch where a hapless creature lies,
Where a hapless creature waits, as the perishing dumbly wait,
A mother unwed—of sons that are born to suffer and hate.

Then over the sapphire sea with the swords of the sun aflame
And out of the languorous mists of the island hills there came
A sudden, an anguished cry of a thousand voices blent
In tortured, terrible prayer for the end of a punishment.

Mother Spain! (it rang), mother Spain! Oh, heed thy daughter's
    tears,
She is bound with the chains of crime and cursed with the yoke
    of years,
Her sons with a birth-wrong strive and shriek for their father's
    name,
The sons of the freedom she might not wed, the lover she loves
    in shame.

Mother Spain! (the desolate wail), oh, heed thy child's desire!
Thou mother of nations free from the gulf to the land of fire.
Oh, harken and heed and save, thou, mother of conquerors dead,
And break the fetters of her who waits and bid her rise and wed!

And I slept again that night in the glow of the magic star,
The gracious midnight god of the Southern heavens afar,
And the starshine bathed my brain with a vision of Cuba free,
As the ship went sailing down on the breast of the sapphire sea.

BOOK XV

Socialism

The most eloquent passages from the pens of those who foresee the definite solution of the problems of economic inequality. Every aspect of the socialist movement is represented.

The March of the Workers
by WILLIAM MORRIS
English poet and artist, 1834-1896

What is this—the sound and rumor? What is this that all men hear,
Like the wind in hollow valleys when the storm is drawing near,
Like the rolling-on of ocean in the eventide of fear?
　　　'Tis the people marching on.

CHORUS

　　Hark the rolling of the thunder!
　　Lo! the sun! and lo! thereunder
　　Riseth wrath, and hope, and wonder,
　　　And the host comes marching on.

Forth they come from grief and torment; on they go towards health
　　and mirth.
All the wide world is their dwelling, every corner of the earth.
Buy them, sell them for thy service! Try the bargain what 'tis
　　worth,
　　　For the days are marching on. (Chorus)

Many a hundred years passed over have they labored deaf and
　　blind;
Never tidings reached their sorrow, never hope their toil might
　　find.
Now at last they've heard and hear it, and the cry comes down the
　　wind
　　　And their feet are marching on. (Chorus)

"Is it war then? Will ye perish as the dry wood in the fire?
Is it peace? Then be ye of us, let your hope be our desire.
Come and live! for life awaketh, and the world shall never tire;
　　　And hope is marching on. (Chorus)

A Marching Song

by CHARLES ALGERNON SWINBURNE

We mix from many lands,
   We march for very far;
In hearts and lips and hands
   Our staffs and weapons are;
The light we walk in darkens sun and moon and star.

It doth not flame and wane
   With years and spheres that roll,
Storm cannot shake nor stain
   The strength that makes it whole,
The fire that moulds and moves it of the sovereign soul. . . .

From the edge of harsh derision,
   From discord and defeat,
From doubt and lame division,
   We pluck the fruit and eat;
And the mouth finds it bitter, and the spirit sweet. . . .

O nations undivided,
   O single people and free,
We dreamers, we derided,
   We mad blind men that see,
We bear you witness ere ye come that ye shall be.

Ye sitting among tombs,
   Ye standing round the gate,
Whom fire-mouthed war consumes,
   Or cold-lipped peace bids wait,
All tombs and bars shall open, every grave and grate. . . .

O sorrowing hearts of slaves,
   We heard you beat from far!
We bring the light that saves,
   We bring the morning star;
Freedom's good things we bring you, whence all good things are. . . .

Rise, ere the dawn be risen;
   Come, and be all souls fed;
From field and street and prison
   Come, for the feast is spread;
Live, for the truth is living; wake, for night is dead.

The Duties of Man

by Giuseppe Mazzini

Italian patriot and statesman, 1805-1872

We improve with the improvement of humanity; nor without the improvement of the whole can you hope that your own moral and material conditions will improve. Generally speaking, you cannot, even if you would, separate your life from that of humanity; you live in it, by it, for it. Your souls, with the exception of the very few men of exceptional power, cannot free themselves from the influence of the elements amid which they exist, just as the body, however robust its constitution, cannot escape from the effects of corrupt air around it. How many of you have the strength of mind to bring up your sons to be wholly truthful, knowing that you are sending them forth to persecution in a country where tyrants and spies bid them conceal or deny two-thirds of their real opinions? How many of you resolve to educate them to despise wealth in a society where gold is the only power which obtains honors, influence, and respect, where indeed it is the only protection from the tyranny and insults of the powerful and their agents? Who is there among you who in pure love and with the best intentions in the world has not murmured to his dear ones in Italy, *Do not trust men; the honest man should retire into himself and fly from public life; charity begins at home,*—and such-like maxims, plainly immoral, but prompted by the general state of society? What mother is there among you who, although she belongs to a faith which adores the cross of Christ, the voluntary martyr for humanity, has not flung her arms around her son's neck and striven to dissuade him from perilous attempts to benefit his brothers? And even if you had strength to teach the contrary, would not the whole of society, with its thousand voices, its thousand evil examples, destroy the effect of your words? Can you purify, elevate your own souls in an atmosphere of contamination and degradation?

And, to descend to your material conditions, do you think they can be lastingly ameliorated by anything but the amelioration of all? Millions of pounds are spent annually here in England, where I write, by private charity, for the relief of individuals who have fallen into want; yet want increases here every year, and charity to individuals has proved powerless to heal the evil—the necessity of collective organic remedies is more and more universally felt. . . .

There is no hope for you except in universal reform and in the brotherhood of all the peoples of Europe, and through Europe of all humanity. I charge you then, O my brothers, by your duty and by your own interest, not to forget that your first duties— duties without fulfilling which you cannot hope to fulfil those owed to family and country—are to humanity. Let your words and your actions be for all, since God is for all, in His love and in His law. In whatever land you may be, wherever a man is fighting for right, for justice, for truth, there is your brother; wherever a man suffers through the oppression of error, of injustice, of tyranny, there is your brother. Free men and slaves, *you are all brothers.*

The Communist Manifesto
by KARL MARX AND FREDERICK ENGELS

The Communists disdain to conceal their views and aims. They openly declare that their ends can be attained only by the forcible overthrow of all existing social conditions. Let the ruling classes tremble at a Communistic revolution. The proletarians have nothing to lose but their chains. They have a world to win.

Workingmen of all countries, unite!

The Workingman's Program
by FERDINAND LASSALLE
Lassalle was arrested and sentenced to prison for delivering the address from which the following paragraph is taken.

Whoever invokes the idea of the working-class as the ruling principle of society, does not put forth a cry that divides and separates the classes of society. On the contrary, he utters a cry of reconciliation, a cry which embraces the whole of the community, a cry for the abolishing of all the contradictions in every circle of society; a cry of union, in which all should join who do not wish for privileges, for the oppression of the people by privileged classes; a cry of love, which having once gone up from the heart of the people, will forever remain the true cry of the people, and whose meaning will still make it a cry of love, even when it sounds as the people's war cry.

Poverty Makes All Unhappy
by JOHN RUSKIN

For my own part, I will put up with this state of things, passively, not an hour longer. I am not an unselfish person, nor an evangelical one; I have no particular pleasure in doing good; neither do I dislike doing it so much as to expect to be rewarded for it in another world. But I simply cannot paint, nor read, nor look at minerals, nor do anything else I like, and the very light of the morning sky has become hateful to me, because of the misery that I know of, and see signs of where I know it not, which no imagination can interpret too bitterly.

Land Titles
by HERBERT SPENCER

It can never be pretended that the existing titles to landed property are legitimate. The original deeds were written with the sword, soldiers were the conveyancers, blows were the current coin given in exchange, and for seals, blood. Those who say that "time is a great legaliser" must find satisfactory answers to such questions as—How long does it take for what was originally wrong to become right? At what rate per annum do invalid claims become valid?

The Rights of Labor
by ABRAHAM LINCOLN

It is assumed that labor is available only in connection with capital; that nobody labors unless somebody else, owning capital, somehow by the use of it, induces him to labor. This assumed, it is next considered whether it is best that capital shall hire laborers, and thus induce them to work by their own consent, or buy them and drive them to do it without their consent. Having proceeded so far, it is naturally concluded that all laborers are either hired laborers or what we call slaves.

Now, there is no such relation between capital and labor as here assumed. . . . Labor is prior to and independent of capital. Capital is only the fruit of labor, could never have existed if labor had not first existed. Labor is the superior of capital, and deserves much the higher consideration.

The Working Day
(From "Capital")
by KARL MARX

What is a working day? What is the length of time during which capital may consume the labor-power whose daily value it buys? How far may the working-day be extended beyond the working time necessary for the reproduction of labor-power itself? It has been seen that to these questions capital replies: the working day contains the full twenty-four hours with the deduction of the few hours of repose without which labor-power absolutely refuses its services again. Hence it is self-evident that the laborer is nothing else, his whole life through, than labor-power; that therefore all his disposable time is by nature and law labor-time, to be devoted to the self-expansion of capital. Time for education, for intellectual development, for the fulfilling of social functions and for social intercourse, for the free-play of his bodily and mental activity, even the rest time of Sunday (and that in a country of Sabbatarians!)—moonshine! But in its blind, unrestrainable passion, its were-wolf hunger for surplus-labor, capital oversteps not only the moral, but even the merely physical maximum bounds of the working-day. It usurps the time for growth, development, and healthy maintenance of the body. It steals the time required for the consumption of fresh air and sunlight. It higgles over a meal-time, incorporating it where possible with the process of production itself, so that food is given to the laborer as to a mere means of production, as coal is supplied to the boiler, grease and oil to the machinery. It reduces the sound sleep needed for the restoration, reparation, refreshment of the bodily powers, to just so many hours of torpor as the revival of an organism, absolutely exhausted, renders essential. It is not the normal maintenance of the labor-power which is to determine the limits of the working-day; it is the greatest possible daily expenditure of labor-power, no matter how diseased, compulsory and painful it may be, which is to determine the limits of the laborers' period of repose. Capital cares nothing for the length of life of labor-power. All that concerns it is simply and solely the maximum of labor-power, that can be rendered fluent in a working-day. It attains this end by shortening the extent of the laborer's life, as a greedy farmer snatches increased produce from the soil by robbing it of its fertility.

The Internationale

by Eugene Pottier

French author, 1816-1887. Hymn of revolutionary workers' movements around the world.

Arise, ye pris'ners of starvation!
  Arise, ye wretched of the earth,
For Justice thunders condemnation,
  A better world's in birth.
No more tradition's chains shall bind us,
  Arise, ye slaves! No more in thrall!
The earth shall rise on new foundations,
  We have been naught, we shall be all.

Refrain

'Tis the final conflict,
  Let each stand in his place,
The International Party
  Shall be the human race.

Behold them seated in their glory,
  The kings of mine and rail and soil!
What would you read in all their story
  But how they plundered toil?
Fruits of the people's work are buried
  In the strong coffers of a few;
In voting for their restitution
  The men will only ask their due. (Refrain)

Toilers from shops and fields united,
  The party we of all who work;
The earth belongs to us, the people,
  No room here for the shirk.
How many on our flesh have fattened!
  But if the noisome birds of prey
Shall vanish from our sky some morning,
  The blessed sunlight still will stay. (Refrain)

The One Duty
(From "The Measure of the Hours")
by MAURICE MAETERLINCK
Belgian poet and dramatist, Nobel Prize for Literature 1911; 1862-1949

Let us start fairly with the great truth: for those who possess there is only one certain duty, which is to strip themselves of what they have so as to bring themselves into the condition of the mass that possesses nothing. It is understood, in every clear-thinking conscience, that no more imperative duty exists; but, at the same time, it is admitted that this duty, for lack of courage, is impossible of accomplishment.

For the rest, in the heroic history of duties, even at the most ardent period, even at the beginning of Christi   d in the majority of the religious orders that made a special cult of poverty, this is perhaps the only duty that has never been completely fulfilled. It behooves us, therefore, when considering our subsidiary duties, to remember that the essential one has been knowingly evaded. Let this truth govern us. Let us not forget that we are speaking in shadow, and that our boldest, our utmost steps will never lead us to the point at which we ought to have been from the first.

The Organization of Labor
by LOUIS BLANC
Early French Utopian Socialist, 1811-1882

What is competition, from the point of view of the workman? It is work put up to auction. A contractor wants a workman; three present themselves.

"How much for your work?"

"Half a crown; I have a wife and children."

"Well; and how much for yours?"

"Two shillings; I have no children, but I have a wife."

"Very well; and now how much for yours?"

"One and eightpence are enough for me; I am single."

"Then you shall have the work."

It is done; the bargain is struck. And what are the other two workmen to do? It is to be hoped they will die quietly of hunger. But what if they take to thieving? Never fear; we have the police. To murder? We have the hangman. As for the lucky one, his triumph is only temporary. Let a fourth workman make his appearance, strong enough to fast every other day, and his price will run down still lower; there will be a new outcast, perhaps a new recruit for the prison.

From Revolution to Revolution
by GEORGE D. HERRON

Under the socialist movement there is coming a time, and the time may be even now at hand, when improved conditions or adjusted wages will no longer be thought to be an answer to the cry of labor; yes, when these will be but an insult to the common intelligence. It is not for better wages, improved capitalist conditions, or a share of capitalist profits that the socialist movement is in the world; it is here for the abolition of wages and profits, and for the end of capitalism and the private capitalist. Reformed political institutions, boards of arbitration between capital and labor, philanthropies and privileges that are but the capitalist's gifts—none of these can much longer answer the question that is making the temples, thrones and parliaments of the nations tremble. There can be no peace between the man who is down and the man who builds on his back. There can be no reconciliation between classes; there can only be an end of classes. It is idle to talk of good will until there is first justice, and idle to talk of justice until the man who makes the world possesses the work of his own hands. The cry of the world's workers can be answered with nothing save the whole product of their work.

Jurgis Hears a Socialist Speech
(From "The Jungle")
by UPTON SINLCAIR

It was like coming suddenly upon some wild sight of nature —a mountain forest lashed by a tempest, a ship tossed about upon a stormy sea. Jurgis had an unpleasant sensation, a sense of confusion, of disorder, of wild and meaningless uproar. The man was tall and gaunt, as haggard as his auditor himself; a thin black beard covered half of his face, and one could see only two black hollows where the eyes were. He was speaking rapidly, in great excitement; he used many gestures—as he spoke he moved here and there upon the stage, reaching with his long arms as if to seize each person in his audience. His voice was deep, like an

organ; it was some time, however, before Jurgis thought of the
voice—he was too much occupied with his eyes to think of what
the man was saying. But suddenly it seemed as if the speaker had
been pointing straight at him, as if he had been singled out particularly for his remarks; and so Jurgis became suddenly aware
of the voice, trembling, vibrant with emotion, with pain and
longing, with a burden of things unutterable, not to be com-
passed by words. To hear it was to be suddenly arrested, to be
gripped, transfixed.

"You listen to these things," the man was saying, "and you say,
'Yes, they are true, but they have been that way always.' Or you
say 'Maybe it will come, but not in my time—it will not help
me.' And so you return to your daily round of toil, you go back
to be ground up for profits in the world-wide mill of economic
might! To toil long hours for another's advantage; to live in
mean and squalid homes, to work in dangerous and unhealthful
places; to wrestle with the spectres of hunger and privation, to
take your chances of accident, disease and death. And each day
the struggle becomes fiercer, the pace more cruel; each day you
have to toil a little harder, and feel the iron hand of circumstance close upon you a little tighter. Months pass, years maybe
—and then you come again; and again I am here to plead with
you, to know if want and misery have yet done their work with
you, if injustice and oppression have yet opened your eyes! I
shall still be waiting—there is nothing else that I can do. There
is no wilderness where I can hide from these things, there is no
haven where I can escape them; though I travel to the ends of
the earth, I find the same accursed system,—I find that all the fair
and noble impulses of humanity, the dreams of poets and the
agonies of martyrs, are shackled and bound in the service of
organized and predatory Greed! And therefore I cannot rest, I
cannot be silent; therefore I cast aside comfort and happiness,
health and good repute—and go out into the world and cry out
the pain of my spirit! Therefore I am not to be silenced by
poverty and sickness, not by hatred and obloquy, by threats and
ridicule—not by prison and persecution, if they should come—
not by any power that is upon the earth or above the earth, that
was, or is, or ever can be created. If I fail tonight, I can only
try tomorrow; knowing that the fault must be mine—that if once
the anguish of its defeat were uttered in human speech, it would
break the stoutest barriers of prejudice, it would shake the most

sluggish soul to action! It would abash the most cynical, it would terrify the most selfish; and the voice of mockery would be silenced, and fraud and falsehood would slink back into their dens, and the truth would stand forth alone! For I speak with the voice of the millions who are voiceless! Of them that are oppressed and have no comforter! Of the disinherited of life, for whom there is no respite and no deliverance, to whom the world is a prison, a dungeon of torture, a tomb! With the voice of the little child who toils tonight in a Southern cotton-mill, staggering with exhaustion, numb with agony, and knowing no hope but the grave! Of the mother who sews by candle-light in her tenement garret, weary and weeping, smitten with the mortal hunger of her babes! Of the man who lies upon a bed of rags, wrestling in his last sickness and leaving his loved ones to perish! Of the young girl who, somewhere at this moment, is walking the streets of this horrible city, beaten and starving, and making her choice between the brothel and the lake! With the voice of those, whoever and wherever they may be, who are caught beneath the wheels of the juggernaut of Greed! With the voice of humanity, calling for deliverance! Of the everlasting soul of Man, arising from the dust; breaking its way out of its prison—rending the bands of oppression and ignorance—groping its way to the light!"

Renovating the State
by RALPH WALDO EMERSON

What is strange, there never was in any man sufficient faith in the power of rectitude, to inspire him with the broad design of renovating the State on the principle of right and love. All those who have pretended this design have been partial reformers, and have admitted in some manner the supremacy of the bad State. I do not call to mind a single human being who has steadily denied the authority of the laws on the simple ground of his own moral nature. Such designs, full of genius and full of fate as they are, are not entertained except avowedly as air-pictures. If the individual who exhibits them dare to think them practicable, he disgusts scholars and churchmen; and men of talent, and women of superior sentiments, cannot hide their contempt. Not the less does nature continue to fill the heart of youth with suggestions of this enthusiasm.

The Revolution in the Mind and Practice
of the Human Race
by ROBERT OWEN
English Utopian Socialist, 1771-1858

The Past has been inevitable, and necessary to produce the Present; as the Present will necessarily produce the Future state of human existence. The past has produced a repulsive, unorganized, ignorant, and to a great extent, miserable state of society, over the world, as now existing. The present, however, has been made to develop all the materials requisite to produce an attractive, organized, enlightened and happy future, for the human race, in all parts of the globe.

Those informed know that all the materials are amply prepared, ready to create a happy future; but that to effect this result, the materials must be wisely applied, to form a scientific arrangement of society, based on an accurate knowledge of human nature. Means are, therefore, now required to induce the public to investigate this important subject, which is in direct opposition to the false and fatal association of ideas which, from birth, have been forced into the minds and upon the habits of people.

Mutual Aid as a Factor in Evolution
by PETER KROPOTKIN

As soon as we study animals—not in laboratories and museums only, but in the forest and prairie, in the steppe and in the mountains—we at once perceive that though there is an immense amount of warfare and extermination going on amidst various species, and especially amidst various classes of animals, there is, at the same time, as much, or perhaps even more, of mutual support, mutual aid, and mutual defense amidst animals belonging to the same species or, at least, to the same society. Sociability is as much a law of nature as mutual struggle. Of course it would be extremely difficult to estimate, however roughly, the relative numerical importance of both these series of facts. But if we resort to an indirect test, and ask Nature: "Who are the fittest: those who are continually at war with each other, or those who support one another?" we at once see that those animals which acquire habits of mutual aid are undoubtedly the fittest. They have more chances to survive, and they attain, in their respective classes, the highest development and bodily organization. If the numberless facts which can be brought forward to support this view are taken into account, we may safely say that mutual aid is as much a law of animal life as mutual struggle; but that as a factor of evolution, it most probably has a far greater importance, inasmuch as it favors the development of such habits and characters as insure the maintenance and further development of the species, together with the greatest amount of welfare and enjoyment of life for the individual, with the least waste of energy.

Co-operation and Nationality
by GEORGE W. RUSSELL ("A.E.")

Wherever there is mutual aid, wherever there is constant give and take, wherever the prosperity of the individual depends directly and obviously on the prosperity of the community about him, there the social order tends to produce fine types of character, with a devotion to public ideas; and this is the real object of all government. The worst thing which can happen to a social community is to have no social order at all, where every man is for himself and the devil may take the hindmost. Generally in such a community he takes the front rank as well as the stragglers.

New Worlds for Old
by H. G. WELLS

Socialism is to me a very great thing indeed, the form and substance of my ideal life and all the religion I possess. I am, by a sort of predestination, a Socialist. I perceive I cannot help talking and writing about Socialism, and shaping and forwarding Socialism. I am one of a succession—one of a growing multitude of witnesses, who will continue. It does not—in the larger sense —matter how many generations of us must toil and testify. It does not matter, except as our individual concern, how individually we succeed or fail, what blunders we make, what thwartings we encounter, what follies and inadequacies darken our private hopes and level our personal imaginations to the

Oliver Twist Asks for More, *George Cruikshank*

dust. We have the light. We know what we are for, and that the light that now glimmers so dimly through us must in the end prevail.

Why I Voted the Socialist Ticket
by VACHEL LINDSAY

I am unjust, but I can strive for justice.
My life's unkind, but I can vote for kindness.
I, the unloving, say life should be lovely.
I, that am blind, cry out against my blindness.

Man is a curious brute—he pets his fancies—
Fighting mankind to win sweet luxury;
So he will be, tho' law be clear as crystal,
Tho' all men plan to live in harmony.

Come, let us vote against our human nature,
Crying to God in all the polling places
To heal our everlasting sinfulness
And make us sages with transfigured faces.

Progressivism and After
by WILLIAM ENGLISH WALLING
American socialist writer, 1877-1936

A certain measure of progress is to be expected through the self-interest of the governing classes. This is the national, or industrial, efficiency movement.

Far greater progress is to be expected from the successive rise into power and prosperity of new elements of the middle-class —and of the upper layers of the wage-earners. This is the progressive and the Laborite movement.

By far the greatest progress is to be expected as a direct or indirect result of the revolt of the lower classes. For this is the only force that can be relied upon to put an end to class government and class exploitation of industry, and to establish that social democracy which is the real or professed aim of every progressive movement.

From the Magnificat
by MARY, MOTHER OF JESUS

He hath showed strength with his arm; he hath scattered the proud in the imagination of their hearts. He hath put down the mighty from their seats, and exalted them of low degree. He hath filled the hungry with good things, and the rich he hath sent empty away.

Jimmie Higgins
by BEN HANFORD

A New York printer who literally gave his life for the socialist movement, dying of consumption caused by overwork. He was the party's candidate for Vice-president in 1904.

A comrade who shall be called Jimmie Higgins because that is not his name, and who shall be styled a painter for the very good reason that he is not a painter, has perhaps had a greater influence in keeping me keyed up to my work in the labor movement than any other person.

Jimmie Higgins is neither broad-shouldered nor thick-chested. He is neither pretty nor strong. A little, thin, weak, pale-faced chap. But he is strong enough to support a mother with equal physical disabilities. Strong enough to put in ten years of unrecognized and unexcelled service to the cause of Socialism.

What did he do? Everything.

He has made more Socialist speeches than any man in America. Not that he did the talking; but he carried the platform on his bent shoulders when the platform committee failed to be on hand.

Then he hustled around to another branch and got their platform out. Then he got a glass of water for "the speaker." That same evening or the day before he had distributed hand-bills advertising the meeting.

Previously he had informed his branch as to "the best corner" in the district for drawing a crowd. Then he distributed leaflets at the meeting, and helped to take the platform down and carry it back to headquarters, and got subscribers for Socialist papers.

The next day the same, and so on all through the campaign, and one campaign after another. When he had a job, which was none too often, for Jimmie was not an extra good workman and was always one of the first to be laid off, he would distribute Socialist papers among his fellows during the noon hour, or take a run down to the gate of some factory and give out Socialist leaflets to the employees who came out to lunch.

What did he do? Jimmie Higgins did everything, anything. Whatever was to be done, THAT was Jimmie's job.

The Marseillaise
by CLAUDE JOSEPH ROUGET DE LISLE

French captain of engineers, 1760-1836. He composed this most famous of all revolutionary songs in 1792 when the French republicans were resisting the might of all Europe's monarchs.

Ye sons of toil, awake to glory!
  Hark, hark, what myriads bid you rise;
Your children, wives and grandsires hoary--
  Behold their tears and hear their cries!
Shall hateful tyrants, mischief breeding,
  With hireling hosts, a ruffian band,—
Affright and desolate the land,
While peace and liberty lie bleeding?

CHORUS

  To arms! to arms! ye brave!
    Th' avenging sword unsheathe!
  March on, march on, all hearts resolved
    On Victory or Death.

With luxury and pride surrounded,
  The vile, insatiate despots dare,
Their thirst for gold and power unbounded,
  To mete and vend the light and air;
Like beasts of burden would they load us,
  Like gods would bid their slaves adore,
  But Man is Man, and who is more?
Then shall they longer lash and goad us? (Chorus)

O Liberty! can man resign thee,
  Once having felt thy generous flame?
Can dungeons' bolts and bars confine thee,
  Or whips thy noble spirit tame?
Too long the world has wept bewailing,
  That Falsehood's dagger tyrants wield;
  But Freedom is our sword and shield,
And all their arts are unavailing! (Chorus)

The Necessity of Socialism
by SIDNEY WEBB
Pioneer of Fabian Socialism, 1859-1947

Why are these reformers not Socialists? Why do they hesitate to join the only party of social reform which has definite principles of action, and a clear vision of the course of economic evolution? Have they not paved the way by their progressive restrictions of the despotism of the private employer? And are they not constantly extending the sphere of social industry in the post office, the telegraphs, telephones, tramways, docks, harbors, markets, schools, the supply of gas, water, and electricity, and many other public undertakings? Are they not steadily increasing the local taxation of realized property, and recovering rent ,for public use, by the rates on rent for education, parks, free libraries, public baths, meals for school children and other social conveniences?

All these are Socialistic measures, that is they tend either to the recovery of some portion of the tribute which landlord and capitalist now levy or to the assumption by the community of the control of lands and industrial capital. These measures we would extend by increased taxation, and by the additions to such communal administration, in the hope of leavening the Individualist society in which we have to work. Such advances serve as palliatives of existing evils, as educational examples to the slow of understanding, as encouragements to the cautious and conservative. But whether the advance be slow or rapid, this we hold indisputable, that until the workers of this and every other country collectively own and control the instruments they must work with, till then are liberty and manhood impossible for the majority; and that until we cease to pay to non-effectives the half of our annual sustenance, it will be impossible for the many to obtain that existence and education in youth, that security and leisure in old age, and those opportunities for human and appreciative life, which the resources of our country and our civilization are amply sufficient to yield them.

Democracy and Socialism

(From a speech made to the Twenty-seventh Party Congress, February 1986)

BY MIKHAIL GORBACHEV

Last President of the Union of Soviet Socialist Republics, he introduced
democratic reforms. He was awarded the Nobel Peace Prize in 1990
for his efforts in ending the Cold War; born 1931

Democracy is the wholesome and pure air without which a socialist public organization cannot live a full-blooded life.

The Curse of Free Enterprise

(From "One-Dimensional Man")

BY HERBERT MARCUSE

American professor and political philosopher, 1898-1979

Freedom of enterprise was from the beginning not altogether a
blessing. As the liberty to work or to starve, it spelled toil, insecurity,
and fear for the vast majority of the population. If the individual
were no longer compelled to prove himself on the market, as a free
economic subject, the disappearance of this freedom would be one
of the greatest achievements of civilization.

BOOK XVI

Struggle for Equality

America has been and remains the center of one of man's greatest struggles for freedom and equality. It was the magnificent fight for the abolition of slavery, and today it is continued as the historic struggle for equality between men of all colors and races.

The Freedom

(Negro Slave Song)

Oh! Freedom, oh! Freedom,
Oh! Freedom, over me;
And before I'll be a slave
I'll be buried in my grave,
And go home to my God
And be free.

The Vow I Take

by WILLIAM LLOYD GARRISON

America's most ardent anti-slavery agitator, 1805-1879. The following pronouncement, presented in its entirety, marked the beginning of the anti-slavery campaign;
it appeared as the editorial statement in the first issue of *The Liberator*.

In the month of August, I issued proposals for publishing
The Liberator in Washington City; but the enterprise, though
hailed in different sections of the country, was palsied by public
indifference. Since that time, the removal of the *Genius of
Universal Emancipation* to the Seat of Government has rendered
less imperious the establishment of a similar periodical in that
quarter.

During my recent tour for the purpose of exciting the minds
of the people by a series of discourses on the subject of slavery,
every place that I visited gave fresh evidence of the fact that a
greater revolution in public sentiment was to be effected in the
free States—*and particularly in New England*—than in the South.
I found contempt more bitter, opposition more active, detraction
more relentless, prejudice more stubborn, and apathy more
frozen, than among slave-owners themselves. Of course, there
were individual exceptions to the contrary. This state of things
afflicted, but did not dishearten me. I determined at every hazard
to lift up the standard of emancipation in the eyes of the
nation, *within sight of Bunker Hill and in the birthplace of
liberty*. That standard is now unfurled; and long may it float,
unhurt by the spoliations of time or the missiles of a desperate
foe—yea, till every chain be broken, and every bondman set free!
Let Southern oppressors tremble—let their secret abettors tremble

—let their Northern apologists tremble—let all enemies of the persecuted blacks tremble.

I deem the publication of my original Prospectus unnecessary, as it has obtained a wide circulation. The principles therein inculcated will be steadily pursued in this paper, excepting that I shall not array myself as the political partisan of any man. In defending the great cause of human rights, I wish to derive the assistance of all religions and of all parties.

Assenting to the "self-evident truth" maintained in the American Declaration of Independence, "that all men are created equal, and endowed by their Creator with certain inalienable rights— among which are life, liberty, and the pursuit of happiness," I shall strenuously contend for the immediate enfranchisement of our slave population. In Park Street Church, on the Fourth of July, 1829, in an address on slavery, I unreflectingly assented to the popular but pernicious doctrine of *gradual* abolition. I seize this opportunity to make a full and unequivocal recantation and thus publicly to ask pardon of my God, of my country, and of my brethren, the poor slaves, for having uttered a sentiment so full of timidity, injustice and absurdity. A similar recantation, from my pen, was published in the *Genius of Universal Emancipation* at Baltimore, in September, 1829. My conscience is now satisfied.

I am aware that many object to the severity of my language; but is there not cause for severity? I *will be* as harsh as truth, and as uncompromising as justice. On this subject, I do not wish to think, or speak, or write, with moderation. No! no! Tell a man whose house is on fire to give a moderate alarm; tell him to moderately rescue his wife from the hands of the ravisher; tell the mother to gradually extricate her babe from the fire into which it has fallen;—but urge me not to use moderation in a cause like the present. I am in earnest—I will not equivocate—I will not excuse—I will not retreat a single inch—AND I WILL BE HEARD. The apathy of the people is enough to make every statue leap from its pedestal and to hasten the resurrection of the dead.

It is pretended that I am retarding the cause of emancipation by the coarseness of my invective and the precipitancy of my measures. *The charge is not true.* On this question my influence —humble as it is—is felt at this moment to a considerable extent, and shall be felt in coming years—not perniciously, but beneficially—not as a curse, but as a blessing; and posterity will bear witness that I was right. I desire to thank God that He enables me to disregard "the fear of man which bringeth a snare," and to speak his truth in its simplicity and power.

And here I close with this fresh dedication:

Oppression! I have seen thee, face to face,
And met thy cruel eye and cloudy brow;
But thy soul-withering glance I fear not now—
For dread to prouder feelings doth give place
Of deep abhorrence! Scouring the disgrace
Of slavish knees that at thy footstool bow,
I also kneel—but with far other vow
Do hail thee and thy herd of hirelings base:—
I swear, while life-blood warms my throbbing veins,
Still to oppose and thwart, with heart and hand,
The brutalizing sway—till Africa's chains
Are burst, and Freedom rules the rescued land,—
Trampling Oppression and his iron rod:
Such is the vow I take—SO HELP ME GOD!

The True Face of Slavery
by FREDERICK DOUGLASS
Ex-slave who became the most inspiring Black fighter for
emancipation, 1817–1895

It was the interest and business of the slaveholders to study human nature, and the slave nature in particular, with a view to practical results; and many of them attained astonishing proficiency in this direction. They had to deal not with earth, wood, and stone, but with MEN; and by every regard they had for their safety and prosperity they had need to know the material on which they were to work. So much intellect as the slaveholder had round him required watching. Their safety depended on their vigilance.

Conscious of the injustice and wrong they were every hour perpetrating, and knowing what they themselves would do if they were the victims of such wrongs, they were constantly looking out for the first signs of dread retribution. They watched, therefore, with skilled and practiced eyes, and learned to read, with great accuracy, the state of mind and heart of the slave through his sable face. Unusual sobriety, apparent abstraction, sullenness, and indifference,—indeed, any mood out of the common way,—afforded ground for suspicion and inquiry. Relying on their superior position and wisdom, they would often hector the slave into a confession by affecting to know the truth of their accusations.

"You have got the devil in you, and we'll whip him out of you," they would say. I have often been put thus to the torture on bare suspicion.

This system had its disadvantages as well as its opposite—the slave being sometimes whipped into a confession of offenses which he never committed. It will be seen that the good old rule, "A man is to be held innocent until proved guilty," did not hold good on the slave plantation. Suspicion and torture were the approved methods of getting at the truth there.

He Shall Deliver the Needy
by HARRIET BEECHER STOWE

American writer, 1811-1896. *Uncle Tom's Cabin* was the single most important literary work to crystallize the opposing forces of abolition and pro-slavery prior to the Civil War; the following is from the preface to that novel.

The scenes of this story, as its title indicates, lie among a race hitherto ignored by the associations of polite and refined society; an exotic race, whose ancestors, born beneath a tropic sun, brought with them, and perpetuated to their descendants, a character so essentially unlike the hard and dominant Anglo-Saxon race, as for many years to have won from it only misunderstanding and contempt.

But another and better day is dawning; every influence of literature, of poetry, and of art, in our times, is becoming more and more in unison with the great master chord of Christianity, "good will to man."

The poet, the painter, and the artist now seek out and embellish the common and gentler humanities of life, and, under the allurements of fiction, breathe a humanizing and subduing influence, favorable to the development of the great principles of Christian brotherhood.

The hand of benevolence is everywhere stretched out, searching into abuses, righting wrongs, alleviating distresses, and bringing to the knowledge and sympathies of the world the lowly, the oppressed, and the forgotten.

In this general movement, unhappy Africa at last is remembered; Africa, who began the race of civilization and human progress in the dim, gray dawn of early time, but who, for centuries, has lain bound and bleeding at the foot of civilized and Christianized humanity, imploring compassion in vain.

But the heart of the dominant race, who have been her conquerors, her hard masters, has at length been turned towards her in mercy; and it has been seen how far nobler it is in nations to protect the feeble than to oppress them. Thanks be to God, the world has at last outlived the slave-trade!

The object of these sketches is to awaken sympathy and feeling for the African race, as they exist among us; to show their wrongs and sorrows, under a system so necessarily cruel and unjust as to defeat and do away the good effects of all that can be attempted for them, by their best friends, under it.

In doing this, the author can sincerely disclaim any invidious feeling towards those individuals who, often without any fault of their own, are involved in the trials and embarrassments of the legal relations of slavery.

Experience has shown her that some of the noblest of minds and hearts are often thus involved; and no one knows better than they do, that what may be gathered of the evils of slavery from sketches like these, is not the half that could be told, of the unspeakable whole.

In the northern states, these representations may, perhaps, be thought caricatures; in the southern states are witnesses who know their fidelity. What personal knowledge the author has had, of the truth of incidents such as here are related, will appear in its time.

It is a comfort to hope, as so many of the world's sorrows and wrongs have, from age to age been lived down, so a time shall come when sketches similar to these shall be valuable only as memorials of what has long ceased to be.

When an enlightened and Christianized community shall have, on the shores of Africa, laws, language, and literature, drawn from among us, may then the scenes of the house of bondage be to them like the remembrance of Egypt to the Israelite,—a motive of thankfulness to Him who hath redeemed them!

For, while politicians contend, and men are swerved this way and that by conflicting tides of interest and passion, the great cause of human liberty is in the hands of One, of whom it is said:

"He shall not fail nor be discouraged
Till He have set judgment in the earth."
"He shall deliver the needy when he crieth,
The poor, and him that hath no helper."
"He shall redeem their soul from deceit and violence,
And precious shall their blood be in His sight."

The Lynching
by CLAUDE MCKAY
Black American poet, 1890–1948

His spirit in smoke ascended to high heaven,
His father, by the cruelest way of pain,
Had bidden him to his bosom once again;
The awful sin remained still unforgiven.
All night a bright and solitary star
(Perchance the one that ever guided him,
Yet gave him up at last to Fate's wild whim),
Hung pitifully o'er the swinging char.
Day dawned, and soon the mixed crowds came to view
The ghostly body swaying in the sun:
The women thronged to look, but never a one
Showed sorrow in her eyes of steely blue;
And little lads, lynchers that were to be,
Danced round the dreadful thing in fiendish glee.

Pride in Race
by BOOKER T. WASHINGTON
Black American educator and writer, born a slave, c. 1859–1915

From any point of view, I had rather be what I am, a member
of the Negro race, than be able to claim membership with the
most favored of any other race. I have always been made sad
when I have heard members of any race claiming rights and
privileges, or certain badges of distinction, on the ground simply
that they were members of this or that race, regardless of their
own individual worth or attainments. I have been made to feel
sad for such persons because I am conscious of the fact that mere
connection with what is known as a superior race will not perma-

nently carry an individual forward, and mere connection with what is regarded as an inferior race will not finally hold an individual back if he possesses intrinsic individual merit. Every persecuted individual and race should get much consolation out of the great human law, which is universal and eternal, that merit, no matter under what skin found, is, in the long run, recognized and rewarded. This I have said here, not to call attention to myself as an individual, but to the race to which I am proud to belong.

The Strife of Honorable Men
(From "The Souls of Black Folk")
by W. E. BURGHARDT DU BOIS

Leading Black American sociologist, 1868–1963; one of the founders of the Niagara movement, which led to the National Association for the Advancement of Colored People.

The world-old phenomenon of the contact of diverse races of men is to have new exemplification during the new century. Indeed, the characteristic of our age is the contact of European civilization with the world's undeveloped peoples. Whatever we may say of the results of such contact in the past, it certainly forms a chapter in human action nor pleasant to look back upon. War, murder, slavery, extermination, and debauchery,—this has again and again been the result of carrying civilization and the blessed gospel to the isles of the sea and the heathen without the law. Nor does it altogether satisfy the conscience of the modern world to be told complacently that all this has been right and proper, the fated triumph of strength over weakness, of righteousness over evil, of superiors over inferiors. It would certainly be soothing if one could readily believe all this; and yet there are too many ugly facts for everything to be thus easily explained away. We feel and know that there are many delicate differences in race psychology, numberless changes that our crude social measurements are not yet able to follow minutely, which explain much of history and social development. At the same time, too, we know that these considerations have never adequately explained or excuse the triumph of brute force and cunning over weakness and innocence.

It is, then, the strife of all honorable men of the twentieth century to see that in the future competition of races the survival

A Slave Auction in Virginia

of the fittest shall mean the triumph of the good, the beautiful, and the true; that we may be able to preserve for future civilization all that is really fine and noble and strong, and not continue to put a premium on greed and impudence and cruelty. To bring this hope to fruition, we are compelled daily to turn more and more to a conscientious study of the phenomena of race contact,—to a study frank and fair, and not falsified and colored by our wishes or our fears. And we have in the South as fine a field for such a study as the world affords,—a field, to be sure, which the average American scientist deems somewhat beneath his dignity, and which the average man who is not a scientist knows all about, but nevertheless a line of study which by reason of the enormous race complications with which God seems about to punish this nation must increasingly claim our sober attention, study, and thought, we must ask, what are the actual relations of whites and blacks in the South? and we must be answered, not by apology or fault-finding, but by a plain, unvarnished tale.

In the civilized life of today the contact of men and their relations to each other fall in a few main lines of actions and communication: there is, first, the physical proximity of homes and dwelling places, the way in which neighborhoods group themselves and the contiguity of neighborhoods. Secondly, and in our age chiefest, there are the economic relations,—the methods by which individuals cooperate for earning a living, for the mutual satisfaction of wants, for the production of wealth. Next, there are the political relations, the cooperation in social control, in group government, in laying and paying the burden of taxation. In the fourth place there are the less tangible, but highly important, forms of intellectual contact and commerce, the interchange of ideas through conversation and conference, through periodicals and libraries; and, above all, the gradual formation for each community of that curious *tertium quid* which we call public opinion. Closely allied with this come the various forms of social contact in everyday life, in travel, in theatres, in house gatherings, in marrying and giving in marriage. Finally, there are the varying forms of religious enterprise, of moral teaching and benevolent endeavor. These are the principal ways in which men living in the same communities are brought into contact with each other. It is my present task, therefore, to indicate, from my point of view, how the black race in the South meets and mingles with the whites in these matters of everyday life.

First, as to physical dwelling. It is usually possible to draw in nearly every Southern community a physical color-line on the map, on the one side of which whites dwell and on the other Negroes. The winding and intricacy of the geographical color-line varies, of course, in different communities. I know some towns where a straight line drawn through the middle of the mainstreet separates nine-tenths of the whites fron nine-tenths of the blacks. In other towns the older settlement of whites has been encircled by a broad band of blacks; in still other cases little settlements or nuclei of blacks have sprung up amid surrounding whites. Usually in cities each street has its distinctive color, and only now and then do the colors meet in close proximity. Even in the country something of this segregation is manifest in the smaller areas, and of course in the larger phenomena of the Black Belt.

All this segregation by color is largely independent of that natural' clustering by social grades common to all communities. A Negro slum may be in dangerous proximity to a white residence quarter, while it is quite common to find a white slum planted in the heart of a respectable Negro district. One thing, however, seldom occurs: the best of the whites and the best of the Negroes almost never live in anything like close proximity. It thus happens that in nearly every Southern town and city, both whites and blacks see commonly the worst of each other. This is a vast change from the situation in the past, when, through the close contact of master and house-servant in the patriarchal big house, one found the best of both races in close contact and sympathy, while at the same time the squalor and dull round of toil among the field-hands was removed from the sight and hearing of the family. One can easily see how a person who saw slavery thus from his father's parlors, and sees freedom on the streets of a great city, fails to grasp or comprehend the whole of the new picture. On the other hand, the settled belief of the mass of Negroes that the Southern white people do not have the black man's best interests at heart has been intensified in later years by the continual contact of the better class of blacks with the worst representatives of the white race. . . .

I should be the last one to deny the patent weaknesses and shortcomings of the Negro people; I should be the last to withhold sympathy from the white South in its efforts to solve its intricate social problems. I freely acknowledged that it is possible, and sometimes best, that a partially undeveloped people should be ruled by the best of their stronger and better neighbors for their own good, until such time as they can start and fight the world's battles alone. I have already pointed out how sorely in need of such economic and spiritual guidance the emancipated Negro was, and I am quite willing to admit that if the representatives of the best white Southern public opinion were the ruling and guiding powers in the South today the conditions indicated would be fairly well fulfilled. But the point I have insisted upon, and now emphasize again, is that the best opinion of the South today is not the ruling opinion. That to leave the Negro helpless and without a ballot today is to leave him, not to the guidance of the best, but rather to the exploitation and debauchment of the worst; that this is no truer of the South than of the North,—of the North than of Europe: in any land, in any country under modern free competition, to lay any class of weak and despised people, be they white, black, or blue, at the political mercy of their stronger, richer, and more resourceful fellows, is a temptation which human nature seldom has withstood and seldom will withstand.

Lynching in Arkansas
by WALTER F. WHITE
President for many years of the National Association for the Advancement of Colored People, a Black of white appearance who refused to desert his race in social difficulties; 1893–1955

A narrow escape during an investigation of an alleged plot by Negroes in Arkansas to "massacre" all the white people of the State. It later developed that the Negroes had simply organized a cooperative society to combat their economic exploitation by landlords, merchants, and bankers, many of whom openly practiced peonage. I went as a representative of a Chicago newspaper to get the facts. Going first to the capital of the State, Little Rock, I interviewed the Governor and other officials and then proceeded to the scene of the trouble, Phillips County, in the heart of the cotton-raising area, close to the Mississippi.

As I stepped from the train at Elaine, the county seat, I was

Negro Slave Ship

closely watched by a crowd of men. Within half an hour of my arrival I had been asked by two shopkeepers, a restaurant waiter, and a ticket agent why I had come to Elaine, what my business was, and what I thought of the recent riot. The tension relaxed somewhat when I implied I was in sympathy with the mob. Little by little suspicion was lessened and then, the people being eager to have a metropolitan newspaper give their side of the story, I was shown "evidence" that the story of the massacre plot was well-founded, and not very clever attempts were made to guide me away from the truth.

Suspicion was given new birth when I pressed my inquiries too insistently concerning the share-cropping and tenant-farming system, which works somewhat as follows: Negro farmers enter into agreements to till specified plots of land, they to receive usually half of the crop for their labor. Should they be too poor to buy food, seed, clothing and other supplies, they are supplied these commodities by their landlords at designated store. When the crop is gathered the landowner takes it and sells it. By declaring that he has sold it at a figure far below the market price and by refusing to give itemized accounts of the supplies purchased during the year by the tenant, a landlord can (and in that region almost always does) so arrange it that the bill for supplies always exceeds the tenant's share of the crop. Individual Negroes who had protested against such thievery had been lynched. The new organization was simply a union to secure relief through the courts, which relief those who profited from the system meant to prevent. Thus the story of a "massacre" plot.

Suspicion of me took definite form when word was sent to Phillips County from Little Rock that it had been discovered that I was a Negro, though I knew nothing about the message at the time. I walked down West Cherry Street, the main thoroughfare of Elaine, one day on my way to the jail, where I had an appointment with the sheriff, who was going to permit me to interview some of the Negro prisoners who were charged with being implicated in the alleged plot. A tall, heavy-set Negro passed me and, *sotto voce*, told me as he passed that he had something important to tell me, and that I should turn to the right at the next corner and follow him. Some inner sense bade me obey. When we had got out of sight of other persons the Negro told me not to go to the jail, that there was great hostility in the town against me and that they planned harming me. In the man's manner there was something which made me certain he was telling the truth. Making my way to the railroad station, since my interview with the prisoners (the sheriff and jailer being present), was unlikely to add anything to my story, I was able to board one of the two trains a day out of Elaine. When I explained to the conductor—he looked at me so inquiringly—that I had no ticket because delays in Elaine had given me no time to purchase one, he exclaimed, "Why, Mister, you're leaving just when the fun is going to start! There's a damned yaller nigger down there passing for white and the boys are going to have some fun with him."

I asked him the nature of the fun.

"Wal, when they get through with him," he explained grimly, "he won't pass for white no more."

Back to Harlem
by JAMES BALDWIN
American essayist and novelist, 1924–1987

Harlem, physically at least, has changed very little in my parents' lifetime or in mine. Now as then the buildings are old and in desperate need of repair, the streets are crowded and dirty, there are too many human beings per square block. Rents are 10 to 58 per cent higher than anywhere else on the city; food, expensive everywhere, is more expensive here and of an inferior quality; and now that the war is over and money is dwindling, clothes are carefully shopped for and seldom bought. Negroes, traditionally the last to be hired and the first to be fired, are finding jobs harder to get, and while prices are rising implacably, wages are going down. All over Harlem now there is felt the same bitter expectancy with which, in my childhood, we awaited winter: it is coming and it will be hard; there is nothing anyone can do about it.

All of Harlem is pervaded by a sense of congestion, rather like the insistent, maddening, claustrophobic pounding in the skull that comes from trying to breathe in a very small room with all the windows shut. Yet the white man walking through Harlem is not at all likely to find it sinister or more wretched than any other slum.

Harlem wears to the casual observer a casual face; no one remarks that—considering the history of black men and women and the legends that have sprung up about them, to say nothing of the ever-present policemen, wary on the street corners—the face is, indeed, somewhat excessively casual and may not be as open or as careless as it seems. If an outbreak of more than usual violence occurs, as in 1935 or in 1943, it is met with sorrow and surprise and rage; the social hostility of the rest of the city feeds on this as proof that they were right all along, and the hostility increases; speeches are made, committees are set up, investigations ensue. Steps are taken to right the wrong, without, however, expanding or demolishing the ghetto. The idea is to make it less of a social liability, a process about as helpful as make-believe to a leper. Thus we have the Boys' Club on West 134th Street, the playground at West 131st and Fifth Avenue; and, since Negroes will not be allowed to live in Stuyvesant Town, Metropolitan Life is thoughtfully erecting a housing project called Riverton in the center of Harlem; however, it is not likely that any but the professional class of Negroes—and not all of them—will be able to pay the rent.

If We Must Die
by CLAUDE McKAY

If we must die—let it not be like hogs
  Hunted and penned in an inglorious spot,
While round us bark the mad and hungry dogs,
  Making their mock at our accursed lot.
If we must die—oh, let us nobly die,
  So that our precious blood may not be shed
In vain; then even the monsters we defy
  Shall be constrained to honor us though dead!

Oh, Kinsmen! We must meet the common foe;
  Though far outnumbered, let us still be brave,
And for their thousand blows deal one death-blow!
  What though before us lies the open grave?
Like men we'll face the murderous, cowardly pack,
  Pressed to the wall, dying, but—fighting back!

An Appeal for Human Rights

A full-page advertisement that appeared in *Atlanta Constitution*, on March 9, 1960
—an historic document in the struggle for Negro rights.

We, the students of the six affiliated institutions forming the
Atlanta University Center—Clark, Morehouse, Morris Brown,
and Spelman Colleges, Atlanta University, and the Interdenomi-
national Theological Center—have joined our hearts, minds, and
bodies in the cause of gaining those rights which are inherently
ours as members of the human race and as citizens of these
United States.

We pledge our unqualified support to those students in this
nation who have recently been engaged in the significant movement to secure certain long-awaited rights and privileges. This
protest, like the bus boycott in Montgomery, has shocked many
people throughout the world. Why? Because they had not quite
realized the unanimity of spirit and purpose which motivates the
thinking and action of the great majority of the Negro people.
The students who instigate and participate in these sit-down
protests are dissatisfied, not only with the existing conditions, but
with the snail-like speed at which they are being ameliorated.
Every normal human being wants to walk the earth with dignity
and abhors any and all proscriptions placed upon him because
of race or color. In essence, this is the meaning of the sit-down
protests that are sweeping this nation today.

We do not intend to wait placidly for these rights which are
already legally and morally ours to be meted out to us one at
a time. Today's youth will not sit by submissively, while being
denied all of the rights, privileges, and joys of life. We want to
state clearly and unequivocally that we cannot tolerate, in a
nation professing democracy and among people professing Christianity, the discriminatory conditions under which the Negro is
living today in Atlanta, Georgia—supposedly one of the most
progressive cities in the South.

Among the inequalities and injustices in Atlanta and in
Georgia against which we protest, the following are outstanding
examples:

(1) Education:
In the Public School System, facilities for Negroes and whites
are separate and unequal. Double sessions continue in about
half of the Negro Public Schools, and many Negro children

travel ten miles a day in order to reach a school that will admit them.

On the university level, the state will pay a Negro to attend a school out of the state rather than admit him to the University of Georgia, Georgia Tech, the Georgia Medical School, and other tax-supported public institutions.

According to a recent publication, in the fiscal year 1958 a total of $31,632,057.18 was spent in the State institutions of higher education for whites only. In the Negro State Colleges only $2,001,177.06 was spent. The publicly supported institutions of higher education are interracial now, except that they deny admissions to Negro Americans.

(2) Jobs:
Negroes are denied employment in the majority of city, state, and federal governmental jobs, except in the most menial capacities.

(3) Housing:
While Negroes constitute 32% of the population of Atlanta, they are forced to live within 16% of the area of the city.

Statistics also show that the bulk of the Negro population is still:

a. locked into the more undesirable and overcrowded areas of the city;
b. paying a proportionally higher percentage of income for rental and purchase of generally lower quality property;
c. blocked by political and direct or indirect racial restrictions in its efforts to secure better housing.

(4) Voting:
Contrary to statements made in Congress recently by several Southern Senators, we know that in many counties in Georgia and other southern states, Negro college graduates are declared unqualified to vote and are not permitted to register.

(5) Hospitals:
Compared with facilities for other people in Atlanta and Georgia, those for Negroes are unequal and totally inadequate.

Reports show that Atlanta's 14 general hospitals and 9 related institutions provide some 4,000 beds. Except for some 430 beds at Grady Hospital, Negroes are limited to the 250 beds in three private Negro hospitals. Some of the hospitals barring Negroes were built with federal funds.

(6) Movies, Concerts, Restaurants:

Negroes are barred from most downtown movies and segregated in the rest.

Negroes must even sit in a segregated section of the Municipal Auditorium.

If a Negro is hungry, his hunger must wait until he comes to a "colored" restaurant, and even his thirst must await its quenching at a "colored" water fountain.

(7) Law Enforcement:

There are grave inequalities in the area of law enforcement. Too often, Negroes are maltreated by officers of the law. An insufficient number of Negroes is employed in the law-enforcing agencies. They are seldom, if ever, promoted. Of 830 policemen in Atlanta only 36 are Negroes.

We have briefly mentioned only a few situations in which we are discriminated against. We have understated rather than overstated the problems. These social evils are seriously plaguing Georgia, the South, the nation, and the world.

We hold that:

(1) The practice of racial segregation is not in keeping with the ideals of Democracy and Christianity.

(2) Racial segregation is robbing not only the segregated but the segregator of his human dignity. Furthermore, the propagation of racial prejudice is unfair to the generations yet unborn.

(3) In times of war, the Negro has fought and died for his country; yet he still has not been accorded first-class citizenship.

(4) In spite of the fact that the Negro pays his share of taxes, he does not enjoy participation in city, county, and state government at the level where laws are enacted.

(5) The social, economic, and political progress of Georgia is retarded by segregation and prejudices.

(6) America is fast losing the respect of other nations by the poor example which she sets in the area of race relations.

It is unfortunate that the Negro is being forced to fight, in any way, for what is due him and is freely accorded other Americans. It is unfortunate that even today some people should hold to the erroneous idea of racial superiority, despite the fact that the world is fast moving toward an integrated humanity.

The time has come for the people of Atlanta and Georgia to

take a good look at what is really happening in this country, and to stop believing those who tell us that everything is fine and equal, and that the Negro is happy and satisfied.

It is to be regretted that there are those who still refuse to recognize the over-riding supremacy of the Federal Law.

Our churches, which are ordained by God and claim to be the houses of all people, foster segregation of the races to the point of making Sunday the most segregated day of the week.

We, the students of the Atlanta University Center, are driven by past and present events to assert our feelings to the citizens of Atlanta and to the world.

We, therefore, call upon all people in authority—State, County, and City officials; all leaders in civic life—ministers, teachers, and business men; and all people of good will to assert themselves and abolish these injustices. We must say in all candor that we plan to use every legal and non-violent means at our disposal to secure full citizenship rights as members of this great Democracy of ours.

I Dream

by LANGSTON HUGHES

I dream
A world where man
No other man will scorn,
Where love will bless the earth
And peace its paths adorn.
I dream a world where all
Will know sweet freedom's way,
Where greed no longer saps the soul
Nor avarice blights our day.
A world I dream where black or white,
Whatever race you be,
Will share the bounties of the earth
And every man is free,
Where wretchedness will hang its head
And joy, like a pearl,
Attends the needs of all mankind—
Of such I dream, my world!

Letter from Birmingham Jail

(From " Why We Can't Wait")
BY MARTIN LUTHER KING, JR.
Leader of American civil rights movement, 1929-1968

Law and order exist for the purpose of establishing justice ... when they fail in this purpose they become dangerously structured dams that block the flow of social progress.

The Culture of Discrimination

(From "The Other America")
BY MICHAEL HARRINGTON

To be a Negro is to participate in a culture of poverty and fear that goes far deeper than any law for or against discrimination . . . . After racist statutes are all struck down, after legal equality has been achieved in the schools and in the courts, there remains the profound institutionalized and abiding wrong that white America has worked on the Negro for so long.

(From "Lady Sings the Blues," written with William Duffy)

BILLIE HOLIDAY
American singer who really could sing the blues.

You can be up to your boobies in white satin, with gardenias in your hair and no sugar cane for miles, but you can still be working on a plantation.

Soul Force

(From a letter written in 1957)
BY MARTIN LUTHER KING, JR.

It is my hope that as the Negro plunges deeper into the quest for freedom and justice he will plunge even deeper into the philosophy of non-violence. The Negro all over the South must come to the point that he can say to his white brother: "We will match your capacity to inflict suffering with our capacity to endure suffering. We will meet your physical force with soul force. We will not hate you, but we will not obey your evil laws. We will soon wear you down by the pure capacity to suffer.

Not Just an American Problem, but a World Problem

(From a speech given on February 16, 1965, shortly before his assassination)

BY MALCOLM X

American Black leader who was part of the Black Muslim movement that advocated separatism. He later converted to orthodox Islam; 1925–1965

...we realize that we have to fight against the evils of society that has failed to produce brotherhood for every member of that society. This in no way means that we're antiwhite, antiblue, antigreen, or antiyellow. We're antiwrong. We're antidiscrimination. We're anti-segregation. We're against anybody who wants to practice some form of segregation or discrimination against us because we don't happen to be a color that's acceptable to you. We believe in fighting that.

We don't judge a man because of the color of his skin. We don't judge you because you're white. We don't judge because you're Black. We don't judge you because you're brown. We judge you because of what you do, what you practice. And as long as you practice evil, we're against you. And to us, the worst form of evil is the evil that's based upon judging a man because of the color of his skin. I don't think anybody here can deny that we're living in a society that just doesn't judge a man according to his talent, according to his know-how, according to his academic background, or lack of academic background. This society judges a man solely upon the color of his skin. If you're white, you can go forward, if you're Black, you have to fight your way every step of the way, and you still don't go forward.

We're not against people because they're white. But we're against those who practice racism.

Suppression of Women

(From "In Search of Our Mother's Gardens")
BY ALICE WALKER
American author and poet

As for those who think the Arab world promises freedom, the briefest study of its routine traditional treatment of blacks (slavery) and women (purdah) will provide relief from all illusion. If Malcolm X had been a black woman, his last message to the world would have been entirely different. The brotherhood of Moslem men—all colors—may exist here, but part of the glue that holds them together is the thorough suppression of women.

(From a letter from Birmingham jail, 1963)

BY MARTIN LUTHER KING, JR.

We were here before the mighty words of the Declaration of Independence were etched across the pages of history. Our forebears labored without wages. They made cotton "king." And yet out of bottomless vitality, they continued to thrive and develop. If the cruelties of slavery could not stop us, the opposition we now face will surely fail ...

The goal of America is freedom, abused and scorned tho' we may be, our destiny is tied up with America's destiny.

BOOK XVII

The Freedoms

The search for human dignity continues on many fronts. Man aspires to freedom from fear, freedom of expression, freedom to read.

Fredome

by John Barbour
English poet, c. 1316-1396

A! Fredome is a nobill thing!
Fredome mayse man to haiff liking!
Fredome all solace to man giffis:
He levys at ese that frely levys;
A noble hart may haiff nane ease,
Na ellys nocht that may him plese,
Gyff fredome failythe: for fre liking
Is yearnyt ow'r all othir thing
Na he, that ay hase levyt fre,
May nocht knaw weill the propyrte,
The angry, na the wretchyt dome,
That is cowplyt to foule thyrldome.
Bot gyff he had assayit it,
Than all perquer he suld it wyt;
And suld think fredome mar to pryse
Than all the gold in warld that is.

By Gunnar Myrdal
Swedish sociologist, author of most important
single study of American race relations, 1898–1987

The Negro problem is not only America's greatest failure but
also America's incomparably great opportunity for the future. If
America should follow its own deepest convictions, its well-being
at home would be increased directly. At the same time America's
prestige and power abroad would rise immensely. The century-
old dream of American patriots, that America should give to the
entire world its own freedoms and its own faith, would come true.
America can demonstrate that justice, equality and cooperation
are possible between white and colored persons. . . .

*America is free to choose whether the Negro shall remain her
liability or become her opportunity.*

The Four Freedoms
by Franklin Delano Roosevelt

In the future days, which we seek to secure, we look forward to a world founded upon four essential freedoms.

The first is freedom of speech and expression—everywhere in the world.

The second is freedom of every person to worship God in his own way—everywhere in the world.

The third is freedom from want, which, translated into world terms, means economic understandings which will secure to every nation a healthy peacetime life for its inhabitants—everywhere in the world.

The fourth is freedom from fear, which, translated into world terms, means a world-wide reduction of armaments to such a point and in such a thorough fashion that no nation will be in a position to commit an act of physical aggression against any neighbor—anywhere in the world.

This is no vision of a distant millenium. It is a definite basis for a kind of world attainable in our own time and generation. That kind of world is the very antithesis of the so-called new order of tyranny which the dictators seek to create with the crash of a bomb.

The Belief in Heresy
by Carey McWilliams
Contemporary American author and editor, born 1905

The belief in heresy is tantamount to the belief in original sin. It is a variation of the notion that people can be divided into categories of the "damned" and the "elect" for it implies that there are "good" ideas and "bad" ideas and that problems are merely the result of bad ideas. Thus problems are not to be solved by the application of scientific method but by the application of thought control, for if enough people have the right ideas, how can there be any problems? The heresy manual of the inquisitor with its neatly graduated scale of punishments for a vast specification of heresies was the counterpart of the medieval conception of a purgatory in which endless special punishments had been worked out for an unending catalogue of minutely defined sins and punishments. The belief in heresy is a form of intellectual predestination and, as such, it is the one real heresy.

By a strange but understandable paradox, the more we yield to the anti-Communist hysteria, the more we minimize the differences between democracy and Communism. The more violently we "fight Communism," as a heresy, the more we are compelled to borrow and apply the methods of the police state. Already a note of official "correctness" has begun to invade even informal political discussions and nearly everyone is nowadays concerned to avoid, if possible, any criticism of the main tenets of the anti-Communist ideology. Today it is quite clear that any criticism of social conditions is likely to be met with a charge of Communism and the knowledge that this can happen has had a clear tendency to stifle social criticism. The differences between democracy and Communism are still great; but they need to be clarified, not confused.

Before we proceed any further along the road that leads to the police state, it might be well to consider a figure of speech suggested by Jeremiah Burroughs which can be read today as a parable. "It is with the saints here," he wrote, "as with the boughs of trees in time of storm. You shall see the boughs beat one upon another as if they would beat one another to pieces, as if armies were fighting; but this is but while the wind, while the tempest lasts; stay awhile, you shall see every bough standing in its own order and comeliness; why? because they are all united in one root; if any bough be rotten, the storm breaks it." The boughs grind against each other because the storm drives them; they do not drive the storm. It is with the storm, not with the beating of the boughs, that we should be concerned; for it is only while the wind, while the tempest lasts, that the boughs beat one upon the other.

The House Afire
by Harold L. Ickes
Bull Moose Republican who became a major New Dealer, 1874-1952

What constitutes an American? Not color nor race nor religion. Not the pedigree of his family nor the place of his birth. Not the coincidence of his citizenship. Not his social status nor his bank account. Not his trade nor his profession. An American is one who loves justice and believes in the dignity of man. An American is one who will fight for his freedom and that of his neighbor. An American is one who will sacrifice prosperity, ease and security in order that he and his children may retain the rights of free men.

An American is one in whose heart is engraved the immortal second sentence of the Declaration of Independence.

Americans have always known how to fight for their rights and their way of life. Americans are not afraid to fight. They fight joyously in a just cause.

We Americans know that freedom, like peace, is indivisible. We cannot retain our liberty if three-fourths of the world is enslaved. Brutality, injustice and slavery, if practiced as dictators would have them, universally and systematically, in the long run would destroy us as surely as a fire raging in our nearby neighbor's house would burn ours if we didn't help to put out his.

The Freedom to Read

An Open Letter to Prime Minister Mackenzie King of Canada on the banning in Canada of Farrell's novel, *Bernard Clare*

by JAMES T. FARRELL
American novelist, 1904–1979

For some years now, the prejudiced forces of censorship have been straining at the leash in the United States in order to begin a new witch hunt against serious and honest writing. These forces need only governmental precedents in order to come out into the open and to begin a reactionary campaign of legal book lynching in this country. If your government does not rescind this unwarranted ban on my book, it can well provide the necessary example. And if this happens, it will be clear where the public responsibility for such a campaign can be laid. Because of facts such as these which I present in my letter, the action of Canadian customs officials is one which does and must concern the public of both the United States and Canada. I therefore regard it as my duty to protest this banning, to call it to the attention of the writers and the readers of both the United States and the Dominion of Canada and to call upon them to give me public support in my effort to have this ban rescinded.

In conclusion, may I stress the fact that governmental censorship of serious works of literature can only lead one to conclude that such censorship is based on distrust of those who read books, fear that they are not free enough, decent enough, to read serious works without being deleteriously affected. If this is the case, then one must look for the reason in the conditions of life, the conditions of freedom, and the conditions of education in a country which resorts to this practice of book banning. Further, distrust of the people, expressed through censorship, can lead to ever deepening reaction; it can only create fear in the hearts and minds of creative artists. It can only put hypocrisy in place of frankness and a dedication to truth.

Permit me, thus, in the light of these considerations, formally to request that the ban on my novel, *Bernard Clare*, be removed.

The Competition of Ideas
by ADLAI E. STEVENSON
American statesman, 1900–1965

A free society means a society based on free competition and there is no more important competition than competition of ideas, competition in opinion. This form of competition is essential to the preservation of a free press. Indeed, I think the press should set an example to the nation in increasing opposition to uniformity.

What I think I detect is a growing uniformity of outlook among publishers—a tendency toward the trade-association mentality of uniformity of attitude toward the public, the customer, if not toward one another as producers of consumer goods. I doubt if this shoe fits the peculiar function of the newspaper.

I think you will agree that we cannot risk complacency. We need to be rededicated every day to the unfinished task of keeping our free press truly free. We need to work even harder for the time when all editors will honor their profession, when all publishers will have a sense of responsibility equal to their power and thus regain their power, if I may put it that way.

It's not honest convictions honestly stated that concern me. Rather it is the tendency of many papers, and I include columnists, commentators, analysts, feature writers, and so on, to argue editorially from the personal objective, rather than from the whole truth. As the old jury lawyer said: "And these, gentlemen, are the conclusions on which I base my facts."

In short, it seems to me that facts, truth, should be just as sacred in the editorial column as the news column. And, as I have said, happily most papers, but by no means all, do struggle with sincerity for accuracy in the news. Coming from Chicago, of course, I am not unfamiliar with the phenomenon of an editorial in every news column!

What I am saying is that the press cannot condemn demagoguery, claptrap, distortion and falsehood in politicians and public life on the one hand and practice the same abuses on the public themselves, on the other. I know the people are smarter than many politicians think and sometimes I suspect that even editors underestimate them.

Sexual Freedom
(From "Sex Without Guilt")
by ALBERT ELLIS
American psychologist and authority on sex problems, born 1913

Every human being, just because he exists, should have the right to as much (or as little), as varied (or as monotonous), as intense (or as mild), as enduring (or as brief) sex enjoyments as he prefers—as long as, in the process of acquiring these preferred satisfactions, he does not needlessly, forcefully, or unfairly interfere with the sexual (or non-sexual) rights and satisfactions of others.

This means, more specifically, that in my estimation society should not legislate or invoke social sanctions against sex acts performed by individuals who are reasonably competent and well-educated adults: who use no force or duress in the course of their sex relations; who do not, without the consent of their partners, specifically injure these partners; and who participate in their sex activities privately, out of sight and sound of unwilling observers.

If this and only this kind of limitation were applied in modern communities, only a few distinct sex acts would be considered to be illegal or illegitimate. Included among these antisocial activities would be seduction of a minor by an adult; rape; sexual assault and murder; and exhibitionism or other forms of public display....

In actual practice (alas!), our own society is such that, in order to live successfully within its laws and mores, the average highly sexed individual has to curb not merely many but probably the overwhelming majority of his sex desires and practices.

Universal Declaration of Human Rights

Official document adopted by the Third Session of the General Assembly of the
United Nations; reprinted here in full.

Preamble

WHEREAS recognition of the inherent dignity and of the
equal and inalienable rights of all members of the human family
is the foundation of freedom, justice and peace in the world,

WHEREAS disregard and contempt for human rights have
resulted in barbarous acts which have outraged the conscience of
mankind, and the advent of a world in which human beings shall
enjoy freedom of speech and belief and freedom from fear and
want has been proclaimed as the highest aspiration of the common
people,

WHEREAS it is essential, if man is not to be compelled to have
recourse, as a last recourse, to rebellion against tyranny and oppression, that human rights should be protected by the rule of law,

WHEREAS it is essential to promote the development of
friendly relations between nations,

WHEREAS the peoples of the United Nations have in the
Charter reaffirmed their faith in fundamental human rights, in
the dignity and worth of the human person and in the equal
rights of men and women and have determined to promote social
progress and better standards of life in larger freedom,

WHEREAS Member States have pledged themselves to achieve,
in cooperation with the United Nations, the promotion of universal respect for and observance of human rights and fundamental freedoms,

WHEREAS a common understanding of these rights and freedoms is of the greatest importance for the full realisation of this
pledge,

NOW THEREFORE

THE GENERAL ASSEMBLY

proclaims

THIS UNIVERSAL DECLARATION OF HUMAN RIGHTS

as a common standard of achievement for all peoples and all nations, to the end that every individual and every organ of society,
keeping this Declaration constantly in mind, shall strive by teaching and education to promote respect for these rights and freedoms and by progressive measures, national and international, to
secure their universal and effective recognition and observance,

both among the peoples of the Member States themselves and among the peoples of territories under their jurisdiction.

ARTICLE 1   All human beings are born free and equal in dignity and rights. They are endowed with reason and conscience and should act towards one another in a spirit of brotherhood.

ARTICLE 2   Everyone is entitled to all the rights and freedoms set forth in this Declaration, without distinction of any kind, such as race, colour, sex, language, religion, political or other opinion, national or social origin, property, birth or other status. Furthermore, no distinction shall be made on the basis of the political, jurisdictional or international status of the country or territory to which a person belongs, whether it be independent, trust, non-self-governing or under any other limitation of sovereignty.

ARTICLE 3   Everyone has the right to life, liberty and security of person.

ARTICLE 4   No one shall be held in slavery or servitude; slavery and the slave trade shall be prohibited in all their forms.

ARTICLE 5   No one shall be subjected to torture or to cruel, inhuman or degrading treatment or punishment.

ARTICLE 6   Everyone has the right to recognition everywhere as a person before the law.

ARTICLE 7   All are equal before the law and are entitled without any discrimination to equal protection of the law. All are entitled to equal protection against any discrimination in violation of this Declaration and against any incitement to such discrimination.

ARTICLE 8   Everyone has the right to an effective remedy by the competent national tribunals for acts violating the fundamental rights granted him by the constitution or by law.

ARTICLE 9   No one shall be subjected to arbitrary arrest, detention or exile.

ARTICLE 10   Everyone is entitled in full equality to a fair and public hearing by an independent and impartial tribunal, in the determination of his rights and obligations and of any criminal charge against him.

ARTICLE 11 (1)   Everyone charged with a penal offense has the right to be presumed innocent until proved guilty according to law in a public trial at which he has had all the guarantees necessary for his defence.

(2) No one shall be held guilty of any penal offence on account of any act or omission which did not constitute a penal offence, under national or international law, at the time when it was committed. Nor shall a heavier penalty be imposed than the one that was applicable at the time the penal offence was committed.

ARTICLE 12   No one shall be subjected to arbitrary interference with his privacy, family, home or correspondence, nor to attacks upon his honour and reputation. Everyone has the right to the protection of the law against such interference or attacks.

ARTICLE 13 (1)   Everyone has the right to freedom of movement and residence within the borders of each state.

(2)   Everyone has the right to leave any country, including his own, and to return to his country.

ARTICLE 14 (1)   Everyone has the right to seek and to enjoy in other countries asylum from persecution.

(2)   This right may not be invoked in the case of prosecutions genuinely arising from non-political crimes or from acts contrary to the purposes and principles of the United Nations.

ARTICLE 15 (1)   Everyone has the right to a nationality.

(2)   No one shall be arbitrarily deprived of his nationality nor denied the right to change his nationality.

ARTICLE 16 (1)   Men and women of full age, without any limitation due to race, nationality or religion, have the right to marry and to found a family. They are entitled to equal rights as to marriage, during marriage and at its dissolution.

(2)   Marriages shall be entered into only with the free and full consent of the intending spouses.

(3)   The family is the natural and fundamental group unit of society and is entitled to protection by society and the State.

ARTICLE 17 (1)   Everyone has the right to own property alone as well as in association with others.

(2)   No one shall be arbitrarily deprived of his property.

ARTICLE 18   Everyone has the right to freedom of thought, conscience and religion; this right includes freedom to change his religion or belief, and freedom, either alone or in community with others and in public or private, to manifest his religion or belief in teaching, practice, worship and observance.

ARTICLE 19   Everyone has the right to freedom of opinion and expression: this right includes freedom to hold opinions without interference and to seek, receive and impart information and ideas through any media and regardless of frontiers.

ARTICLE 20 (1)   Everyone has the right to freedom of peaceful assembly and association.

(2)   No one may be compelled to belong to an association.

ARTICLE 21 (1)   Everyone has the right to take part in the government of his country, directly or through freely chosen representatives.

(2)   Everyone has the right of equal access to public service in his country.

(3)   The will of the people shall be the basis of the authority of government; this will shall be expressed in periodic and genuine elections which shall be by universal and equal suffrage and shall be held by secret vote or by equivalent free voting procedures.

ARTICLE 22   Everyone, as a member of society, has the right to social security and is entitled to realisation, through national effort and international co-operation and in accordance with the organisation and resources of each State, of the economic, social and cultural rights indispensable for his dignity and the free development of his personality.

ARTICLE 23 (1)   Everyone has the right to work, to free choice of employment, to just and favourable conditions of work and to protection against unemployment.

(2)   Everyone, without any discrimination, has the right to equal pay for equal work.

(3)   Everyone who works has the right to just and favourable remuneration insuring for himself and his family an existence worthy of human dignity, and supplemented, if necessary, by other means of social protection.

(4)   Everyone has the right to form and to join trade unions for the protection of his interests.

ARTICLE 24   Everyone has the right to rest and leisure, including reasonable limitation of working hours and periodic holidays with pay.

ARTICLE 25 (1)   Everyone has the right to a standard of living adequate for the health and well-being of himself and of his family, including food, clothing, housing and medical care and necessary social services, and the right to security in the event of unemployment, sickness, disability, widowhood, old age or other lack of livelihood in circumstances beyond his control.

(2)   Motherhood and childhood are entitled to special care and assistance. All children, whether born in or out of wedlock, shall enjoy the same social protection.

ARTICLE 26 (1)   Everyone has the right to education. Education shall be free, at least in the elementary and fundamental stages. Elementary education shall be compulsory. Technical and professional education shall be made generally available and higher education shall be equally accessible to all on the basis of merit.

(2)   Education shall be directed to the full development of the human personality and to the strengthening of respect for human rights and fundamental freedoms. It shall promote understanding, tolerance and friendship among all nations, racial or religious groups, and shall further the activities of the United Nations for the maintenance of peace.

(3)   Parents have a prior right to choose the kind of education that shall be given their children.

ARTICLE 27 (1)   Everyone has the right to participate in the cultural life of the community, to enjoy the arts and to share in scientific advancement and its benefits.

(2)   Everyone has the right to the protection of the moral and material interests resulting from any scientific, literary or artistic production of which he is the author.

ARTICLE 28   Everyone is entitled to a social and international order in which the rights and freedoms set forth in this Declaration can be fully realized.

ARTICLE 29 (1)   Everyone has duties to the community in which alone the free and full development of his personality is possible.

(2)   In the exercise of his rights and freedoms, everyone shall be subject only to such limitations as are determined by law solely for the purpose of securing due recognition and respect for the rights and freedoms of others and of meeting the just requirements of morality, public order and the general welfare in a democratic society.

(3)   These rights and freedoms may in no case be exercised contrary to the purpose and principles of the United Nations.

ARTICLE 30   Nothing in this Declaration may be interpreted as implying for any State, group or person any right to engage in any activity or to perform any act aimed at the destruction of any of the rights and freedoms set forth herein.

Respect

(From "Racism: the Cancer that is Destroying America")
BY MALCOLM X

The common goal of twenty-two million Afro-Americans is respect as *human beings*, the God-given right to be a human being. Our common goal is to obtain the *human rights* that America has been denying us. We can never get civil rights in America until our *human rights* are first restored. We will never be recognized as citizens there until we are first recognized as *humans*.

Speak Out

BY NADINE GORDIMER
South African author who won the 1991 Nobel Prize for Literature, born 1923

In a democracy—even if it is a so-called democracy like our white-elitist one—the greatest veneration one can show the rule of law is to keep a watch on it, and to reserve the right to judge unjust laws and the subversion of the function of the law by the power of the state. That vigilance is the most important proof of the respect for the law.

From a speech to the United States Senate in 1966

BY J. WILLIAM FULBRIGHT
American politician known for the Fulbright Act of 1946 that established an exchange program between scholars from the United States and other countries, as well as his opposition to the Vietnam conflict, 1905-1995

In a democracy dissent is an act of faith. Like medicine, the test of its value is not from its taste, but from its effects.

BOOK XVIII

The New Day

The deliverance of humanity and the triumph of labor enfranchised; passages from Utopias new and old, and the raptures of poets and prophets contemplating "the good time coming."

As a Strong Bird on Pinions Free
by WALT WHITMAN

Beautiful World of new, superber Birth, that rises to my eyes,
Like a limitless golden cloud, filling the western sky....
Thou Wonder World, yet undefined, unformed—neither do I
    define thee;
How can I pierce the impenetrable blank of the future?
I feel thy ominous greatness, evil as well as good;
I watch thee, advancing, absorbing the present, transcending the
    past;
I see thy light lighting and thy shadow shadowing, as if the entire
    globe;
But I do not undertake to define thee—hardly to comprehend
    thee;
I but thee name—thee prophesy—as now!

The New Colossus
by EMMA LAZARUS
American Jewish poet, 1849-1887. This sonnet is engraved on a tablet on the
pedestal of the Statue of Liberty.

Not like the brazen giant of Greek fame,
With conquering limbs astride from land to land,
Here at our sea-washed, sunset gates shall stand
A mighty woman with a torch, whose flame
Is the imprisoned lightning, and her name
Mother of Exiles. From her beacon hand
Glows world-wide welcome; her mild eyes command
The air-bridged harbor that twin cities frame.
"Keep, ancient lands, your storied pomp!" cries she
With silent lips. "Give me your tired, your poor,
Your huddled masses yearning to breathe free,
The wretched refuse of your teeming shore.
Send these, the homeless, tempest-tost to me,
I lift my lamp beside the golden door."

579

On a Steamship
by Upton Sinclair

All night, without the gates of slumber lying,
I listen to the joy of falling water,
And to the throbbing of an iron heart.

In ages past, men went upon the sea,
Waiting the pleasure of the chainless winds:
But now the course is laid, the billows part;
Mankind has spoken: "Let the ship go there!"

I am grown haggard and forlorn, from dreams
That haunt me, of the time that is to be,
When man shall cease from wantonness and strife,
And lay his law upon the course of things.
Then shall he live no more on sufferance,
An accident, the prey of powers blind;
The untamed giants of nature shall bow down—
The tides, the tempest and the lightning cease
From mockery and destruction, and be turned
Unto the making of the soul of man.

By Thomas Carlyle

We must some day, at last and forever, cross the line between Nonsense and Common Sense. And on that day we shall pass from Class Paternalism, originally derived from fetish fiction in times of universal ignorance, to Human Brotherhood in accordance with the nature of things and our growing knowledge of it; from Political Government to Industrial Administration; from Competition in Individualism to Individuality in Co-operation; from War and Despotism, in any form, to Peace and Liberty.

By Isaiah

They shall not hurt nor destroy in all my holy mountain: for the earth shall be full of the knowledge of the Lord, as the waters cover the sea.

In Memoriam
by ALFRED, LORD TENNYSON

Ring out, wild bells, to the wild sky,
  The flying clouds, the frosty light:
  The year is dying in the night;
Ring out, wild bells, and let him die.

Ring out the old, ring in the new,
  Ring, happy bells, across the snow:
  The year is going, let him go;
Ring out the false, ring in the true.

Ring out the grief that saps the mind,
  For those that here we see no more;
  Ring out the feud of rich and poor,
Ring in redress to all mankind. . . .

Ring out false pride in place and blood,
  The civic slander and the spite;
  Ring in the love of truth and right,
Ring in the common love of good.

Ring out old shapes of foul disease;
  Ring out the narrowing lust of gold;
  Ring out the thousand wars of old,
Ring in the thousand years of peace.

Ring in the valiant man and free,
  The larger heart, the kindlier hand;
  Ring out the darkness of the land,
Ring in the Christ that is to be.

FROM THE BOOK OF LEVITICUS

Proclaim liberty throughout all the land unto all the inhabitants thereof.

I Have a Dream

by MARTIN LUTHER KING, JR.

Contemporary American, leader of civil rights movement, born 1929

Now is the time to make real the promises of democracy. Now is the time to rise from the dark and desolate valley of segregation to the sunlit path of racial justice. Now is the time to lift our nation from the quicksands of racial injustice to the solid rock of brotherhood. Now is the time to make justice a reality of all of God's children.

There will neither be rest nor tranquility in America until the Negro is granted his citizenship rights. The whirlwinds of revolt will continue to shake the foundations of our nation until the bright day of justice emerges.

And that is something that I must say to my people who stand on the threshold which leads to the palace of justice. In the process of gaining our rightful place we must not be guilty of wrongful deeds. . . .

We can never be satisfied as long as our children are stripped of their selfhood and robbed of their dignity by signs stating "for whites only." We cannot be satisfied as long as the Negro in Mississippi cannot vote and the Negro in New York believes he has nothing for which to vote.

No, we are not satisfied and we will not be satisfied until justice rolls down like water and righteousness like a mighty stream.

I have a dream that one day on the red hills of Georgia the sons of former slaves and the sons of former slave-owners will be able to sit down together at the table of brotherhood.

I have a dream that one day even the state of Mississippi, a state sweltering with the people's injustice, sweltering with the heat of oppression, will be transformed into an oasis of freedom and justice.

I have a dream that my four little children will one day live in a nation where they will not be judged by the color of their skin, but by the content of their character.

This is our hope. This is the faith that I go back to the South with—with this faith we will be able to hew out of the mountain of despair a stone of hope.

The Desire of Nations
by EDWIN MARKHAM

Earth will go back to her lost youth,
And life grow deep and wonderful as truth,
When the wise King out of the nearing Heaven comes
To break the spell of long millenniums—
To build with song again
The broken hope of men—
To hush and heroize the world,
Beneath the flag of brotherhood unfurled.
And He will come some day;
Already is His star upon the way!
He comes, O world, He comes!
But not with bugle-cry nor roll of doubling drums....

And when He comes into the world gone wrong,
He will rebuild her beauty with a song.
To every heart He will its own dream be:
One moon has many phantoms in the sea.
Out of the North the norns will cry to men:
"Baldur the Beautiful has come again!"
The flutes of Greece will whisper from the dead:
"Apollo has unveiled his sunbright head!"
The stones of Thebes and Memphis will find voice:
"Osiris comes: O tribes of Time, rejoice!"
And social architects who build the State,
Serving the Dream at citadel and gate,
Will hail Him coming through the labor-hum.
And glad quick cries will go from man to man:
"Lo, he has come, our Christ the Artisan,
The King who loved the lilies, He has come!"

By ISAIAH

The Lord hath anointed me to preach good tidings unto the
meek; he hath sent me to bind up the brokenhearted, to proclaim
liberty to the captives. They shall build the old wastes, they shall
raise up the former desolations, and they shall repair the waste
cities.

The Perfect City
(From "The Republic")
by PLATO

Greek philosopher, 429-347 B.C. His "Republic" is the first, and perhaps the most famous, of all efforts to portray an ideal society. The argument is in the form of a discussion between Socrates and some of his friends and pupils.

First, then (said Socrates), let us consider in what manner those who dwell in the city shall be supported. Is there any other way than by making bread and wine, and clothes and shoes, and building houses? They will be nourished, partly with barley, making meal of it, and partly with wheat, making loaves, boiling part, and toasting part, putting fine loaves and cakes over a fire of stubble, or over dried leaves, and resting themselves on couches strewed with smilax and myrtle leaves. They and their children will feast, drinking wine, and crowned, and singing to the Gods; and they will pleasantly live together, begetting children not beyond their substance, guarding against poverty or war.

Glauco, replying, said: You make the men to feast, as it appears, without meats.

You say true, said I: for I forget that they need have meats likewise. They shall have salt and olives and cheese, and they shall boil bulbous roots and herbs of the field; and we set before them desserts of figs and vetches and beans; and they toast at the fire myrtle berries and the berries of the beech-tree, drinking in moderation. Thus passing their life in peace and health, and dying, as is likely, in old age, they will leave to their children another such life.

If you had been making, Socrates, said he, a city of hogs, what else would have fed them but these things?

But how should we do, Glauco, said I?

What is usually done, said he. They must, as I imagine, have their beds and tables, and meats and desserts, as we now have, if they are not to be miserable.

Be it so, said I: I understand you. We consider, it seems, not only how a city may exist, but a luxurious city; and perhaps it is not amiss; for in considering such a one, we may probably see how justice and injustice have their origin in cities. The true city seems to me to. be such as we have described, like one who is healthy; but if you prefer that we likewise consider a city that is corpulent, nothing hinders it. For these things will not, it seems, please some, nor this sort of life satisfy them; but there

shall be beds and tables and all other furniture, seasonings, oint-
ments, and perfumes, mistresses, and confections: and various
kinds of these. And we must no longer consider as alone necessary what we mentioned at the first, houses and clothes and shoes,
but painting, too, and all the curious arts must be set agoing,
and carving, and gold, and ivory; and all these things must be
got, must they not?

Yes, said he.

Must not the city, then, be larger? For that healthy one is no
longer sufficient, but is already full of luxury, and of a crowd of
such as are in no way necessary to cities; such as all kinds of
sportsmen, and the imitative artists, many of them imitating
in figures, and colors; and others in music; and poets too, and
their ministers, rhaps'odists, actors, dancers, undertakers, workmen of all sorts of instruments and what hath reference to female
ornament, as well as other things. We shall need likewise many
more servants. Do you not think they will need pedagogues, and
nurses, and tutors, hairdressers, barbers, victuallers too, and
cooks? And further still, we shall want swineherds likewise; of
these there were none in the other city (for there needed not);
but in this we shall want these, and many other sorts of herds
likewise, if any eat the several animals, shall we not?

Why not?

Shall we not, then, in this manner of life be much more in
need of physicians than formerly?

Much more.

And the country, which was then sufficient to support the inhabitants, will, instead of being sufficient, become too little; or
how shall we say?

Just so, said he.

Must we not then encroach upon the neighboring country, if
we want to have sufficient for plough and pasture, and they in
like manner upon us, if they likewise suffer themselves to accumulate wealth to infinity, going beyond the boundaries of
necessaries?

There is great necessity for it, Socrates.

Shall we afterwards fight, Glauco, or how shall we do?

We shall certainly, said he.

We say nothing, said I, whether war does any evil or any good,
but this much only: *that we have found the origin of war, from
which most especially arise the greatest mischiefs to states, both
private and public.*

Utopia

by SIR THOMAS MORE

The word "Utopia" means "No Place." It was first used in this book, and has come to be a general name for pictures of a future society. The book was written in Latin, and first published in Belgium in 1516. This translation was published in England in 1551.

Every Cytie is devided into foure equall partes or quarters. In the myddes of every quarter there is a market place of all maner of things. Thether the workes of every familie be brought into certeyne houses. And everye kynde of thing is layde up severall in bernes or store houses. From hence the father of everye familye, or every householder fetchethe whatsoever he and his have neade of, and carieth it away with him without money, without exchaunge, without any gage, pawne, or pledge. For whye shoulde any thing be denyed unto him? Seynge there is abundance of all things, and that it is not to bee feared, leste anye man wyll aske more then he neadeth. For whie should it be thoughte that that man woulde aske more then anough, which is sewer never to lacke? Certeynely in all kyndes of lyving creatures either feare of lacke dothe cause covetousnes and ravyne, or in man only pryde, which counteth it a glorious thinge to pass and excel other in the superfluous and vayne ostentation of thinges. The whyche kynde of vice amonge the Utopians can have no place.

Nowe I have declared and described unto you, as truelye as I coulde the fourme and ordre of that common wealth, which verely in my judgment is not only the beste, but also that which alone of good right maye claime and take upon it the name of a common wealth or publique weale. For in other places they speake stil of the common wealth. But every man procureth his owne private gaine. Here where nothinge is private, the commen affaires bee earnestlye loked upon. . . . For there nothinge is distributed after a nyggyshe sorte, neither there is anye poore man or beggar. And thoughe no man have anye thinge, yet everye man is ryche. For what can be more ryche, than to lyve joyfully and merely, without al griefe and pensifenes: not caring for his owne lyving, nor vexed or troubled with his wifes importunate complayntes, nor dreadynge povertie to his sonne, nor sorrowyng for his doughters dowrey?

Cities, Old and New
(From "In the Days of the Comet")
by H. G. WELLS

Where is that old world now? Where is London, that somber city of smoke and drifting darkness, full of the deep roar and haunting music of disorder, with its oily, shining, mud-rimmed, barge-crowded river, its black pinnacles, and blackened dome, its sad wildernesses of smut-grayed houses, its myriads of draggled prostitutes, its millions of hurrying clerks? The very leaves upon its trees were foul with greasy black defilements. Where is the lime-white Paris, with its green and disciplined foliage, its hard unflinching tastefulness, its smartly organized viciousness, and the myriads of workers, noisily shod, streaming over the bridges in the gray cold light of dawn? Where is New York, the high city of clangor and infuriated energy, wind swept and competition swept, its huge buildings jostling one another and straining ever upward for a place in the sky, the fallen pitilessly overshadowed? Where are its lurking corners of heavy and costly luxury, the shameful bludgeoning bribing vice of its ill ruled underways, and all the gaunt extravagant ugliness of its strenuous life? . . .

All these vast cities have given way and gone, even as my native Potteries and the Black Country have gone, and the lives that were caught, crippled, starved, and maimed amidst their labyrinths, their forgotten and neglected maladjustments, and their vast, inhuman, ill-conceived industrial machinery have escaped—to life. Those cities of growth and accident are altogether gone, never a chimney smokes about our world today, and the sound of the weeping of children who toiled and hungered, the dull despair of overburdened women, the noise of brute quarrels in alleys, all shameful pleasures and all the ugly grossness of wealthy pride have gone with them, with the utter change of our lives. As I look back into the past I see a vast exultant dust of house-breaking and removal rise up into the clear air; I live again the Year of Tents, the Years of Scaffolding, and like the triumph of a new theme in a piece of music—the great cities of our new days arise.

The Soul of Man Under Socialism
by OSCAR WILDE

The fact is, that civilization requires slaves. The Greeks were quite right there. Unless there are slaves to do the ugly, horrible, uninteresting work, culture and contemplation become almost impossible. Human slavery is wrong, insecure, and demoralizing. On mechanical slavery, on the slavery of the machine, the future of the world depends.

By ALFRED, LORD TENNYSON

The old order changeth, yielding place to new
And God fulfils Himself in many ways,
Lest one good custom should corrupt the world.

Caesar and Cleopatra
by GEORGE BERNARD SHAW

The Romans have set fire to the Library of Alexandria

THEODOTUS:—What is burning there is the memory of mankind.
CAESAR:—A shameful memory. Let it burn.
THEODOTUS (*wildly*):—Will you destroy the past?
CAESAR:—Ay, and build the future with its ruins.

Incentives
by CHARLES FOURIER

Up to the present time politicians and philosophers have not dreamed of rendering industry attractive; to enchain the mass to labor, they have discovered no other means, after slavery, than the fear of want and starvation; if, however, industry is the destiny which is assigned to us by the creator, how can we think that he would wish to force us to it by violence, and that he has no notion how to put in play some more noble lever, some incentive capable of transforming its occupations into pleasures?

A Festival in Utopia
(From "News from Nowhere")
by WILLIAM MORRIS

"Once a year, on May-day, we hold a solemn feast in those easterly communes of London to commemorate the Clearing of Misery, as it is called. On that day we have music and dancing, and merry games and happy feasting on the site of some of the worst of the old slums, the traditional memory of which we have kept. On that occasion the custom is for the prettiest girls to sing some of the old revolutionary songs, and those which were the groans of discontent, once so hopeless, on the very spots where those terrible crimes of class-murder were committed day by day for so many years. To a man like me, who has studied the past so diligently, it is a curious and touching sight to see some beautiful girl, daintily clad, and crowned with flowers from the neighboring meadows, standing among the happy people, on some mound where of old time stood the wretched apology for a house,—a den in which men and women lived packed among the filth like pilchards in a cask; lived in such a way that they could only have endured it, as I said just now, by being degraded out of humanity. To hear the terrible words of threatening and lamentation coming from her sweet and beautiful lips, and she unconscious of their real meaning; to hear her singing Hood's 'Song of the Shirt,' and think all the time she does not understand what it is all about—a tragedy grown inconceivable to her and her listeners. Think of that if you can, and of how glorious life is grown!"

"Indeed," said I, "it is difficult for me to think of it."

The Utopian City
(From "A Modern Utopia")
by H. G. WELLS

Here will be one of the great meeting places of mankind. Here —I speak of Utopian London—will be the traditional center of one of the great races in the commonality of the World State— and here will be its social and intellectual exchange. There will be a mighty University here, with thousands of professors and tens of thousands of advanced students, and here great journals of thought and speculation, mature and splendid books of philosophy and science, and a glorious fabric of literature will be woven and shaped, and with a teeming leisureliness, put forth. Here will be stupendous libraries, and a mighty organization of museums. About these centers will cluster a great swarm of people, and close at hand will be another center,—for I who am an Englishman must needs stipulate that Westminster shall still be a seat of world Empire, one of several seats, if you will—where the ruling council of the world assembles. Then the arts will cluster round this city, as gold gathers about wisdom, and here Englishmen will weave into wonderful prose and beautiful rhythms and subtly atmospheric forms, the intricate, austere and courageous imagination of our race.

One will come into this place as one comes into a noble mansion. They will have flung great arches and domes of glass above the wider spaces of the town, the slender beauty of the perfect metal-work far overhead will be softened to a fairy-like unsubstantiality by the mild London air. It will be the London air we know, clear of filth and all impurity, the same air that gives our October days their unspeakable clarity and makes every London twilight mysteriously beautiful. We shall go along avenues of architecture that will be emancipated from the last memories of the squat temple boxes of the Greek, the buxom curvatures of Rome; the Goth in us will have taken to steel and countless new materials as kindly as once he took to stone. The gay and swiftly moving platforms of the public ways will go past on either hand, carrying sporadic groups of people, and very speedily we shall find ourselves in a sort of central space, rich with palms and flowering bushes and statuary. We shall look along an avenue of trees, down a wide gorge between the cliffs of crowded hotels that are still glowing with internal lights, to where the shining morning river streams dawnlit out to sea.

The New Nationalism

by THEODORE ROOSEVELT
President of the United States; 1858-1919

Practical equality of opportunity for all citizens, when we achieve it, will have two great results. First, every man will have a fair chance to make himself all that in him lies; to reach the highest point to which his capacities, unassisted by special privilege of his own and unhampered by the special privilege of others, can carry him, and to get for himself and for his family substantially what he has earned. Second, equality of opportunity means that the commonwealth will get from every citizen the highest service of which he is capable. No man who carries the burden of the special privileges of another can give to the commonwealth that service to which it is fairly entitled.

Looking Backward
by EDWARD BELLAMY
A story of the experience of a man who goes to sleep and wakes up a hundred years later.

"How do you regulate wages?" I asked.

Dr. Leete did not reply till after several moments of meditative silence. "I know, of course," he finally said, "enough of the old order of things to understand just what you mean by that question; and yet the present order is so utterly different at this point that I am a little at a loss how to answer you best. You ask me how we regulate wages: I can only reply that there is no idea in the modern social economy which at all corresponds with what was meant by wages in your day."

"I suppose you mean that you have no money to pay wages in," said I. "But the credit given the worker at the Government storehouse answers to his wages with us. How is the amount of credit given respectively to the workers in different lines determined? By what title does the individual claim his particular share? What is the basis of allotment?"

"His title," replied Dr. Leete, "is his humanity. The basis of his claim is the fact that he is a man."

"The fact that he is a man!" I repeated, incredulously. "Do you possibly mean that all have the same share?"

"Most assuredly." . . .

"But what inducement," I asked, "can a man have to put forth his best endeavors when, however much or little he accomplishes, his income remains the same? High characters may be moved by devotion to the common welfare under such a system, but does not the average man tend to rest back on his oar, reasoning that it is of no use to make a special effort, since the effort will not increase his income, nor its withholding diminish it?"

"Does it then really seem to you," answered my companion, "that human nature is insensible to any motives save fear of want and love of luxury, that you should expect security and

equality of livelihood to leave them without possible incentives
to effort? Your contemporaries did not really think so, though
they might fancy they did. When it was a question of the grandest
class of efforts, the most absolute self-devotion, they depended on
quite other incentives.

"Not higher wages, but honor and hope of men's gratitude,
patriotism and the inspiration of duty, were the motives which they
set before their soldiers when it was a question of dying for the
nation; and never was there an age of the world when these
motives did not call out what is best and noblest in men. And
not only this, but when you come to analyze the love of money
which was the general impulse to effort in your day, you find
that the dread of want and desire of luxury were two of several
motives which the pursuit of money represented; the others, and
with many the more influential, being desire of power, of social
position and reputation for ability and success. So you see that
though we have abolished poverty and the fear of it, and inordinate luxury with the hope of it, we have not touched the greater
part of the motives which underlay the love of money in former
times, or any of those which prompted the supremer sorts of
effort. The coarser motives, which no longer move us, have been
replaced by high motives wholly unknown to the mere wage
earners of your age. Now that industry of any sort is no longer
self-service, but service of the nation, patriotism, passion for humanity, impel the workers as in your day they did the soldier.
The army of industry is an army, not alone by virtue of its perfect organization, but by reason also of the ardor of self-devotion
which animates its members.

"But as you used to supplement the motives of patriotism with
the love of glory, in order to stimulate the value of your soldiers,
so do we. Based as our industrial system is on the principle of
requiring the same unit of effort from every man, that is, the
best he can do, you will see that the means by which we spur the
workers to do their best must be a very essential part of our
scheme. With us, diligence in the national service is the sole
and certain way to public repute, social distinction, and official
power. The value of a man's services in society fixes his rank in
it. Compared with the effect of our social arrangements in im-
pelling men to be zealous in business, we deem the object-lessons
of biting poverty and wanton luxury on which you depended a
device as weak and uncertain as it was barbaric."

The Social Revolution and After
by KARL KAUTSKY
German socialist leader and anti-Bolshevik Marxist, 1854-1938

Freedom of education and of scientific investigation from the fetters of capitalist dominion; freedom of the individual from the oppression of exclusive, exhaustive physical labor; displacement of capitalist industry in the intellectual production of society by the free unions—along this road proceeds the tendency of the proletarian régime. . . .

Regulation of social chaos and liberation of the individual—these are the two historical tasks that capitalism has placed before society. They appear to be contradictory, but they are simultaneously soluble because each of them belongs to a different sphere of social life. Undoubtedly whoever should seek to rule both spheres in the same manner would find himself involved in insoluble contradictions. . . .

Communism in material production, anarchism`in intellectual. This is the type of the Socialist productive system which will arise from the dominion of the proletariat.

Liberty in Utopia
(From "A Modern Utopia")
by H. G. WELLS

The idea of individual liberty is one that has grown in importance and grows with every development of modern thought. To the classical Utopists freedom was relatively trivial. Clearly they considered virtue and happiness as entirely separable from liberty, and as being altogether more important things. But the modern view, with its deepening insistence upon individuality and upon the significance of its uniqueness, steadily intensifies the value of freedom, until at last we begin to see liberty as the very substance of life, that indeed it is life, and that only the dead things, the choiceless things, live in absolute obedience to law. To have free play for one's individuality is, in the modern view, the subjective triumph of existence, as survival in creative work and offspring is its objective triumph. . . .

A Utopia such as this present one, written on the opening of the Twentieth Century, and after the most exhaustive discussion —nearly a century long—between Communistic and Socialistic ideas on the one hand, and Individualism on the other, emerges upon a sort of effectual conclusion to these controversies. . . . In the very days when our political and economic order is becoming steadily more Socialistic, our ideals of intercourse turn more and more to a fuller recognition of the claims of individuality. The State is to be progressive, it is no longer to be static, and this alters the general condition of the Utopian problem profoundly; we have to provide not only for food and clothing, for order and health, but for initiative. The factor that leads the World State on from one phase of development to the next is the interplay of individualities; to speak teleologically, the world exists for the sake of and through initiative, and individuality is the method of initiative. . . . The State is for Individuals, the law is for freedoms, the world is for experiment, experience and change: these are the fundamental beliefs upon which a modern Utopia must go.

The Understanding of Nature
by JEAN LEON JAURÈS
French socialist hero, victim of fanatic assassin, 1859-1914

When Socialism has triumphed, when conditions of peace have succeeded to conditions of combat, when all men have their share of property in the immense human capital, and their share of initiative and of the exercise of free-will in the immense human activity, then all men will know the fullness of pride and joy; and they will feel that they are co-operators in the universal civilization, even if their immediate contribution is only the humblest manual labor; and this labor, more noble and more fraternal in character, will be so regulated that the laborers shall always reserve for themselves some leisure hours for reflection and for a cultivation of the sense of life.

They will have a better understanding of the hidden meaning of life, whose mysterious aim is the harmony of all consciences, of all forces, and of all liberties. They will understand history better and will love it, because it will be their history, since they are the heirs of the whole human race. Finally, they will understand the universe better; because, when they see conscience and spirit triumphing in humanity, they will be quick to feel that this universe which has given birth to humanity cannot be fundamentally brutal and blind; that there is spirit everywhere, soul everywhere, and that the universe itself is simply an immense confused aspiration toward order, beauty, freedom, and goodness. Their point of view will be changed; they will look with new eyes not only at their brother men, but at the earth and the sky, rocks and trees, animals, flowers, and stars.

The Future of Art
(From "Collectivism and Industrial Evolution")
by EMILE VANDERVELDE
Belgian socialist leader, 1866-1938

Many a time it has been said that art under all its forms is only the mirror, more or less distorted, yet always faithful, of society. Today it reflects the discouragements of a dying *bourgeoisie,* the torments, the anguish, and also the hopes of a proletariat which lives and grows in the midst of suffering. Tomorrow, it will reflect the calm and peace of happy generations which, escaped from the mire of poverty, will have founded through their own efforts the sovereignty of labor and the reign of brotherhood.

Art After the Revolution
(From "Syndicalism and the Co-operative Commonwealth")
by EMILE PATAUD AND EMILE POUGET
French trade union leaders, early Twentieth Century

Life was now to take its revenge. The human being was no longer riveted to the chain of wages; his aim in life passed beyond the mere struggle for a living. Industry was no longer his master, but his servant. Freed from all hindrances, he would be able to develop without constraint.

And there was no need to fear that the level of art would be lowered as it became universalized. Far from this, it would gain in extent and depth. Its domain would be unlimited. It would enter into all production. It would not restrict itself to painting large canvasses, to sculpturing marble, to moulding bronze. There would be art in everything.

And we should no longer see great artists stifled by misery, lost in the quicksands of indifference, as was too often the case formerly.

Punishment in Utopia
(From "A Modern Utopia")
by H. G. WELLS

You see the big convict steamship standing in to the Island of Incurable Cheats. The crew are respectfully at their quarters, ready to lend a hand overboard, but wide awake, and the captain is hospitably on the bridge to bid his guests good-bye and keep an eye on the movables. The new citizens for this particular Alsatia, each no doubt with his personal belongings securely packed and at hand, crowd the deck and study the nearing coast. Bright, keen faces would be there, and we, were we by any chance to find ourselves beside the captain, might recognize the double of this great earthly magnate or that, Petticoat Lane and Park Lane cheek by jowl. The landing part of the jetty is clear of people, only a government man or so stands there to receive the boat and prevent a rush; but beyond the gates a number of engagingly smart-looking individuals loiter speculatively. One figures a remarkable building labeled Custom House, an interesting fiscal revival this population has made, and beyond, crowding up the hill, the painted walls of a number of comfortable inns clamor loudly. One or two inhabitants in reduced circumstances would act as hotel touts, there are several hotel omnibuses and a Bureau de Change, certainly a Bureau de Change. And a small house with a large board, aimed point-blank seaward, declares itself a Gratis Information Office, and next to it rises the graceful dome of a small Casino. Beyond, great hoardings proclaim the advantages of many island specialties, a hustling commerce, and the opening of a Public Lottery. There is a large cheap-looking barrack, the school of Commercial Science for gentlemen of inadequate training. . . .

Altogether a very go-ahead looking little port it would be, and though this disembarkation would have none of the flow of hilarious good fellowship that would throw a halo of genial noise about the Islands of Drink, it is doubtful if the new arrivals would feel anything very tragic in the moment. Here at last was scope for adventure after their hearts.

This sounds more fantastic than it is. But what else is there to do, unless you kill? You must seclude, but why should you torment? All modern prisons are places of torture by restraint, and the habitual criminal plays the part of a damaged mouse at the mercy of the cat of our law. He has his little painful run, and back he comes again to a state more horrible even than destitution. There are no Alsatias left in the world. For my own part I can think of no crime, unless it is reckless begetting or the wilful transmission of contagious disease, for which the bleak terrors, the solitudes and ignominies of the modern prison do not seem outrageously cruel. If you want to go as far as that, then kill. Why, once you are rid of them, should you pester criminals to respect an uncongenial standard of conduct? Into such islands of exile as this a modern Utopia will have to purge itself. There is no alternative that I can contrive.

The Triumph of Love
(From "Labor")
by ÉMILE ZOLA

In this novel the French writer gives his solution of the labor problem, in the story of a young engineer who is led by the study of Fourier to found a co-operative steel mill, which in the course of time replaces all the old competitive establishments, and brings about a reign of human brotherhood.

The triumphant spectacle that Luc had now always before his eyes, that city of happiness, the gaily colored roofs of which were spread out before his window, was admirable. The march of progress which a former generation, sunk in ancient error, and contaminated by an iniquitous environment, had so mournfully begun in the midst of many obstacles and former hatreds, was to be pursued by their children, instructed and disciplined by the schools and workshops, advancing with a cheerful step, even to the attainment of aims formerly declared chimerical. The long effort of struggling humanity resulted in the free expansion of the individual, in a society completely satisfied; in man being fully man, and living his life in its entirety. The happy city was thus realized in the religion of life; the religion of humanity, freed at length from dogmas, became in itself all glory and all joy. . . .

Authority was at an end; the new social system had no other foundation than the tie of labor accepted as necessary by all, their law and the object of their worship. A number of groups adopted the new system, breaking off from the old groups of builders, dealers in clothing, metalworkers, artisans, and farm laborers, each group increasing in number, each different, each making itself essential to the rest, and satisfying individual wants as well as the needs of a community. Nothing impeded any man's expansion; a citizen working as a laborer might unite himself with as many groups as he thought proper. . . .

And in the city all was love. A pervading sense of love, increasing, wholesome, purifying, became the perfume and the sacred flame of daily life. Love, general and universal, had its birth in youth; then it passed on and became mother love, father love, filial love; it spread to relations, to neighbors, to fellow-citizens, to all men upon earth, and as its waves swept on and became stronger, it seemed to become a great sea of love, bathing the shores of the whole earth. Charity—that is, love of one's neighbors—was like the fresh air which fills the lungs of all who breathe it; everywhere there was this feeling of brotherly love; love alone had proved able to realize the unity men had so long dreamed of, bringing all into divine harmony. The human race, at last as well balanced as the planets in their orbits by the law of attraction, the laws of justice, solidarity, and love, would go joyfully on its round through the ages of eternity. Such was the harvest ever renewed and renewing, the great harvest of tenderness and loving kindness, that Luc every morning saw growing up around him in spots where he had sown his seed so bountifully in his early days. In his whole city, in his school-rooms, in his work-shops, in each house, and almost in each heart, for many years he had been sowing the good seed with lavish hands.

The City of the Sun
by Tomasso Campanella

Love is foremost in attending to the charge of the race. He sees that men and women are joined together, that they bring forth the best offspring. Indeed, they laugh at us who exhibit a studious care for our breed of horses and dogs, but neglect the breeding of human beings. Thus the education of children is under his rule. So also is the medicine that is sold, the sowing and collecting of fruits of the earth and of trees, agriculture, pasturage, the preparations for the months, the cooking arrangements, and whatever has any reference to food, clothing, and the intercourse of the sexes. Love himself is ruler, but there are many male and female magistrates dedicated to these arts.

A Preface to Politics
by WALTER LIPPMANN

You don't have to preach honesty to men with a creative purpose. Let a human being throw the energies of his soul into the making of something, and the instinct of workmanship will take care of his honesty. The writers who have nothing to say are the ones you can buy; the others have too high a price. A genuine craftsman will not adulterate his product; the reason isn't because duty says he shouldn't, but because passion says he couldn't.

Love in Utopia
(From "News from Nowhere")
by WILLIAM MORRIS

"Ah," said I, "no doubt you wanted to keep them out of the Divorce Court; but I suppose it often has to settle such matters?"

"Then you suppose nonsense," said he. "I know that there used to be such lunatic affairs as divorce courts; but just consider, all the cases that came into them were matters of property quarrels; and I think, dear guest, that though you do come from another planet, you can see from the mere outside look of our world that quarrel about private property could not go on among us in our days."

Indeed, my drive from Hammersmith to Bloomsbury, and all the quiet, happy life I had seen so many hints of, even apart from my shopping, would have been enough to tell me that "the sacred rights of property," as we used to think of them, were now no more. So I sat silent while the old man took up the thread of the discourse again. . . .

"You must understand once for all that we have changed these matters; or rather, that our way of looking at them has changed within the last two hundred years. We do not deceive ourselves, indeed, or believe that we can get rid of all the trouble that besets the dealings between the sexes. We know that we must face the unhappiness that comes of man and woman confusing the relations between natural passion and sentiment, and the friendship which, when things go well, softens the awakening from passing illusions; but we are not so mad as to pile up degradation

on that unhappiness by engaging in sordid squabbles about livelihood and position, and the power of tyrannizing over the children who have been the results of love or lust." . . .

He was silent for some time, and I would not interrupt him.
At last he began again: "But you must know that we of these
generations are strong and healthy of body, and live easily; we
pass our lives in reasonable strife with nature, exercising not one
side of ourselves only, but all sides, taking the keenest pleasure
in all the life of the world. So it is a point of honor with us not
to be self-centered,—not to suppose that the world must cease
because one man is sorry; therefore we should think it foolish,
or if you will, criminal, to exaggerate these matters of sentiment
and sensibility; we are no more inclined to eke out our sentimental sorrows than to cherish our bodily pains; and we recognize that there are other pleasures besides love-making. You must
remember, also, that we are long-lived, and that therefore beauty
both in man and woman is not so fleeting as it was in the days
when we were burdened so heavily with self-inflicted diseases. So
we shake off these griefs in a way which perhaps the sentimental-
ist of other times would think contemptible and unheroic, but
which we think necessary and manlike. As on the one hand,
therefore, we have ceased to be commercial in our love-matters,
so also we have ceased to be artificially foolish. The folly which
comes by nature, the unwisdom of the immature man, or the
older man caught in a trap, we must put up with that, nor are
we much ashamed of it; but to be conventionally sensitive or
sentimental—my friend, I am old and perhaps disappointed, but
at least I think that we have cast off *some* of the follies of the
older world."

The Free Woman
by Walt Whitman

She is less guarded than ever, yet more guarded than ever,
The gross and soil'd she moves among do not make her gross and
    soiled,
She knows the thoughts as she passes, nothing is concealed from
    her,
She is none the less considerate or friendly therefor,
She is the best belov'd, it is without exception; she has no reason
    to fear, and she does not fear.

Thus Spake Zarathustra
by Friedrich Nietzsche

When Zarathustra came into the next city, which lay beside the forest, he found in that place much people gathered together in the market; for they had been called that they should see a rope-dancer. And Zarathustra spoke thus unto the people:

"*I teach ye the Over-man.* The man is something who shall be overcome. What have ye done to overcome him?

"All being before this made something beyond itself: and you will be the ebb of this great flood, and rather go back to the beast than overcome the man?

"What is the ape to the man? A mockery or a painful shame. And even so shall man be to the Over-man: a mockery or a painful shame.

"Man is a cord, tied between Beast and Over-man—a cord above an abyss.

"A perilous arriving, a perilous traveling, a perilous looking backward, a perilous trembling and standing still.

"What is great in man is that he is a bridge, and no goal; what can be loved in man is that he is a going-over and a going-under.

"I love them that know not how to live, be it even as those going under, for such are those going across.

"I love them that are great in scorn, because these are they that are great in reverence, and arrows of longing toward the other shore!"

Woman in Freedom
by Edward Carpenter

There is no solution except the freedom of woman—which means of course also the freedom of the masses of the people, men and women, and the ceasing altogether of economic slavery. There is no solution which will not include the redemption of the terms "free woman" and "free love" to their *true* and rightful significance. Let every woman whose heart bleeds for the sufferings of her sex, hasten to declare herself and to constitute herself, as far as she possibly can, a free woman. Let her accept the term with all the odium that belongs to it; let her insist on her right to speak, dress, think, act, and above all to use her sex, as she deems best; let her face the scorn and ridicule; let her "lose her own life" if she likes; assured that only so can come deliverance, and that only when the free woman is honored will the prostitute cease to exist. And let every man who really would respect his counterpart, entreat her also to act so; let him never by word or deed tempt her to grant as a bargain what can only be precious as a gift; let him see her with pleasure stand a little aloof; let him help her to gain her feet; so at last, by what slight sacrifices on his part such a course may involve, will it dawn upon him that he has gained a real companion and helpmate on life's journey.

The Feminine Urge to Freedom
by MARGARET SANGER
American birth control advocate, 1879–1966

Woman has, through her reproductive ability, founded and perpetuated the tyrannies of the Earth. Whether it was the tyranny of a monarchy, an oligarchy or a republic, the one in-dispensable factor of its existence was, as it is now, hordes of human beings—human beings so plentiful as to be cheap, and so cheap that ignorance was their natural lot. Upon the rock of an unenlightened, submissive maternity have these been founded; upon the product of such a maternity have they flourished.

No despot ever flung forth his legions to die in foreign conquest, no privilege-ruled nation ever erupted across its borders, to lock in death embrace with another, but behind them loomed the driving power of a population too large for its boundaries and its natural resources.

No period of low wages or of idleness with their want among the workers, no peonage or sweatshop, no child-labor factory, ever came into being, save from the same source. Nor have famine and plague been as much "acts of God" as acts of too prolific mothers. They, also, as all students know, have their basic causes in over-population.

The creators of over-population are the women, who, while wringing their hands over each fresh horror, submit anew to their task of producing the multitudes who will bring about the *next* tragedy of civilization.

While unknowingly laying the foundations of tyrannies and providing the human tinder for racial conflagrations, woman was also unknowingly creating slums, filling asylums with insane, and institutions with other defectives. She was replenishing the ranks of the prostitutes, furnishing grist for the criminal courts and inmates for prisons. Had she planned deliberately to achieve this tragic total of human waste and misery, she could hardly have done it more effectively.

Woman's passivity under the burden of her disastrous task was almost altogether that of ignorant resignation. She knew virtually nothing about her reproductive nature and less about the consequences of her excessive child-bearing. It is true that, obeying the inner urge of their natures, *some* women revolted. They went even to the extreme of infanticide and abortion. Usually their revolts were not general enough. They fought as individuals, not as a mass. In the mass they sank back into blind and hopeless subjection. They went on breeding with staggering rapidity those numberless, undesired children who become the clogs and the destroyers of civilizations.

Today, however, woman is rising in fundamental revolt. Even her efforts at mere reform are . . . steps in that direction. Underneath each of them is the feminine urge to complete freedom. Millions of women are asserting their right to voluntary motherhood. They are determined to decide for themselves whether they shall become mothers, under what conditions and when. This is the fundamental revolt referred to. It is for woman the key to the temple of liberty.

Catastrophe and Debasement
by LEWIS MUMFORD
American social philosopher, 1895–1990

Modern civilization has been arrested in mid-flight; its technical advances in saving labor, perfecting automatism, mechanizing the daily processes of life, multiplying the arts of destruction, and dehumanizing the personality have been responsible for this arrest. The rise of the machine and the fall of man are two parts of the same process: never before have machines been so perfect, and never before have men sunk so low, for the sub-

The Liberatress, *Théophile Alexandre Steinlen*

human conduct that the Nazis have exhibited in the torture and extermination of their victims drops below any level of merely animal brutality. That degradation is shared by those who passively condone this sub-human conduct, by belittling its horror and denying its terrible significance.

This catastrophe and this debasement have no parallels in earlier history; for now, for the first time, the entire world is involved. All consolations that are based on past recoveries are meaningless. What happened to Greece, Rome, China, or India has no parallel in the world today: when these civilizations collapsed, they were surrounded by neighbors that had reached nearly equal levels of culture, whereas if Western civilization should continue its downward course it will spread ruin to every part of the planet; and its going will consume the very forces and ideas within its own tradition that might have given a start to its successor.

The present crisis has long been visible. Jacob Burckhardt observed its early stages in the middle of the nineteenth century: in the series of brilliant essays, now published in English under the title, *Force and Freedom*, he not merely diagnosed the malady but accurately predicted its outward manifestations. In a letter written to Henry Osborn Taylor in 1905, Henry Adams remarked: "At the present rate of progression since 1600, it will not need another century or half century to tip thought upside down. Law, in that case, would disappear as theory or *a priori* principle and give place to force. Morality would become police. Explosives would reach cosmic violence. Disintegration would overcome integration." Henry Adams did not live to observe fascism: he anticipated it. He knew that the detonators of violence and destruction were present in every part of the social structure of Western society.

Like the die-hards of fourth century Rome, most of our contemporaries are still unaware of the dimensions of the present catastrophe. They were so completely self-hypnotized by pride in man's control over nature that they overlooked all the palpable evidence of the fact that this control did not extend to his own self and his own very life: they were unprepared to believe that a fiendish barbarism could arise in the midst of an advanced scientific country like Germany; and they were unable to analyze in their own reactions to this the characteristic symptoms of decay: a moral inertia, a flight from reality, an unwillingness to face danger or hardship on behalf of an ideal cause. The democratic peoples, inheritors of a universal culture that had actually spread throughout the globe, were willing to barter all their advances for the sake of "peace." When they finally found that the choice was not in their hands, they made ready to fight—but skeptically, reluctantly, stupidly, as men answer an alarm when still thick with sleep. This feeble response to the challenge of barbarism was as much a sign of disintegration as the barbarism itself.

A Boot on a Face
(From "1984")
by GEORGE ORWELL
English novelist and social critic, 1903-1950

"How does one man assert his power over another, Winston?" Winston thought. "By making him suffer," he said.

"Exactly. By making him suffer. Obedience is not enough. Unless he is suffering, how can you be sure that he is obeying your will and not his own? Power is inflicting pain and humiliation. Power is in tearing human minds to pieces and putting them together again in new shapes of your own choosing. Do you begin to see, then, what kind of world we are creating? It is the exact opposite of the stupid hedonistic Utopias that the old reformers imagined. A world of fear and treachery and torment, a world of trampling and being trampled upon, a world which will grow not less but *more* merciless as it refines itself. Progress in our world will be progress toward more pain. The old civilizations claimed that they were founded on love or justice. Ours is founded upon hatred. In our world there will be no emotions except fear, rage, triumph, and self-abasement. Everything else we shall destroy—everything. Already we are breaking down the habits of thought which have survived from before the Revolution. We have cut the links between child and parent, and between man and man, and between man and woman. No one dares trust a wife or a child or a friend any longer. But in the future there will be no wives and no friends. Children will be taken from their mothers at birth, as one takes eggs from a hen. The sex instinct will be eradicated. Procreation will be an annual formality like the renewal of a ration card. We shall abolish the orgasm. Our neurologists are at work upon it now. There will be no loyalty, except loyalty toward the Party. There will be no love, except the love of Big Brother. There will be no laughter, except the laughter of triumph over a defeated enemy. There will be no art, no literature, no science. When we are omnipotent we shall have no more need of science. There will be no distinction between beauty and ugliness. There will be no curiosity, no enjoyment of the process of life. All competing pleasures will be destroyed. But always—do not forget this, Winston—always there will be the intoxication of power, constantly increasing and constantly growing subtler. Always, at every moment, there will be the thrill of victory, the sensation of trampling on an enemy who is helpless. If you want a picture of the future, imagine a boot stamping on a human face—forever."

The Newly Won Freedom
(From "The Sane Society")
by ERICH FROMM
American exponent of socially-oriented psychoanalysis, 1900–1980

Today, when man seems to have reached the beginning of a new, richer, happier human era, his existence and that of the generations to follow is more threatened than ever. How is this possible?

Man had won his freedom from clerical and secular authorities, he stood alone with his reason and his conscience as his only judges, but he was afraid of the newly won freedom; he had achieved "freedom from"—without yet having achieved "freedom to"—to be himself, to be productive, to be fully awake. Thus he tried to escape from freedom. His very achievement, the mastery over nature, opened up the avenues for his escape.

In building the new industrial machine, man became so absorbed in the new task that it became the paramount goal of his life. His energies, which once were devoted to the search for God and salvation, were now directed toward the domination of nature and ever-increasing material comfort. He ceased to use production as a means for a better life, but hypostatized it instead to an end in itself, an end to which life was subordinated. In the process of an ever-increasing division of labor, ever-increasing mechanization of work, and an ever-increasing size of social agglomerations, man himself became a part of the machine, rather than its master. He experienced himself as a commodity, as an investment; his aim became to be a success, that is, to sell himself as profitably as possible on the market. His value as a person lies in his salability, not in his human qualities of love, reason, or in his artistic capacities. Happiness became identical with consumption of newer and better commodities, the drinking in of music, screen plays, fun, sex, liquor and cigarettes. Not having a sense of self except the one which conformity with the majority can give, he is insecure, anxious, depending on approval. He is alienated from himself, worships the product of his own hands, the leaders of his own making, as if they were above him, rather than made by him. He is in a sense back where he was before the great human evolution began in the second millenium B.C.

He is incapable to love and to use his reason, to make decisions, in fact incapable to appreciate life and thus ready and even willing to destroy everything. The world is again fragmentalized, has lost its unity; he is again worshiping diversified things, with the only exception that now they are man-made, rather than part of nature. . . .

Our only alternative to the danger of robotism is humanistic communitarianism. The problem is not primarily the legal problem of property ownership, nor that of sharing *profits;* it is that of sharing *work,* sharing *experience.* Changes in ownership must be made to the extent to which they are necessary to create a community of work, and to prevent the profit motive from directing production into socially harmful directions. Income must be equalized to the extent of giving everybody the material basis for a dignified life, and thus preventing the economic differences from creating a fundamentally different experience of life for various social classes. Man must be restituted to his supreme place in society, never being a means, never a thing to be used by others or by himself. Man's use by man must end, and economy must become the servant for the development of man. Capital must serve labor, things must serve life. Instead of the exploitative and hoarding orientation, dominant in the nineteenth century, and the receptive and marketing orientation dominant today, the *productive orientation* must be the end which all social arrangements serve. . . .

Man today is confronted with the most fundamental choice; not that between Capitalism or Communism, but that between *robotism* (of both the capitalist and the communist variety), or **Humanistic Communitarian Socialism.** Most facts seem to indicate that he is choosing robotism, and that means, in the long run, insanity and destruction. But all these facts are not strong enough to destroy faith in man's reason, good will and sanity. As long as we can think of other alternatives, we are not lost; as long as we can consult together and plan together, we can hope. But, indeed, the shadows are lengthening; the voices of insanity are becoming louder. We are in reach of achieving a state of humanity which corresponds to the vision of our great teachers; yet we are in danger of the destruction of all civilization, or of robotization. A small tribe was told thousands of years ago: "I put before you life and death, blessing and curse—and you chose life." This is our choice too.

The Challenge to Democracy
by ELEANOR ROOSEVELT
Social reformer and American delegate to the United Nations, often called "the First Lady of the world," 1884-1962

In the United States we are the showcase for the possibilities inherent in a free world, in democracy. If the lives of our people are not better in terms of basic satisfactions as well as in material ways than the lives of people anywhere in the world, then the uncommitted peoples we need on our side will look for leadership elsewhere.

BOOK XIX

Man Will Prevail

More than ever before, mankind is asking: Will humanity prevail? It is a question which has become frighteningly meaningful in the age of atomic warfare. Philosophers and poets alike are answering it in the affirmative.

Adapt or Perish
by H. G. WELLS

If *Homo sapiens* is such a fool that he cannot realize what is before him now and set himself urgently to save the situation while there is still some light, some freedom of thought and speech, some freedom of movement and action left in the world, can there be the slightest hope that in fifty or a hundred years hence, after he has been through two or three generations of accentuated fear, cruelty and relentless individual frustration, with ever diminishing opportunity of apprehending the real nature of his troubles, he will be collectively any less of a fool? Why should he undergo a magic change when all the forces, within him as without, are plainly set against it?

There is no reason whatever to believe that the order of nature has any greater bias in favor of man than it had in favor of the ichthyosaur or the pterodactyl. In spite of all my disposition to a brave looking optimism, I perceive that now the universe is bored with him, is turning a hard face to him, and I see him being carried less and less intelligently and more and more rapidly, suffering as every ill-adapted creature must suffer in gross and detail, along the stream of fate to degradation, suffering and death.

That, compactly, is the human outlook, the only possible alternative to the willful and strenuous adaptation by re-education of our species now—forthwith—that I am urging in this book. Adapt or perish, that is and always has been the implacable law of life for all its children. Either the human imagination and the human will to live, rises to the plain necessity of our case, and a renascent *Homo sapiens* struggles on to a new, a harder and a happier world dominion, or he blunders down the slopes of failure through a series of unhappy phases, in the wake of all the monster reptiles and beasts that have flourished and lorded it on the earth before him, to his ultimate extinction. Either life is just beginning for him or it is drawing very rapidly to its close. This is no guess that is put before you, no fantasy; it is a plain and reasoned assembling of known facts in their natural order and relationship. It faces you. Meet it or shirk it, this is the present outlook for mankind.

The Triumph
(From "On a Note of Triumph")
by NORMAN CORWIN
American poet and dramatist, born 1910

Lord God of trajectory and blast
Whose terrible sword has laid open the serpent
So it withers in the sun for the just to see,
Sheathe now the swift avenging blade with the names
        of nations writ on it,
And assist in the preparation of the ploughshare.

The Humane Illusion
by THOMAS MANN
German novelist and anti-Nazi, Nobel Prize for Literature 1929; 1875-1955

Democracy as a whole is still far from acquiring a clear conception of this fascist concentration, of the fanaticism and absolutism of the totalitarian state. It willingly sacrifices all culture and humanity for the sake of power and victory, and secures for itself in this unfair way advantages and advances in the battle of life such as have never been seen before, whose effect upon civilization is wholly bewildering. And yet, in order to be able to survive, democracy must understand this new thing in all of its thoroughly vicious novelty. Democracy's danger is the humane illusion, the virtuous belief that compromise with this new creature is possible, that it can be won over to the idea of peace and collective reconstruction by forbearance, friendliness, or amicable concessions. That is a dangerous mistake which is founded on the wholly different throught-process of the democratic and of the fascist mentality. Democracy and fascism live, so to speak, on different planets, or, to put it more accurately, they live in different epochs. The fascist interpretation of the world and of history is one of absolute force, wholly free of morality and reason and having no relation to them. Its demands cannot be satisfied and quieted with concessions, but are thoroughly vague, indefinable, and boundless. The thoughts of democracy and fascism cannot meet because the latter is deeply and unqualifiedly involved in the concept of power and hegemony as the aim and substance of politics, at a period when democracy is no longer interested in power and hegemony, nor in politics as a means toward gaining them, but is interested only in peace.

The People, Yes
by CARL SANDBURG

The people, yes—
Born with bones and hearts fused in deep and violent secrets
Mixed from a bowl of sky blue dreams and sea slime facts—
A seething of saints and sinners, toilers, loafers, oxen, apes
In a womb of superstition, faiths, genius, crime, sacrifice—
The one and only source of armies, navies, work-gangs,
The living flowing breath of the history of nations,
Of the little Family of Man hugging the little ball of Earth,
And a long hall of mirrors, straight, convex and concave,
Moving and endless with scrolls of the living,
Shimmering with phantoms flung from the past,
Shot over with lights of babies to come, not yet here.
The honorable orators, the gazettes of thunder,
The tycoons, big shots and dictators,
Flicker in the mirrors a few moments
And fade through the glass of death
For discussion in an autocracy of worms
While the rootholds of the earth nourish the majestic people
And the new generations with names never heard of
Plow deep in broken drums and shoot craps for old crowns,
Shouting unimagined shibboleths and slogans,
Tracing their heels in moth-eaten insignia of bawdy leaders—
Piling revolt on revolt across night valleys,
Letting loose insurrections, uprisings, strikes,
Marches, mass-meetings, banners, declared resolves,
Plodding in a somnambulism of fog and rain
Till a given moment exploded by long-prepared events—
Then again the overthrow of an old order
And the trials of another new authority
And death and taxes, crops and droughts,
Chinch bugs, grasshoppers, corn borers, boll weevils,
Top soil farms blown away in a dust and wind,
Inexorable rains carrying off rich loam,
And mortgages, house rent, groceries,
Jobs, pay cuts, layoffs, relief
And passion and poverty and crime
And the paradoxes not yet resolved
Of the shrewd and elusive proverbs,

The have-you-heard yarns,
The listen-to-this anecdote
Made by the people out of the roots of the earth,
Out of dirt, barns, workshops, time-tables,
Out of lumberjack payday jamborees,
Out of joybells and headaches the day after,
Out of births, weddings, accidents,
Out of wars, laws, promises, betrayals,
Out of mists of the lost and anonymous,
Out of plain living, early rising and spare belongings.

To Endure and to Prevail
by WILLIAM FAULKNER

American novelist of southern life, Nobel Prize for Literature 1949; 1897-1962; the
following is his Nobel Prize acceptance speech, in full.

I feel that this award was not made to me as a man, but to
my work—a life's work in the agony and sweat of the human
spirit, not for glory and least of all for profit, but to create out
of the materials of the human spirit something which did not exist
before. So this award is only mine in trust.

It will not be difficult to find a dedication for the money part
of it commensurate with the purpose and significance of its origin.
But I would like to do the same with the acclaim, too, by using
this moment as a pinnacle from which I might be listened to by
young men and women already dedicated to the same anguish and
travail, among whom is already that one who will some day stand
where I am standing.

Our tragedy today is a general and universal fear so long
sustained by now that we can even bear it. There are no longer
problems of the spirit. There is only the question: When will I
be blown up? Because of this, the young man or woman writing
today has forgotten the problems of the human heart in conflict
with itself which alone can make good writing because only that
is worth writing about, worth the agony and the sweat.

He must learn them again. He must teach himself that the
basest of all things is to be afraid: and, teaching himself that,
forget it forever, leaving no room in his workshop for anything
but the old verities and truths of the heart, the universal truths
lacking which any story is ephemeral and doomed—love and
honor and pity and pride and compassion and sacrifice. Until

he does, he labors under a curse. He writes not of love but of lust, of defeats in which nobody loses anything of value, of victories without hope and, worst of all, without pity or compassion. His griefs grieve on no universal bones, leaving no scars. He writes not of the heart but of the glands.

Until he learns these things, he will write as though he stood among and watched the end of man. I decline to accept the end of man. It is easy enough to say that man is immortal simply because he will endure; that when the last ding-dong of doom has clanged and faded from the last worthless rock hanging tideless in the last red and dying evening, that even then there will still be one more sound; that of his puny inexhaustible voice, still talking. I refuse to accept this.

I believe that man will not merely endure; he will prevail. He is immortal, not because he alone among creatures has an inexhaustible voice, but because he has a soul, a spirit capable of compassion and sacrifice and endurance. The poet's, the writer's, duty is to write about these things. It is his privilege to help man endure by lifting his heart, by reminding him of the courage and honor and hope and pride and compassion and pity and sacrifice which have been the glory of his past. The poet's voice need not merely be the record of man, it can be one of the props, the pillars to help him endure and prevail.

Where Hope Remains Undimmed
by BERTRAND RUSSELL
English mathematician, philosopher and pacifist, Nobel Prize for Literature 1950; born 1872

To die for a cause is noble if the cause is good and your death promotes it. If it is practically certain that your death will not promote it, your action shows merely fanaticism. It is particularly obvious in the case of those who say explicitly that they would prefer the extinction of our species to a Communist victory, or, alternatively, to an anti-Communist victory. Assuming Communism to be as bad as its worst enemies assert, it would nevertheless be possible for improvement to occur in subsequent generations. Assuming anti-Communism to be as bad as the most excessive Stalinists think it, the same argument applies. There have been many dreadful tyrannies in past history, but, in time, they have been reformed or swept away. While men continue to exist, improvement is possible; but neither Communism or anti-Communism can be built upon a world of corpses...

There are those who say: "War is part of human nature, and human nature cannot be changed. If war means the end of man, we must sigh and submit." This is always said by those whose sigh is hypocritical. It is undeniable that there are men and nations to whom violence is attractive, but it is not the case that anything in human nature makes it impossible to restrain such men and nations. Individuals who have a taste for homicide are restrained by the criminal law, and most of us do not find life intolerable because we are not allowed to commit murder. The same is true of nations, however disinclined warmongers may be to admit it. Sweden has never been at war since 1814. None of the Swedes that I have known has shown any sign of suffering from thwarted instinct for lack of war. There are many forms of peaceful competition which are not to be deplored, and in these, men's combative instincts can find full satisfaction. Political contests in a civilized country often raise just the kind of issues that would lead to war if they were between different nations. Democratic politicians grow accustomed to the limitations imposed by law. The same would be true in international affairs if there were political machinery for settling disputes and if men had become accustomed to respecting it. Not long ago, private disputes were often settled by duels, and those who upheld dueling maintained that its abolition would be contrary to human nature. They forgot, as present upholders of war forget, that what is called "human nature" is, in the main, the result of custom and tradition and education, and in civilized men, only a very tiny fraction is due to primitive instinct. If the world could live for a few generations without war, war would come to seem as absurd as dueling has come to seem to us. No doubt there would still be some homicidal maniacs, but they would no longer be heads of governments. ...

If the danger of war were removed, there would be a transition period during which men's thoughts and emotions were still molded by the turbulent past. During this transition period, the full benefit to be expected from the ending of war could not be realized. There would still be an excess of competitive feeling, and the older generation, at least, would not readily adapt their minds to the new world that would be in process of being created.

While the work of reorientation was going on, there would be need of an effort, possibly involving some limitation of freedom, to bring about the necessary adaptation. I do not think, however, that this adaptation would prove impossible. Human nature is at least nine-tenths nurture, and only the remaining tenth is genetic. The part which is due to nurture can be dealt with by education. Probably, in time, even the part that is genetic will prove amenable to science. Let us suppose that the transition period has been successfully traversed, and ask ourselves what sort of a world might be hoped for as a result.

How would art and literature and science fare in such a world? I think we may hope that liberation from the load of fear, private economic fear and public fear of war, would cause the human spirit to soar to hitherto undreamt of heights. Men, hitherto, have always been cramped in their hopes and aspirations and imagination by the limitations of what has been possible. They have sought relief from pain and sorrow in the hope of an after-life in heaven. As the Negro spiritual says, "I'm going to tell God all of my troubles, when I go home." But there is no need to wait for heaven. There is no reason why life on earth should not be filled with happiness. There is no reason why imagination should have to take refuge in myth. In such a world as men could now make, if they chose, it could be freely creative within the framework of our terrestrial existence. In recent times, knowledge has grown so fast that its acquisition has been confined to a tiny minority of experts, few of whom have had the energy or capacity to impregnate it with poetic feeling and cosmic insight. The Ptolemaic system of astronomy found its best poetic expression in Dante, and for this it had to wait some fifteen hundred years. We are suffering from undigested science. But in a world of more adventurous education this undigested mass would be assimilated and our poetry and art could be enlarged to embrace new worlds to be depicted in new epics. The liberation of the human spirit may be expected to lead to new splendors, new beauties, and new sublimities impossible in the crammed and fierce world of the past. If our present inadequacies can be conquered, man can look forward to a future immeasurably longer than his past, inspired by a new breadth of vision, a continuing hope perpetuated by a continuing achievement. Man has made a beginning creditable for an infant—for, in a biological sense, man, the latest of species, is still an infant. No limit can be set to what he may achieve in the future. I see, in my mind's eye, a world of glory and joy, a world where minds expand, where hope remains undimmed, and what is noble is no longer condemned as treachery to this or that paltry aim. All this can happen if we will let it happen. It rests with our generation to decide between this vision and an end decreed by folly.

Extremism

(From "The Pursuit of Justice")
BY ROBERT F. KENNEDY

Ultimately, America's answer to the intolerant man is diversity, the very diversity which our heritage of religious freedom has inspired.

The Call of History

(From "Living in Truth")
BY VACLAV HAVEL

Life cannot be destroyed for good, neither can history be brought entirely to a halt. A secret streamlet trickles on beneath the heavy lid of inertia and pseudo-events, slowly and inconspicuously undercutting it. It may be a long process, but one day it must happen: the lid will no longer hold and will start to crack. This is the moment when something once more begins visibly to happen, something truly new and unique ... something truly historical, in the sense that history again demands to be heard.

BOOK XX

Civil Disobedience

by HENRY DAVID THOREAU

New England essayist and naturalist, 1817-1862, who went to prison because he refused to pay taxes to a government which returned fugitive slaves to the South. This work, presented in its entirety, is the most important single document in the development of the theory of nonviolent resistance which has strongly influenced liberation movements in India, the United States, and elsewhere.

I heartily accept the motto, "That government is best which governs least"; and I should like to see it acted up to more rapidly and systematically. Carried out, it finally amounts to this, which also I believe,—"That government is best which governs not at all"; and when men are prepared for it, that will be the kind of government which they will have. Government is at best but an expedient; but most governments are usually, and all governments are sometimes, inexpedient. The objections which have been brought against a standing army, and they are many and weighty, and deserve to prevail, may also at last be brought against a standing government. The standing army is only an arm of the standing government. The government itself, which is only the mode which the people have chosen to execute their will, is equally liable to be abused and perverted before the people can act through it. Witness the present Mexican war, the work of comparatively a few individuals using the standing government as their tool; for, in the outset, the people would not have consented to this measure.

The American government,—what is it but a tradition, though a recent one, endeavoring to transmit itself unimpaired to posterity, but each instant losing some of its integrity? It has not the vitality and force of a single living man; for a single man can bend it to his will. It is a sort of wooden gun to the people themselves. But it is not the less necessary for this; for the people must have some complicated machinery or other, and hear its din, to satisfy that idea of government which they have. Governments show thus how successfully men can be imposed on, even impose on themselves, for their own advantage. It is excellent, we must all allow. Yet this government never of itself furthered any enterprise, but by the alacrity with which it got out of its way. *It* does not keep the country free. *It* does not settle the West. *It* does not educate. The character inherent in the American people has done all that has been accomplished; and it would have done somewhat more, if the government had not sometimes got in its way. For government is an expedient by which men would fain succeed in letting one another alone; and, as has been said, when it is most expedient, the governed are most let alone by it. Trade and commerce, if they were not made of india-rubber, would never manage to bounce over the obstacles which legislators are continually putting in their way; and, if one were to judge these men wholly by the effects of their actions and not partly by their intentions, they would deserve to be classed and punished with those mischievous persons who put obstructions on the railroads.

But, to speak practically and as a citizen, unlike those who call themselves no-government men, I ask for, not at once no government, but *at once* a better government. Let every man make known what kind of government would command his respect, and that will be one step toward obtaining it.

After all, the practical reason why, when the power is once in the hands of the people, a majority are permitted, and for a long period continue, to rule is not because they are most likely to be in the right, nor because this seems fairest to the minority, but because they are physically the strongest. But a government in which the majority rule in all cases cannot be based on justice, even as far as men understand it. Can there not be a government in which majorities do not virtually decide right and wrong, but conscience?—in which majorities decide only those questions to which the rule of expediency is applicable? Must the citizen ever for a moment, or in the least degree, resign his conscience to the legislator? Why has every man a conscience, then? I think that we should be men first, and subjects afterward. It is not desirable to cultivate a respect for the law, so much as for the right. The only obligation which I have a right to assume is to do at any time what I think right. It is truly enough said that a corporation has no conscience; but a corporation of conscientious men is a corporation *with* a conscience. Law never made men a whit more just; and, by means of their respect for it, even the well-disposed are daily made the agents of injustice. A common and natural result of an undue respect for law is, that you may see a file of soldiers, colonel, captain, corporal, privates, powder-monkeys, and all, marching in admirable order over hill and dale to the wars, against their wills, ay, against their common sense and consciences, which makes it very steep marching indeed, and produces a palpitation of the heart. They have no doubt that it is a damnable business in which they are concerned; they are all peaceably inclined. Now, what are they? Men at all? or small movable forts and magazines, at the service of some unscrupulous man in power? Visit the Navy-Yard, and behold a marine, such a man as an American government can make, or such as it can make a man with its black arts,—a mere shadow and reminiscence of humanity, a man laid out alive and standing, and already, as one may say, buried under arms with funeral accompaniments, though it may be,—

> "Not a drum was heard, not a funeral note,
>   As his corse to the rampart we hurried;
> Not a soldier discharged his farewell shot
>   O'er the grave where our hero we buried."

The mass of men serve the state thus, not as men mainly, but as machines, with their bodies. They are the standing army, and the militia, jailers, constables, *posse comitatus*, etc. In most cases there is no free exercise whatever of the judgment or of the moral sense; but they put themselves on a level with wood and earth and stones; and wooden men can perhaps be manufactured that will serve the purpose as well. Such command no more respect than men of straw or a lump of dirt. They have the same sort of worth only as horses and dogs. Yet such as these even are commonly esteemed good citizens. Others—as most legislators, politicians, lawyers, ministers, and office-holders—serve the state chiefly with their heads; and, as they rarely make any moral distinctions, they are as likely to serve the devil, without *intending* it, as God. A very few—as heroes, patriots, martyrs, reformers in the great sense, and *men*—serve the state with their consciences also, and so necessarily resist it for the most part; and they are commonly treated as enemies by it. A wise man will only be useful as a man, and will not submit to be "clay," and "stop a hole to keep the wind away," but leave that office to his dust at least:—

> "I am too high-born to be propertied,
>   To be secondary at control,
> Or useful serving-man and instrument
>   To any sovereign state throughout the world."

He who gives himself entirely to his fellow-men appears to them useless and selfish; but he who gives himself partially to them is pronounced a benefactor and philanthropist.

How does it become a man to behave toward this American government to-day? I answer, that he cannot without disgrace be associated with it. I cannot for an instant recognize that political organization as *my* government which is the *slave's* government also.

All men recognize the right of revolution; that is, the right to refuse allegiance to, and to resist, the government, when its tyranny or its inefficiency are great and unendurable. But almost all say that such is not the case now. But such was the case, they think, in the Revolution of '75. If one were to tell me that this was a bad government because it taxed certain foreign commodities brought to its ports, it is most probable that I should not make an ado about it, for I can do without them. All machines have their friction; and possibly this does enough good to counterbalance the evil. At any rate, it is a great evil to make a stir about it. But when the friction comes to have its machine, and oppression and robbery are organized, I say, let us not have such a machine any longer. In other words, when a sixth of the population of a nation which has undertaken to be the refuge of liberty are slaves, and a whole country is unjustly overrun and conquered by a foreign army, and subjected to military law, I think that it is not too soon for honest men to rebel and revolutionize. What makes this duty the more urgent is the fact that the country so overrun is not our own, but ours is the invading army.

Paley, a common authority with many on moral questions, in his chapter on the "Duty of Submission to Civil Government," resolves all civil obligation into expediency; and he proceeds to say that "so long as the interest of the whole society requires it, that is, so long as the established government cannot be resisted or changed without public inconveniency, it is the will of God . . . that the established government be obeyed,—and no longer. This principle being admitted, the justice of every particular case of resistance is reduced to a computation of the quantity of the danger and grievance on the one side, and of the probability and expense of redressing it on the other." Of this, he says, every man shall judge for himself. But Paley appears never to have contemplated those cases to which the rule of expediency does not apply, in which a people, as well as an individual, must do justice, cost what it may. If I have unjustly wrested a plank from a drowning man I must restore it to him though I drown myself. This, according to Paley, would be inconvenient. But he that would save his life, in such a case, shall lose it. This people must cease to hold slaves, and to make war on Mexico, though it cost them their existence as a people.

In their practice, nations agree with Paley; but does any one think that Massachusetts does exactly what is right at the present crisis?

"A drab of state, a cloth-o'-silver slut,
  To have her train born up, and her soul trail in the dirt."

Practically speaking, the opponents to a reform in Massachusetts are not a hundred thousand politicians at the South, but a hundred thousand merchants and farmers here, who are more interested in commerce and agriculture than they are in humanity, and are not prepared to do justice to the slave and to Mexico, *cost what it may.* I quarrel not with far-off foes, but with those who, near at home, cooperate with, and do the bidding of, those far away, and without whom the latter would be harmless. We are accustomed to say, that the mass of men are unprepared; but improvement is slow, because the few are not materially wiser or better than the many. It is not so important that many should be as good as you, as that there be some absolute goodness somewhere; for that will leaven the whole lump. There are thousands who are *in opinion* opposed to slavery and to the war, who yet in effect do nothing to put an end to them; who, esteeming themselves children of Washington and Franklin, sit down with their hands in their pockets, and say that they know not what to do, and do nothing; who even postpone the question of freedom to the question of free trade, and quietly read the prices-current along with the latest advices from Mexico, after dinner, and, it may be, fall asleep over them both. What is the price-current of an honest man and patriot to-day? They hesitate, and they regret, and sometimes they petition; but they do nothing in earnest and with effect. They will wait, well disposed, for others to remedy the evil, that they may no longer have it to regret. At most, they give only a cheap vote, and a feeble countenance and God-speed, to the right, as it goes by them. There are nine hundred and ninety-nine patrons of virtue to one virtuous man. But it is easier to deal with the real possessor of a thing than with the temporary guardian of it.

All voting is a sort of gaming, like checkers or backgammon, with a slight moral tinge to it, a playing with right and wrong, with moral questions; and betting naturally accompanies it. The character of the voters is not staked. I cast my vote, perchance, as I think right; but I am not vitally concerned that that

right should prevail. I am willing to leave it to the majority. Its
obligation, therefore, never exceeds that of expediency. Even
voting *for the right* is *doing* nothing for it. It is only expressing
to men feebly your desire that it should prevail. A wise man will
not leave the right to the mercy of chance, nor wish it to prevail
through the power of the majority. There is but little virtue in
the action of masses of men. When the majority shall at length
vote for the abolition of slavery, it will be because they are indifferent to slavery, or because there is but little slavery left to
be abolished by their vote. *They* will then be the only slaves.
Only *his* vote can hasten the abolition of slavery who asserts his
own freedom by his vote.

I hear of a convention to be held at Baltimore, or elsewhere,
for the selection of a candidate for the Presidency, made up
chiefly of editors, and men who are politicians by profession; but
I think, what is it to any independent, intelligent, and respectable man what decision they may come to? Shall we not have
the advantage of his wisdom and honesty, nevertheless? Can we
not count upon some independent votes? Are there not many
individuals in the country who do not attend conventions? But
no: I find that the respectable man, so called, has immediately
drifted from his position, and despairs of his country, when his
country has more reason to despair of him. He forthwith
adopts one of the candidates thus selected as the only *available*
one, thus proving that he is himself *available* for any purposes
of the demagogue. His vote is of no more worth than that of any
unprincipled foreigner or hireling native, who may have been
bought. O for a man who is a *man,* and, as my neighbor says, has
a bone in his back which you cannot pass your hand through!
Our statistics are at fault: the population has been returned too
large. How many *men* are there to a square thousand miles in this
country? Hardly one. Does not America offer any inducement
for men to settle here? The American has dwindled into an
Odd Fellow,—one who may be known by the development of his
organ of gregariousness, and a manifest lack of intellect and cheerful self-reliance; whose first and chief concern, on coming into
the world, is to see that the almshouses are in good repair; and,
before yet he has lawfully donned the virile garb, to collect a
fund for the support of the widows and orphans that may be; who,
in short, ventures to live only by the aid of the Mutual Insurance
company, which has promised to bury him decently.

It is not a man's duty, as a matter of course, to devote himself to the eradication of any, even the most enormous, wrong; he may still properly have other concerns to engage him; but it is his duty, at least, to wash his hands of it, and, if he gives it no thought longer, not to give it practically his support. If I devote myself to other pursuits and contemplations, I must first see, at least, that I do not pursue them sitting upon another man's shoulders. I must get off him first, that he may pursue his contemplations too. See what gross inconsistency is tolerated. I have heard some of my townsmen say, "I should like to have them order me out to help put down an insurrection of the slaves, or to march to Mexico;—see if I would go;" and yet these very men have each, directly by their allegiance, and so indirectly, at least, by their money, furnished a substitute. The soldier is applauded who refuses to serve in an unjust war by those who do not refuse to sustain the unjust government which makes the war; is applauded by those whose own act and authority he disregards and sets at naught; as if the state were penitent to that degree that it hired one to scourge it while it sinned, but not to that degree that it left off sinning for a moment. Thus, under the name of Order and Civil Government, we are all made at last to pay homage to and support our own meanness. After the first blush of sin comes its indifference; and from immoral it becomes, as it were, *un*moral, and not quite unnecessary to that life which we have made.

The broadest and most prevalent error requires the most disinterested virtue to sustain it. The slight reproach to which the virtue of patriotism is commonly liable, the noble are most likely to incur. Those who, while they disapprove of the character and measures of a government, yield to it their allegiance and support are undoubtedly its most conscientious supporters, and so frequently the most serious obstacles to reform. Some are petitioning the State to dissolve the Union, to disregard the requisitions of the President. Why do they not dissolve it themselves,—the union between themselves and the state,—and refuse to pay their quota into its treasury? Do not they stand in the same relation to the State that the State does to the Union? And have not the same reasons prevented the State from resisting the Union which have prevented them from resisting the State?

How can a man be satisfied to entertain an opinion merely, and enjoy *it*? Is there any enjoyment in it, if his opinion is that he is aggrieved? If you are cheated out of a single dollar by your neighbor, you do not rest satisfied with knowing that you are cheated, or with saying that you are cheated, or even with petitioning him to pay you your due; but you take effectual steps at once to obtain the full amount, and see that you are never cheated again. Action from principle, the perception and the performance of right, changes things and relations; it is essentially revolutionary, and does not consist wholly with anything which was. It not only divides States and churches, it divides families; ay, it divides the *individual,* separating the diabolical in him from the divine.

Unjust laws exist: shall we be content to obey them, or shall we endeavor to amend them and obey them until we have succeeded, or shall we transgress them at once? Men generally, under such a government as this, think that they ought to wait until they have persuaded the majority to alter them. They think that, if they should resist, the remedy would be worse than the evil. But it is the fault of the government itself that the remedy *is* worse than the evil. *It* makes it worse. Why is it not more apt to anticipate and provide for reform? Why does it not cherish its wise minority? Why does it cry and resist before it is hurt? Why does it not encourage its citizens to be on the alert to point out its faults, and *do* better than it would have them? Why does it always crucify Christ, and excommunicate Copernicus and Luther, and pronounce Washington and Franklin rebels?

One would think, that a deliberate and practical denial of its authority was the only offense never contemplated by government; else, why has it not assigned its definite, its suitable and proportionate, penalty? If a man who has no property refuses but once to earn nine shillings for the State, he is put in prison for a period unlimited by any law that I know, and determined only by the discretion of those who placed him there; but if he should steal ninety times nine shillings from the State, he is soon permitted to go at large again.

If the injustice is part of the necessary friction of the machine of government, let it go, let it go; perchance it will wear smooth,—certainly the machine will wear out. If the injustice has a spring, or a pulley, or a rope, or a crank, exclusively for itself then perhaps you may consider whether the remedy will not be worse than the evil; but if it is of such a nature that it requires you to be the agent of injustice to another, then, I say, break the law. Let your life be a counter-friction to stop the machine. What I have to do is to see, at any rate, that I do not lend myself to the wrong which I condemn.

As for adopting the ways which the State has provided for remedying the evil, I know not of such ways. They take too much time, and a man's life will be gone. I have other affairs to attend to. I came into this world, not chiefly to make this a good place to live in, but to live in it, be it good or bad. A man has not everything to do, but something; and because he cannot do *everything*, it is not necessary that he should do *something* wrong. It is not my business to be petitioning the Governor or the Legislature any more than it is theirs to petition me; and if they should not hear my petition, what should I do then? But in this case the State has provided no way: its very Constitution is the evil. This may seem to be harsh and stubborn and unconciliatory; but it is to treat with the utmost kindness and consideration the only spirit that can appreciate or deserves it. So is all change for the better, like birth and death, which convulse the body.

I do not hesitate to say, that those who call themselves Abolitionists should at once effectually withdraw their support, both in person and property, from the government of Massachusetts, and not wait till they constitute a majority of one, before they suffer the right to prevail through them. I think that it is enough if they have God on their side, without waiting for that other one. Moreover, any man more right than his neighbors constitutes a majority of one already.

I meet this American government, or its representative, the State government, directly, and face to face, once a year—no more —in the person of its tax-gatherer; this is the only mode in which a man situated as I am necessarily meets it; and it then says distinctly, Recognize me; and the simplest, the most effectual, and, in the present posture of affairs, the indispensablest mode of treating with it on this head, of expressing your little satisfaction with and love for it, is to deny it then. My civil neighbor, the tax-gatherer, is the very man I have to deal with,—for it is, after all, with men and not with parchment that I quarrel,—and he has voluntarily chosen to be an agent of the government. How shall he ever know well what he is and does as an officer of the government, or as a man, until he is obliged to consider whether he shall treat me, his neighbor, for whom he has respect, as a neighbor and well-disposed man or as a maniac and disturber of the peace, and see if he can get over this obstruction to his neighborliness without a ruder and more impetuous thought or speech corresponding with his action. I know this well, that if one thousand, if one hundred, if ten men whom I could name,—if ten *honest* men only, —ay, if *one* HONEST man, in this State of Massachusetts, *ceasing to hold slaves*, were actually to withdraw from this copartnership, and be locked up in the county jail therefor, it would be the abolition of slavery in America. For it matters not how small the beginning may seem to be: what is once well done is done forever. But we love better to talk about it: that we say is our mission. Reform keeps many scores of newspapers in its service, but not one man. If my esteemed neighbor, the State's ambassador, who will devote his days to the settlement of the question of human rights in the Council Chamber, instead of being threatened with the prisons of Carolina, were to sit down the prisoner of Massachusetts, that State which is so anxious to foist the sin of slavery upon her sister,—though at present she can discover only an act of inhospitality to be the ground of a quarrel with her,—the Legislature would not wholly waive the subject the following winter.

Under a government which imprisons any unjustly, the true place for a just man is also a prison. The proper place to-day, the only place which Massachusetts has provided for her freer and less desponding spirits, is in her prisons, to be put out and locked out of the State by her own act, as they have already put themselves out by their principles. It is there that the fugitive slave, and the Mexican prisoner on parole, and the Indian come to plead the wrongs of his race should find them; on that separate, but more free and honorable, ground, where the State places those who are not *with* her, but *against* her,—the only house in a slave State in which a free man can abide with honor. If any think that their influence would be lost there, and their voices no longer afflict the ear of the State, that they would not be as an enemy within its walls, they do not know by how much truth is stronger than error, nor how much more eloquently and effectively he can combat injustice who has experienced a little in his own person. Cast your whole vote, not a strip of paper merely, but your whole influence. A minority is powerless while it conforms to the majority; it is not even a minority then; but it is irresistible when it clogs by its whole weight. If the alternative is to keep all just men in prison, or give up war and slavery, the State will not hesitate which to choose. If a thousand men were not to pay their tax-bills this year, that would not be a violent and bloody measure, as it would be to pay them, and enable the State to commit violence and shed innocent blood. This is, in fact, the definition of a peaceable revolution, if any such is possible. If the tax-gatherer, or any other public officer, asks me, as one has done, "But what shall I do?" my answer is, "If you really wish to do anything, resign your office." When the subject has refused allegiance, and the officer has resigned his office, then the revolution is accomplished. But even suppose blood should flow. Is there not a sort of blood shed when the conscience is wounded? Through this wound a man's real manhood and immortality flow out, and he bleeds to an everlasting death. I see this blood flowing now.

I have contemplated the imprisonment of the offender, rather than the seizure of his goods,—though both will serve the same purpose,—because they who assert the purest right, and consequently are most dangerous to a corrupt State, commonly have not spent much time in accumulating property. To such the State renders comparatively small service, and a slight tax is wont to appear exorbitant, particularly if they are obliged to earn it by special labor with their hands. If there were one who lived wholly without the use of money, the State itself would hesitate to demand it of him. But the rich man—not to make any invidious comparison—is always sold to the institution which makes him rich. Absolutely speaking, the more money, the less virtue; for money comes between a man and his objects, and obtains them for him; and it was certainly no great virtue to obtain it. It puts to rest many questions which he would otherwise be taxed to answer; while the only new question which it puts is the hard but superfluous one, how to spend it. Thus his moral ground is taken from under his feet. The opportunities of living are diminished in proportion as what are called the "means" are increased. The best thing a man can do for his culture when he is rich is to endeavor to carry out those schemes which he entertained when he was poor. Christ answered the Herodians according to their condition. "Show me the tribute-money," said he;—and one took a penny out of his pocket;—if you use money which has the image of Caesar on it, and which he has made current and valuable, that is, *if you are men of the State,* and gladly enjoy the advantages of Caesar's government, then pay him back some of his own when he demands it. "Render therefore to Caesar that which is Caesar's, and to God those things which are God's,"—leaving them no wiser than before as to which was which; for they did not wish to know.

When I converse with the freest of my neighbors, I perceive that, whatever they may say about the magnitude and seriousness of the question, and their regard for the public tranquillity, the long and the short of the matter is, that they cannot spare the protection of the existing government, and they dread the consequences to their property and families of disobedience to it. For my own part, I should not like to think that I ever rely on the protection of the State. But, if I deny the authority of the State when it presents its tax-bill, it will soon take and waste all my property, and so harass me and my children without end. This is hard. This makes it impossible for a man to live honestly, and at the same time comfortably, in outward respects. It will not be worth the while to accumulate property; that would be sure to go again. You must hire or squat somewhere, and raise but a small crop, and eat that soon. You must live within yourself, and depend upon yourself always tucked up and ready for a start, and not have many affairs. A man may grow rich in Turkey even, if he will be in all respects a good subject of the Turkish government. Confucius said: "If a state is governed by the principles of reason, poverty and misery are subjects of shame; if a state is not governed by the principles of reason, riches and honors are the subjects of shame." No: until I want the protection of Massachusetts to be extended to me in some distant Southern port, where my liberty is endangered, or until I am bent solely on building up an estate at home by peaceful enterprise, I can afford to refuse allegiance to Massachusetts, and her right to my property and life. It costs me less in every sense to incur the penalty of disobedience to the State than it would to obey. I should feel as if I were worth less in that case.

Some years ago, the State met me in behalf of the Church, and commanded me to pay a certain sum toward the support of a clergyman whose preaching my father attended, but never I myself. "Pay," it said, "or be locked up in the jail." I declined to pay. But, unfortunately, another man saw fit to pay it. I did not see why the schoolmaster should be taxed to support the priest, and not the priest the schoolmaster; for I was not the State's schoolmaster, but I supported myself by voluntary subscription. I did not see why the lyceum should not present its tax-bill, and have the State to back its demand, as well as the Church. However, at the request of the selectmen, I condescended to make some such statement as this in writing:—"Know all men by these presents, that I, Henry Thoreau, do not wish to be regarded as a member of any incorporated society which I have not joined." This I gave to the town clerk; and he has it. The State, having thus learned that I did not wish to be regarded as a member of that church, has never made a like demand on me since; though it said that it must adhere to its original presumption that time. If I had known how to name them, I should then have signed off in detail from all the societies which I never signed on to; but I did not know where to find a complete list.

I have paid no poll-tax for six years. I was put into a jail once on this account, for one night; and, as I stood considering the walls of solid stone, two or three feet thick, the door of wood and iron, a foot thick, and the iron grating which strained the light, I could not help being struck with the foolishness of that institution which treated me as if I were mere flesh and blood and bones, to be locked up. I wondered that it should have concluded at length that this was the best use it could put me to, and had never thought to avail itself of my services in some way. I saw that, if there was a wall of stone between me and my townsmen, there was a still more difficult one to climb or break through before they could get to be as free as I was. I did not for a moment feel confined, and the walls seemed a great waste of stone and mortar. I felt as if I alone of all my townsmen had paid my tax. They plainly did not know how to treat me, but behaved like persons who are underbred. In every threat and in every compliment there was a blunder; for they thought that my chief desire was to stand the other side of that stone wall. I could not but smile to see how industriously they locked the door on my meditations, which followed them out again without let or hindrance, and *they* were really all that was dangerous. As they could not reach me, they had resolved to punish my body; just as boys, if they cannot come at some person against whom they have a spite, will abuse his dog. I saw that the State was half-witted, that it was timid as a lone woman with her silver spoons, and that it did not know its friends from its foes, and I lost all my remaining respect for it, and pitied it.

Thus the State never intentionally confronts a man's sense, intellectual or moral, but only his body, his senses. It is not armed with superior wit or honesty, but with superior physical strength. I was not born to be forced. I will breathe after my own fashion.

Let us see who is the strongest. What force has a multitude? They only can force me who obey a higher law than I. They force me to become like themselves. I do not hear of *men* being *forced* to live this way or that by masses of men. What sort of life were that to live? When I meet a government which says to me, "Your money or your life," why should I be in haste to give it my money? It may be in a great strait, and not know what to do: I cannot help that. It must help itself; do as I do. It is not worth the while to snivel about it. I am not responsible for the successful working of the machinery of society. I am not the son of the engineer. I perceive that, when an acorn and a chestnut fall side by side, the one does not remain inert to make way for the other, but both obey their own laws, and spring and grow and flourish as best they can, till one, perchance, overshadows and destroys the other. If a plant cannot live according to its nature, it dies; and so a man.

The night in prison was novel and interesting enough. The prisoners in their shirt-sleeves were enjoying a chat and the evening air in the doorway, when I entered. But the jailer said, "Come, boys, it is time to lock up;" and so they dispersed, and I heard the sound of their steps returning into the hollow apartments. My room-mate was introduced to me by the jailer as a "first-rate fellow and a clever man." When the door was locked, he showed me where to hang my hat, and how he managed matters there. The rooms were whitewashed once a month; and this one, at least, was the whitest, most simply furnished, and probably the neatest apartment in the town. He naturally wanted to know where I came from, and what brought me there; and, when I had told him, I asked him in my turn how he came there, presuming him to be an honest man, of course; and, as the world goes, I believe he was. "Why," said he, "they accuse me of burning a barn; but I never did it." As near as I could discover, he had probably gone to bed in a barn when drunk, and smoked his pipe there; and so a barn was burnt. He had the reputation of being a clever man, had been there some three months waiting for his trial to come on, and would have to wait as much longer; but he was quite domesticated and contented, since he got his board for nothing, and thought that he was well treated.

He occupied one window, and I the other; and I saw that if one stayed there long, his principal business would be to look out the window. I had soon read all the tracts that were left there, and examined where former prisoners had broken out, and where a grate had been sawed off, and heard the history of the various occupants of that room; for I found that even here there was a history and a gossip which never circulated beyond the walls of the jail. Probably this is the only house in the town where verses are composed, which are afterward printed in a circular form, but not published. I was shown quite a long list of verses which were composed by some young men who had been detected in an attempt to escape, who avenged themselves by singing them.

I pumped my fellow-prisoner as dry as I could, for fear I should never see him again; but at length he showed me which was my bed, and left me to blow out the lamp.

It was like traveling into a far country, such as I had never expected to behold, to lie there for one night. It seemed to me that I never had heard the town clock strike before, nor the evening sounds of the village; for we slept with the windows open, which were inside the grating. It was to see my native village in the light of the Middle Ages, and our Concord was turned into a Rhine stream, and visions of knights and castles passed before me. They were the voices of old burghers that I heard in the streets. I was an involuntary spectator and auditor of whatever was done and said in the kitchen of the adjacent village inn,—a wholly new and rare experience to me. It was a closer view of my native town. I was fairly inside of it. I never had seen its institutions before. This is one of its peculiar institutions; for it is a shire town. I began to comprehend what its inhabitants were about.

In the morning, our breakfasts were put through the hole in the door, in small oblong-square tin pans, made to fit, and holding a pint of chocolate, with brown bread, and an iron spoon. When they called for the vessels again, I was green enough to return what bread I had left; but my comrade seized it, and said that I should lay that up for lunch or dinner. Soon after he was let out to work at haying in a neighboring field, whither he went every day, and would not be back till noon; so he bade me good-day, saying that he doubted if he should see me again.

When I came out of prison,—for some one interfered, and paid that tax,—I did not perceive that great changes had taken place on the common, such as he observed who went in a youth and emerged a tottering and gray-headed man; and yet a change had to my eyes come over the scene,—the town, and State, and country,—greater than any that mere time could effect. I saw yet more distinctly the State in which I lived. I saw to what extent the people among whom I lived could be trusted as good neighbors and friends; that their friendship was for summer weather only; that they did not greatly propose to do right; that they were a distinct race from me by their prejudices and superstitions, as the Chinamen and Malays are; that in their sacrifices to humanity they ran no risks, not even to their property; that after all they were not so noble but they treated the thief as he had treated them, and hoped, by a certain outward observance and a few prayers, and by walking in a particular straight though useless path from time to time, to save their souls. This may be to judge my neighbors harshly; for I believe that many of them are not aware that they have such an institution as the jail in their village.

It was formerly the custom in our village, when a poor debtor came out of jail, for his acquaintances to salute him, looking through their fingers, which were crossed to represent the grating of a jail window, "How do ye do?" My neighbors did not thus salute me, but first looked at me, and then at one another, as if I had returned from a long journey. I was put into jail as I was going to the shoemaker's to get a shoe which was mended. When I was let out the next morning, I proceeded to finish my errand, and, having put on my mended shoe, joined a huckleberry party, who were impatient to put themselves under my conduct; and in half an hour,—for the horse was soon tackled,—was in the midst of a huckleberry field, on one of our highest hills, two miles off, and then the State was nowhere to be seen.

This is the whole history of "My Prisons."

I have never declined paying the highway tax, because I am as desirous of being a good neighbor as I am of being a bad subject; and as for supporting schools, I am doing my part to educate my fellow-countrymen now. It is for no particular item in the tax-bill that I refuse to pay it. I simply wish to refuse allegiance to the State, to withdraw and stand aloof from it effectually. I do not care to trace the course of my dollar, if I could, till it buys a man or a musket to shoot one with,—the dollar is innocent,—but I am concerned to trace the effects of my allegiance. In fact, I quietly declare war with the State, after my fashion, though I will still make what use and get what advantage of her I can, as is usual in such cases.

If others pay the tax which is demanded of me, from a sympath with the State, they do but what they have already done in th own case, or rather they abet injustice to a greater extent than the State requires. If they pay the tax from a mistaken interest in the individual taxed, to save his property, or prevent his going to jail, it is because they have not considered wisely how far they let their private feelings interfere with the public good.

This, then, is my position at present. But one cannot be too much on his guard in such a case, lest his action be biased by obstinacy or an undue regard for the opinions of men. Let him see that he does only what belongs to himself and to the hour.

I think sometimes, Why, this people mean well, they are only ignorant; they would do better if they knew how: why give your neighbors this pain to treat you as they are not inclined to? But I think again, This is no reason why I should do as they do, or permit others to suffer much greater pain of a different kind. Again, I sometimes say to myself, When many millions of men, without heat, without ill will, without personal feeling of any kind, demand of you a few shillings only, without the possibility, such is their constitution, of retracting or altering their present demand, and without the possibility, on your side, of appeal to any other millions, why expose yourself to this overwhelming brute force? You do not resist cold and hunger, the winds and the waves, thus obstinately; you quietly submit to a thousand similar necessities. You do not put your head into the fire. But just in proportion as I regard this as not wholly a brute force, but partly a human force, and consider that I have relations to those millions as to so many millions of men, and not of mere brute or inanimate things, I see that appeal is possible, first and instantaneously, from them to the Maker of them, and, secondly, from them to themselves. But if I put my head deliberately into the fire, there is no appeal to fire or to the Maker of fire, and I have only myself to blame. If I could convince myself that I have any right to be satisfied with men as they are, and to treat them accordingly, and not according, in some respects, to my requisitions and expectations of what they and I ought to be, then, like a good Mussulman and fatalist, I should endeavor to be satisfied with things as they are, and say it is the will of God. And, above all, there is this difference between resisting this and a purely brute or natural force, that I can resist this with some effect; but I cannot expect, like Orpheus, to change the nature of the rocks and trees and beasts.

I do not wish to quarrel with any man or nation. I do not wish to split hairs, to make fine distinctions, or set myself up as better than my neighbors. I seek rather, I may say, even an excuse for conforming to the laws of the land. I am but too ready to conform to them. Indeed, I have reason to suspect myself on this head; and each year, as the tax-gatherer comes round, I find myself disposed to review the acts and position of the general and State governments, and the spirit of the people, to discover a pretext for conformity.

> "We must affect our country as our parents,
> And if at any time we alienate
> Our love or industry from doing it honor,
> We must respect effects and teach the soul
> Matter of conscience and religion,
> And not desire of rule or benefit."

I believe that the State will soon be able to take all my work of this sort out of my hands, and then I shall be no better a patriot than my fellow-countrymen. Seen from a lower point of view, the Constitution, with all its faults, is very good; the law and the courts are very respectable; even this State and this American government are, in many respects, very admirable, and rare things, to be thankful for, such as a great many have described them; but seen from a point of view a little higher they are what I have described them; seen from a higher still, and the highest, who shall say what they are, or that they are worth looking at or thinking of at all?

However, the government does not concern me much, and I shall bestow the fewest possible thoughts on it. It is not many moments that I live under a government, even in this world. If a man is thought-free, fancy-free, imagination-free, that which *is not* never for a long time appearing *to be* to him, unwise rulers or reformers cannot fatally interrupt him.

I know that most men think differently from myself; but those whose lives are by profession devoted to the study of these or kindred subjects content me as little as any. Statesmen and legislators, standing so completely within the institution, never distinctly and nakedly behold it. They speak of moving society, but have no resting-place without it. They may be men of a certain experience and discrimination, and have no doubt invented ingenious and even useful systems, for which we sincerely thank them; but all their wit and usefulness lie within certain not very wide limits. They are wont to forget that the world is not governed by policy

and expediency. Webster never goes behind government, and
so cannot speak with authority about it. His words are wisdom
to those legislators who contemplate no essential reform in the
ng government; but for thinkers, and those who legislate for
me, he never once glances at the subject. I know of those
whose serene and wise speculations on this theme would soon reveal the limits of his mind's range and hospitality. Yet, compared
with the cheap professions of most reformers, and the still cheaper
wisdom and eloquence of politicians in general, his are almost
the only sensible and valuable words, and we thank Heaven for
him. Comparatively, he is always strong, original, and, above all,
practical. Still his quality is not wisdom but prudence. The
lawyer's truth is not Truth, but consistency or a consistent expediency. Truth is always in harmony with herself, and is not
concerned chiefly to reveal the justice that may consist with wrong-
doing. He well deserves to be called, as he has been called, the
Defender of the Constitution. There are really no blows to be
given by him but defensive ones. He is not a leader, but a follower.
His leaders are the men of '87. "I have never made an effort," he
says, "and never propose to make an effort; I have never count-
enanced an effort, and never mean to countenance an effort, to
disturb the arrangement as originally made, by which the various
States came into the Union." Still thinking of the sanction which
the Constitution gives to slavery, he says, "Because it was a part
of the original compact,—let it stand." Notwithstanding his special
acuteness and ability, he is unable to take a fact out of its merely
political relations, and behold it as it lies absolutely to be disposed
of by the intellect,—what, for instance, it behooves a man to do
here in America to-day with regard to slavery,—but ventures, or
is driven, to make some such desperate answer as the following,
while professing to speak absolutely, and as a private man,—from
which what new and singular code of social duties might be in-
ferred? "The manner," says he, "in which the governments of
those States where slavery exists are to regulate it, is for their own
consideration, under their responsibility to their constituents, to
the general laws of propriety, humanity, and justice, and to God.
Associations formed elsewhere, springing from a feeling of humanity, or any other cause, have nothing whatever to do with it. They
have never received any encouragement from me, and they never
will."

They who know of no purer sources of truth, who have traced

up its stream no higher, stand, and wisely stand, by the Bible and the Constitution, and drink at it there with reverence and humility; but they who behold where it comes trickling into this lake or that pool, gird up their loins once more, and continue their pilgrimage toward its fountain-head.

No man with a genius for legislation has appeared in America. They are rare in the history of the world. There are orators, politicians, and eloquent men, by the thousand; but the speaker has not yet opened his mouth to speak who is capable of settling the much-vexed questions of the day. We love eloquence for its own sake, and not for any truth which it may utter, or any heroism it may inspire. Our legislators have not yet learned the comparative value of free trade and of freedom, of union, and of rectitude, to a nation. They have no genius or talent for comparatively humble questions of taxation and finance, commerce and manufactures and agriculture. If we were left solely to the wordy wit of legislators in Congress for our guidance, uncorrected by the seasonable experience and the effectual complaints of the people, America would not long retain her rank among the nations. For eighteen hundred years, though perchance I have no right to say it, the New Testament has been written; yet where is the legislator who has wisdom and practical talent enough to avail himself of the light which it sheds on the science of legislation?

The authority of government, even such as I am willing to submit to,—for I will cheerfully obey those who know and can do better than I, and in many things even those who neither know nor can do so well,—is still an impure one: to be strictly just, it must have the sanction and consent of the governed. It can have no pure right over my person and property but what I concede to it. The progress from an absolute to a limited monarchy, from a limited monarchy to a democracy, is a progress toward a true respect for the individual. Even the Chinese philosopher was wise enough to regard the individual as the basis of the empire. Is a democracy, such as we know it, the last improvement possible in government? Is it not possible to take a step further towards recognizing and organizing the rights of man? There will never be a really free and enlightened State until the State comes to recognize the individual as a higher and independent power, from which all its own power and authority are derived, and treats him accordingly. I please myself with imagining a State at last which can afford to be just to all men, and to treat the individual with respect as a neighbor; which even would not think it inconsistent with its own repose if a few were to live aloof from it, not meddling with it, nor embraced by it, who fulfilled all the duties of neighbors and fellow-men. A State which bore this kind of fruit, and suffered it to drop off as fast as it ripened, would prepare the way for a still more perfect and glorious State, which also I have imagined, but not yet anywhere seen.

INDEXES

Index of Authors

Index of Titles

651